THE ELECTION THAT SHAPED GUJARAT

&

NARENDRA MODI'S RISE TO NATIONAL STARDOM

Also by Ramesh N. Rao

Secular 'Gods' Blame Hindu 'Demons': The Sangh Parivar through the Mirror of Distortion (2001)

Coalition Conundrum: The BJP's Trials, Tribulations and Triumphs (2001)

Gujarat after Godhra: Real Violence, Selective Outrage (2002): Co-edited with Koenraad Elst

THE ELECTION THAT SHAPED GUJARAT

&

NARENDRA MODI'S RISE TO NATIONAL STARDOM

BY

Ramesh N. Rao

&

Vishal Sharma

Mount Meru Publishing

Copyright © 2015 by Ramesh N. Rao

All rights reserved. No part of this book may be reproduced or transmitted in any form or by any means, electronic or mechanical, including copying, photocopying, scanning, and recording or by any information storage and retrieval system without written permission from the author, except for the inclusion of brief quotations for research or review.

The views expressed in this book belong solely to the authors and do not necessarily reflect the views of the publisher. Neither the authors nor publisher are liable for any loss or damages resulting from the use of information presented in this book. Neither the authors nor publisher make any representation or warranty with respect to the accuracy or completeness of the information presented in this book.

Cover design by Sugam Garg

Published in 2015 by:

Mount Meru Publishing
P.O. Box 30026
Cityside Postal Outlet PO
Mississauga, Ontario
Canada   L4Z 0B6
Email: mountmerupublishing@gmail.com

ISBN 978-0-9684120-1-5

CONTENTS

Acknowledgements vii

Foreword viii

Preface xi

Introduction 1

Chapter I – Gujarat's Relevance, India's Context 8

Chapter II -- Shifting Fortunes and their Aftermath 49

Chapter III -- Wages of Personality Politics 57

Chapter IV -- Rekindling Pride in the Wake of a Quake 60

Chapter V -- Modi's Hundred Days in Office 63

Chapter VI -- Seeking a Mandate: The Rajkot By-Elections 70

Chapter VII -- Godhra and its Aftermath 73

Chapter VIII -- The Riots 81

Chapter IX -- Media Bias and Selective Outrage 93

Chapter X – The Demand for Modi's Resignation 102

Chapter XI – A "Super Cop" to Advise Modi 114

Chapter XII -- The Historic Goa Meeting 123

Chapter XIII -- Vaghela becomes Gujarat Congress Party's President 128

Chapter XIV – State Assembly Dissolved 133

Chapter XV -- Gujarati Honor 137

Chapter XVI – The Election Commission Visits 144

Chapter XVII -- Congress' soft Hindutva 149

Chapter XVIII -- The Forty- Page Commandment:

        Thou shalt not hold Elections 152

Chapter XIX -- The GGY: Na Bhuto, Na Bhavishyati 158

Chapter XX -- Waiting for the Polls... 172

Chapter XXI – The Rath Yatra of Lord Jagannath 182

Chapter XXII – Surveys 185

Chapter XXIII – Akshardham 190

Chapter XXIV --Ticket distribution.. 210

Chapter XXV -- Narendra Modi in Hospital... 222

Chapter XXVI -- VHP in the Forefront... 226

Chapter XXVII -- *Hum Paanch, Humare Pachees* (We five, our twenty-five) 232

Chapter XXVIII – Electioneering and the Elections..................................... 236

Chapter XXIX – Ends, Means, Justifications and the Future of India 266

        Appendix: Questionnaire – Narendra Modi 273

        Bibliography... 278

        Subject Index... 289

        About the authors 298

ACKNOWLEDGEMENTS

Many people were kind and generous in giving us their time and sharing with us their knowledge of events and people in Gujarat, when we conducted interviews for this book in 2003. These included then Chief Minister of Gujarat Narendra Modi and members of his Cabinet, former Gujarat government ministers, members of the Opposition Congress Party, officers in the Gujarat government, academics, and ordinary Gujaratis – from doctors and engineers, to artists and home-makers.

This book was first suggested by Dr. Mahesh Mehta, who enabled the meeting with Chief Minister Narendra Modi, other politicians, as well as administrators and ordinary citizens in Gujarat. Dasu Krishnamoorty, who served as senior editor at the Indian Express and Times of India, as political commentator for All India Radio, and taught at the Indian Institute of Mass Communication, did a careful reading of the manuscript and suggested relevant edits. Dr. Tom Dolan, Professor, Department of Political Science and Public Administration, Columbus State University, read the manuscript carefully and suggested further edits. Any remaining mistakes are our own.

Dr. Raja Ram Mohan Roy, an engineer by training and an expert on India's sacred texts, a long time friend, came in the guise of a publishing expert to change the moth of a manuscript into the butterfly of a book. Sugam Garg, design and graphic expert, provided the colors and the power of the book cover to make this book attractive.

Prof. Vamsee Juluri of the University of San Francisco, author of the seminal "Rearming Hinduism", keen observer of and expert commentator on the culture and contexts of India and the Indian Diaspora, has weighed in with a foreword to put this book and its times in brilliant perspective.

Both of us thank our families for their support and encouragement.

FOREWORD

The premise of this book might appear deceptively modest at first glance. What significance, one might ask, can a book about an election in an Indian state over a decade ago have for anyone except the most diligent graduate student in political science or history? The fact that this election marked the beginning of the rise of Narendra Modi might expand its interest somewhat to include fans of India's new and charismatic Prime Minister. Does it offer clues about his campaign strategy, or how he beat the odds to win at that time? Or, as critics might wonder about the same thing, does this book ignore the context of what was happening at that time to offer a merely technocratic account of an effective politician's rise?

Ramesh Rao and Vishal Sharma begin with a question substantially larger than any of these presumptions; the idea of the "end of history" that floated around the upper echelons of the global debate in the decade before most of us had even heard about Narendra Modi. It was a bold claim, born out of that utterly inward looking way in which the privileged circles of the post-colonial, Cold War era chose to speak about the lives and destinies of billions on the planet. The Soviet Union had collapsed, the West had won, and all was well, it was presumed.

Their bubble burst, in many ways on 9/11/2001.

But for one sixth of the world's people, there was never a bubble to hide under in the first place. India, in its march from centuries of colonialism to some sense of itself again, was in some ways far removed from such luxurious pontifications. Its history did not end at all when the Cold War ended. But something powerful, complex, and even in 2002, hardly clear at all, did start to happen.

The significance of this book is not simply a man or a footnote in his rise, but really in the prescient way in which the Gujarat of 2002 educates the reader about the massive paradigm shifts that are taking place at present in the Indian public sphere. If I had read this manuscript in 2002, much of it might have seemed outlandish to me. It would have torn at every bit of commonsense that dominated the academic consensus on South Asia at that point. But I suspect, it would have resonated, if expressed in suitable idioms, with the ordinary people of India even back then. Such is the power of its truth-claim, and such is the troubled state of our world that time alone tells truth when its time has come.

This is not, however, a mystical or mystifying book at all. It is erudite, logical, and engages with the scholarship on Indian politics and history precisely to give us a picture of the present that is still not fully clear to many people in academia and journalism, apparently. While it shares in parts the fast political action-narratives we find in some recent biographies of Narendra Modi, its importance lies in the fact that it is in many ways an outline of a new India that has already happened, though the South Asianist canon in academia has obdurately refused to recognize it. Maybe the book could have been called "The Reality of India," to give it its rightful place on the shelf as the best response so far to an earlier system of thought that got rather stuck on an "Idea"! This book simply put, is a recognition, in a well thought-out global sense, of what India is today, its politics, society, and thinking, and where it is going. It shows us that what Modi's election in 2002 was about was not just some simplistic fight between communalism and secularism, as the dominant discourses made it out to be, but something far more complex, and reflective of what might still be something like hope for India and the world.

That hope is not necessarily about an individual, and this book does not reduce it in that manner either. It is about the hope of a country that rises to make the tools of modernity, tainted as they are with the violence and ignorance of colonial degradation, work for itself and for its own deep and still-breathing sense of itself as a civilization. All around the arguments this book makes about reconsidering the established canonical narratives on Modi and his rise is a sense of India itself straining to move beyond the straitjacket of a divisive, violent calculus of political chicanery masquerading as democracy. To make this case, the authors engage with several themes that need to be revisited, examined, and now talked about assertively in the public sphere against the tide of a rising outburst of calculated propaganda and identity-based hate in large parts of the Indian media and academia. This book addresses the attack on the train in Godhra and the riots, and takes it out of the flawed calculus of "religious hatred" to remind us of the very dangerous context of global terror in which it took place. It addresses the bizarre and recklessly unprofessional way in which a media demonization campaign started at that time, and names the political interests surrounding it. It outlines the viciously fragmented nature of Indian and Gujarati electoral politics, the old British "divide and rule" now reinvented and kept running for five decades in free India as a cynical system of "divide and get votes." It addresses the "fault-lines" of religion and caste that "experts" had said Modi and his "brand" of politics would push to a dangerous and explosive point.

But the only thing that has exploded, it seems, is an old system of morally corrosive identity politics. This book shows us that what Modi brought to the 2002 election was not some simplistic religious hatred against minorities, but a sense of a new kind of nationalism, one which was neither "secular" in the old flawed and divisive sense, nor was it "religious" in the textbook sense. It was this sort of thinking, deeply reflective of where a new India which is young, optimistic, and eager to go beyond the old pseudo-

The Election That Shaped Gujarat

modern calculations of identity politics, that one sees in the Prime Ministerial candidate of 2014, and the Prime Minister of today. As the authors point out in their new introduction, there has been very little scholarly understanding yet of the Modi phenomenon; with observers either demonizing a fiction of him, or sympathizers merely struggling to find inadequate comparisons of him with Reagan or Thatcher. This book begins to spell out the worldview and politics that are starting to express themselves around him. Future scholarship might find, in time, a whole wealth of hitherto ignored or suppressed voices in India's intellectual journey that have gone into the making of Modi, such as the Integral Humanism of Pandit Deendayal Upadhyaya. For now, with this book, a clear foundation has been laid for the study of the reality we see today.

The fundamental truth of today is that a new kind of Indian politics has emerged, and with it has ended a long-lingering and malignant phase of the colonial legacy.

For some of us, history is just beginning, still.

Vamsee Juluri
October 9, 2015

PREFACE

"It is not the critic who counts; not the man who points out how the strong man stumbles, or where the doer of deeds could have done them better. The credit belongs to the man who is actually in the arena, whose face is marred by dust and sweat and blood; who strives valiantly; who errs, who comes short again and again, because there is no effort without error and shortcoming; but who does actually strive to do the deeds; who knows great enthusiasms, the great devotions; who spends himself in a worthy cause; who at the best knows in the end the triumph of high achievement, and who at the worst, if he fails, at least fails while daring greatly, so that his place shall never be with those cold and timid souls who neither know victory nor defeat"[1] -- *Theodore Roosevelt*

This book recounts and analyzes the events leading up to and the results of the elections to the Gujarat State Assembly in 2002. Despite Modi's meteoric rise since then, the events in Gujarat leading up to the elections in 2002, still cast a long shadow. This inquiry recounts and analyzes that crucial period in Gujarat's history and explains how Gujarat is a crucible for understanding and testing the sustainability of democratic traditions in the context of a multicultural society buffeted by global events.

The manuscript for this book was finalized in 2004, much closer to the actual historical events. We believe time has enhanced its value, not diminished it. We offer it as a contribution to understanding and analyzing not only what happened in Gujarat in 2002 but how such an analysis might guide large, multi-ethnic, multi-religious societies to manage change and strengthen governance in a democracy.

First suggested in 2003, and quickly followed up with a visit to India by the primary author, interviews were conducted with lay people as well as administrators and activists, and capped by a two-hour-long discussion with Mr. Narendra Modi. The Gujarat Chief Minister had recently been returned to office with a landslide victory but was still under the microscope, if not in the crosshairs, of a variety of forces seeking to keep him in the uncomfortable corner they had pushed him into.

Ten years and two more Gujarat Assembly elections later, Narendra Modi who had been entrenched in his office in Gandhinagar, led a blistering and bruising campaign, creating the "Moditva" wave that swept him into Panchavati, the official residence of the Prime Minister at 7, Race Course Road in New Delhi on May 17, 2014. In this

---

[1] Roosevelt, T. (1910). Excerpt from the speech, "Citizenship in a Republic".

context, it is imperative to understand what brought Mr. Modi to power in Gujarat, and what Modi might accomplish as the Prime Minister of India.

Much has transpired between 2004 and 2015 and we have not made any major revisions to the manuscript to comment upon and analyze events and actors in those intervening years. Politics has a déjà vu quality, and the only difference over time, it may seem, is the different set of actors acting out the plot in a different set of circumstances. However, changes in the economic and social arena provide better indicators of what has transpired in the lives of citizens. We have dwelt on these matters only in passing, since there are now reports and analyses by academics and think tanks on the nature and indices of those developments.[2]

We believe, however, our work can provide the lay reader and the ordinary citizen the context for understanding Gujarat and Indian politics, and the nature of democracy in a tumultuous, large, diverse nation. We are not interested in weighing the worth and impact of Narendra Modi on India and the larger world, but we acknowledge that he has indeed become a larger than life figure. He is not the scion of a political family, no one offered him the mantle of leadership, and he did not have connections to and relationship with the rich and the powerful. In many ways he should be considered the embodiment of what it means to be a self-made man. However, he was demonized, vilified, and caricatured, and the United States made him *persona non grata* denying him a visa to travel there for ten long years. In the hallowed halls and the cushy rooms in which the political and social elite of India planned the fate of their countrymen, Modi was mocked, and plots were hatched to keep him in his state, in a state of beleaguerment. Why was that? He was portrayed the villain, a dangerous man with "fascist tendencies", by the Western media – and a convenient whipping boy for the political establishment and academe in the US and Western Europe that seek to save India from itself, or redefine India according to their fantasies of an ideal "Third World Democracy". But as his fortunes changed last year, and he spearheaded the massive win of the Bharatiya Janata Party and its National Democratic Alliance partners, some commentators began to compare him with Ronald Reagan or Margaret Thatcher -- seeing in him a determined, self-made man, with a right of center leaning. Those comparisons and analogies are rather superficial, simply because the Indian milieu is vastly different than the American or the British political, social, and economic contexts. Narendra Modi grew up in a divided India – divided between the elite, urban, ensconced in privilege men and women, who spoke English, were educated in fancy private schools, and kept jetting off to foreign locales to meet and eat or to receive awards bestowed by foreign men and women who were happy to find these sophisticated Indians who spoke of local and global matters in glib and acceptable ways,

---

[2] For examples, Panagariya, A. "Narendra Modi's Real Report Card," *Business Standard*, October 28, 2013

Preface

and the rest – the vast majority of Indians in the teeming cities, towns, and villages where every kind of mish-mash and contaminated gruel are still fed in schools and colleges by men and women who have consumed the same concoction, and where the other institutions of a liberal democracy – a strong judiciary, a well-administered bureaucracy, etc., mostly exist on paper.

Our book will not provide the immediacy of a biography nor the kind of page-turning, blow-by-blow account of an investigative report. However, it provides the much necessary political and social context for understanding what made Modi's leadership of a fractious society tenable and why he may therefore be able to bring his twelve years of experience and the Gujarat model of governance to bear upon the larger battleground that is India.

A small number of biographies in English of Narendra Modi have appeared, some laudatory, some critical, and the fulminations against the man reached a crescendo in the political campaign as we awaited the completion of the nine-phase General Election for the sixteenth Lok Sabha, which ended on May 12, 2014 with the results being announced on May 16, 2014. Even his most determined critics had to acknowledge that the 2014 exercise in choosing members to the sixteenth Lok Sabha was very much centered on Modi. His personal story is fascinating, yet slim, almost bare in the details of his struggles and his identity. Some of it has been captured in the pages of M.V. Kamath and K. Randeri's book, *Narendra Modi: The Architect of a Modern State* (2009)[3]; his political philosophy and response to the vagaries of Indian politics are presented in Andy Marino's (2014) book, *Narendra Modi: A Political Biography*[4]; and the planning and orchestration of the Lok Sabha win is described in Lance Price's (2015) book, *The Modi Effect: Inside Narendra Modi's Campaign to Transform India*[5].

Providing the necessary historical and political context to the life and politics of Narendra Modi and to the understanding of the political dynamics in India, drawn from our account of the Gujarat State Assembly elections in 2002, we believe is important, and we hope we have contributed to that task here, as the Narendra Modi-led government seeks to corral anarchic and petulant forces within the country, and master the art of winning and retaining international friends, collaborators and benefactors, given the little experience that Modi's ministers have in governance, and given their status as members of the teeming, barely literate India.

Ramesh N. Rao
October 10, 2015

---

[3] Kamath, M.V. & Randeri, K. (2009). Narendra Modi: The Architect of a Modern State. New Delhi: Rupa & Co.

[4] Marino, A. (2014). Narendra Modi: A Political Biography. Harper Collins Publishers India.

[5] Price, L. (2015). The Modi Effect: Inside Narendra Modi's Campaign to Transform India.

INTRODUCTION

Politics is the art of the possible, and surely anyone with a faint heart cannot enter the political kitchen where knives are out, sharpened in back-alleys and corners, and cooks stabbed in the back by plotting, scheming characters who are one day friends and collaborators and sworn enemies the next. In such a context, any story that anyone tells is a selective act of communication. When we say selective, we mean that no particular account of any event, even the narrative of a fairly small event and one narrow in scope, is full or complete. There are always more details, always more interpretations, and always something else that someone else wants to add. We can quote and describe the works of myriad Western philosophers on these matters, or just point to the writing of the *Arthashastra*[6] by Chanakya (also known popularly as Kautilya), the third century BCE philosopher and adviser to the great king Chandragupta, and his son, Bindusara.

History is contested, and the writing of it is fraught with challenges, and mired in controversy. In the past it was the "winners" who were privileged to tell or pay others to tell stories of their victories. But in a world which witnesses endless battles in one corner or another, and where there are no clear winners and a lot of bruised leaders and followers waiting for their day in the sun, story-telling and history writing have become even more contentious. Those works which win the "authentic", "scholarly" or "expert" label are products that are not necessarily "true" or "accurate," but owe their status to how the ingredients are packaged – in the choice of language and the theoretical framework analyzing and showcasing them. While we are chary of summarily dismissing the work of expert historians and investigative reporters, and the analyses of human rights groups and non-governmental organizations (NGOs), we have reservations in accepting all of their accounts as fair and balanced, for, the "complete truth" in these human matters is hard to find.

In telling the story of the events that forced the elections in Gujarat in 2002, as an aftermath of the massacre of Hindus on the Sabarmati Express on February 27, 2002, and recalling the four days of bloody riots that followed, we surely had to be selective. How selective our narrative is and whether it passes the test of "fairness, accuracy, and balance" is not for us to say.

The Godhra train massacre is not the center of our account here nor is it focused on the resultant riots that followed it. Instead, it is the story of the viability and strength of modern nation-states faced with threats from outside and fractures and friction from within, including factions of one's own party.

It was declared with much fanfare that after the collapse of the Soviet Union history as we knew it would come to an end, and that democratic forms of government

---

[6] Kautilya (2000). *Arthashastra*. Penguin Classics.

would supplant the remaining few authoritarian, feudal and totalitarian governments around the world sooner than expected. India is the world's largest democracy where faith-inspired terrorism, and neighbors ruled by authoritarians and extremists have seriously impaired the pace of its development. India is a nation with many fault-lines that divide its people: religion, caste, region, language, history, and social and cultural practices. How is it possible to strengthen Indian democracy, and who is going to fight the battle to keep India democratic? Is democracy enough to make a state strong or are there other requirements – for instance, a strong economy, institutions that assure effective law and order, education, alleviation of poverty, equality and justice? The Gujarat elections raised all of these questions, and therefore the retelling of that election story is important to underline its relevance to the sustenance of democracy and the governance of a tumultuous nation in troubled times.

If the Bharatiya Janata Party (BJP) and its Gujarat chief Narendra Modi had lost the elections, we would have seen a hundred books celebrating the triumph of "secularism" over "communalism". But the BJP and Narendra Modi won, inviting unsubstantiated demonization and calumny spread around the world by self-proclaimed secularists and progressives indicating how the Gujarat elections were a travesty of the democratic process. Their version of the Gujarat story got much media space, and much academic spotlight. Since they had their say, we, therefore, have to tell the story of the real "winners" and why that win was important in the local context of Gujarat and the global context of democracies threatened by fundamentalist forces.

Our story is not Narendra Modi-centric, though he can be considered the main protagonist in this narrative. In fact, a neologism was coined in India to describe the influence of Modi in the Gujarat elections: it was "Moditva", or the power and influence of Modi. However, the BJP's win was not the fallout of any particular political "wave" that marked many Indian elections, nor was it merely due to Modi's popularity, though that part of the dynamic should not be ignored or minimized.

More important than the personality of Modi, and the relevance and impact of his leadership style, are the concerns about the vulnerabilities of a democratic and open society. In India, anyway, the evaluation of leadership is fairly superficial: the analyses are mostly in terms of caste affiliation, position in the party, money, social clout, previous experience and offices held, and organizational abilities of the party. Or we have the strange and self-deprecating phenomenon of political scientists, journalists, and U.N. officials continuing to produce tomes on Jawaharlal Nehru and Mahatma Gandhi, regarding them as the architects of modern India. The Nehru cottage industry has become global, and the most dangerous fallout of this "Nehru-mania" is ironically, cult politics, feudalism, authoritarianism, and intolerance of alternative viewpoints.

The political planks of parties are rarely or thoroughly analyzed nor the leadership style and quality adequately understood or described. In a country where a large majority of the population is still illiterate, both politicians and media continue to believe that short and simplistic slogans for eliminating poverty (the famous Indira Gandhi slogan of *"garibi hatao"* made popular in the 1970s) or for building the Ram temple in Ayodhya can seduce the electorate. If indeed such slogans yield miracles, we don't know why some politicians using them win, and why others using the same lose. There are no careful rhetorical analyses of speeches Indian politicians deliver, and media commentators do not take the time, for example, to "unpack" carefully as they do in the U.S., the claims and assertions politicians make in their public presentations. In this regard, it is important to understand the popularity of Modi or his influence in terms of his leadership style and his public rhetoric.

The quality and characteristics of Indian leaders have changed over time. From freedom fighters and activists of the independence era to the agitationists of the 1960s and 1970s (student agitationists, Naxalites, language chauvinists, and others), to pretenders winning elections on caste appeal in the 1980s and 1990s we have arrived at a juncture in Indian history where new forms of leadership are emerging. Modi is the harbinger of this trend -- a surprising phenomenon considering that he is not from a powerful caste group; not the scion of any influential or royal family; not the alumnus of any elite schools; not well-connected politically; not owner of a record of winning elections till he became Chief Minister of Gujarat; and not a career politician either, who had run for office till he was actually forced to do so after he was anointed by his party elders to go manage a fast-collapsing state. On the other hand, Modi comes off as a self- made man, belonging to a political group reviled and abused for long (with its own internal wrangling, jockeying for power, and ideological confusion), a man interested in technology, is disciplined and hardworking, and with a clear vision for his country's future. The Bharatiya Janata Party only faintly embraced the project of *integral humanism*, propounded by its ideologue, Deendayal Upadhyaya, and which is purportedly the BJP's "official philosophy". The middle ground that Upadhyaya sought, between unbridled individualism and stifling socialism, drawing from the fount of Indian traditions and wisdom, integral humanism builds on the idea that the ends of life include *kama* (desire), *artha* (wealth), *dharma* (law and ethics), and *moksha* (liberation/salvation). Western political philosophies and political planks seem primarily to focus on aspects of production and management of *artha* and aspects of maintaining law and order. There is very little written about Upadhyaya's philosophy, and the blame can be assigned both the BJP and its leadership as well as Indian academics who have sold themselves wholesale to the Western and Continental philosophies and political ideologies.[7]

Indian secularists deliberately attribute the outcome of Gujarat elections to the use of the communal (religion) card, whereas Modi attributes it to the surging nationalism that rendered communalism irrelevant. Indian nationalism has many versions – for example Gandhian nationalism, secular nationalism, and Hindu nationalism – but few are those who negotiate the nuances and employ that advantage to appreciate the

---

[7] Sen, G. (September 02, 2015). "Integral Humanism of Deendayal Upadhyaya". *Indiafacts*.

electoral planks of political parties. How would one interpret the kind of nationalism that, for instance, Muslims and Christians of India support? Are they all secular nationalists? These questions do not trouble the secularists at all because in their anxiety to blame only certain sections of the Hindus for advocating the "wrong" brand of nationalism ("Hindu nationalism") they exonerate everyone else, even those who are striving to Balkanize India.

The quick urge and simple anxiety to label the BJP as advocates of "Hindu nationalism" (though there are forces within the party who do want that) belies the complex contemporary Indian dynamic that characterizes the BJP's appeal anchored to a nationalist plank. The appeal to nationalism should be seen in the context of threats from outside forces to wreak havoc on a resurgent and vibrant democracy, and in the context of aspirations of some within the country to divide it on a variety of economic, social, and political fault-lines. Importantly, this new nationalism should be understood as a response to the colonial constructs of India which post-independence, India's so-called secularists and progressives, ironically, have sought to reify.

This work therefore is placed before the public to draw the attention of both informed and lay readers to the vulnerabilities and strengths of democratic nations in the twenty-first century. The Godhra massacre was orchestrated to bring down not only the Modi government but also to dismember India. The post-Godhra riots tested the strength of the Indian law and order machinery and the compartmentalized relationships, professionalism, and independent procedural systems for resolving disputes. The Gujarat elections repulsed the attempts of forces – both well-meaning and calculating – to undermine Indian democratic traditions and pluralistic identity. Pluralism can survive and thrive only when religious traditions and political ideologies exclusively appropriating claims to God and "equality" are considered the greatest threats to the survival and well-being of people all over the world. Certain sections of Muslim societies at present make monopolistic claims to God violently and viciously. Their claims find easy acceptance among gullible "believers" around the world.

Next, the monopolistic claim to usher in "equality" as dreamed by Marx has come unhinged everywhere in the world except in parcels of the academic landscape. For Indian academics and their Western collaborators plying their Marxist trade, "Hindu nationalists" are the only ones who stand between them and their utopia in India. Therefore, they embark on discrediting their chosen targets without the least concern for preserving the democratic traditions that they so assiduously assert are their creation and goal.

The events of September 11, 2001 made Americans aware of the global threat of terrorism. National security has become one of the top U.S. priorities. India has suffered a thousand blows from both organized terrorism and maverick "militants". For a long time, the world ignored India's woes. The 9/11 attacks happened at a time when the radical changes introduced in 1991 in India had begun to fructify and the economy showed signs of wriggling out of the socialist stranglehold. A major catalyst in this economic change was India's role in the new world of high technology. National security concerns and economic partnership with the world's most powerful and largest democracy therefore have brought India and the U.S. closer. This demands that the two evolve a long-term strategy to sustain the tempo of such partnership.

That long-term strategy should not become hostage to any myopic or partisan analysis of the state of India. There are a number of forces, both inside the U.S. and in India, who wish to see the partnership between the two derailed. These forces include not only the old-school socialists and Marxists who are still dreaming of the perfect world of "stateless communities" where equality and happiness reign, but also religious fundamentalists who see pluralistic and diverse India a hunting ground to collect scalps in the name of their God. The Godhra massacre was the work of those who wish to see India divided, if not burned down. Unfortunately, the violent incidents following the Godhra massacre gained more attention and traction in the media, academe and among some influential policy makers than the initial torch that triggered them. These influential constituencies have the potential to slow down the process of a mutually beneficial partnership between the world's two largest democracies, or to even try and shut it down, if U.S. leaders are not wary.

We witnessed the heartening spectacle of U.S. support for a dialogue between India and Pakistan, starting from the later Clinton years, and continuing into the Bush presidency. An increase in the range and frequency of India-U.S. dialogues became evident. These dialogues covered both global and regional matters, as also long term and near-term issues. What was more significant was the changed atmosphere of the dialogue between the two countries: they addressed each other with the confidence and candor of friends and partners. The dialogue, based on respect and equality, was successful precisely because both sides recognized that there is no fundamental conflict of interest between the two democracies. Over the past five years, however, the U.S.-India relationship has frayed, and given the decade long U.S. policy to keep Mr. Modi on his back foot, it would be interesting to see how balance is regained and a new, positive dynamic created. Despite the travails of the past five years the Indo-U.S. relationship reflects the growing maturity that marks their friendship. The U.S. realizes that a serious threat to India can undermine balance and stability in Asia. Europe, while more quick to begin building bridges with Narendra Modi, is not as nimble and open a partner as the U.S. has been and still can continue to be.[8]

Both countries are exploring new areas of mutual interest such as medicine, renewable energy and advanced engineering. The most visible case is "business process outsourcing" (BPO), which arguably is a win-win situation for both the countries. Software accounts for 22 percent of India's total exports. With outsourcing, the U.S. can offer cheaper products to its customers by using the less expensive technically

---

[8] Kapur, D. "Europe's India Aversion," April 13, 2014, *The Business Standard.*

qualified labor pool available in India. In turn, India benefits economically as well as socially. Outsourcing is expected to generate over one million jobs in India. This helps India reduce her rate of unemployment that directly translates into better, safer and healthier living conditions for Indians. As Thomas Friedman wrote in *The New York Times*, referring to the false goals pursued at the Davos conference in 2003: "The last elephant to crash were the anti-globalization protesters, who almost shut Davos down the last two years. This year, they were nowhere. May be it was because this year it was the Western business executives who were besieging their colleagues from India and China. They wanted to hear from the Indians about how Western firms can shift more service jobs -- ranging from software design to reading X-rays -- to India, and from the Chinese how they can absorb more manufacturing. With the world's two biggest developing countries doing so well by globalizing in their own ways, it's no wonder much of the hot air has come out of the anti-globalization movement, which never did have any real alternative growth strategy".[9]

Social activists and academics should therefore see Narendra Modi's efforts at wooing business and manufacturing to park at Gujarat, one of the most developed states in India, in this light rather than rewarding it with slander and demagoguery. The Indian economy doubled between 1994 and 2004, making it the fourth largest in the world in terms of purchasing power parity. The country's external reserves crossed the $100 billion mark and were increasing by a billion dollars every two weeks. A rapidly developing India has a stake in strengthening its partnership with the world's largest economy. These links will gain further strength rapidly as India's economic growth creates new opportunities for investment and joint ventures. On both sides, there is recognition of the strong strategic value of this collaboration. Narendra Modi's focus on good and efficient governance, and a small government with a big footprint, has earned kudos from internationally renowned economists, and his leadership therefore might do wonders in the larger context of the Indian economy.[10]

We should not therefore let those whose grand idealism is merely a masked version of authoritarianism undermine or weaken vibrant societies. These "pie in the sky" idealists propose that governments and leaders provide everyone with everything at the same time. They deliberately sabotage the liberal and pluralistic communities and practices by harping on what is not right with them, even as they gloss over the most oppressive and dangerous ideas and practices espoused and implemented by fundamentalist groups. Thus, to this day, not one academic of any standing has bothered to seriously investigate who engineered the Godhra massacre and for what

---

[9] Friedman, T. Elephants Can't Fly", *The New York Times*, January 29, 2004.

[10] See Panagariya, A. "The Narendra Modi economic model offers a compelling alternative to the mess at the Centre," *The Economic Times*, June 29, 2013

reasons. Instead, they have pilloried one man: his smile is characterized as a smirk, his serious demeanor is described as murderous, his humorous and sarcastic responses to such demonization labeled cynical, and his attempts to re-energize and rebuild Gujarat dismissed as marginal.

Political scientists and historians argue that democracy has worked or survived only in those nations which were economically developed, which had fashioned a civil society, whose people were ethnically homogeneous, and so on. India, which did not meet any of these requirements at the time of independence, has proven to be a resilient democracy. Pakistan, which was carved out from India, and which therefore had some similarities with India, has mostly been ruled by military dictators, who reduced its democratic institutions to tatters. What ingredients have made India a resilient democracy? Some argue that it is the legacy of Mahatma Gandhi and the vision of Jawaharlal Nehru which made India democratic and kept it that way. However, it is not the influence of Gandhi and Nehru alone but also the efforts of great leaders of pre-independence India -- Vallabhbhai Patel, Rajagopalachari, Kripalani, Ambedkar, and a multitude of others. But, leaders alone do not make a nation. It needs some ingredients within the society that keep the people away from pulling down institutions and downsizing leaders. What have kept Indians democratic are not only civil institutions but their religious ethic. Indic traditions have, unlike Semitic traditions, enabled the people to accept and celebrate diversity. So, when we hear the RSS and BJP leaders harp on "Hindtuva" we know that what they are seeking to highlight is the "catholicity" of Hindu peoples, their willingness to embrace and celebrate diversity. Of course, we cannot discount the "hot heads" or the illiberal in the company of the BJP but within every group we find such a mix, and their influence and ambit cannot be discounted.

It is this wider context which it is the aim of this book to discuss to facilitate an understanding of the political and social dynamic of Gujarat and draw lessons in the cause of democracy and good governance. Narendra Modi and the coalition of parties headed by the Bharatiya Janata Party has emerged victorious, and the Indian political scene is beginning to be redrawn and repainted – with many old actors still playing their part in different corners of the country, but an energetic man whose focus is on good governance, seeking justice for all but special treatment to none, shaking up Lutyens' Delhi.

CHAPTER I – GUJARAT'S RELEVANCE, INDIA'S CONTEXT

The few days of communal frenzy that shook Gujarat in 2002, after the Godhra train massacre[11], kindled the hopes of the country's oldest political party, the Congress Party, to regain power by unsettling the incumbent National Democratic Alliance (NDA) coalition. In this effort, it forged an unethical ideological liaison with unprincipled political fragments, an ultra-radical campus crowd, and with the backing of a media that abjured all norms of social responsibility known to the profession. This combination unleashed a no-holds- barred debate, remarkable for its accent on suppression of truth and circulation of lies. Every political concept was turned on its head to launch a new interpretation of democracy that jettisons its emphasis on the primacy of the majority and anoints minority interest as the primary ingredient of democracy. This distorted political and media debate on Gujarat intentionally overlooked uncomfortable facts that would weaken their questionable thesis on such milestones of Indian history as the thousand years of foreign rule, the partition of the country on the basis of religion, and the consequent rise of fundamentalism. Conveniently sidelined were the presence of a hostile neighbor who forced three wars on a country devoted to refashioning its economy and social structures. Both the media and the political parties hungering for power mischievously delinked growing global terrorism from every discussion on Gujarat. An obsession with conflict deprived the media of sanity, credibility and sensitivity to its constituents. To pretend to import sense into the Gujarat debate without co-opting these factors would amount to unabashed hypocrisy and an ambitious exercise in disinformation.

It is against this backdrop that elections took place to Gujarat Assembly in December 2002 evoking a mélange of reactions, some branding the elaborate exercise as an unmitigated travesty of the democratic process, and others as a supreme exemplar of the people's determination to express their free will in the face of concerted campaign to revile the Hindus, to bloody the nose of a politician and the political party he represented, and to wreck the basis of liberal structures in the state.

In the face of results that refuted the skewed analyses of certain media outlets, some political pundits sought to explain them away in the tired old way of counting the number of votes cast in different constituencies, how different castes had exercised their franchise in what ways, what percentage of swing votes swung the results in one way or the other, and why the Gujarat "model" cannot be and will not be replicated elsewhere.[12] Mistaking the woods for the trees, these analyses tried to ignore the big

---

[11] R. Rao & Elst, K. (Eds.) (2002). Gujarat after Godhra: Real Violence, Selective Outrage. New Delhi: Har-Anand Publications.

[12] See, for example, essay by Yadav, Y. "The Patterns and Lessons", *Frontline*, December 21, 2002.

issues that exercised the minds and hearts of Gujaratis. Moreover, they overlooked some of the major political dynamics within the country, and how a combination of political, cultural, religious, social, and economic factors shaped and influenced the election campaigns of the two major parties that vied for power: Bharatiya Janata Party (BJP) and the Congress Party.

What were these factors? They included prevailing tensions between populism and efficient governance, the fuzzy nature of secular ideology in India and the indifference to the spiritual traditions of India, the influence of casteism and "communalism" (what is known in India as "communalism" is the conflict between the different religions, principally Hinduism and Islam), corruption of the political process, security threats to the nation from neighboring countries, and the effects of globalization. Not all of these factors were similarly or equally influential in the election campaign, nor do they exercise the concerns of the citizens of Gujarat and of India with equal force.

Whether at the forefront or merely subliminal, these factors need to be studied carefully for making sense of the chaotic and election-driven nature of Indian democracy, and the dangers facing the second largest nation in the world, and the world's largest nation. We will take these up seriatim but begin with a quick summary of the nature of democracy and constitutional liberalism.

Democracy and Constitutional Liberalism

Since the time humankind sought to live in groups and foraged together, the problem of resolving conflicting goals and reconciling altercating demands has engaged the minds and talents of people. It is a cliché that all life is connected and conflicted, and that the human quest for order is an enduring concern. Every student of political science goes through the required couple of courses about the human endeavor to live in groups amicably. Speculation about unrecorded and unremembered endeavors of the past and analyses of known attempts to create forms of governance to meet human needs test students' ability to travel with philosophers and historians into the past, and to make sense of the ambiguous nature of such past efforts. How the modern state came into being and what are the broad contours of debate about its nature is a little less ambiguous but not any less troubling. It seems, however, that an uneasy but broad consensus has emerged that democratic governance is the best of imperfect options available to strike a balance between order and freedom.

Democracy is a political system marked by free and fair elections. But liberal democracy or constitutional liberalism has come to also mean the rule of law, a separation of powers between the executive, legislature and the judiciary, and the protection of certain fundamental rights like freedom of speech, assembly, religion, and property. Democracy, however, does not guarantee liberty, according to some.

The challenges to democratic governance are many. Stable and effective democratic rule is difficult to accomplish, and problems get further compounded when the state is large, the population diverse, and the history of the peoples conflicted. Add to the mix the dynamics of the twenty-first century with forces of religious fundamentalism seeking to wage holy war on heathen peoples, and economic globalization taking its toll on command economies which had secured lifelong sinecures to many and we have the ingredients for large scale destabilization, chaos and violence.

In an interesting analysis of the confluence of globalization and fundamentalism-driven terrorism, Barber[13] argues that tribalism and mass consumerism are a deadly mix, and the pull of these two major socio-political forces upon the citizenry of the world could lead to the extinction of democracy. "Jihad", according to Barber, represents the extreme tribalist nature of fundamentalist cultures. Their only goal is to ensure the preservation of their own culture and to influence those from outside through their belief system. The result is warring tribes. "Jihad" leaves no room for a freethinking civil democracy and absolutely abhors influences from outside its realm. Hence its ardent distrust of Western consumerist ideology, Barber argues.

With the fall of the Soviet Union some predicted an end to history, believing that democracy and capitalism had won, and that the world would basically be organized around those two philosophies -- political and economic. Fukuyama who proposed such a future, asserts that history is directional and that its endpoint is capitalist liberal democracy.[14]

Then came warnings that with the collapse of the Soviet Union the balance of world power had veered toward the West. However, these analysts argued that instead of democratic forces prevailing across the world, a reversion to religious fundamentalism would precipitate a clash of civilizations.[15] Islamic fundamentalism, with its center in Wahhabi Saudi Arabia, and with an agenda as grand as the Western colonial attempt to remake the world, has now taken its toll and brought religion-inspired terrorism to many parts of the world.

After the world-shaking events of September 11, 2001 and America's invasion of Afghanistan to rid it of its Taliban regime, and then of Iraq to dethrone Saddam Hussein, debate now rages in many policy circles between those who call themselves realists, and those for whom culture is destiny and the Middle East a dangerous mess. Still others, who are also critical of Arab states, advocate a new American initiative to remake the region. A third faction includes scholars who believe that Arab reformers can remake the Middle East without Western or outside intervention. Democracy has not come to the Middle East, and in many parts of the world it is a fragile veneer for

---

[13] Barber, B.R. (1996). *Jihad vs. McWorld*. Ballantine Books.

[14] Fukuyama, F. (1993). *The End of History and the Last Man*. New York: Penguin Books.

[15] Huntington, S. (1996). *The Clash of Civilizations and the Remaking of World Order*. New York: Simon & Schuster

incompetent and unruly governance, evidenced by the rigged elections in many African countries, and the wholesale homage to a variety of vote banks in India.

Democracy is fragile where systems and institutions have not first come into place and where the people are unfamiliar with them, according to Lee Kuan Yew, the former Prime Minister of Singapore. Political analysts like Fareed Zakaria[16] have renewed the debate about the efficacy of adult franchise in weak democracies. He argues that although we take the concept of "liberal democracy" for granted, the two components -- liberalism and democracy -- have not always worked well in tandem. "Constitutional liberalism" is responsible for rule of law and protection of human rights but it has not always been associated with democracy, he argues. In turn, democracy is not always or necessarily connected to liberalism.

Zakaria's argument that "democracy is not inherently good" indicates that democracy is not a result or a product but a process. Some have criticized his argument that elections sometimes serve not as a "guarantee of liberty, but a legitimization of tyranny" by pointing out that an election that "legitimizes tyranny" is in effect a self-refuting concept. Either elections were not truly democratic -- not allowing for free and open decision-making by the people -- or the results of elections indicated the true will of the people, even if their choice of authoritarian or religious parties curtailed some or all freedoms for some or all sections of the people. We can point out to the election of Hamas in the Gaza Strip or of the Muslim Brotherhood in Egypt. In the former case, democracy is a sham, and in the latter it worked as it should. However, those who offer this argument conflate "democracy" with "constitutional liberalism" which guarantees equal rights and freedoms for all citizens, and the basic principle of which cannot be undermined by parties or individuals who claim to be democratic but who favor some form of authoritarianism.

Zakaria's other argument that "liberty depends less on the will of the majority than it does on the institutional safeguards for the rights of minorities" is fraught with problems. The question arises as to what kinds of minority rights need protection. Should it be that a Muslim minority in a Christian majority country have the right of polygamy or the right to slaughter animals the "halal" way because of religious edicts?

Should it be that minorities be allowed to use their pulpits to spread hate against the majority? Common civil and criminal law, as well as the quick and efficient dispensation of justice, are what protect both minorities and majorities. Minority rights that Zakaria propounds are at best an argument for moral relativism and at worst a prescription for balkanization of a country. The 2004 French legislation banning overt religious symbols in public schools was a direct result of the havoc wrought by radical

---

[16] Zakaria, F. (2003) *The Future of Freedom: Illiberal Democracy at Home and Abroad.* W. W. Norton & Company

minority groups seeking to abuse both democracy and constitutional liberalism.[17] The French ban was ratified recently by the European Court.[18]

Zakaria, for example, passes strictures against the Bharatiya Janata Party (BJP) government in Gujarat and accuses it of state sponsored pogrom against Muslims, while ignoring the obvious reason for the retaliatory violence against Muslims in the state: the burning to death of 59 Hindu pilgrims in a train carrying them back from a journey across the country to visit the Hindu holy city of Ayodhya. The massacre on the train was perpetrated by a Muslim mob of more than 2,000 in the Gujarat town of Godhra. Similarly, Zakaria blames the rise of "Hindu nationalism" for attacks against Muslims, and completely ignores the fact that India was partitioned at the behest and express desire of the Muslim elite led by Mohammed Ali Jinnah (ironically fully detailed in his father, Rafiq Zakaria's book)[19], and three wars fought between Pakistan and India. Zakaria's Muslim identity influences his evaluation of Indian events and mars his otherwise trenchant analysis of the threats to liberal democracy. Incidentally, Zakaria has changed his mind and is now supportive of Narendra Modi as a man and as an administrator, though his praise is carefully parsed to ensure that he does not fall into the bad graces of the politically fashionable.[20]

Some historians and political scientists are now arguing that the quest for a separate homeland was not merely at the behest of the Muslim elite but also because of Hindu nationalists.[21] But this revisionist history is justification in hindsight in the light of new dangers allegedly posed by Hindu nationalists. Khilnani says, "Secular and Hindu nationalisms have invariably assigned primary responsibility for Partition to Muslim 'communalism' and separatism. Yet recent historical research has complicated the conventions of this picture…. It is true that a Muslim argument for a homogenous Muslim nation, which presumed a different interpretation of the historical past, was made at different times over the past century…. But this did not amount to a coherent impulse towards an independent nation state for all Muslims on the subcontinent" (p. 162). Was there a coherent impulse towards an independent nation state for all Hindus on the subcontinent? Khilnani asserts as much: Hindu nationalists, upon whom "secularist" scholars have heaped dung, have been easy targets and whipping boys for every ill that beset India, and for everything that went wrong before India became

---

[17] Sciolino, E. (February 11, 2004), "Ban passed on religious symbols in schools", *The New York Times*.

[18] "European Court upholds France's face veil ban," *Aljazeera*, July 1, 2014.

[19] Zakaria, R. (1998). *The Price of Partition: Recollection and Reflections*. Bharatiya Vidya Bhavan.

[20] Zakaria, F. "Is India's bold Prime Minister bold enough?" *The Washington Post*, September 18, 2014.

[21] Khilnani. S. (1997). *The Idea of India*, p. 161-164. New York: Farrar, Straus & Giroux.

independent. Khilnani too indulges in this favorite pastime and so the assertion that Congress rule in the Indian provinces after the 1937 elections encouraged Muslim political alienation, that the "political and intellectual weight of the Hindu nationalist imagination, with its desire for a clear definition of Indianness based on an exclusive sense of culture and of an historical past, was decisive in imposing an artificial cohesion to the diverse local Muslim identities on the subcontinent: indeed, Jinnah himself protested that the idea of Pakistan was foisted upon him by Hindu public opinion" (p. 163).

Rafiq Zakaria, however, portrays in vivid detail the cynical machinations of Jinnah to carve out an independent and Islamic Republic of Pakistan. But since apportioning blame on one party is not acceptable in modern scholarship, the elder Zakaria too manages to find culprits if not villains among the Hindu/secular leadership who succumbed to Jinnah's machinations. He maintains without evidence that V. P. Menon and V. K. Menon convinced Vallabhbhai Patel and Nehru that the partition of India was inevitable. Venkat Dhulipala's magisterial new book puts all these poorly substantiated arguments to rest.[22] Democracy is rule by majority. It seems clear from Jinnah's and the Muslim elite's pronouncements that Muslims did not want rule by the Hindu majority in the subcontinent. They believed that since Hindus were in a majority, Muslims would be marginalized if not discriminated against. This was despite the fact that the Congress Party itself was not a "Hindu" political party, and the Hindu nationalist groups were too disparate, reflecting the diverse nature of Hindu beliefs and customs.

We do know that democracy, as a political principle or arrangement, is the ideal form of governance. However, in practice it can be both messy and unsure of justice, equality, and the well-being of all citizens. Without a moral compass (well thought out constitutional safeguards to protect everyone in the country) democracies can become debased and defunct. A majority can make tragically wrong decisions as in the case of Germany in the 1930's or minorities can wreak havoc as they did in apartheid South Africa. That Muslims felt threatened is not unnatural. However, the resistance of the Muslim leadership to work for constitutional safeguards that would make India a nation state where everyone -- Hindu, Muslim, Christian or Sikh -- could live and prosper without discrimination, and Pakistan's expulsion of its minorities, in contrast to their prosperity in India, should be a clear barometer of the nature of Muslim impulse and Hindu accommodation.

Finally, the threat of adherents of various hegemonistic faiths or violent cults or terrorists to open societies is another danger that faces democracies.[23] We also need to

---

[22] Dhulipala, V. (2015). *Creating a New Medina: State Power, Islam, and the Quest for Pakistan in Late Colonial North India.* Cambridge University Press.

[23] Berman, P. (2003). *Terror and Liberalism.* W. W. Norton & Company.

listen to Daniel Boorstin[24] to understand some of the challenges all democracies face. The biggest problem in a democracy is what Boorstin terms "overcommunication". Everyone has an opinion, everyone wants to express it, and the media want to convey as many disparate opinions as possible because there is "news" in conflict. "Good manners consist not only in our willingness to say what we *are* expected to say, but just as much in our self-control in keeping ourselves from saying what we really feel and really want to say, but which might hurt others", Boorstin warns us. We have, however, come to believe that more communication is better. Any malcontent, with even the minimal communication skills, gets media space. Conflict is encouraged for it sells newspapers. Reporters have become commentators, and commentary has replaced news. The idea that democracy thrives on selective communication is frowned upon if not vilified as the view of authoritarians. These disparate voices blame one another and project a view of the world that is one of irredeemable horror or crisis or desperation. There is no doubt that those who read too many newspapers or watch too much television seem unhappier with the world than those who consume "communication" in moderation.

Politicians and administrators who try to bring normality to a community which has seen violence or conflict are thus faced with the stupendous task of achieving it in the face of constant barrage of "news" and "opinion" that exacerbate that conflict. As Chief Minister of Gujarat, Narendra Modi faced such a task, and opinion makers wanted him to fail so that they could turn around and say that their predictions came true: a self-fulfilling prophecy of the most dangerous kind.

Populism vs. Effective Governance
Populism can be loosely defined as surrender to public view, pandering to the public's temporary or sectarian desires, or bowing to public pressure and making decisions on emotional and impractical grounds. In India, the public is divided into so many *jatis* (wrongly translated as *caste*), identified with religions and regions, with language and customs, color and sex, as rural or urban, and the lettered and the illiterate. Many of these divisions have been assiduously cultivated by politicians, and encouraged by many in the media and in academe. Populism and political correctness drives or misdirects Indian democracy, and the cost as a whole is detrimental to the country's long term growth if not survival.

In India, polls and surveys have still not achieved the kind of power they have in the U.S., where the continuous monitoring of the public's "feelings, wishes, desires, speculations, and compulsions" has led to a fractured polity and a short term "let us win the election at any cost" approach to politics. Polls do not have the same clout in India

---

[24] Boorstin, D. (1974). *Democracy and Its Discontents: Reflections on Everyday America*. New York: Random House

as they do in the U.S., nor do Indians flood their legislators' email boxes or jam their telephone lines with complaints. Yet, caste and religious affiliation and a variety of other social factors manifest in the distribution of "tickets" by political parties to individuals wanting to contest elections. They also influence the doling out of ministerial posts and sinecures like chairmanship of boards of various public sector corporations and commissions. They direct legislation that increases the percentage of quotas for entry into colleges, for government jobs, and for a variety of subsidies. All these have debased Indian politics. Such practices have reduced the Indian citizen to a seeker of "labels" and doles; merit and sheer need be damned.

Fareed Zakaria claims that Western democracies are getting hollowed at the core as politicians bend to a variety of interest groups, and are constantly in a campaign mode -- raising money for the next election. Just as in the West, in India too, there are many who claim that more of democracy is better, and that from the divvying up of the public cake, the field will be leveled for all, and that equality and prosperity will be the outcome. It will happen in the long run, they assert. However, they ignore the rapid erosion of the democratic fabric by a variety of vested interests, and by the lumpen and criminal elements capturing power. Academics who predict that order will come out of chaos rely on false analogies, unproven theories, and do so waving the banner of "secularism and liberalism".

To flourish, liberal democracies need freedom as well as order, a focus on duties as much as on rights, and a steady gaze at the long term while dealing with short-term pressures. Fareed Zakaria tells his readers that his book is not an argument against democracy as much as a warning and reminder that too much democracy is not necessarily healthy. Galbraith, former U.S. ambassador to India, in a memorable expression, said that India was a "functioning anarchy". India continues to function but anarchy continues to grow, and with the pressure of a billion people seeking remedies for a variety of ailments, something surely is going to give.

It is in this context that we need to analyze the 2002 Gujarat elections. They were different because Narendra Modi tried to appeal to all Gujaratis: his mantra throughout the election campaign was about the "five crore (fifty million) Gujaratis", and not about pleasing the Patels or the Scheduled Castes, or mollifying the minorities. This appeal to the whole population, and not to the myriad divisions in society, sought to stop the populist train in its wayward tracks. Some political analysts argued that "the Congress (I)'s tried and tested KHAM (Kshatriya, Harijan, Adivasi, Muslim) formula (and) failed this time, mainly because the party did not take a firm stand against violence". The cause-effect logic is specious at best because while it may make sense to argue that Muslims moved away from the Congress Party for not taking a stance against attacks against them, it ignores the factors that persuaded the Kshatriyas, Harijans, and Adivasis ("*Vanavasis*" as the BJP and the RSS label them) to vote against the Congress Party.

Partisan analysts, who for too long marketed the idea of quotas, reservations, subsidies, and sinecures, termed the appeal to Gujarati "pride", and warnings about threats that the state faced from terrorists, as populist. Sure, appeals to nationalism and patriotism can become scare tactics to promote divisive politics. That was what was said about Narendra Modi's slogan "Modi or Musharraf", implying that voting against him would be a vote for forces that would weaken Indian security and allow General Musharraf to wage another war against India, as he did in Kargil in 1999.

But the smear of populism cannot be applied at will. Pakistan has posed and continues to pose a serious threat to India's security. Its leaders and terrorist outfits have appealed to their Muslim brethren in India to undermine India's national interests. Gujarat is a border state, and Pakistan-based terrorists and criminal gangs have infiltrated India through Gujarat. Careful investigation has shown that some of the Muslim groups in Gujarat, especially in the town of Godhra, were armed, trained, and abetted by Pakistani forces. The large cache of arms recovered from a number of Muslim houses and individuals indicates too that there is a security threat not only to Gujarat but also to the rest of India. The point is not whether there is such a threat but when and how seriously India will suffer when the attack comes. The attack on Parliament building in New Delhi in 2001 was the most ambitious in a series of attacks against Indian targets. With the possibility of weapons of mass destruction (chemical, biological, or nuclear) falling into the hands of one of the terrorist groups aided and abetted by the Pakistani establishment being real, it is not just idle speculation or wanton scare-mongering to suggest that such attacks are in the offing.

Effective governance means the creation and sustenance of institutions that will pursue goals of long term good of the state and the people. The implication is that these institutions will not succumb to the manipulation of politicians and pressure groups. Effective governance means not kowtowing to sectional or sectarian interests, or succumbing to privileges and power of office. Effective governance means identifying and enabling people of merit to guide and implement policy. Politics of caste and religion, natural disasters, like the devastating earthquake of 2001 that killed more than 20,000 people and the cyclone of 1998 that took the lives of more than 2,500 people have debilitated Gujarat.

Partisan analysts and politicians, however, blamed the BJP-led governments between 1998 and 2004 for Gujarat's woes. They claimed that Gujarat's Gross Domestic Product grew by only 1.1 per cent in 2000-01, compared to a growth of 20 percent in 1994-95. These claims ignored the ruin the earthquake had inflicted on Gujarat. Even as they asserted that agricultural growth was only one percent, and was very unstable, given the frequency of drought, they turned around and opposed the State's attempt to build a dam across Narmada River and provide succor to Gujarat's farmers. Worse yet, they made wild claims that the State was losing "Rs. 25,000 crores (Rs. 250 billion) in the communal carnage" of 2002.[25] When they said "Development

---

[25] Bunsha, D. "Hindutva's Triumph", *Frontline*, December 21, 2002.

work is at a standstill since the government is too bankrupt to clear contractors' bills," they ignored the massive loans that the State had to borrow to begin rehabilitate the quake-hit economy. Similarly, the fiscal deficit that burgeoned to Rs. 47,000 crores (Rs. 470 billion) was not due to mismanagement of the exchequer but due to the earthquake which cost Gujarat $5.5 billion or more ($1 = Rs. 50; 1 crore = 10 million; $5.5 billion = Rs. 27,500 crores).[26] The Federation of Indian Chambers of Commerce and Industry (FICCI) not only put the losses in the earthquake-ravaged state at about $5.5 billion, but its secretary general Amit Mitra said that in addition to this amount, there was a daily production loss of about $111 million. The Confederation of Indian Industry (CII) said it was impossible to calculate the destruction caused by the quake, and that the entire Kutch region was ravaged, with all the houses, colleges and schools completely in a shambles. Now, it is pertinent to ask: was it administrative inefficiency that was the cause of Gujarat's burgeoning deficit or was the deficit due to the earthquake and sectarian violence?

With a confluence of vested interests – political, social and religious -- unleashing constant and orchestrated attacks against the government, BJP leaders experienced great difficulty managing the affairs of the state.

Secularism in India

Secularism is the child of partition and gift of Jawaharlal Nehru to India and is unique for its vulnerability to multiple interpretations. One gloss on it persuaded Nehru to include Articles 25 to 30 and 370 into the Constitution which are antithetical to secularism and which guarantee certain rights to the minorities on the basis of their faith even while they deny the same rights to the majority community. The minorities freely interpreted these guarantees to mean a license to embark on a proselytization drive regardless of the Constitution and a Supreme Court ruling that freedom to practice religion does not include the right to convert. The Muslim minority became so vocal that Rajiv Gandhi had to undo a Supreme Court verdict in the Shah Bano case through an amendment to the Constitution.[27] Such developments, in addition to the vote bank politics of the Congress Party, raised apprehensions in the minds of the majority community about the future of their cultural and religious heritage. Added to this is the provision in the Constitution to reserve jobs and berths in educational institutions for certain sections of the Hindu society that resulted in a depletion of the ranks of the majority community as the beneficiaries of this provision began disowning their religious origin encouraged by the church as well as the media. The open appeal by secular parties for votes on the basis of caste to further divide the Hindu society paved the way for Hindu resurgence.

---

[26] "India: Damage Costs $5.5 billion or higher", *CNN*, January 30, 2001.

[27] Anand, U. "From Shah Bano to Salma," *The Indian Express,* March 26, 2010.

The Election That Shaped Gujarat

India gained independence on August 15, 1947 after almost two hundred years of colonial rule (if we were to trace the British control of India to the Battle of Plassey in 1757). The bloody partition of India into Muslim-majority Islamic Republic of Pakistan and a Hindu-majority secular India has proved expensive to secular India. In the name of Islam, Pakistani rulers (mostly military dictators) throttled human rights, crushed civil liberties, waged three wars against India, funded and exported sectarian violence to Indian Kashmir and incited sections of Indian Muslims. Muslim separatism and Islam-inspired dreams of a Muslim hegemony in the region triggered a Hindu backlash and a resurgence of Hindu suspicion and anger. Indian secularism, guaranteed not just by constitutional liberalism but by a variety of later amendments (as in the Shah Bano case - see below) to the Indian Constitution, turns minority rights on their head. These laws deny the Hindus freedoms and rights that are constitutionally guaranteed to minorities, such as laws conferring on the minorities the right to run their own religious institutions.

What threatens Indian democracy and democratic institutions therefore is not majority chauvinism as much as security threats from hostile neighbors; religious hegemony practiced by the adherents of the world's two most powerful monotheistic faiths -- Christianity and Islam; the challenge to India's spiritual traditions by forces of political totalitarianism and religious fundamentalism; the immediate fallout from globalization; and the undermining of democratic institutions through corruption and criminalization.

Let us start with the problem of secularism in the Indian context. The Indian Constitution did not contain the word "secularism" initially. The word "secular" figures only once in the document: to denote an aspect of religious practice. The forty-second amendment added the terms "secular" and "socialist" to the Constitution at the height of the internal emergency (1975-1977) Indira Gandhi imposed, with the help of a pliant Parliament in 1976.

The word "secular" is derived from the Latin "*saeculum*" which means "an age". By extension, it also means "the world". The Bible introduces the idea of the world as "divine creation". Being created, the world is separate from divinity, and is thus "secularized". The world, as we know it, is thus secular. Secularism as a modern ideology emerged in the late Middle-ages as a result of conflict between religious faith and human reason. While serious scholars did not reject religion completely, they sought to bind it within the "limits of reason". It was also cast as a call for and a cause of "human emancipation". T. N. Madan believes that secularism can be defined positively as "a reasonable theory about human agency" rather than just as an "anti-religious ideology".[28]

---

[28] Madan, T. N. (1998). *Modern Myths, Locked Minds: Secularism and Fundamentalism in India*. Oxford University Press.

The Protestant Reformation Martin Luther spearheaded led to the privatization of religion. This meant that the individual no longer needed the Church to be his agent for salvation. So, what was a matter of faith, i.e., the individual being responsible for his/her salvation, led to the secular notion of the "perfectibility of humankind". This individual responsibility and indeed challenge to seek God did not mean it should create a "non- religious" less so an "anti-religious" nation/state or body politic.

The word "secularization" was first used in the Treaty of Westphalia (1648), and it referred to the transfer of lands and other church properties to the exclusive control of the princes. Later, by the end of eighteenth century, and after the French Revolution, secularity came to be considered as "the rational basis of social life and therefore an imperative". Much later, sociologists in the nineteenth century like Comte, Durkheim, Weber, and Marx adumbrated further on the concept, with the last proclaiming that the correct understanding of religion is through demystifying it and locating it "within a framework of class antagonism". Therefore Marxist scholars in India assert that the only secularists are Marxists.[29] Ironically, Marx himself acknowledged that the sociological perspective explaining the endeavor to free society from its religious moorings suffered from self-contradictoriness. After all, how is the "classless and unalienated world" of Marx different from the "redemptive world" of the Christian and Jewish religions?

Secularism has now become an ideology. Like any ideology, it is made up of "ideas, world images, and value judgments," and is not simply descriptive of a particular and/or contemporary situation. Every ideology is rooted in historical experience. Ideologies are "comprehensive, even totalizing, blueprint(s) for living and for action," says Madan (1998). Finally, ideologies are rhetorical in form: they seek to convince and persuade people about the desirability of a particular world image. Those wedded to the ideology of secularism wish to circumscribe if not remove religion and the sacred from society. They believe secularization enlarges the material, institutional and intellectual areas of life, and that it does so through a process that progressively limits the role of religion and the sacred. "Secularity" is the resultant state of social being: it is a mind-set that incorporates ways of behavior. Finally, secularists argue that secularism is a historical inevitability, and that States, nations, and peoples will be secularized progressively: something akin to the Marxian notion of the inevitable death of the state.

In the West secularism is an outcome of Enlightenment and Protestantism. But what secularism means in India depends on who uses the word and in what context. Madan says that there are three assumptions made about Indian secularism: one, that secularism is an anti- or non-religious universal ideal with culturally specific expressions, and that what has worked in the West for four hundred years should work in India too; two, it is assumed that all right-thinking people will embrace secularism; and three,

---

[29] Ahmad, A. (1994) *In Theory: Classes, Nations, Literatures.* London: Verso

despite its faltering progress it is assumed that secularism will succeed in India if corrective measures are taken.

Each of these assumptions is mistaken if not false. We have seen that secularism in the West is neither non-religious nor anti-religion. Even the shining star of secular constitutions, the U.S. Constitution, is presented in the name of God. Despite the clear separation sought of Church and State, in practice the U.S. people and their lawmakers readily invoke God -- from the presidents who take the oath of office with their hand on the Bible to the handsomely paid Chaplain in the U.S. Congress who opens every session with a prayer. One could point out that unlike many of the Western countries that still owe allegiance to particular churches (like Britain and its connection with the Church of England) the U.S. Constitution specifically desists from such a relationship. But what is barred at the front gates is usually allowed entry through various other entrances.

Moreover, given the overwhelming proportion/percentage of Christians (of various denominations) in the U.S., there is very little chance that "secularism" will be tested like it is in India or Serbia or the Sudan. In the preliminary debates of the Republican Party candidates in 1999/2000 three of the six candidates proclaimed their faith in Jesus Christ as their philosopher and guide. Not to be outdone in that sphere, Democratic Party candidate Vice President Al Gore threw his own hat in the Christian ring saying that he is a born-again Christian. In many Western countries that have monarchs as Heads of State the country has an affiliation to a particular church.

The second assumption that all right-thinking people will embrace secularism is equally problematic. Many of the "die-hard" secularists are basically agnostics or atheists. People who are essentially Westernized, Anglicized, and non-religious have foisted secularism on India. That others have climbed on to the bandwagon for political expediency does not make this assertion any weaker.

Gandhian vs. Nehruvian Secularism

Gandhi has been inaccurately labeled a secularist. He would have rejected any ideology that demarcated boundaries between the sacred and the secular domains. His vision was holistic. Religion, for him, meant altruism (*sevadharma*), self-assurance through inner conviction (*atmatushti*), and faith in the saving grace of God (*Rama nama*). He believed that God permeated everything, including politics. He believed that God's work and "true" religion demanded that we should partake of politics.[30] For Gandhi, it was the citizens' sense of moral responsibility for their actions that determined the character of the state. Gandhi felt that Western liberal democracies were rooted in individual

---

[30] T. N. Madan, "Hinduism", in Mark Juergensmeyer (Ed.) *Global Religions: An Introduction,* p. 59, 2003. Oxford University Press.

selfishness and a materialist conception of the "good life". He was not at all enthusiastic about recommending that path.

A Gandhian would say secularism has faced difficulties because the state is too much with us. Gandhi was, however, against a state religion or state support for any religion. Both "Hindu nationalists" as well as "secular nationalists" have glorified the state. Gandhi would have thus rejected both. Gandhi believed that a secularized world was inherently unstable because it elevated instrumental values to the realm of ultimate values.

Nehru, on the other hand, was against institutional religion, ritual, and mysticism, and did not consider himself a religious person. He was an agnostic subscribing to a rationalist/historicist (Marxian) worldview. Gandhi's religiosity annoyed Nehru. He considered the idea of a personal God "odd", and had implicit confidence in the process of secularization. He believed that the economic bond was stronger than the national one, and when he did acknowledge the problem of religious conflict, he saw it merely as an expression of class interest. Religion was not "scientific" and was therefore not attractive to him. We could say that he subscribed to a version of religion that was a combination of diluted Marxism and the Enlightenment view. He attacked bigotry and what he termed the dogmatism of religion; but on rare occasions he acknowledged that religion stood for higher things in life too. Nehru was beholden to Marx and Lenin (as he acknowledged in his autobiography) but was not a copybook Marxist.

In 1949, after watching the disastrous results of partition, Nehru asked, "Do we believe in a national state which includes people of all religions and shades of opinion and is essentially a secular state, or do we believe in the religious, theocratic conception of the state?" He firmly stated, "We shall proceed on secular and national lines". It then became the guiding principle for many of the framers of the Constitution. However, people like Sarvepalli Radhakrishnan thought it strange that "our government should be secular while our culture is rooted in spiritual values". Radhakrishnan wanted to focus on a different facet of secularism, with "stress on the universality of spiritual values which may be attained in a variety of ways".

For Gandhi and Radhakrishnan religious pluralism entailed inter-religious understanding and mutual respect. For Nehru, religiosity was the "badge of social backwardness". Nehru also adopted his stand on secularism not objectively but as a counter to Hindutva (defined by Savarkar as "Hinduness" of those who considered India both their spiritual home and motherland). Nehru once proclaimed himself culturally and by inclination more of a Muslim than a Hindu.

Constitutional Provisions

Madan points out that there is a contradiction between Articles 25 to 30 and Article 44. Articles 25 to 30 guarantee citizens the right to profess and practice religion, and the guarantee of the State to support some of these activities as it pertains to minorities.

Article 44 proposes a Uniform Civil Code. After more than 50 years of constitutional rule there is no uniform civil code in sight. The resistance to such a code has mainly come from Muslims.

The framers of the Indian Constitution overlooked the tenability that in a democratic society the state may reflect the character of the society, and therefore a communally divided society is anathema to a secular state. Also, they ignored or played down the role of *"majoritarianism"* or *"minoritarianism"* (minority veto and/or minority appeasement). For example, Article 48 prohibits slaughter of cows and calves. Does this constitute an appeasement of the majority? What about Article 47 that contains a directive about prohibition of consumption of intoxicants? Is this meant to cater to Muslim sensibilities?

Rajiv Gandhi nullified the Supreme Court verdict in Shah Bano case by passing the Muslim Women (Protection of Rights) Act in 1986 to pacify the conservative Muslim lobby. In this regard, Madan believes that both Nehru and Gandhi had the same attitude towards minorities, especially Muslims. He terms the Congress legacy of providing special treatment to Muslims the "benign elder brother" attitude.

Since Indian polity is differentiated (if not divided) majority and minority demands can never be reconciled. Sayyid Ahmed, in 1887, argued for two nations, the Hindu and the Muslim. He claimed that the Muslims otherwise would come under Hindu domination. Sixty years later, the Muslims got Pakistan, and made it an Islamic Republic. Many million Muslims stayed back in India, the secular state. Pakistan does not have to live up to any secular ideal. No nation that calls itself an Islamic Republic need be secular. Pakistan is an Islamic state. It has driven out most of the Hindus and other minorities from the country, and made the *Sharia* (Islamic law) the law of the land.

In India, the minorities look upon the Hindu majority as a threat. However, people who wish to derive mileage out of the heterogeneity of Hindus contest even the idea of a "majority". Ambedkar claimed that minorities "have loyally accepted the rule of the majority which is basically a communal majority and not a political majority. It is for the majority to realize its duty not to discriminate against minorities". As Madan points out, "the majority and the minorities thus stood defined, though in a somewhat Humpty Dumpty fashion". Prof. V.V. John says (in *Modern Myths, Locked Minds,* p. 254-255) that we should protect *human rights* rather than *minority rights*. According to him, the leaders of the minority communities practice "selective secularism" and demand from Hindus what they do not themselves practice. The privileged status of "minority" may seem a concoction of the fertile imagination of Hindu nationalists. But as Madan points out, Article 29 which protects the minorities' right to establish and administer educational institutions is not available to the majority. Thus the Ramakrishna Mission petitioned the West Bengal High Court to be recognized as a minority institution and won permission. The Supreme Court overturned the decision and left the problem of *"minoritarianism"* on the front-burner. Similarly, Article 334 which allows caste-based reservations deals a body blow to secularism. Given the vote bank politics of the country is there even a prospect of ending caste-based reservations?

Finally, Article 370, which gave Jammu and Kashmir special status, was intended as a temporary measure. Article 370 is now said to protect *"Kashmiriyat"* or Kashmiri identity. One wonders why Kashmiri identity needs special protection any more than a Bengali or a Tamil identity, unless it is taken to mean Kashmiri *Muslim* identity. The clamor for this "identity" has led to the ethnic cleansing of the Hindu minority in Kashmir, and a semi-permanent state of emergency in the Valley. Human rights observers blame the Indian Army for rights abuses while ignoring the rights of the over quarter million Hindus driven out of the Valley. This decades-long ethnic cleansing of the Hindus has not drawn worldwide protests. Such a calamity befalling Muslims of the Valley would have made headline news.

The justification for protecting "unequal" minority rights has been offered too simplistically to stand up to any close scrutiny. Thus, Sunil Khilnani can assert, "Indians who belonged to smaller religious communities had to be protected against the totalitarian potentials of mass democracy" (p. 177) without a shred of evidence to support the assertion. According to Khilnani, permitting a Muslim male to have four wives, and Muslims and Christians control over their own religious institutions while keeping Hindu temples under government control constitutes "protection" of minorities. These kinds of assertions earn serious "intellectual" and civic space only in India, and nowhere else in the world.

Khilnani can therefore maintain that, "Communities would in time open themselves up to reform; but they had to retain the right to decide when" (p. 177). But this concession is available only to the minorities and not the Hindu community! Similarly, when Khilnani attacks Madan, without naming him (p. 180), for arguing that "secularism" was imposed by a minority on the majority, he fails to appreciate Madan's careful argument against "selective secularism".

Minoritarianism also encourages selective attacks by academics and politicians who condemn the destruction of the Babri masjid in Ayodhya by Hindus while condoning the retaliatory bombings in Mumbai (which killed more than 300 and injured more than 2000) by Muslims or the bombing of the famous Meenakshi temple in Madurai by Islamic terrorists. We can also point out the silence that greeted the Godhra arson and the worldwide campaign against people who attacked Muslims in retaliation for that massacre.[31] Notably, even the attack on the Akshardham temple in the capital of Gujarat was explained away as a response by "individuals" angry over the "state sponsored pogrom" against Muslims.[32]

---

[31] Rao, R., & Elst, K. (2002). *Gujarat after Godhra: Real Violence, Selective Outrage.* Har-Anand Publications.

[32] Bunsha, D., & Swami, P. "The Terror Trail", *Frontline*, October 12, 2002.

Madan notes that one major reason for the rise of religious fundamentalism is the *excesses* of ideological secularism, and its emergence as dogma or a religion. Thus, unprincipled and ideologically bankrupt coalitions of rump parties claiming to be "secular" get media space while the "Hindu nationalists" face an endless barrage of invectives. Such attitudes buttress Madan's argument that "by subverting religion as generally understood, secularism sets off a reaction in the form of fundamentalism, which usually is a perversion of religion." That Islam and Hinduism do not recognize the sacred-secular divide that Christianity does queer the political pitch further.

Civil Religion

Are there any solutions to the problem of selective or "pseudo-secularism"? For example, "civil religion," as it is practiced in the U.S. publicly acknowledges the religious foundations of the American state. Everyone knows which God it is that most Americans "trust", which values they swear affinity to, and which civilizational divide they occupy. Can there be such a "civil religion" in India? Madan thinks that it is too late for such a development. The furor over the singing of the *Saraswati Vandana* in 1998 at the Education Ministers' Conference and the hostility expressed to the proposed adoption of *Vande Mataram* as a national song shows the enormity of the opposition to such a "civil religion". Moreover, the idea of a "civil religion" is Western and is a poor fit for the Indian ethos.

Madan says that if in the West intellectuals are calling for reconciliation through "exchange of memories," "promotion of plural readings of founding events," "narrative hospitality," and "forgiveness," may be Indian intellectuals can do the same. Till now, a left/liberal/secular combine has commandeered Indian universities, especially the elite campuses. The easy use of the labels "fundamentalist," "Nazi," "fascist," and "obscurantist," has replaced careful debate, and after the destruction of the Babri masjid in 1992, there has been shrill and continued exchange of invectives across the political and religious divide. The idea of finding middle ground, of reconciliation and rapprochement is anathema to self-proclaimed secularists, and the concerted campaign to undermine the elected government in Delhi these past five years (since 1998) is indicative of the unprincipled approach to bridging the religious and political divide in India.

We do note that there is a kind of religious pluralism practiced by the common people of India. From the visit to a *dargha* and a rooster sacrifice by Hindus for the cure of epilepsy to the pilgrimage to Sabarimala by Muslims and Christians do indicate the willingness of people to cross religious and cultural boundaries. However, nineteenth century intellectuals and their twentieth century descendants have decried these interfaith manifestations as "superstitious" belief. Also, such behavior can be seen as temporary and very context-specific.

What about the idea of *Hindutva* as a form of "civil religion"? *Hindutva* has been described variously as a "way of life," and as encompassing all the peoples who live in the land of Bharat or India. According to RSS Chief K.S. Sudarshan, "Anyone who is the national of this country, irrespective of being a Shaiva, Shakta, Vaishnava, Sikh, Jain, Muslim, Christian, Parsi, Buddhist or Jew by way of his creed or mode of worship, is a Hindu.... If only we accept this proposition and call ourselves Hindus by race, it would be the greatest triumph for secularism."

Sudarshan quotes the Archbishop of Ernakulam, Joseph Cardinal Parecattil, who said the "Church had to draw its cultural nourishment from the local soil -- the rich resources of Hinduism," and claims that the Archbishop affirms that all Indians including Christians and Muslims should imbibe this national culture of the soil. However, he also admits, "there is no lack of political leaders who consider the idea of Hindu *rashtra* as rank communalism and the biggest threat to secularism". Whatever the case may be, will the concept of *Hindutva* find resonance with the majority of the peoples of India? Nearly 140 million Muslims, 25 million Christians, now with affiliations and connections to churches and institutions across the world cannot be brought under the *Hindutva* umbrella without serious repercussions in the country.

To conclude, secularism is an ideal better achieved in academic treatises than in reality. At present all that people do is to pay lip service to it. No nation in the world is truly and completely secular. If some claim they are, it is because they have made sure that their allegiance to certain religions and civilizational values are beyond predation. The monarch of England, mother of parliamentary democracies, owes allegiance to the Church of England. Sweden, Norway, Denmark and others follow suit. So does Japan. Then there are the Islamic republics from Saudi Arabia to Indonesia. China, North Korea, and Cuba and the remaining communist countries, don't need secularism. China controls its minorities with an iron hand. The U.S. will permit diversity as long as its "Judeo-Christian" worldview is not threatened. The U.S. has a uniform civil law.

Muslims cannot practice polygamy or divorce their wives through the practice of *talaq* in the U.S. France, scared about the growing ghettoization of its Muslim citizens, and the threat they pose to "Judeo-Christian" values, has barred any kind of clothing that is considered to indicate religiosity in schools.

Caste and Religion

Caste is a concept that is unique to India and one that a non-Indian hardly can comprehend. It is vocational nomenclature in ancient times. Just as we refer to a person who paints or draws or sings as an artist, a person who adopts learning as pursuit was called Brahmana, a person associated with commerce was called Vyshya, a person who is drafted to defend the ruler's territory was called Kshatriya and a person who performs none of the above tasks is known as Shudra. Through ages, this vocational horizontal division acquired rigidity and attributes of hierarchy. The severest critics of caste discrimination refuse to marry into any other caste. Over centuries, whether it is due to the low level of their contribution to production or low level of economic returns from their services, the Shudras came to be relegated to the bottom of the pyramid. The worst product of casteism is untouchability. The British tried to improve their lot by classifying them as backward and by offering Shudras opportunities not available to other castes. The missionaries tried to impart education to them but only succeeded to seduce them from the Hindu fold.

A remarkable feature of Hindu society is its inbuilt mechanisms for self-reform. From Raja Rammohan Roy and Mahatma Phule to Mahatma Gandhi, Hindu society has seen a galaxy of reformers who strived to rid it of evils like sati, child marriages, untouchability etc., and succeeded to achieve enactment of laws to punish these evils. Despite such efforts, a large section of Hindu society remained backward and suffered its consequences. When India became independent, its leaders adopted a policy of reservations, enshrined in the Constitution, for improving the lot of backward sections. These reservations were to remain in operation for ten years. Unfortunately, the reservations were extended as frequently as they expired, mainly for two reasons: first, irrespective of their ideologies, all political parties found in the system a goldmine of electoral dividends; second, backward classes themselves developed a stake in remaining backward for the effortless benefits that reservations conferred on them.

It is difficult to elevate a community that is determined to remain backward for the benefits that accrue from backwardness. There are now more than 4,000 castes in the place of the original four castes. A direct consequence of the reservations policy is the further hardening of the lines demarcating castes. Even the Christian church in India and the Muslim clergy recognize caste among the converts. They remain Christian Dalits and carry the same disabilities even after conversion as is evident from separate pews and in some places separate churches for Dalits in the south. Today, both Christian and Muslim Dalits are clamoring for benefits that are the due of Hindu Dalits. Therefore, what began as an ameliorative measure has now become a permanent drag on society and the exchequer, not to mention the distortions it has introduced into the education system and a slump in national productivity as a result of heartburning caused to those classes denied these benefits.

Blaming all of India's ills on the caste system is like blaming only the Whites for poverty and crime in the United States. As long as the energies of social and political commentators in India are focused on berating Hinduism for the ills of social discrimination then little cheer can be brought into the lives of the poor and downtrodden in India, and the influence of caste will remain untouched. Caste is a social formation that can be traced to the thirteenth verse in the *Purusha Sukta* of the *Rig Veda*. This is the most controversial verse, and any interpretation of it is fraught with political implications. A straightforward translation of the verse is:

*brāhmaṇo asya mukhamāsīt | bāhū rājanyaḥ kṛtaḥ
ūru tadasya yadvaiśyaḥ | padbhyām śūdro ajāyata*

"From his mouth came forth men of learning; from his arms were warriors made; from his thighs came the merchants (traders); and his feet gave birth to servants".

Is this ordained by God or Brahman or does this verse reflect the societal system prevalent in the past? Faith is a matter of individual choice. To rely on experts to tell us about something that was written two thousand or five thousand years ago merely prolongs and perpetuates the debate, to no useful purpose as there is nothing new said about it. The fact and the reality now is that we do have a caste system, and that system still plays an oppressive role, especially in villages and small towns of India. For example, a recent report said that there was an increase in the practice of untouchability in Karnataka, and that the State government had embarked on a statewide survey in villages to try and eradicate it. The problem refuses to go away because the guilty are not punished.

Egregious cases of discrimination can still be identified, as in the case of Thattekere village in Hunsur district of Karnataka where upper caste people in the village boycotted schools because the government appointed *Dalit* (or Scheduled Caste) cooks to manage the primary mid-day meal programs. Hunsur district has a majority of Vokkaliga (the Shudra land-owning caste) population. The Chief Minister of Karnataka was a Vokkaliga, which made it difficult to resolve the problem. *Dalits* have not been allowed into the local temples, and in many villages across India, *Dalits* have not been allowed to draw water from the same well as others, and there is still a major taboo in marrying across caste divisions.

At a meeting on "Challenges before the Dalit Community" organized by India's leading software company, *Infosys*, speakers expressed concern over a system that exploits *Dalits*. According to Narayana Murthy, Infosys Chairman, around 50 per cent of all *Dalit* households in the country live below the poverty line. Nearly two-thirds of *Dalits* are illiterate and just 30 per cent of *Dalit* households have access to electricity.

The caste system served certain purposes in the past, does so today (including enabling large numbers to take advantage of "reservations" based on their caste status), and most probably will have its role to play in the future. Discrimination is a way of life, and the way the human mind organizes information. We both generalize and particularize. We note differences, and also ignore differences. But how do we make sure that discrimination is not used to oppress others?

The call for a "casteless society" sounds politically and morally correct, but cannot simply be implemented by law or edict. The Constitution makes discrimination based on caste punishable. It does not abolish caste. It cannot. Just like we cannot excise certain passages from the *Bible* or the *Koran* we cannot excise the thirteenth verse of the *Purusha Sukta* from the *Rig Veda*. Nor can we imprison people who firmly believe that the *Purusha Sukta*, for all times, lays down the nature of different kinds of groups. The problem of caste got compounded when *jati* got identified and conflated with *varna*. Each caste (*jati*) -- birth-unit -- is an endogamous group into which one is born and will marry within. There are approximately 3,000 *jatis* in India. By contrast, *varna* is the typical functional division of an advanced society. It is one of the four large caste groups (Brahman, Kshatriya, Vaishya, and Shudra) from which most *jatis* are believed to derive.[33] So, how can we pragmatically and realistically deal with the "problem" of caste? The Belgian author Koenraad Elst says that Hinduism survived foreign onslaughts because of caste formation.[34] He argues that while caste is perceived as based on an "exclusion-from" model, it is first of all a form of "belonging-to". For this reason, Christian and Muslim missionaries found it very difficult to lure Hindus away from their communities. Elst points out that sometimes castes were collectively converted to Islam, and Pope Gregory XV (1621-23) decreed that the missionaries could tolerate caste distinction among Christian converts. However, caste remained an effective hurdle to the destruction of Hinduism through conversion. That is why the missionaries started attacking the institution of caste, particularly the Brahmin caste. This propaganda has bloomed into full-fledged anti-Brahminism, an Indian equivalent of anti-Semitism.

Every caste had a large measure of autonomy, with its own judiciary, duties and privileges, and often its own temples, and inter-caste affairs were settled at the village council by consensus; even the lowest caste had veto power. "This autonomy of intermediate levels of society is the antithesis of the totalitarian society in which the individual stands helpless before the all-powerful state. This decentralized structure of civil society and of the Hindu religious commonwealth has been crucial to the survival of Hinduism under Muslim rule", Elst argues.

Caste-based Reservation
Reservations for Scheduled Castes and Scheduled Tribes, which were to be for a period of ten years in the beginning, have now flourished for more than fifty years, and more than 3,000 "other backward castes" swelled the ever-growing list of the "oppressed" in India. This expansion of the scope and longevity of reservations, instead of alleviating the ills of the caste system, has both legitimized and strengthened the caste system. The call for a "casteless society" therefore will be opposed now not by Brahmins but by other caste groups. Caste is now a passport to certain privileges, just like it has been in the past, but with an interesting twist: the "oppressed" now enjoy those privileges that the "oppressors" have lost. "This is justice", some think, and they insist that we should continue this practice of reserving jobs in government service and seats in educational

---

[33] Flood, G.D. (1996). *An Introduction to Hinduism*. Cambridge University Press.

[34] Elst, K. "Caste: Verdict from Belgium", *Hinduism Today*, September 1994.

institutions for as long as it takes to "level the playing field". *The Hindu* reported on the Congress Party's preparation for the 2004 election saying, "On the Kerala and Karnataka models, the party seems in favor of extending reservation to minorities as a part of the overall reservation granted to the Other Backward Castes".[35]

Those berating the caste system will hopefully note the irony: people who want to neutralize the oppressive nature of the caste system are not only reinforcing caste distinctions but want such reinforcement for an unstated period of time. Moreover, discrimination against *Dalits* and the oppressed is mostly practiced by "other backward castes". Studies have shown that the real tormentors in the vast rural hinterland of India are the land-owning middle castes, now called "Backward". *Dalits* have suffered at the hands of Brahmins only in areas where the latter have owned land or engaged in farming. Chandra Bhan Prasad, a *Dalit* intellectual, says that when he inquired of a *Dalit* friend from Karnataka who the biggest tormentors of *Dalits* in the Karnataka countryside were, the friend said that it was "mostly Shudras or what we call Backward Classes".[36] Bhan says that nearly 80 per cent of *Dalits* in Karnataka live in the countryside, and a majority of them are landless agricultural laborers, who are harassed and exploited by the Shudras.

Can we solve the problems of caste in any other manner? Studies show that economic and educational opportunities would minimize, if not eliminate, discrimination based on caste. That means primary and secondary education should become a national priority. Without basic education, opportunities to earn a living, to move out of oppressive rural settings, to vote intelligently, and to make effective political and life choices (including having a small family) are minimal if not nil.

Therefore wasting time and energy churning out the same old theses and arguments about the oppressive nature of caste system and of its two thousand or four thousand or six thousand year-old heritage makes little sense. Those who do so are interested less in liberating the downtrodden than in exacting revenge. Vengeance against history and against large groups of people, however, cannot be pursued without paying a very heavy price and without any surety about the exact outcome.

Arun Shourie's analysis of the Mandal Commission Report on caste-based reservation and V.P. Singh's acceptance of it is one of the most thorough critiques of the commission's infamous recommendations.[37] Basically, the report recommended that fifty percent of the posts in the government sector should be reserved on the basis of caste and should be given to those who, by definition, are unqualified to hold those positions.

---

[35] Ansari, J. M. (July 8, 2003). "Congress begins fine-tuning poll strategy", *The Hindu*.

[36] Prasad, C. B. "Are Brahmins Still our Shatrus?" *The Pioneer*, July 20, 2003.

[37] Shourie, A. (1992). *State as Charade*: V. P. Singh, Chandra Shekhar and the Rest. New Delhi: ASA

According to Mandal, 27 percent of all posts in the government must be reserved for members from "Other Backward Classes" (OBCs); that those OBC candidates recruited on the basis of merit should not be adjusted against the OBC quota of 27 percent; that they should not be adjusted against the 22.5 percent reserved for Scheduled Castes and Tribes; that the quota was to be applied not only at the time of recruitment but also "to promotion at all levels", and that if a sufficient number of those sub-standard OBCs were not available to fill the posts during a particular year, the unfilled margin should be carried forward for three years. Mandal also recommended that the government set up separate financial institutions to help these OBCs. Furthermore, he suggested that the Central Government advise the State governments to similarly set up financial institutions, as well as a separate Backward Classes Development Corporation. He recommended too that separate ministries be created to administer OBC affairs, and that development programs, on the lines already in place for Scheduled Castes and Tribes, be financed by the Central Government.

Mandal determined that 52 percent of the total population of India belonged to the OBC category. The first Backward Classes Commission set up in 1953 identified 2,399 castes as backward. Criticizing the methodology used by that commission, Mandal assumed that the rate of growth of each caste was identical since 1931 when the last such caste-based census was taken. He therefore concluded that more than half of India's population was backward, excluding the 22.5 percent Scheduled Castes and Tribes who had already been categorized as backward initially. Final tally: three quarters of all Indians belonged to "backward" castes and tribes.

Shourie analyzed the survey administered by the Mandal Commission to identify the backward caste groups. He points out how poorly the questionnaires were constructed. With such a poorly constructed survey, the Commission was able to come up with a list of 3,743 backward castes. These 3,743 castes were just Hindus. There were others from other religious groups that Mandal said he was looking for and would publish the results. Shourie makes the very important point that the Indian Constitution does not provide for the reservation of seats either in education or in the government for "other backward castes". The relevant Articles are as follows:

> Article 16 (1): There shall be equality of opportunity for all citizens in matters relating to employment or appointment to any office under the State.
>
> Article 16 (4): Nothing in this Article shall prevent the State from making any provision for the reservation of appointments or posts in favor of any backward *classes* of citizens which in the opinion of the State, is not adequately represented in the services under the State.

There is no mention of "backward castes" in these Articles. Moreover, even Article 46 that guarantees promotion of educational and economic interests of Scheduled Castes and Tribes is circumscribed by Article 335 stipulating that the claims by those groups "shall be taken into consideration, consistently with the maintenance of efficiency of administration". Shourie points out that the Supreme Court in *M.R. Balaji v. State of Mysore* took the view that caste is not class, and though caste could be identified for assessing backwardness it was backwardness that should be primarily identified. Mandal simply ignored it all.

The Southern States have been at the forefront of guaranteeing government jobs and seats in colleges, including engineering and medical schools, on the basis of caste. Shourie notes that in Tamil Nadu the number of Backward Castes grew from 11 in 1883 to 39 in 1893, from 46 in 1903 to 122 in 1913, from 131 in 1923 to 182 in 1933, and from 238 in 1943 to 270 in 1953. The Mandal Commission listed 288 castes as backward in Tamil Nadu.

Reservation of jobs for the Scheduled Castes and Tribes was supposed to be valid for a period of ten years. It has been extended for fifty years now, and the National Democratic Alliance government has assured the continuation of this reservation policy. In Karnataka the two most dominant and powerful castes, Lingayats and Vokkaligas (Gowdas), were included among the backward caste category. The Havanur Commission which was asked to recommend changes removed the two castes from the "backward castes" list. Violence followed, and the two castes were made "backward" again.

Caste consideration is rampant in the distribution of tickets by political parties during elections, and the appointment of ministers to the cabinet by a party after it has won the elections. Newspapers report these matters without expressing even a little bit of concern. In Karnataka, a leader of the Lingayat caste was reported to have been angry that no person from his caste was awarded a ministerial berth in the Central Cabinet chosen by Prime Minister Vajpayee. A newspaper report had this to say: "Congress leader and the president of Veerashaiva Mahasabha Bhimanna Khandre (said) that not a single Lingayat was inducted into the A. B. Vajpayee ministry today and it was (an) insult to the community". Khandre said Karnataka had elected 10 NDA MPs in the elections out of which four belonged to Lingayat community.[38]

Like caste considerations, religious affiliations too are influential in the formation of a ministry. For example, in Karnataka it was reported that, "the main feature of the Congress ministry would be more or rather proper representation to the Muslims. As many as 12 Muslims have been elected to the assembly from different parts of the State".[39]

In Gujarat, under Congress Party rule, a combination of caste and religious groups influenced political outcomes. This led to the appeasement of various constituencies in

---

[38] "State ministry likely in two stages," DH News Service, *Deccan Herald*, October 14th, 1999

[39] "40-odd member Cabinet to be sworn-in on Sunday: Muslims to get major representation in State", DH News Service, *Deccan Herald*, Oct 16, 1999

The Election That Shaped Gujarat

the form of subsidies, reservations, and berths in the cabinet. The Congress catered to the combination known as "KHAM" – constituting the Kshatriya, Harijan (Dalit), Adivasi, and Muslim groups. Adivasis and Dalits make up 15 percent and 7.5 percent of the total voters in Gujarat while Muslims count another 12.5 percent in the state. OBCs account for 45 percent of the state's electorate. Kshatriyas comprise 20 percent of the population and have traditionally supported the Congress Party. Modi realized how difficult it was to rule the state without catering to these caste and religious groups. He thus launched his campaign appealing to all fifty million Gujaratis, focusing on their common interests, rather than their sectarian interests.

Punishing Merit

Shourie reported that of the 20,000 persons who wrote exams for the 700 seats available in Kerala's medical colleges in the 1980s, a "forward caste" candidate had to rank 412 or higher to get a seat, an Ezhava "backward caste" candidate had to rank 1605 or higher, a Muslim OBC 1752 or higher, a Latin Catholic 2653 or higher, a scheduled caste candidate 4409 or higher, and a scheduled tribe candidate 14,246 or higher.

At the prestigious Post-Graduate Institute of Medical Education and Research, candidates of backward castes, Scheduled Caste and Scheduled Tribe do not even have to score minimum marks to secure admission to the institute. What happens when these unqualified candidates not only get to enter colleges, even professional colleges, but also get absorbed into government services? In Uttar Pradesh, for example, a doctor belonging to a backward caste was appointed Chief Medical Officer of a large city superseding 1,500 doctors!

These last two examples may give the readers a taste of what emerges under the system of reservations: a backward caste employee in Ahmedabad got two promotions in one day. In Delhi, a person who *joined* the government in 1957 was superseded by a woman who was *born* in 1966. V. P. Singh promulgated the Mandal recommendations not out of conviction but to be acclaimed a savior of the backward castes, and to defeat BJP. What followed were riots and public demonstrations. Singh was out of office by November 7, 1990. But he had put in place what is now difficult to remove. Consequently, the BJP has also bought into the system. Modi's battle therefore is uphill.

Nehru said that the system of reservations was not just "folly, but disaster". Caste cannot be wished away, but what can be done is to minimize the discrimination based on caste affiliation. However, Indian leaders now use caste to create vote banks and win elections. For the first time since Gujarat became a separate state, the caste factor was played down as much as possible in the election campaign, and the small and compact cabinet of fourteen ministers makes sure that caste equations are kept to the minimum.

The "Right" to Proselytize
Religious conflict has become more fierce, especially so after the partition of the country. Both the political parties and the media have to share the blame for the low level of inter- religious relations in the country. Gujarat is not the sole scene of Hindu-Muslim irascibility. There is bad blood throughout the country. Muslim leaders have not been successful in dispelling the suspicion that terrorism enjoys their blessings. The new element in this uneasy scenario is the Christian missionaries' aggressive conversion drive blessed by the Vatican. The evangelists ingeniously combine proselytization with service. While the Constitution does not endorse conversions, the Hindu community has its own apprehensions about the possible shift in the country's demographic profile as a result of unhindered conversion programs. The country has seen how regions where minorities are the majority became centers of secessionist movements in Kashmir, Punjab and North-East region. East Timor is an example where the missionaries converted the natives and prodded them to press for a separate state. Today, the Christian minority has internationalized its demands seeking intervention from such agencies as the US Commission on International Religious Freedom, and in fact the USCIRF has been at the forefront of publishing recycled reports from its Christian and Muslim interlocutors demonizing Narendra Modi. American administrations have, in the name of human rights, linked economic and political relation to the status of Christian rights in India. Apart from this history, no community can remain passive to the depletion of its ranks or ridicule and contempt heaped on its culture and heritage. Conversion is not a right in the Constitution and resistance to it cannot be unconstitutional.

India has been a rich arena for harvesters of souls not only because Indian rulers and religions have been open to outside influences but diversity has been the hallmark of Indian spirituality. Aggressive monotheistic faiths that purvey their monopolistic claims to God, and Christian missionaries especially who mark India as a target for converting "heathens" have invited both individual and organized protests in India.[40] The extent to which Christianity and Islam have become the largest and most influential religious faiths in the world, and the manner in which they have achieved their status – through violence and through seduction as no doubt through "persuasion" – is surely cause for concern for those who believe in and practice other faiths.

Despite India's openness there is also native to the Indian tradition a powerful culture of inquiry and resistance to the marketing of spurious ideas and claims. That Jesus is the only son of God and Mohammed the last prophet are claims that Hindus can look at skeptically since their faith tradition extends back millennia before Christ or Mohammed. Islam and Christianity dismiss if not abhor the idea of incarnation of Gods and of imagery and image worship. Without image, there is no worship. Hindus worship their Gods – they bathe them, dress them, kiss them, adorn them, and adore

---

[40] Shourie, A. (2000). *Harvesting our souls: Missionaries, their design, their claims*. New Delhi: ASA Publications

them. For Christians and Muslims, God is a distant being/idea. However, they demand that the rest of the world accept their God or be doomed as "sinners" or demonized as "kafirs".

Gauchet[41] whose Christian-centric worldview enables him to claim that monotheistic religion was a form of social revolution leading to the birth of modernity and to freedom, says that God's "otherness" (a white bearded old man sitting somewhere in outer space called "heaven" and whose antecedents we cannot know and whose "mercy" we have to beg and accept) has allowed humans to become "free" or "modern". In fact, such speculation ignores Indian traditions of spirituality, and disregards the ground reality of the world where Christian proselytizers roam the world in search of heathens to save, and practice in their own backyards a variety of "primitive" rituals to rid their world of "Satan". Christian theologians cannot seem to acknowledge that their belief system is a house of straw built on sand.

Freedom for Gauchet seems to mean simply freedom from restrictions imposed by the Church. "Out of sight, out of mind", the old adage, seems to summarize Gauchet's esoteric and exotic argument about God being "put away" in some far away "Heaven". In Indian traditions "freedom" can be achieved when we break the shackles of greed, envy, fear, and desire, and not by sending God away. The enormous difference in approaches to the idea of "freedom" is indicative of the vast divide between the Western (especially Christian) traditions and Indic traditions. While this book is not a treatise on religion and psychology, it is important to point out in succinct terms that what the West and its religious traditions have marketed is nothing but hatred of and disenchantment with every other form of worship and prayer. That it has been done with such violence and has led to such societal upheaval is recorded in fine detail by Regina Schwartz.[42]

Monotheism is not just the belief in a single Divine Person. One who thinks of the Divine as an impersonal "essence" is not a monotheist, nor one who thinks of the Divine as a woman or maiden, child or boy. In monotheism, the divine person has to be a "Father", rather elderly, and who resides in "heaven".[43] "Monotheism contemplates the Divine in heaven and polytheism contemplates the Divine in the Universe", says Bose, and the placing of the Divine in some far away abode called "heaven" is what Gauchet claims "frees" humans from the divine – by taking "Him" out of the midst of humans. This is the kind of "freedom" that the West seeks to introduce to the "heathens" of India by sending missionaries who have sought to

---

[41] Gauchet, M. (1997). *The Disenchantment of the World: A Political History of Religion*. Princeton, NJ: Princeton University Press.

[42] Schwartz, R. (1998). *The Curse of Cain: The Violent Legacy of Monotheism*. Chicago: University of Chicago Press.

[43] Bose, A. C. (1954). *The Call of the Vedas*. Bombay: Bhavan's Book University.

proselytize Hindus over a period of centuries, and continue to do so even more aggressively now.[44]

The assertion of the Vatican, in response to a law passed in the Indian state of Tamil Nadu, that there is restriction of religious freedom in India is an allegation in the tradition of Christian manipulative politics. Ignoring the sovereign status of India, and meddling in India's internal affairs, the Vatican charged that, "Free exercise of the natural right to religious freedom" is prohibited in India. A similar concern was registered in the report of the United States' Commission on International Religious Freedom (USCIRF), which has declared India as a Country of Particular Concern (CPC) for the past six years.

Writing in the *Indian Express* Swami Dayananda Saraswati pointed out that both the Vatican and the USCIRF ignore that Tamil Nadu law makes only "the use of force or allurement or fraudulent means" unlawful in conversion activities. He asks, "Which just-minded person would not applaud a State's efforts to prohibit the use of such means? Is it not, then an embarrassment to those involved in conversion activities that the state finds it necessary to issue an ordinance prohibiting these?"[45]

It has never embarrassed Christian missionaries to use fraudulent means to convert people.[46] In 1974, a mission strategist, Ralph Winter, advised that Christians turn their attention from areas exposed to Christ to "unreached people groups". In 1989 another missionary, Luis Bush, claimed that 97 percent of the "unevangelized" lived in a "window" between the 10th and 40th latitudes, and said that the majority of those living in that region were "enslaved" by Islam, Hinduism and Buddhism, and, ultimately, by Satan.

Similarly, Shourie (2000) quotes from the Texas-based magazine *Gospel for Asia*: "The Indian sub-continent with one billion people is a living example of what happens when Satan rules the entire culture... India is one vast purgatory in which millions of people... are literally living a cosmic lie! Could Satan have devised a more perfect system for causing misery?"

Addressing the first world religion conference during his historic visit to the U.S. in 1893, Swami Vivekananda condemned such characterization of Hinduism: "Part of the Sunday School education for children here (in the U.S.) consists in teaching them to hate everybody who is not a Christian, and the Hindus especially, so that, from their very childhood they may subscribe their pennies to the missions. What is meant by those pictures in the school-books for children where the Hindu mother is painted as throwing her children to the crocodiles in the Ganga? The mother is black, but the

---

[44] Shashikumar, V.K. "Preparing for the Harvest..." *Tehelka*, February 07, 2004

[45] Swami Dayananda Saraswati (July 9, 2003). "The spectre of religious freedom". *The Indian Express*.

[46] Biema, D. V. "Missionaries Under Cover", *Time*, June 30, 2003.

baby is painted white, to arouse more sympathy and get more money. What is meant by those pictures that paint a man burning his own wife at a stake with his own hands, so that she may become a ghost and torment the husband's enemy? If all India stands up, and takes all the mud that is at the bottom of the Indian Ocean and throws it up against the Western countries, it will not be doing an infinitesimal part of that which you are doing to us" (Shourie, 2000).

Christian missionaries have always assumed and exercised complete freedom to evangelize and convert. That they have felt entitled to do so by any means is old news. However, the anger of many right-thinking people all over the world at the arrogance and blind hostility of the missionaries to other religions, couched in the verbiage of "Christian love and concern," seems to have had little bearing or impact on even the most powerful of Christian institutions, the Catholic Church.

Swami Dayananda Saraswati says that he is not against the freedom to "manifest one's religion or belief in teaching, practice, worship and observance," as stipulated in Article 18 of the United Nations Declaration of Human Rights. But he is opposed to those who consider themselves subject to a mandate to convert people to one's own faith because they espouse a worldview that does not permit religious freedom. Such proselytizers do not have any place for the practice of religions other than their own. The Swamiji pointed out the contradiction in the Pope's message that not only appeals for evangelism, but also for a democracy to support it that has "respect for religious freedom, for this is the right which touches on the individual's most private and sovereign interior freedom." He pointed out that the Pope, while recognizing an individual's religious freedom as "most private and sovereign," exhorted Christian missionaries to invade this private, sacred space. "The contradiction reveals a form of religious arrogance, known as fundamentalism," the Swamiji argued. The Swamiji, who passed away recently,[47] was one of the few vocal leaders who was able to make some impact on this issue, but in a world where religious conversion is accepted and practiced by the majority of religions, the Hindu voice has been ignored in the cacophony of the book-thumpers.

Integral to a converting religion is conversion, Dayananda Saraswati reminds us, and that ethnic religions across the world do not now, nor have they ever evangelized. The practitioners of such religions are not driven by religious intolerance as the practitioners of the two "great" monotheistic faiths. So, how should one deal with these aggressive and intolerant religions? Confronted with the paradox of religious freedom and the intolerance espoused by certain religions, the "objection to conversion from any indigenous religious leadership is an urgently necessary and long-overdue assertion, not a violation, of human rights," the Swamiji argued. He pointed out that a

---

[47] Gurumurthy, S. (September 25, 2015). "Swami Dayananda: The Patriot Saint". *The New Indian Express*.

Hindu is free from malice toward other forms of religious practice, and that Hindus do not have a religious mandate to bring other religionists to the Hindu fold. Therefore, a Hindu is fundamentally accommodating in terms of religious pursuits. Yet, if a Hindu wants his or her religious privacy respected and not intruded upon, the specter of a suppression of fundamental rights is raised around the globe, and in institutions that are basically commandeered by Christians, as the USCIRF is. The commissioners of USCIRF (which had no Hindu nor Buddhist representation, nor of any native traditions, till Ms. Preeta Bansal was appointed a commissioner after the urging of the Hindu community) have urged the United States government to use economic sanctions against India to ensure adequate "religious freedom" for their evangelism and conversion programs.

A Confluence of Anti-Hindu Forces
The more benign and amateurish the Hindu response is to the campaign of conversion and abridgement of Hindu influence in India, the more vicious the campaign of demonization carried out by Christian groups and organizations, who have connived with other fundamentalists to encircle and defeat Hindu activists. For example, a conference organized by the Indian Muslim Council-USA on June 28, 2003 in the San Francisco Bay Area, gave a call for uniting India's minorities (everyone from Christians and Muslims to Sikhs, *Dalits* and women) and for building a coalition to fight the "growing menace of Hindu extremism". Well-known Hindu-baiters harangued the sizable crowd of Muslims from India and Pakistan to safeguard their interests, and end the "oppression and suppression of minorities in India". It also appealed to the American people and government not to cooperate with authorities in India and Gujarat because they claimed that the Gujarat government had sponsored the massacre of minorities.

People who have appropriated the label of "secularist" but who are merely anti-Hindu, continue to raise the specter of "communalism" in India. That the news and analyses of events of 2002 in Gujarat was broadcast all over the world by these "secularists" is indicative of the challenges to good governance not just in Gujarat but in the rest of India.

Corruption of the Political Process
For a long time now, people writing letters to the editors of Indian newspapers have bemoaned that while the Indian Constitution puts faith in the value of democratic politics, the politicians are unfaithful and disloyal to the Constitution.

A former Election Commissioner, G.V.G. Krishnamurthy, said that there were 684 registered political parties in India. As of March 12, 2014 there were 1,616 political parties, the majority of them unrecognized. The fragmenting of parties, the floating of new parties, the permutations and combinations of these "non-serious" parties who wish to cash in by supporting one or other of the major parties during a crucial vote are at the root of instability and divisiveness in Indian society. The Election Commission seriously considered de-recognizing such "non-serious" parties but has not done so for fear that it is unconstitutional. Some frustrated citizens feared that unless the number of serious political parties at the national level was limited to not more than three, by amending the Constitution, India would not have stable democratic governance.

Would such a proposal be taken seriously? For example, almost all political pundits and media commentators proclaimed that the contest for the thirteenth Lok Sabha (1999-2004) would be between BJP and the Congress (I) and that regional parties would fare especially poorly. For example, *The Tribune*[48] reported that the Star Insight (exit poll) had predicted seats in the range of 295-305 for the NDA, and 145-155 for the Congress and its allies. On the other hand, the Doordarshan-DRS (exit poll) predicted 287 seats for the NDA and 174 for the Congress-led alliance. But both surveys agreed that the gains to BJP and the Congress will be at the cost of 'other' players. These other players are basically the variety of regional and caste-based parties who have splintered the Indian electorate. Given the enormous costs of conducting a general election in India (estimated between Rs. 9 billion and Rs. 10 billion, or $250 million), and the unconscionable and frivolous attitude of these "other" players that has led to the coarsening of the political and democratic ethos in the country, serious consideration should be given to the imperative of reducing the number of political parties to three of four.

There would certainly be a stampede for the position of "centrist" party with the Congress Party arguing that BJP is a conservative or a right-wing Hindu party, and BJP arguing that it has Muslims in its ranks and it is following the economic and social policies first adopted by the Congress Party. The debate for such positioning would be interesting because it would force the parties to adumbrate their economic and social policies that would help the country decide who is centrist in what terms, and who is conservative in what other terms. The problem of implementing such a plan is enormous as it would need a constitutional amendment. Regional parties like the Dravida Munnetra Kazhagam (DMK), the All India Anna Dravida Munnetra Kazhagam (AIADMK), the Telugu Desam Party and others would be especially wary of such a national dispensation. The other possibility is that the three or four party formula would be only for the national parliament and that states could let other political parties contest for state assemblies. Considering the rather large role that bit players still play we may have to wait for yet another general election to see if the electorate makes up its mind about such regional and caste-based parties.

---

[48] *The Tribune*, "Exit Polls are here to stay", October 11, 1999.

Too many Elections

Every time there is a midterm election, citizens angrily complain that what should have been avoided in the interest of the nation was forced on it, that the country was not prepared for yet another midterm election, costing the nation hundreds of millions of rupees of taxpayers' money. And yet others hope that midterm elections would perhaps be a blessing in disguise. They hope that the people will realize the selfishness and shortsightedness of politicians, and punish those politicians and their parties by not voting for them.

Why is India saddled with a messy democracy? Commentators have pointed out that the theory of modernization was developed primarily by American political scientists studying third world countries in the post-second World War period, and that the theory expected political development in new states to follow the path laid down by Western industrialized democracies. The theory failed not just because a large number of developing countries did not follow the prescribed path, but countries like India began to show political tendencies and characteristics that could not be explained by the modernization theory.

When democracy is transplanted it sometimes looks different in the new soil compared to the original. One such difference is the disturbing feature of political parties forming alliances without the least regard for ideology or policy issues. Pursuit of power at any cost has acquired legitimacy with long and widespread practice. This goes against the fundamentals of democratic governance, wherein the electorate is supposed to elect on the basis of ideological and/or policy issues and preferences.

S. R. Choudhury points out that while in all democracies political parties seek power they do it on the basis of an ideology, or a policy stance, as a means to the attainment of power. In India, most political parties do not have any such qualms or any such beliefs.[49] Thus, the AIADMK, part of a coalition led by BJP, overnight switched to seeking a coalition with the Congress Party, which was in the Opposition. The Congress Party was open to forming a government with the support of a party which till recently was part of the coalition to which the Congress was in the Opposition. The DMK, which was part of the NDA-led coalition government in the 1990s, sought to join hands with the Congress Party, and the AIADMK was all set to join the NDA to contest the 2004 general elections.

Misalliances and joint ventures of this kind are not just unthinkable in the West but unworkable (though the Cameron government which took office in 2010 is a coalition between the Conservative Party and Liberal Democrats). These "arrangements" shortchange the electorate; secondly, with increasing shifts in party alliances such political incest becomes institutionalized and acceptable. Thus there has been very little discussion about such unscrupulous practices and what it does to the fundamental principles of democratic governance. The media did not carry out any sustained

---

[49] Choudhury, S. R. "Whose Democracy?" *The Hindu*, April 28, 1999.

campaign against such practices at the time of the crisis that brought the BJP-led government down in 1999, while people were too passive and cynical to bring pressure on politicians to make a difference.

Coalition governments have been successful in the Netherlands, Switzerland, Belgium and Austria. Coalition experience in these countries has hinged primarily upon a politics of accommodation. Though such accommodation does not enjoy a comprehensive political consensus, it still makes sense because there isn't a complete absence of consensus. Is such consensus, essential to the quality and endurance of the political fabric, shared by India's politicians? Unfortunately, it is not so. For example, the Lok Dal decided to withdraw support to the BJP in January of 1999 and then changed its mind only to support it again during the confidence motion. The Bahujan Samaj Party (BSP) reneged on its pledge to abstain from voting during the confidence motion. Coalition logic should be based not just on a shared commitment to the maintenance of the system but more importantly on that crucial element: political trust.

In matters of politics leadership is the *sine qua non* for democratic governance. Hangers-on, criminals, and corrupt bureaucrats have entered the political arena since the time Indira Gandhi decided to dump the Congress Party's "Old Guard" and assume the mantle of "supreme leader" of the Congress Party. The birth of unprincipled coalition politics should be traced thus to the late 1960s. This is the same political dynamics that propelled Sonia Gandhi, a woman with little political experience, to be elevated as the president of the Congress Party, and as the party's candidate for prime minister. Not only did she have any message of her own to convey to the country but in the beginning she was even unable to read even those messages prepared by her colleagues. The Congress Party was willing, nay eager, to let Sonia Gandhi become prime minister because she is Indira Gandhi's daughter-in-law. It is the same political dynamic that made the BJP seek the support of a woman (Jayalalithaa) against whom not one but several corruption cases were pending. That act of hubris, which many BJP sympathizers have tried to play down, was what brought the BJP-led government down in 1999. That Jayalalithaa got back in the BJP fold soon after tells us of the unprincipled and unregulated political alignments that make governance in India such a hazardous affair.

Finally, the criminalization of Indian politics is a fall-out of "too much democracy". That every political party has succumbed to expediency was clear when 21 major political parties representing the entire spectrum of Indian politics came together in a rare show of unity to reject unanimously the Election Commission's order making it mandatory for candidates seeking election to declare their financial assets, their criminal antecedents, and their educational background along with their nomination forms.[50]

---

[50] Shahin, S. "The Criminalization of Indian Politics", *The Asian Age*, July 12, 2002.

Roughly 10 percent of legislators at both the central and state level are believed to be hardened criminals facing charges of murder, rape and armed robbery. Some 700 State Assembly members and 40 Central Parliament members had a criminal background in 2004. Equally troubling is the fact that almost all legislators are believed to be corrupt. It was estimated that a politician spent about 50 million rupees ($1 million) for campaigning a decade ago, and in the recently concluded elections it was estimated that some candidates spent anywhere from $10 million to $20 million.[51] Their legislative careers then become a way of recovering what they have spent, and more.

The practice of democracy in India has produced such distortions that it is dangerous to try and explain them away as "imperfections brought on by importing institutions". While democratic political structures are the most widely accepted design for governance in the world at the turn of the millennium, political practices in India contradict the logic on which those structures are set up. That academics and intellectuals in India ignore these trends and instead train their guns on a person like Narendra Modi, known for his simple lifestyle, discipline, and energy, is indicative of the idiosyncratic and illiberal nature of Indian politics.

Security Threats to the Nation
Campaign slogans not only have to be catchy, but if they have to have any impact they should have to have a strong kernel of truth. When Narendra Modi coined the slogan, "Modi or Musharraf", he homed in on one of the most important concerns of not just Gujaratis but all Indians: and that is the threat from neighboring Pakistan, and the Islamic jihadi forces trained and supported by Pakistanis.

The partition of India on the basis of religion – Pakistan for Muslims, and India for the rest – hurriedly executed by the British doomed India and Hindu-Muslim relations. Optimists, mostly Indians, still try hard to reconcile Pakistani ambitions with the Indian reality – that of being home to the third largest Muslim population in the world, after Indonesia and Pakistan. Pakistani attempts to disaffect Indian Muslims have had limited success, but generated among the Muslims a sense of siege and suspicion in India.

When Jinnah proclaimed that Hindus and Muslims are two different nations, he seemed to appeal to not only large sections of the Muslim elite and intelligentsia but also to the Muslim masses whom he despised. Mulk Raj Anand, in an afterword to Rafiq Zakaria's book, *The Price of Partition*, writes that "Truly amazing to me, even now (March 1998), is this phenomenon of Muslims, old and young, in Bombay being attracted to Jinnah who really despised all underprivileged people, whether they were Muslims or non-Muslims…. More amazing was the metamorphosis that he brought about among the Muslim masses, whom he turned, as if overnight, from friends of Gandhi into his enemies".

---

[51] "Campaign Finance in India: Black Money Power", *The Economist*, May 4, 2014.

The Election That Shaped Gujarat

In the provincial elections of 1945-1946 Muslim League presented a one-point manifesto: "if you want Pakistan, vote for the Muslim League". Jinnah toured the country and tried to unite the Muslim community under the banner of Muslim League. The Congress on the other hand stood for a united India. The Congress swept the polls for the non-Muslim seats, winning more than 80 percent of the general seats and about 91.3 percent of the total general votes. Muslim League, however, managed to win all 30 seats reserved for the Muslims. The results of the provincial election held in early 1946 were not different. Congress won most of the non-Muslim seats while Muslim League captured approximately 95 percent of the Muslim seats. While the majority of Muslims therefore voted for a separate Muslim nation carved out of India, one third of the Muslim population remained in India after the partition of the country. The bellicose and hateful Pakistani attitude towards India that triggered three wars has not only ruined India- Pakistan relations, but has also "created tension and unease among Indian Muslims" according to Rafiq Zakaria.

Zakaria ends his book with a strange comment, reflecting the confusion and conflict of the relationship between Hindus and Muslims in the sub-continent. He says the Muslim leaders in India "instead of bridging the gulf between Hindus and Muslims, are ever ready to widen it. They turn non-issues into crises and whip up religious frenzy. They are neither bothered about the educational backwardness and economic plight of their co-religionists nor are they interested in making the biggest minority of 140 million an integral part of the nation. Pakistanis seem little concerned about the consequences of their tirade against India, which inevitably harms the vital interests of their leftover faithful in India. Here in India in the name of secularism, bogus or genuine, Muslims become either pawns or scapegoats in the power struggle. How long will Indian Muslims have to pay the price of partition?"

Zakaria does not ask the more pertinent question: "How long will Hindus have to pay the price for partition?" Partition claimed the lives of at least half a million Hindus while undemocratic regimes in East Pakistan before and during the struggle for an independent Bangladesh, claimed another million or more. Three wars with Pakistan have cost the Indian exchequer billions of rupees. India is forever burdened with a split community, and because of the nature of Islam itself, and the global reach of the Muslim communities, Indian energies and ingenuity are tested in maintaining relationships with other Muslim nations. Finally, the Pakistani attempt to make Kashmir its own has posed the highest security threat to India. More than 300,000 Kashmiri Hindus have been driven out of Kashmir, and at least 60,000 people have died in the past 10-12 years in the region battling terrorists exported from Pakistan and militants homegrown in Kashmir. When 59 people were burnt to death on a train in Godhra, it was yet another exercise to import instability and mayhem into India. Gujaratis responded with anger and blood lust, killing hundreds of innocent Muslims. Even though the violence was controlled within 72 hours, damage had been done, and

India's self-avowed secularists went on a blame binge without understanding the consequences to India's Hindu-Muslim relations.

When Narendra Modi asked the Gujarat electorate to choose between him and Musharraf, he was asking them to choose between security and a Congress government that would weaken India's security by turning a blind eye to terrorism. That the Congress has been mollifying Muslims is evident from a statement made by Kerala's Congress Chief Minister A. K. Antony's that representatives of the minority community should "take sober positions in view of the general feeling among the majority communities that the minority communities were enjoying several privileges and were using their organized strength to wrest more benefits from the Government". He advised the Indian Union Muslim League's leaders not to shut their eyes to the large-scale economic inequalities that exist in the State. "They should not think that they could make the Government do anything on the basis of their organized strength", he said and pointed out that Kerala politics was much different from that of North India.[52]

Similarly, former Gujarat Chief Minister Chhabildas Mehta, decried in 1995 the Congress Party's appeasement of Muslims. He called for drastic measures by the Congress to win back majority support that, he claimed, the party lost in its search for minority votes. He said that the appeasement policy cost the party dearly in Gujarat: "Though we have done so much for minorities, they feel disillusioned. In the process, we also donated majority votes to BJP. We must now have a clear stand and do away with appeasement policy. The need of the hour is introspection. We have to search a way out to win the confidence of the majority and erase the impression that the Congress caters only to minority interests." More importantly, Mehta's comments about criminal activity among Muslim leadership in Gujarat, directly focus on the security issue that Narendra Modi harped on during the 2002 election campaign. Mehta said, "Some fundamentalist Muslims who have come to occupy important posts in the party are the ones who have done nothing except exploiting the Congress. Several of these leaders have direct links with anti-social elements. Also, investigations into the narcotics seizure in Broach indicated that the couple found with heroin worth crores of rupees had connections with some bigwig. A Maruti car found has been registered in Delhi. I do not want to go into details, but if proper investigations are made, much more can come out".[53]

It is all right for Indian academics and media commentators to proclaim that the only way Hindu-Muslim relations can heal or be turned around is to show Pakistanis how secularism has allowed India to become home for both Hindus and Muslims. Will this exhortation mean anything to Pakistan? One doubts whether Pakistan is going to change its Islamic character and announce any time soon that it is going to be a secular

---

[52] *The Hindu*, "Antony rejects deadline for rehabilitating the displaced in Marad", July 10, 2003.

[53] Trivedi, D. "Chhabildas sticks to his guns on minority votes", *Indian Express*, July 12, 1995

nation. One doubts too whether Pakistani leaders will stop harping on Kashmir, and focus on rebuilding their country and making it economically strong. One doubts too whether the attacks against Hindu modes of worship and culture will stop. In a recently released document, "The Subtle Subversion: The State of Curricula and Textbooks in Pakistan," prepared by the Islamabad-based Sustainable Development Policy Institute, it is reported that in government approved textbooks for schools Hindus are said to worship in temples which are narrow and dark places, and where they worship idols. Only one person can enter the temple at a time, whereas in mosques, on the other hand, all Muslims can say their prayers together. The books also tout that the "religion of the Hindus did not teach them good things" and that Hindus did not respect women. Accusing Hindus of being opportunists who co-operated with the English, the textbooks brainwash young children about India and Hindus.[54]

At best what Indians can do is to work to strengthen the country economically and follow a steady policy on security issues. This means nipping in the bud attempts by anyone to strike liaison with foreign terrorist groups, and imposing strict punishment on anyone attempting to subvert the security of the country. If those caught in such activities happen to be Muslim, it will be incumbent upon the Muslim leadership in India to condemn such attempts and consistently demand of their fellow Muslims to not lose sight of the fact that they are Indians first, and Muslims next. Merely harping on their minority status will simply add to the woes of an already tired nation.

Effects of Globalization

In an interview with the Public Broadcasting Service (PBS), United States, one of the most celebrated and listened to of India's leaders, the chairman of *Infosys*, Narayana Murthy, defended globalization. He said that globalization was good for mankind. If globalization led to fair trade practices, agreed to and adhered to by every country, globalization would usher in prosperity. But he also felt that those people and countries that had nothing to offer to the marketplace were afraid of and did not like globalization.

When asked if global free trade allowed the world's poor to escape from poverty, Murthy said that if a country which is rich and a country that is poor come together in global trade, sooner or later the standard of living of the poor country would go up. Of course, he agreed that if countries did not play by the rules, then globalization would not work. He feared that some of the rules of WTO were rigged in favor of the developed countries. He pointed out that while India would remove all quantitative restrictions by April 1, 2001, the U.S. (whom he did not identify) would retain quotas in areas like textiles until 2005. "Globalization is good, global trade is good, free trade is

---

[54] Bhattacharya, A. "Creating a Pakistan of Distortions", *The Daily Pioneer*, July 12, 2003.

good, competition is good. But at the same time, all of us must play by the... same rules. There must be the same playing field. All of us have to have a common referee; all of us have to follow the same set of rules,"[55] he said.

However, there is strong opposition to globalization in India, not only from Left/Marxist groups but even from many within RSS. It compelled Union Minister for Divestment Arun Shourie to write a scathing essay on what he considered the shortsighted views of some of his erstwhile colleagues in the RSS.[56] Shourie has said that India runs the risk of being isolated if it maintains an attitude of negativism and suspicion about the benefits of effective engagement at WTO. He feels that India has no alternative but to engage the world. One of his colleagues S. Gurumurthy has said that globalization in its present form is a continuation of Western hegemony. He believes that all the problems we face at present are the result of colonialism, and that while present day globalization is presented as a platform for the upliftment of people, it stands on three pillars: first, it is based on exploitation of nature; second, it is based on individual liberty and freedom; and third, on the idea of the survival of the fittest. These principles, he believes, go against the Indian ethos, and would be disastrous in the long run.[57]

The charges against globalization include exploitation of Third World labor, destruction of environment, rules that favor the West and the rich countries, child labor and sweat shops, the weakening of nation states, especially the poor and the small ones, fall in real wages, mechanization, unemployment and underemployment, loss of traditional culture and habits, sex trade and exploitation of women, and many others. It is claimed that globalization is a process that leads to great wealth for a few, marginalization of the many, and polarization (or inequality) between them. Tanzania's President Benjamin Mkapa told an UNCTAD Conference that countries that adopted liberalization and privatization under World Bank-IMF policies suffered immense social costs, including job losses, cuts in health care and education, and "immense possibility of instability". "Opening up of our national economies is also a problem," he added, for "such industries as we have will be affected by imported products that run our companies out of business".

The Human Development Report (HDR) 1996, recently published by the United Nations Development Program (UNDP), also contains data that add empirical weight to the thesis that globalization benefits only a few, makes a lot of people worse off, and generates tremendous inequities. It also questions the conventional wisdom that

---

[55] "The Basis for India's High-Tech Industry" (February 5, 2001). Interview with N. R. Narayana Murthy, *Public Broadcasting Corporation.*

[56] Shourie, A. "The Comfort of Conspiracies", *Daily Excelsior*, February 26, 1999.

[57] Gurumurthy, S. International Seminar on "Bhagavad Gita and Modern Problems", Thiruvananthapuram, 7-10 December, 2000.

economic growth has benefited most of the world's people. It is claimed that over the past three decades, only 15 countries have enjoyed high growth whilst 89 countries were worse off economically than they were ten or more years ago. In 70 developing countries, today's income levels were below those of the 1960s and 1970s. And in 19 of them (including Ghana, Venezuela, Haiti, Nicaragua, Sudan), per capita income was less than it was in 1960 or before.

Before we let such statistics overwhelm us, we need to understand that the sins attributed to globalization are mostly sins committed by dictators, unwieldy command economies, and mismanagement by bureaucrats. With the fall of the Soviet Union, the world saw major, even cataclysmic, changes. Countries formerly in the Soviet orbit, which built up barriers on trade, suddenly faced the prospect of negotiating "international waters". Many were unequipped to do so, and many were unwilling. Moreover, the policies of the World Bank and the International Monetary Fund had sapped the economies of quite a number of developing countries.[58] Stiglitz says that the probability of a major financial crisis has actually increased because the government is more leveraged and liberalization of capital flows allows short-term, "hot" money to flow in and out of the country, which makes for more volatile markets. He points out the hypocrisy of the United States, which asks countries to drop their tariffs and subsidies to enable the U.S. to export goods, keeps tariffs on steel and subsidies for farmers, thus closing the U.S. market for other countries. The central theme of the book is that the current focus of globalization adversely affects developing countries because they incur a disproportionate amount of the costs and long-term risks while well-to-do western bankers and U.S. corporations reap many of the benefits.

The effects of globalization doubly trouble a state like Gujarat, which has seen natural disasters and human conflict, and which is struggling to pay off huge debts. While it struggles to find employment for its people, it also has to face closure of textile and other small industrial units that cannot compete with cheap foreign goods flooding the market. To deal with these problems, the State Government, in cooperation with the Indian Institute of Management, Ahmedabad and the Center for Globalization and Sustainable Development, signed a memorandum of understanding at Gandhinagar on Friday, May 9, 2003. The three parties agreed to initiate research in the following broad areas:

> 1. Developing a macroeconomic growth model for Gujarat economy with a view to developing alternative scenarios and policy options.
> 2. To help in the designing of a new seismic research institute in Gujarat and to work with the Gujarat State Disaster Management Authority on developing suitable disaster management strategies.

---

[58] Stiglitz, J. (2003). *Globalization and its Discontents*. New York: W.W. Norton & Company.

3. Promotion of foreign direct investment in the State, and CGSD's participation in the FDI attracting Mega event planned for September 2003.
4. Studies to develop Special Economic Zones in the State for export promotion.
5. Measures for the development of information technology and biotechnology sectors in the State.
6. Seasonal and inter-annual climate prediction and their impact on the economy.
7. Studies for development and expansion of labor intensive manufacturing in the state.

This would include:

(a) Likely impact on agricultural output at the farm level using crop models to facilitate decisions on crop selection, input-mix, irrigation requirements, etc.
(b) Likely impact on agricultural economy to help decisions on seed and water allocation;
(c) Likely macroeconomic impact on state budget, drought relief, and environment.

These programs are important and necessary for the State as some experts have attributed the ferocity of the sectarian violence of 2002 to the frustration of people hit by unemployment following closure of textile mills in Ahmedabad as a result of economic liberalization. Vandana Shiva, the globetrotting anti-globalization activist, claimed that "one of the fallouts of the insecurities and polarizations created by both 9/11 and globalization is the increased communalization of politics in India and heightened tensions between India and Pakistan". Quick to connect the dots, uneven as they may be, she claimed, "Thousands of Muslims died in communal violence in Gujarat, the state most integrated into the global economy". "The killers were economically globalized but culturally parochial. They drove fancy cars and had mobile phones, their targets were Muslim business establishments," she asserted confusing those newspaper reports that claimed some hooligans driving cars had stopped to loot shops with rioters who had raped and murdered and set businesses on fire.

Vandana Shiva claimed that "the Gujarat genocide (sic) has made it clear that economic integration and economic 'openness' on terms that generate economic inequality and insecurity can go hand in hand with social disintegration and economic and political 'closure' and exclusion". According to her, "undemocratic, unequitable, unjust integration through global markets is precisely what is fueling fundamentalism, intolerance, xenophobia and violence across the world". She argued, "Economic 'openness' for MNCs under the rules of corporate globalization implies 'economic closure' for domestic producers. India's small scale industry is closing down, destroying millions of jobs".

Hyperbole is the hallmark of publicity-seeking activists, Indian or Western. Those against globalization, especially in India, are for taking India back to its command economy, red-tape-bound "license raj" days that let industries produce high-priced shoddy goods, bureaucrats lord over industrialists, and politicians manipulate the market and seek the setting up of huge loss making government corporations. Globalization, like any other social or political change, is a mixed bag. It is left for the leaders in government, business, and society to make globalization work for India, and not lash out in fury and disgust.

Some have argued that what India needs is full internal liberalization, and selective external liberalization. In the short run, it is one's political ideology that will shape the assessment of the impact of globalization. In the long run, one cannot escape changes in the world, which include open borders for goods, capital, and people.

In the following chapters, we lay out in chronological fashion, the developments in Gujarat in the past two years, and how the 2002 elections not only signified a watershed in Gujarat politics but also serve as a case study in the development and sustenance of democratic and open societies. All the above issues we have brought to the fore impacted the campaign for elections in 2002. Unfortunately, most of the media analyses ignored them or touched upon them superficially. The narrowly focused campaign to oust Narendra Modi was both homegrown and internationally supported. Unless we understand the confluence of interests and agendas of both local and global actors in Gujarat, we will fail in grappling with the challenges democracies face everywhere.

The story of the past two years in Gujarat needs to be told in some detail so that we understand the forces that shape and undermine democracy. While some of the details of Gujarati politics may both seem alien and esoteric to some readers, they are to be read keeping in mind the framework we have constructed and presented above.

CHAPTER II -- SHIFTING FORTUNES AND THEIR AFTERMATH

The period intervening between the last Congress government at the center in 1996 and the induction of Narendra Modi as the elected Chief Minister of Gujarat saw a succession of events of great import to the country and its people. Five prime ministers heading hurriedly cobbled and unprincipled coalitions came and went. Suddenly, stability became a central concern. India and Pakistan moved ominously close to a nuclear confrontation. Social equilibrium in Gujarat suffered damaging communal harmony elsewhere in the country. The media embraced evangelism of a questionable kind.

In this chapter we will summarize the important events leading to changes both in New Delhi and Gandhinagar, the capital of Gujarat. This summary will not only provide the context and the framework to discuss and analyze both the nature and fluidity of Indian politics but also the challenges that confront politicians, especially those keen on ushering in more modern, open, and streamlined administrations in a country that is still beset by the vestiges of colonial and feudal experiences harking back to a millennium.

The 1984 general elections, in the aftermath of Indira Gandhi's assassination, proved to be the BJP's Waterloo. Out of 545 seats to the Lok Sabha, BJP could win only two seats. But after that watershed election, and the subsequent adoption of Ayodhya temple as an issue, BJP grew in stature and strength. It has ruled practically all major North Indian states, the Hindi-speaking belt, and the industrial state of Maharashtra. Three times, a BJP Prime Minister has headed the government -- first for 13 days, and then for 13 months when the BJP lost the confidence of the House by a solitary vote. The government fell in 1999 as a result of the vote of a BJP ally turned back-stabber, Saifuddin Soz, a Kashmiri Muslim, a former National Conference (NC) member, and an ally of the BJP-led NDA government. Consequently, the National Conference expelled Soz for life.[59] Queering the pitch was also the vote by Girdhar Gomango, who rode two horses at the same time: as a Congress Member of Parliament and as Chief Minister of Orissa. He should have quit or been removed from Parliament after being sworn-in as Chief Minister, but strangely enough continued to be on the Parliament rolls and was ordered by Sonia Gandhi to vote for the No Confidence Motion.

As the National Democratic Alliance government headed by Atal Bihari Vajpayee was about to complete its full term of five years in office in September-October 2004, Vajpayee called for early elections in April 2004, which led to the defeat of the NDA

---

[59] *Rediff on the Net*, April 19, 1999, "NC expels Soz for life".

Coalition and the coming to power of the UPA Coalition led by the Congress Party. However, Vajpayee earned the distinction of becoming the first non-Congress Prime Minister to complete a full five-year uninterrupted term in office.

From two seats in Parliament to the "throne" of India, the BJP's success was indeed noteworthy. There have been three major benchmarks one can readily identify as having propelled the BJP strategically when acceleration was what was needed: the first was its historic 1989 Nagpur National Executive meeting that decided to raise the issue of building a temple of Lord Rama in the ancient city of Ayodhya, heralding Hindutva politics, a unique strategy to highlight aggressively and boldly the rights of the Hindus. The second event was the nation-wide road trip undertaken by L. K. Advani, the BJP strongman who garnered the credit for rebuilding the party after its 1984 debacle. Advani covered the length and breadth of the country in an effort to heighten public awareness of his party's plan to build the temple at Ayodhya. The tour went on as planned and nearly reached Ayodhya.

Vishwanath Pratap Singh was heading a non-Congress government at that time, and Rajiv Gandhi was the leader of the Opposition. Singh's ascent was a sequel to the "Bofors Gun" import scandal that had severely dented the prestige of the Congress Party and enthroned a non-Congress coalition government, with BJP support. As Advani's temple caravan neared Ayodhya, "secularists" within the government beseeched V.P. Singh to appreciate the grave threat Advani's tour could pose to the country's secular credentials, and stop his journey. Sensing that the Prime Minister was becoming increasingly critical of the Ayodhya movement, BJP issued a veiled threat that any attempt to stop Advani from completing his tour would forfeit its support to the Singh government. Without that support the government would fall. The Congress wanted this to happen, as it would warrant another round of general elections.

As Advani's entourage entered the Ayodhya area, he was stopped and placed under house arrest. The BJP immediately withdrew support to the central government, forcing the Prime Minister to resign. Chandra Shekhar became the next Prime Minister with the support of the Congress Party. The Congress, eager to come back to power, waited for the opportune moment and withdrew support to Chandra Shekhar in 1991. In the end, general elections had to be called in mid-1991. The Congress had expected to win a majority of seats in Parliament, paving the way for Rajiv Gandhi to become the Prime Minister again. However, destiny had other plans. During his election campaign in the Southern state of Tamil Nadu, a woman suicide bomber killed him at the behest of the Sri Lankan separatist group, the Liberation Tigers of Tamil Eelam (LTTE), to avenge Rajiv Gandhi's decision in 1987 to send Indian troops to Sri Lanka to crush the LTTE.

Rajiv Gandhi's assassination unleashed a sympathy wave for the Congress. The Congress, however, failed to get an absolute majority, and hence formed government with support from other parties. As Rajiv Gandhi's widow Sonia Gandhi, an Italian by birth, refused to enter politics at that point, P.V. Narasimha Rao became the Prime Minister.

Major riots broke out in India in 1992 following the demolition of the mosque named after Babar, the Moghul emperor. BJP governments in a number of States were dismissed, and President's rule imposed. The BJP's parent organization, the RSS was banned. This was the third time when the RSS was banned in independent India. The first time was after the assassination of Mahatma Gandhi, when vested interests pointed fingers at the RSS, but subsequently Home Minister Sardar Vallabhbhai Patel absolved the RSS of complicity. The second time was when Indira Gandhi imposed internal emergency between 1975 and 1977, and the third time was when the Babri mosque was brought down. When elections were held in the former BJP-ruled states, the BJP lost and the Congress Party stormed back to power.

The 1996 general elections saw the Congress losing and the BJP increasing its tally even more. BJP now had the industrial state of Maharashtra too under its belt. Since the verdict of the electorate was fractured, no single party could form a government on its own. It was a hung parliament with BJP emerging as the single largest party. The BJP staked its claim to form the government, and for the first time Atal Bihari Vajpayee was sworn in as Prime Minister. Failing to prove its majority in Parliament, the government fell in thirteen days. Later on L.K. Advani would quote in his famous speech in Shivaji Park, Mumbai that people called it a "13-day wonder". Communists and Janata Dal parties came together with outside support to form a government. It was a conglomeration of parties with diametrically opposite views and ideologies. Advani called it a "multiple-party blunder". The internal squabbles saw two Prime Ministers come and go. Both the "humble farmer" from Karnataka H. D. Deve Gowda, and the suave but tepid I. K. Gujral had brief stints at the top post. In the general elections called in 1998, BJP fell short by about 91 seats to get absolute majority. The party formed a coalition government on a national agenda that compelled BJP to keep in abeyance its main concerns -- the abolition of Article 370 of the Indian Constitution conferring special status on Jammu and Kashmir, implementation of a uniform civil code, building a temple in Ayodhya, and a ban on cow slaughter.

Prime Minister Vajpayee had a tough task reining in and assuaging a petulant Mamta Banerjee, and the inscrutable and complex AIADMK leader Jayalalithaa. Amidst the political wrangling that haunted the coalition, the BJP-led government managed to implement one of its manifesto points: equipping India with nuclear arms. India had first conducted nuclear tests in 1974, but voluntarily refrained from arming itself with nuclear weapons. In the 1980s, and early 1990s, India buckled under international pressure and abstained from inducting nuclear weapons.[60]

However, Indian leaders and the security establishment had reasons for building a nuclear deterrent. For example, the 1980s Chinese incursion into Arunachal Pradesh

---

[60] Raja Mohan, C. (2003). *Crossing the Rubicon: The Shaping of India's new Foreign Policy*. Penguin Books

saw the Indian Army in an aggressive mode. Under the command of General Sundarji, the Army launched Operation Falcon against the Chinese occupation of Sumdorong Chu in 1986. Sundarji used the air force's new air-lift capability to land a brigade in Zimithang, north of Tawang. Indian forces took up positions on the Hathung La ridge, across the Namka Chu River, the site of India's humiliating 1962 defeat and manned defenses across the McMahon Line. Taken aback, the Chinese responded with a counter-build-up, and in early 1987 Beijing's tone became ominously similar to that of 1962. Western diplomats predicted war and Prime Minister Rajiv Gandhi's advisers blamed Sundarji as being reckless. But the General stood firm. The Chinese indeed were taken aback. It was an Indian Army very different from what they had met and defeated in 1962.

Then there was Operation Brass Tacks (1986-87) aimed against Pakistan that saw the two countries come very close to war. This is the backdrop for Vajpayee government's decision to conduct nuclear tests, develop nuclear weapons, and label China as enemy number one.[61] The other reason was that when Vajpayee extended his hand to Pakistan through the Lahore-Delhi bus tour, Pakistan reciprocated by sending its troops to occupy Indian positions in the Kargil sector of the Kashmir Valley in the winter of 1998.

In the interim, the differences with Jayalalithaa of the AIADMK (a partner in the Central government) grew, and when she withdrew her support to Vajpayee's government, no one was in a position to provide an alternative in 1998. Lok Sabha was equally divided, but a solitary vote in the 545-member house ousted the BJP government. Vajpayee submitted his resignation but was asked to carry on as caretaker Prime Minister till an alternative coalition could prove its majority on the floor of the house.

Alien and Imperfect

Let us hark back to our introductory chapter, and reiterate that while western democracy remains the model for the rest of the world, that model is imperfectly adopted or manipulated in emerging democracies. In Germany, for example, to vote out a government, an alternative government has to be voted in first. However, such is not the situation in India where election-driven, no-holds-barred attempts to dislodge ruling governments lead to repeated general elections that can cost the Indian tax payers a billion dollars or more, excluding the vast amounts of money spent by political parties in campaigning.

Sonia Gandhi, the Congress Party leader, who authored much of the "undermine the BJP government" campaign, claimed she had the requisite number of 272 MPs to

---

[61] Van Pragh, D. (2003). *Greater game: India's Race with Destiny and China.* McGill Queens University Press.

form a government, but failed to produce their signatures on paper even when President K. R. Narayanan gave her extra time. Narayanan, a former Congressman and diplomat, entered politics and won in three successive general elections in 1984, 1989 and 1991 from the Parliamentary constituency of Ottapalam in Kerala. He was a Member of Parliament from 1985 to 1992.

The Samajwadi Party of Mulayam Singh Yadav, which was beholden to its Muslim vote bank, did not support the Congress Party's initiative for fear of antagonizing its Muslim vote bank in the state of Uttar Pradesh. As no group could get the requisite numbers, the Lok Sabha was dissolved and general elections were called.

In the interim, the Indian Army had to contend with Pakistan's occupation of its positions, and violations of the Line of Actual Control (LoC). Pakistan's military commanders thought that with the political instability in India, time was ripe to initiate action on the Kargil front, and effectively cut off the Buddhist dominated Ladakh from the country. Ladakh is the area that China had attacked in 1962. It still occupies about 38,000 square kilometers of Indian territory. But Pakistan was mistaken. In a democracy, there is no power vacuum even if there is a caretaker government in place and elections are scheduled. The political diversity of India, with its dozens of regions, religions and languages, actually guarantees the democratic future of the country rather than threaten it. In India, democracy has matured from just being a form of government to a way of life. Democratization has enveloped Indian culture too.

Pakistan's military was taken aback when it saw Indian fighter jets carrying out air-strikes. Pakistani forces withdrew after suffering huge losses, but not before the United States brought pressure on Prime Minister Nawaz Sharif, who saw no escape from asking his generals to go back to their bases. But before Nawaz Sharif could complete his task, General Musharraf threw him out in a bloodless coup. In India, elections held in October 1999 saw Prime Minister Vajpayee leading his coalition partners to victory.

In this period, the BJP had mixed fortunes at the state level. Other than Gujarat and to some extent Uttar Pradesh, the BJP could not retain any other state for two consecutive terms. In Maharashtra, the BJP government fell short by 15 members in the 288-member State Assembly to be able to form a government: as many as 24 of its sitting members could not retain their seats in the anti-incumbency wave that swept the state. In the 1999 state elections, the BJP was relegated to fourth position. The party won only six seats in the 2000 Haryana assembly elections. The BJP wave was ebbing as the party began losing state after state. The Congress Party was now under the leadership of Sonia Gandhi and though her Italian descent issue was raised from time to time, there was no real threat to her leadership despite the fact that the party split in 1999 on this very issue.

Despite reversals elsewhere, the BJP captured a sizeable majority in Gujarat. BJP leader Advani contested successfully from Gujarat to enter Parliament. The BJP headed a government in Gujarat twice in the last ten years. Twice, Keshubhai Patel was the Chief Minister, and Suresh Mehta once. When the BJP came to power in 1995

Keshubhai Patel became the Chief Minister, his one-time protégé and the then general secretary of the party's Gujarat unit -- Narendra Modi -- became his right hand man. Modi was by Keshubhai's side at all meetings. Some people believed that Modi was the de-facto Chief Minister.

Modi, being a long time RSS *pracharak* (grass roots worker and teacher), was an asset for Keshubhai. Many in the party disliked Modi's growing importance, and they began to complain in party forums and elsewhere. Shankersinh Vaghela, chief among the dissidents, even took the extreme step of spiriting away a few of the BJP MLAs from Gujarat into hiding at a hotel in Khajuraho in the neighboring state of Madhya Pradesh. This open show of dissent panicked the BJP high command. Efforts to resolve the issue failed. Vaghela would not come back. He broke away from the BJP and formed his own party, the Rashtriya Janata party (RJP).

Vaghela's revolt led to the fall of Keshubhai Patel government after which he manipulated to get elected as Chief Minister with the backing of the Congress Party. Vaghela was an RSS man, which is why his exit came as a shock to the BJP. Since someone had to accept the blame for this unforeseen development, it was thrust on Narendra Modi, who, his critics argued, as the General Secretary of Gujarat BJP, should not have needled Vaghela or "Baapu" as people lovingly called him. Modi was exiled to Delhi. Officially, he became the secretary of the BJP at the national level yielding the Gujarat slot to another RSS man, Sanjay Joshi.

The Vaghela-Congress party honeymoon did not last long either. As ironic as it seems, the law of karma soon caught up with Vaghela, and the Congress Party cut short his term as Chief Minister by withdrawing support. To oust him, the Congress Party cited corruption, an old and ever useful ruse to foist yet another election on the hapless electorate.

In a span of three years, BJP formed government a second time in Gujarat, and this time with Suresh Mehta as Chief Minister. Though many considered Mehta as the candidate of the industrial lobby, his tenure lasted just a year. His resignation paved the way for the 1998 assembly elections.

Assembly elections were held in 2001 in Assam, West Bengal, Tamil Nadu, Kerala, and the Union Territory of Pondicherry. BJP's presence has traditionally been marginal in those four states and in Pondicherry, and though the party won slightly more votes and more seats, the Congress made a triumphant return to power in Assam vanquishing the Asom Gana Parishad (AGP) - BJP combine at the hustings, securing an absolute majority on their own in the 126-member assembly. While the 2001 elections cannot be considered a parameter to judge the BJP's popularity graph, the loss in Assam compounded the woes of the party.

Gujarat after 1998 and the Sabarmati Election

In the 1998 state elections the BJP won by securing 117 of the 182 seats. Keshubhai Patel, the patriarch of the BJP in Gujarat, again became the Chief Minister, but had to make way for Narendra Modi in the fall of 2001. What led to the fall of Keshubhai is an interesting tale indeed.

In the years after forming government in Gujarat, BJP performed miserably in the village and city council elections, losing the prestigious Ahmedabad and Rajkot municipal councils. At the village level too, BJP performed poorly, with the Congress bagging more than seventy five percent of the village councils. The BJP lost badly not just in Gujarat but also in the adjoining state of Rajasthan, with the Congress getting a two-thirds majority. Maharashtra too went the Congress way. It seemed as if the tide was finally turning in favor of the Congress and that the BJP was in retreat. Perhaps what drove the last nail in the coffin of Keshubhai regime was the debacle in Sabarmati Assembly by-elections.

Yatin Oza, a young lawyer in the Gujarat High Court, was also a BJP member from Sabarmati. Satish Verma, a senior police officer, had a fracas with Oza during a public protest. Oza felt humiliated, and wanted action taken against the officer. Haren Pandya, Home Minister at that time, refused to oblige. Oza felt that it was at the behest of Haren Pandya that he was beaten up by the police in full public view, and it was done to damage his public stature. Being an MLA of the ruling party and yet not able to get the police officer punished, left Oza hurt and humiliated. Contrary to rumors, Oza did not become a minister. The seeds of revolt began to sprout.

The 70 year-old Health Minister Ashok Bhatt added fuel to the controversy by claiming in public that the 35-year-old Yatin Oza had decided to call it a day in politics, and would concentrate on his profession as a High Court lawyer. Oza challenged this statement affirming that he had no intention of retiring from politics. The Congress saw an opportunity in Oza's discontent. Its leader Amarsinh Chaudhary said that a young and dynamic lawyer like Oza would be an asset to his party. Oza quit the BJP saying, "I have no regrets of leaving the party and have no desire to defraud the people's mandate, which was for the BJP and therefore thought it fit to hand over the seat back to the party." Oza was firm about his decision to quit the party. The final act of submission of the resignation was peaceful. Speaker Dhirubhai Shah accepted it wondering whether the number 182 (number of assembly seats in Gujarat) was jinxed, with one seat in the assembly usually vacant.

In 1998, BJP's nomination of Yatin Oza as its candidate from Sabarmati constituency created a controversy. His nomination and those of Bharat Barot (Dariapur- Kalupur constituency), Kamlesh Patel (Maninagar constituency) and Gopaldas Bhojwani (Naroda constituency) were challenged because some of them were among the dissident members who had supported Shankersinh Vaghela, and made the journey from Gujarat to the infamous Khajuraho hideout in 1995. In the end, these MLAs remained with BJP but when Vaghela broke away and formed the RJP, they veered towards their mentor. The grudge between Keshubhai Patel and Yatin Oza was thus an old one. Oza revolted against Keshubhai Patel, defected from BJP, and joined the Congress. This defection in mid-2001 resulted in a by-election for the Sabarmati assembly constituency.

Sabarmati constituency is one of the six assembly segments forming the Greater Gandhinagar parliamentary constituency, whose incumbent representative was Deputy Prime Minister Advani. It is thus considered a "VIP" constituency. In the ensuing by-elections caused by Oza's defection, BJP candidate Babubhai Patel lost to Narhari Amin, a Gujarat Congress party strongman. Loss of Sabarmati seat sent alarm bells ringing in Delhi. It was a severe jolt to Advani, who had campaigned for the BJP. He signaled that things had to change in Gujarat. Keshubhai Patel was summoned to Delhi. The high esteem Keshubhai commanded among the BJP cadre could not translate into votes for the BJP. There were ugly rumors about the entourage that surrounded Keshubhai, and eventually he stepped down, albeit reluctantly after clinching an implicit commitment that he would get back the top slot. Yatin Oza got his revenge, but by sacrificing his MLA seat.

One can surmise that the defeats of the BJP in various elections in Gujarat after 1998 made the party bosses uneasy, what with the state elections scheduled in 2003. The BJP had lost Maharashtra, Rajasthan, and Delhi, but the loss of the Sabarmati seat was a rather loud wake-up call. If the BJP could not retain a seat in Advani's own parliamentary constituency, how could it motivate its cadre to fight a rejuvenated Congress? The BJP high command got its act together and decided Keshubhai must relinquish charge in favor of the younger Narendra Modi.

On October 7, 2001, Narendra Damodardass Modi became Chief Minister. Modi had already adopted the role of a "can-do" man. The swearing-in ceremony was broadcast live, not only on television, but also on the Internet for the thousands of Gujaratis all over the world. In his inaugural speech Modi used the slogan, "*Aapnu Gujarat, Aagvu Gujarat*" ("Our united Gujarat, our foremost Gujarat"). It was then that the concept of Gujarati pride was born, in time for a rich harvest in the state elections about 15 months later.

CHAPTER III -- WAGES OF PERSONALITY POLITICS

In a country still under the influence of colonialism and feudalism, personality politics become the single most important factor in fighting and winning elections, in orchestrating the fall and the construction of new ministries, in the divvying out of public largesse, and in conducting day-to-day administration. Leadership, of course, is the *sine qua non* in providing a vision for any institution or administration. But how leadership is cultivated, attained, maintained, and sidelined is a reflection of the cultural and social condition of that particular institution or society. Considering the vast majority of illiterate and poor citizens in India even today politics are still driven by "personality", and defined by caste, pedigree, power and social status. It is not necessarily a manifestation of the capability and abilities of the person that defines leadership in this scenario as much as "name recognition". Process usually gets short-circuited by the person, and democratic principles get buried under a plethora of personal ambitions, connections, and machinations.

Gujarat politics, in this sense, were and are no different from politics anywhere else in the country. Modi continues to be both demonized and deified as a person, and his abilities as a good administrator, therefore, get very little play in the media and in the minds of the electorate. Modi could initially function effectively only if and when he catered to the whims and fancies of the powerful within his own party. If he was to undo the edifice of personality politics, it would not be accomplished overnight, as many of the "progressives" would want him to. There is no magic wand to deal with this problem, and only careful, intelligent, and disciplined work can begin to undo the undue influence of the powerful, the criminal, and the politically connected.

Thus the Gujarat politics of the last decade of the twentieth century can be traced to many events, but let us begin by relating the incidents leading to the emergence of one political personality. Commissioner of Police Jaspal Singh took a tough stance against anti-social elements in Vadodara city. The police could not enter a particular Muslim dominated area of the city, notorious as haven for ciminals, without permission from the local gang lords. Jaspal Singh, an officer of the Indian Police Service (IPS), an elite core of officers, led a police team to clean up this area and almost single-handedly brought the law and order situation under control. His firm resolve to control the anti-social elements endeared him to the people of Vadodara. He soon had a fan following.

Jaspal Singh resigned from government service and contested the assembly elections as a BJP candidate. As predicted, he won, and was inducted into the cabinet. Jaspal Singh showed his mercurial nature even in his new role as a politician. He rattled the local BJP cadre, and many a time threatened to resign. He challenged the Chief Minister, accusing him of corruption, and supported his former police colleagues, including the Director General of Police, C. P. Singh, who accused the VHP and Bajrang Dal leaders of fomenting communal conflict in Vadodara.

But Jaspal Singh also threw his weight around, as evident from a brush he had with a young Indian Administrative Service (IAS) officer. It could be that he was trying to show the IAS officer that though he was a former IPS officer, he was now a minister no longer lower in the bureaucratic hierarchy (IAS officers are ranked higher than IPS officers). The IAS officer was traveling in his official car when his driver passed Jaspal Singh's car because the officer was in a hurry to attend a meeting. This simple act of perceived disrespect angered Jaspal Singh. How dare such an "insubordination" occur?

With sirens blaring Jaspal Singh's car passed the IAS officer's car, and blocked the official's vehicle. A police constable, a lower rank police officer, instantly appeared on the scene and made sure that the IAS official's vehicle would not move till the "Honorable" Jaspal Singh's vehicle went well past ahead. Refusing to take this humiliation lying down, the IAS officer filed a complaint with the Gujarat IAS Officers Association. Only a personal apology from the then Chief Minister Keshubhai Patel soothed tempers among the IAS officers.

Jaspal Singh's tough action against anti-social gangs in Vadodara endeared him to the people, but his mercurial temper was proving to be a liability for the BJP. Singh was supposedly a Modi supporter in the days when Narendra Modi was the BJP general secretary away in exile in Delhi. Singh resigned from the Keshubhai Patel ministry, accusing the Chief Minister and other members of the cabinet of corruption and inefficiency.[62]

It was rumored that Jaspal Singh resigned at the behest of the anti-Keshubhai lobby. When Narendra Modi became Chief Minister, Jaspal Singh wanted his pound of flesh. With Modi in command, there was no need for Jaspal Singh because there could not be two, let alone too many, "strong men" in the Cabinet. Again, Indian politicians continue to practice to some extent the art of wheeling and dealing, and plotting and scheming that thrived in the palaces of erstwhile Indian kings, Muslim or Hindu. Therefore, everyone constantly keeps minding his back, and in turn plots to undermine someone else. Modi's first ministry-making exercise also encountered the usual pressures for inducting a large number of ministers into the cabinet, thus leading to a rather large 39-member ministry.[63]

It was during a subsequent election rally that Modi explained why Jaspal Singh was not made minister. Modi said that according to an intelligence report Singh was seen coming out of the Pakistani Embassy in Delhi. An angry Jaspal sued Modi for defamation, asking for a public apology. Modi declined, and stood by his statement. Towards the end of 2001 Jaspal Singh, disenchanted with Modi, resigned from the party, and joined the Samajwadi party. Singh's resignation from the Vadodara assembly

---

[62]"BJP fears more may follow Jaspal", *The Indian Express,* December 30, 2001

[63] *India Today,* "Mixed Signals", October 20, 2001.

seat led to by-elections there. The by-elections were held in February 2002, two weeks before the Godhra train carnage. The Congress Party fielded Dalsukhbhai Prajapati, a former mayor of Vadodara -- a man considered to have both money and muscle power. Jaspal Singh also contested the election but could not secure even the minimum number of votes to have his security deposit returned. The Congress won the seat convincingly. The by- elections were for filling three assembly seats -- Vadodara, Mahuva (a designated Scheduled Tribe constituency), and Rajkot-II. Narendra Modi contested the first elections of his life from Rajkot-II assembly constituency. He won in Rajkot, but the Congress gained Vadodara and Mahuva.[64]

These developments should be seen against the complexity of political dynamics in India. There is a tendency among editorial writers or social activists or the simply idealistic to criticize a particular political development or a particular politician and demand that matters be set right immediately. Narendra Modi came with some baggage to the position of Chief Minister of Gujarat, and it was not easy to off-load that weight immediately or easily. Though Modi could not dodge pressures from within the party to induct persons with a history of corruption and crime into his ministry, he himself remained untainted by any charge of corruption.

---

[64] Note: Jaspal Singh joined the Aam Aadmi Party in December 2013. After he quit the BJP in 2001 he joined the Samajwadi Party, and later the Samata Party before rejoining the BJP, which he quit again in 2011.

CHAPTER IV -- REKINDLING PRIDE
IN THE WAKE OF A QUAKE

The Vedas proclaim that the hardships of life can be classified into three categories: *Aadi-daivik*, *Aadi-bhautik*, and *Aadhyatmik*. All natural disasters fall under the first category. The second kind of hardship is caused by living entities -- for example, when a person dies of snake bite. And the third one is a man's own making. An example of the first category was the earthquake that struck the Kutch region of Gujarat on January 26, 2001 registering 6.9 on the Richter scale. In less than two minutes the earth unleashed an energy equivalent to 300 Hiroshima type bombs. About 7,633 villages were razed to the ground, and over 13,000 people lost their lives. More than 50,000 artisans lost their livelihood. The affected area was 182,639 square kilometers -- more than the areas of Portugal and Austria put together. Direct losses were computed at $3.3 billion, indirect losses at $ 0.67 billion, and tertiary losses at $ 2.19 billion.[65]

It was the BJP government's task to set about bringing things to normal, and to provide the healing touch to shattered lives. The administration adopted a holistic approach to reconstruction and rehabilitation. Over 167,000 injured were treated and more than 17,000 surgical operations performed. Nearly 28 million kilograms of food grain were distributed within two weeks of the disaster. Cash doles were provided to over 900,000 families and nearly two million truckloads of debris were cleared to enable reconstruction. The government restored 800,000 houses in a year's time. About 40,269 classrooms were repaired in a year's time to ensure that the education of village children did not suffer. About 31,000 beneficiaries were covered under the cotton growers' package, 16,000 beneficiaries under the trade and commerce package, and 131,000 farmers were helped under the agriculture package. More than 35,000 women received economic livelihood restoration packages. Gujarat rehabilitation efforts following the earthquake have no parallel anywhere in the world. For example, the August 17, 1999 earthquake that struck Marmara, Turkey, is said to have affected 14,000 families directly; the Mexico City earthquake of 1985 is said to have affected 24,000 families; the Latur earthquake in Maharashtra, Sepetember 30, 1993 is said to have affected 30,000 families; the January 17, 1995 earthquake that struck Kobe in Japan is said to have affected 31,000 families, while the 2001 Gujarat earthquake is said to have affected 256,400 families. The Gujarat rehabilitation effort, in terms of providing immediate shelter to affected families, was 8.5 times bigger than the Latur exercise, and 11 times more than the Mexico City effort.

When the earthquake struck Gujarat on January 26, 2001, Keshubhai Patel was the

---

[65] GSDMA (2002). "What has changed after Gujarat earthquake 2001?" PowerPoint presentation. http://www.jst.go.jp/astf/document/43pre.pdf

Chief Minister. A year later, Narendra Modi was at the helm of affairs. Modi presented to the people the efforts the BJP government and the Gujarat State Disaster Management Agency (GSDMA) had made to restore normalcy. The government made several presentations to the United Nations, the International Monetary Fund, and to World Bank officials. In New Delhi, various foreign diplomats attended these presentations. There was appreciation for the work done by the BJP government led by Modi. Later, the presentations made at Prime Minister Vajpayee's official residence to the Indian cabinet mesmerized everyone with the sheer magnitude of work done in a year's time. In a way, the speed and magnitude of debris clearance was faster than even the American effort to clear the World Trade Center site after 9/11.

The presentations were professional, incorporating the latest in graphics, design and technology. Modi wanted to persuade all viewers, and especially those involved in funding the rehabilitation efforts. The Chief Minister chose a small and hitherto obscure company -- the Moving Pixels Company -- for creating the publicity material. Under the guidance of the Additional Principal Secretary, Anil Mukim, a team of young people worked hard to produce a series of audio-visual material that highlighted the BJP government's efforts in providing succor to people hit by the devastating earthquake and in bringing normalcy to a tired and weary state. The Gujarat earthquake and its aftermath have been recounted and analyzed in a 2013 book by Edward Simpson. He blames and shames many and is ambivalent about the many efforts and the consequences to rebuild the Kutch region.[66]

Prior to the presentations before a world audience, Modi had personally taken reports from each and every government department involved in the rebuilding work. The Chief Minister held extensive meetings, and exhaustive question and answer sessions for hours on end, grilling officers on each and every count, conducting video conferencing sessions with district and villages level officers through the GSWAN (Gujarat State Wide Area Network), the largest IT infrastructure in all of South East Asia. Mobile VSATs (Very Small Aperture Terminals) were sent on motor vehicles to remote villages so that the Chief Minister could directly interact with the villagers and get feedback first-hand from the affected. Modi introduced a new concept in governance in India: that of taking the head of the government directly to the common man in the village, through the effective use of Information Technology.

A media blitz was unleashed with various magazines and newspapers focusing on the achievements of the government. The Chief Minister was at his best trying to instill pride in the state and confidence in the government. Modi gave top priority to the issue of earthquake rehabilitation. He made the CEO of GSDMA, Dr. P.K. Mishra, his principal secretary.

The message that Gujarat could put its best foot forward, that it had a government

---

[66] Jack, A. (December 1, 2013). "The Political Biography of an Earthquake, by Edward Simpson". *Financial Times*.

The Election That Shaped Gujarat

that could deliver, was clearly intended to make Gujarat visible to the world community, and make investors take note of this state. Narendra Modi embarked on the mission of invoking Gujarati pride -- "Gujarat's Gaurav".

CHAPTER V -- MODI'S HUNDRED DAYS IN OFFICE

Administrative inefficiency, corruption, and poor planning are the bane of most Indian governments. For example, a recent report by the World Bank claims that India loses about $40-50 billion because of poor roads, and that wages constitute sixty to seventy percent of the cost of road construction. The World Bank defines corruption as "using public office for private gain." Therefore, in 1996, while awarding road-building contracts in India, the World Bank made transparent bidding procedures mandatory for disbursing loans.[67]

Corruption in India is of mammoth proportions, and no government has escaped charges of ministerial and bureaucratic corruption. Of the 133 countries listed on the "corruption index" by Transparency International in 2003, India ranked 83, with Finland the least corrupt and ranked number one. To climb down the steep ladder of corruption is a tough task made more difficult by the ubiquity and the quotidian nature of corruption. However, it was reported that India could soon have an "index" to measure the level of corruption in Government departments, public sector units and banks as a move to bring greater transparency in their functioning. The move, initiated by the former Central Vigilance Commissioner, N. Vittal, was at the behest of the former World Bank president, Robert McNamara. At a conference at The Hague, McNamara said that he found that the "corruption perception index" of various countries brought out annually by Transparency International served as a point of reference to the bank in dealing with the countries.

However, by 2013 India had slid down the index to 94th place -- but the list of countries surveyed had risen to 175. Corruption has seeped so much into the vitals of the nation that even the BJP, supposedly the most disciplined of political parties, was caught in a corruption scandal when its party president, Bangaru Laxman, was taped surreptitiously, receiving about $2,000 from journalists posing as arms traders.

The Keshubhai Patel government, of course, was castigated by many, including people within the BJP, for both corruption and inefficiency. One newspaper reported that Keshubhai Patel, as Chief Minister, had installed 40 air-conditioners in his official residence.[68] Moreover, the Gujarat Congress president, Amarsinh Chaudhary, said that a judicial inquiry should probe the allegations of corruption against Vajubhai Vala, Revenue Minister in Keshubhai's Cabinet. Singh also claimed to possess documentary evidence of alleged corrupt practices by Keshubhai and some of his cabinet colleagues, and is said to have shared the knowledge with Narendra Modi when Modi was the BJP national general secretary.

---

[67] The World Bank (June, 2011). "Curbing Fraud, Corruption, and Collusion in the Roads Sector".

[68] "Gujarat Minister speaks out against CM", *The Hindu*, August 09, 2001.

Thus, when Narendra Modi became the youngest Chief Minister of Gujarat on October 7, 2001, he had quite a task to remake the image of his party, and to produce some quick and positive results. He got down to the task energetically, and in the first 100 days in office he instilled a new spirit in the state, both in the administration and among the people. His "tough man" image served as lubricant to the rather rusty and creaky government machinery. In his early days as Chief Minister, Modi projected the image of a man who had excellent relations with the Central Government and was heard by those who mattered. It was thus that he accompanied Prime Minister Vajpayee on his Russian visit – a rather rare privilege for a Chief Minister to be included in such an entourage traveling abroad.

The Russia Visit
Modi visited Russia with Prime Minister Vajpayee and signed a memorandum of understanding with Anatoly Guzhvin, the Governor of Astrakhan.[69] This event marked the successful culmination of an initiative taken by the Chief Minister. Ten areas of mutual co-operation were included in the MoU: (1) Developing the North-South sea transport corridor; (2) Sharing technology in exploration and development of liquid hydrocarbon – oil and natural gas; (3) Shipbuilding technology; (4) Setting up food processing and packaging industry in Astrakhan for commodities produced in Gujarat; (5) Astrakhan providing modern technology for development of fishery in Gujarat; (6) Encouraging drugs and pharmaceuticals manufacturers of Gujarat to set up units in Astrakhan; (7) Encouraging long – term relations in trade, industry and tourism; (8) Human resources development; (9) Cultural exchange; and (10) Exchange of information.

Funds Allocation
The Gujarat urban development department sanctioned over $217.4 million for town planning, reconstruction, and town modernization programs. The government set up a new women and child welfare department, and also allocated about $22 million towards tribal welfare. The tribal groups form a large vote bank in Southern Gujarat, and more than 10 seats in the State Assembly are reserved for the tribal representatives. Hence the Chief Minister's priority list included focus on tribal welfare. Traditionally, the tribal belt was the stronghold of the Congress Party, but of late the BJP has begun making inroads.

Samras
From the first day in office Modi's focus was the election nearly a year and a half away,

---

[69] Government of India (November 6, 2001). "Protocol of Cooperation between the state of Gujarat and the Astrakhan region".

and his strategy was to work upon the traditionally weak areas of his party, and to develop programs that would help his party gain support in those areas. Gujarat, like the rest of India, is divided along a variety of caste and community lines, and Modi was keen that his party identify its own strengths and weaknesses, and work to build a comprehensive strategy for winning the next elections.

Media pundits and academic apologists have now recognized creating and nurturing vote banks as legitimate and valid strategies for winning elections in India. Of course, in every democracy, narrow appeals to religion, race, class, sex, and origin have always figured either subtly or overtly. Though Indian election laws disallow sectarian appeals, they are still made in different venues and through different processes: for example by promising a variety of economic, social, and welfare measures for particular groups. Thus we see the emergence of vote banks – where the majority if not the whole group votes for a particular candidate or a particular party. Analogously, we may point out that Blacks form a vote bank for the Democratic Party in the U.S, and the majority of Southern White men vote for the Republican Party.

How does one upset this particular cart? Parties usually accomplish this by promising to select groups more than what the rival party had promised. Of course, promises are based on the worth of the vote bank, as political pundits and party officials spend countless hours trying to calculate how much of which vote bank can be seduced by promising what. After the 1998 elections, the BJP was on the decline in Gujarat, having lost town councils, assembly seats, and village councils. In fact 80 percent of Gujarat village councils were in the hands of the Congress. The BJP needed a strategy to upset the Congress cart. The strategy Narendra Modi adopted was termed *"Samras"* (Unity).[70]

Modi assumed office in October 2001, and was leading a BJP already on the decline against a Congress Party that was growing in confidence. Modi was not yet a member of the State Assembly. He had six months within which to contest elections and win if he were to continue as Chief Minister. The village council elections were also due. The BJP was aware that if elections were held to the village councils the Congress Party would have an upper hand. A BJP loss would be a further setback to the Modi government, evoking calls from the Opposition parties to oust his government, and dampening the enthusiasm of party workers who had responded positively to the anointing of Modi as Chief Minister.

Modi's government proposed a plan to give additional funds to village councils to be used exclusively for village welfare. Equivalent of $2,000 would be given to each village with a population of more than 5,000, and $1,200 to each village with a population of less than 5,000 provided that the village chose its councilmen and women unanimously. Villages that chose women as council members or council chairperson got

---

[70] *The Financial Express* (January 18, 2002). "Mr. Modi's Samras Gram Yojana pays rich dividends in Rural Gujarat".

additional funds. A significant number of villages where elections were scheduled voted for this option, thereby getting more funds for the development of their village. Modi, in one shrewd stroke, fulfilled the requirement of setting up village councils, avoided a BJP defeat, and provided much needed funds for rural development. Which party won the *gram panchayat* elections was still not clear, as the candidates did not fight on party symbols.

Village council elections are not fought on party labels but by individuals. Only after the elections would council members proclaim allegiance to a particular party. The unanimous selection of council members saves money, prevents bitterness among political rivals, and generates a cordial political environment, claimed the BJP. Thus *samras* helped villages get much needed development funds and kept the political and social dynamics relatively tension-free. The success of this strategy was a setback to the Congress Party and detractors of Modi who had their own misgivings about these elections. With polling for 10,334 village councils scheduled for December 23, 2001 many were wagering that the more Modi talked about *Samras* by avoiding contests the less the chances of the villagers wanting it.[71] As it turned out, elections were held in 7,988 villages while about 2,791 councils were declared elected through consensus. In the previous village council elections 3,408 of the 13,557 councils opted to select council heads unanimously rather than having a contest. The incentive paid to each village council then was a mere 2,000 rupees ($40) whereas what Modi offered was between 60,000 rupees ($1,200) and 100,000 rupees ($2,000).

Opposition members complained that Modi was misusing government machinery by asking bureaucrats to go to villages and convince them about *Samras*. Others asserted that most of the villages that saw no contest were in the Saurashtra region and the reason for opting for consensus varied from "harmonious co-existence" to "bullying by certain castes". Some analysts asserted that it would take just one knock to demolish the *Samras* scheme, if only the Congress chose to deliver that knock. If the Congress party was determined to have elections in each village council it would have been able to encash its growing popularity in the state. Others said that the *Samras* program was a novel idea but not democratic. They complained that only the BJP believed that a democratic contest creates enmity among the people, and that the BJP's real objective was to take away what the Indian Constitution gave every citizen -- the right to contest elections and the right to vote. Some felt that unanimous selections were dangerous because they permitted the dominant communities to take control of the village councils. This was an effort to manufacture consent, detractors argued, and that it undermined the very roots of local democracy.

Democracy in India, we have pointed out, is election-driven, with the result that all

---

[71] *The Times of India* (November 23, 2001). "Modi's noise over Samras may backfire".

political parties are in a perpetual "gearing up for elections" mode though not as obsessively as the Americans! Being election-driven we mean that there is also a constant attempt at undermining elected governments. Grabbing power at any cost and wielding power for power's sake seems to be the prime motivation in Indian politics. Therefore, it would not have come as a surprise if there was a call for Modi's head if the village council chiefs chose to align with the Congress Party instead of the BJP, no matter that one set of elections should not have any bearing on office-holders who have been elected in another set of elections.

Narmada Dam
Another major achievement of Modi early in his tenure as Chief Minister was to project the Narmada river project as one above partisan politics, and as a project that benefited all Gujaratis. This mega dam project faced stiff opposition from Medha Patkar's NBA (Narmada Bachao Andolan) and other NGOs. Medha Patkar demanded better rehabilitation of the tribals affected by the rising waters of the dam. The Supreme Court of India was seized with the matter, and it was only by court orders that the dam's height was increased in phases to enable effective and timely rehabilitation the people. Medha Patkar and her NBA rejected the government's rehabilitation program. Booker prize winning author of the *"God of Small Things"* Arundhati Roy was also associated with this group. Roy was imprisoned symbolically for a day in March, 2002, on the orders of the Supreme Court for contempt of court.[72] She had criticized the Supreme Court's judgement in the Narmada issue and accused it of trying to silencing dissent and harassment.

The Narmada passes through three Indian states -- Madhya Pradesh, Maharashtra, and Gujarat. Madhya Pradesh and Maharashtra have Congress governments, whereas Gujarat has a BJP government. Gujarat is in dire need of Narmada waters, and has dug huge canals to redirect flood waters to other parts of the state affected by constant drought. It is the government's attempt to evenly distribute fresh water from flood areas to drought areas, and in the process generate electricity. According to an agreed arrangement, Gujarat would get water, whereas Madhya Pradesh would get electricity. However, there can be no generation of electricity unless the height of the dam reaches 110 meters. The government awaited court orders to increase the height in phases. The cases the NBA filed against this dam project also delayed the construction of the dam, and hence Medha Patkar became a *persona non-grata* in Gujarat, and both the Congress Party and the BJP opposed her. This was evident from what greeted her when she visited the Sabarmati Ashram in Ahmedabad after the Hindu-Muslim riots that followed the Godhra train carnage. Later, Medha Patkar operated mostly in Madhya Pradesh, which the Congress Party ruled till 2003 with Digvijay Singh as its Chief Minister. He had become somewhat of a darling of social activists, and somewhere along the way,

---

[72] Venkatesan, J. (March 07, 2002). "Arundhati Roy jailed for contempt of court". *The Hindu*.

and mostly probably on the advice of an astrologer, he added an "a" to his name, so he is now Digvijaya Singh.[73]

Gujarat has paid compensation for tribal rehabilitation to Maharashtra and Madhya Pradesh. On taking office, Modi worked to raise the Narmada issue above partisan politics, and succeeded in winning the support of the the Congress governments for an expeditious rehabilitation program for the tribals.

Tele-Fariad

Modi is a tech-savvy leader. Indeed, we have seen an increment in his approach to and use of communication technology and media, including social media like Facebook, and 3-D technology to "appear live" in different venues simultaneously in the run up to, and during the 2014 General Elections. In a country where most politicians do not know how to use even a typewriter, let alone a computer, or where the jewelry of choice for the legislator is a huge flashing ring on his fingers, Modi is different. He carries with him a lap-top computer and, now a smart-phone, and relies on assistants who are well-versed in science and technology. Modi told one of his assistants that he had about fifteen months to complete the work of reaching out to fifty million Gujaratis before the 2002 election. That translated to less than one second to reach out to each and every Gujarati, including thousands of non-resident Gujaratis. That was how a unique complaint redress scheme came to be launched.

The Chief Minister's recorded voice greeted each complainant when they went to record their grievance. Within 72 hours of the complaint being registered, action was initiated. The scheme achieved an initial success of 41 percent, and then climbed to a 64 percent solution rate of the grievances received. The brainchild of a young assistant of Modi, this hi-tech solution can be used by anyone, the old and the infirm, or the illiterate and the disadvantaged. The system used an isolated computer system in the District Collector's office, and connected with four or five special four-digit telephone lines. The Chief Minister's voice greeted every caller. The computer recorded the grievance as a ".wav" file, and compressed it into an ".mpeg" file. It was then e-mailed to the Chief Minister's office in Gandhinagar through the GSWAN network. A team of young people in the Chief Minister's office listened to the grievances and did the transcription. The transcription also segregates the complaint into various departments, and then e-mails it to the respective District Collector's office from whose district the e-mail has emanated. The District Collector's office then has 72 hours to initiate action and provide feedback to the Chief Minister's office. On Modi's advice, this scheme was implemented in the rural district of Banaskantha on the Gujarat-Rajasthan border, along with the urban district of Rajkot. The United Nations Public Service Award was given

---

[73] Dasgupta, S. (December 02, 2003). "Where did Digvijay go wrong?", *Rediff on the Net.*

to the Gujarat Chief Minister's Office in 2010, in recognition of this innovative program.[74]

Welfare of the Girl Child

"If a boy is educated, a person gets educated, but if a girl is educated, the entire family gets educated", says Modi, giving a creative spin to the old adage, "give a fish to a man and he will eat for a day but teach him how to fish and he will never go hungry".

Modi is a self-proclaimed "bachelor" – the marriage at the age of 17 to Jasodaben was not consummated, and his "wife" led a simple life as a school teacher away from Modi, and retired from Rajosana Primary School in 2009. He lives alone. All the gifts given to him by people were collected and deposited in the government treasury. The government periodically held public auctions of these gifts and the money collected was ploughed back into a scheme called the *"Kanya Kelavyani Yojna"* or the "Scheme for the Benefit of the Girl Child". It was the Chief Minister's favorite program as it aims to change the face of Gujarat by targeting illiteracy and the feudal ways of life which still force most women to lead secluded and sharply circumscribed lives.

Modi seeks to set a standard for political leaders. He leads a frugal and simple life but avoids the Indian political habit of masking corruption behind crumpled clothes and/or displaying red, betel stained teeth.[75] No one has accused him of corruption, though in the labyrinth of Indian politics one cannot always avoid being seen in the company of an unsavory character or two. Modi's sympathizers as well as his detractors told us to tell him to be wary of some of those characters with whom he has been seen in public. Not a neophyte in politics, the man surely recognizes this as he tries to achieve probity in public life and even as he sought to bring stability to his government.

Thus, attempts to use modern technology to bring efficiency to administration, coalition building to achieve the state's goals, and some creative and quick thinking to ward off threats to his nascent rule characterized the first 100 days of Modi in office. He still had to face the first election of his life. All through his years as a grass roots worker and later as a man of influence, he was known as a kingmaker, but now he would be taking his first shot at winning an election for himself.

---

[74] Shah, J., & Jha, P.K. (July 4, 2010). "SWAGAT, says UN to Gujarat CMO's initiative". *Daily News and Analysis*.

[75] Prakash, S. (April 21, 2014). "Meeting Modi: Spartan surroundings, No fuss, All business", *Rediff on the Net*.

CHAPTER VI -- SEEKING A MANDATE: THE RAJKOT BY-ELECTIONS

According to Indian election laws a person cannot be a minister for more than six months without being a member of the legislative assembly or legislative council. However, this six-month waiver is available only once. That means a person cannot resign after six months, and then be sworn in again so that he can continue in office for another six months, and so on.

Narendra Modi was sworn in as the Chief Minister of Gujarat on October 07, 2001. He was not a member of the state assembly, and thus by law he would have to contest elections to continue as Chief Minister, and win within six months of being sworn in. Two seats were ready for contest after the resignation of Jaspal Singh from Vadodara, and the death of the MLA from Mahuva constituency. The big question in everyone's mind was which constituency would be chosen for the Chief Minister. In 1998 the BJP contested 182 seats and won 117 seats. One of these seats would have to be vacated for the Chief Minister. One MLA would have to resign.

As a *pracharak*, Modi had worked for years in the city of Ahmedabad. "Sanskarsdham", a school founded by him, is also in Ahmedabad. It is a city Modi calls home. It was thus natural that he should contest the very first election of his life from Ahmedabad. The BJP MLA from Ellisbridge constituency was Haren Pandya. When Haren Pandya was young, it was Modi who groomed him, pleaded on his behalf, and ensured that Pandya became the BJP candidate from Ellisbridge. The Ellisbridge assembly constituency is a traditional BJP stronghold. Any reasonably good candidate contesting on a BJP symbol would win there.

During his tenure as general secretary of the BJP's Gujarat unit, Modi mainly was responsible for the victory of Pandya. However, things had soured between them over time. Modi was eventually asked to leave Gujarat and go to Delhi as the BJP national general secretary. After the 1998 elections, Haren Pandya got the all-important Home Department portfolio. Because of their new enmity, it was rumored that whenever Modi was in town, the intelligence bureau would keep Pandya updated on Modi's whereabouts. In short, Pandya was rumored as using the police intelligence network to keep track of Modi's activities. When Modi became the Chief Minister, he relieved Pandya of his Home Department portfolio and gave him the Revenue Department.

Modi sought to contest from the Ellisbridge constituency for his first election. But for that to happen, Haren Pandya would have to resign his seat which he refused to do. Modi did not take this insult quietly; he refused to meet Pandya, or invite him to any official meetings. It was said that at any venue where Pandya was present Modi would walk out. The BJP therefore chose the Rajkot-II assembly constituency for Modi. It is a Brahmin-dominated constituency and was represented by senior leader Vajubhai Vala.

Vala was facing a number of allegations of corruption and was known to have a large interest in the infamous construction industry. Vala resigned and vacated his seat in favor of Modi. The Congress Party fielded a well-known city doctor, a Brahmin, and a man of repute.

True to form, Modi used information technology in a big way in his election campaign. As Rajkot-II is an urban constituency, more people have access to computers and telephones. Modi commissioned an auto-dialer system. The system dialed numbers and played Modi's pre-recorded tape. Specific e-mail addresses were surveyed and a database made of those addresses. Narendra Modi had a special photo-session for this campaign. He knew that he had a "strong man" image, and that he had to portray his more humane and sensitive facets. So the photo sessions focused on capturing a smiling Modi. This was the face that was used on all BJP posters, placards and hoardings for the by-elections. E-mails with the picture of a smiling Modi reached Rajkot-II Internet users, and cyber cafes. A "Narendra Modi Internet Fan Club" came into being virtually overnight and it carried out this task.

The charisma of Modi attracted BJP supporters and party workers from all over India to campaign in the elections. One of those workers was Bharat Mata Mohan, who was with the BJP unit in Tamil Nadu. Mohan runs a residential school in Tamil Nadu. Mohan and Modi completed their final year of training at the same time at the RSS headquarters in Nagpur. Founded in 1925 by Dr. Keshav Baliram Hedgewar, the RSS is India's largest NGO. Its aims include building the character of citizens and spreading the message of patriotism to the masses. The collective membership of the RSS, along with its associated organizations numbers over 30 million. The BJP is an RSS off-shoot in the field of politics; the VHP (Vishwa Hindu Parishad) or World Hindu Council is involved in bringing various Hindu sects and groups to work together; the Van-Bandhu Parishad (Tribal Welfare Organization) is involved in tribal welfare; and the Akhil Bharatiya Vidyarthi Parishad (All India Students Organization) is the RSS off-shoot in student politics/activities. India's largest trade union, the Bharatiya Mazdoor Sangh, is also associated with the RSS. The RSS runs orphanages, homes for widows, medical centers, women's organizations, human resource development centers, and training institutes.

The RSS was founded in Nagpur at a time when Muslims and Hindus were at loggerheads. Hedgewar believed that the root cause for attacks by foreign invaders was the internal fragmentation of the Hindu polity. He felt that social fragmentation, the advent of industrialization, and the centuries-long occupation of India by Muslim and Christian invaders and militaries left Hindus vulnerable and weak. Hedgewar, who led the organization from 1925 to 1940, believed that a properly trained cadre of nationalists would lead the movement for change.

Hedgewar launched the RSS in September 1925, recruiting young men and boys from a local neighborhood in Nagpur. These youngsters were encouraged to attend "*akharas*" (gymnasiums) regularly, and listen to lectures on politics and culture on

The Election That Shaped Gujarat

Sundays and Thursdays, taking their oath in front of the saffron flag and the pictures of Ramdas Swami (a seventeenth century Hindu saint) and of Hanuman (a sacred deity and symbol of strength and devotion). The RSS program was planned to instill discipline, build organizational strength, and to channel the energies of adolescents and young men.[76]

Mohan and Modi were friends from their RSS days. Though of modest means, Mohan spent his own money campaigning in Rajkot-II constituency among the South Indian residents there, showcasing RSS brotherhood and lifelong filial bonds.

By-elections were held in three constituencies, Mahuva (a reserved seat for Scheduled Tribes), Vadodara, and Rajkot-II. Modi won from Rajkot-II with a margin of about 14,000 votes, which was a modest victory. The BJP lost the other two. There were rumors that the great patriarch and dethroned king of Gujarat BJP, the erstwhile Chief Minister Keshubhai Patel, was still disgruntled, and did not do much to help Modi's campaign. Rajkot-II is in the Saurashtra region of Gujarat, which is a Keshubhai stronghold. And since Modi had replaced Keshubhai, the latter's refusal to actively campaign for Modi was not unexpected. Modi scraped through to a win, and so had little reason to relish victory. Worse yet, bigger trouble was round the corner.

---

[76] Rao, R. N. (2001) *Secular 'Gods' Blame Hindu 'Demons': The Sangh Parivar through the Mirror of Distortion*. New Delhi: Har-Anand Publications.

CHAPTER VII -- GODHRA AND ITS AFTERMATH

Barely had Narendra Modi begun to breathe a brief sigh of relief, having won the Rajkot- II seat, than a crowd of Muslims, instigated by local politicians and mullahs, set fire to a train carrying Hindu pilgrims at Godhra, barely 200 kilometers from Gandhinagar, the capital of Gujarat, on February 27, 2002. Fifty-nine Hindu pilgrims -- men, women and small children -- were burnt alive. They were returning from a pilgrimage to Ayodhya, where in 1992 Hindus, mostly supporters of the BJP and RSS, tore down a mosque. It is said that a lieutenant of Babur, the Mughal King, built it in the fifteenth century by knocking down the temple to Rama, revered as an incarnation of Vishnu by Hindus.[77]

The Godhra carnage was the most gruesome act of mass murder on a train, since the days of partition, when ghost trains with mutilated bodies crossed the just demarcated borders between Pakistan and India, in 1947. Unfortunately, the global and Indian media's reaction to the ghastly crime was muted. But Gujaratis responded with a blood lust that caught the attention of the world, which quickly foisted the blame on Modi, twisting every word and utterance of his to suit their own purpose of demonizing the Hindus and vilifying the BJP. The media ignored the original act of horror that fueled the reprisal massacre of some 700 Muslims. There was a lot of grandstanding and editors and politicians as well as sundry activists bemoaned the bloodlust of ordinary Gujaratis. "Civilised societies do not allow anger to descend into barbarism"[78], intoned one editor, and blamed Modi for his "insensitive utterances". "Gujarat witnessed the transformation of prejudice into bloody slaughter. It should shame and warn every Indian", the editorial rebuked but shied away from warning about the nature of the dangers that the country faced. As if to make up for the incompleteness of that editorial, the same issue of the magazine carried another editorial which warned that "for the Indian middle class, religious frenzy is now the No.1 cause of concern". Either the focus on the "middle class" was reflective of the concerns of the magazine's readers or it was a pointer to something else. That something else included the assertion that after the events of September 11, 2001 the global community "is less tolerant of religious bigotry and the violence it foments". Once again, the editorial failed to ask the more important question: who would gain from stoking religious conflict in India?

In the North Gujarat town of Himmatnagar there were calls for BJP leaders and Modi to resign and go on a *Haj* pilgrimage to Saudi Arabia. They were trying to shame the Chief Minister and his party for failure to protect the Hindus, for failure to save

---

[77] Elst, K. (1990). *Ram Janmabhoomi vs. Babri Masjid*. New Delhi: Voice of India.

[78] Purie, A. "Primal Fear", *India Today*, March 18, 2002.

Hindu children and women returning from their pilgrimage to Ayodhya. Just as Muslims consider the pilgrimage to Mecca and Medina as holy, just as Christians regard the pilgrimage to Nazareth and Bethlehem religious, and just as Jews regard it a mandate to fight and keep control of Jerusalem, Hindus attach both religious and political significance to visiting Ayodhya and recovering the holy site of the Ramajanmabhoomi (birthplace of Rama). Hindus believe that the Moghuls under Babur destroyed the temple dedicated to Rama, and built a mosque there in the sixteenth century. No Muslim offered prayers in the mosque since the 1950s when the Hindus installed their idols in the premises of the mosque. A Hindu mob destroyed the Babri mosque in 1992. The matter was unresolved and finally the Allahabad High Court gave its verdict in 2010. The Ram- Janmabhoomi Nyas, the All India Babri Masjid Action Committee (AIBMAC), and the All India Muslim Personal Law Board (AIMPLB) engaged in a hotly contested law suit with each of them claiming ownership of the site. Hindus demanded that a temple be built there, and the Vishwa Hindu Parishad (VHP) organized numerous Hindu prayer sessions at the site, even as the Muslim groups sought the restoration of the place as a mosque. Some wanted a temple and mosque adjoining each other, while still others favored the place to be used for public good by building a hospital, a school or a park. It was one such VHP pilgrim group that was returning from Ayodhya when their train was set on fire as it reached Godhra.

Various reports in the media alleged that Muslims traveling in the same train were provoked all along the route and they were only waiting for their brethren at Godhra to exact revenge. Newspaper columnists and academics around the world have equivocated on the gruesome murder or even sought to rationalize it based on rumors that the Hindu pilgrims had taunted the Muslim passengers. Ironically, the same commentators upbraid and demonize Modi who said that the killing and maiming of hundreds of Muslims was a reaction to the massacre on the train. Modi said that the violence following the Godhra massacre could not be termed riots as much as some kind of mass agitation.[79]

Some said that the Hindu pilgrims drank tea at Godhra station and did not pay for it, leading to a brawl with some Muslim vendors, who then instigated the vendors to burn down the train supposedly at 07:45 on a winter morning. Other reports claimed that some men kidnapped or tried to kidnap and molest a Muslim girl, and therefore the train was burnt, while a third version of the story claims that some Hindus had pulled the beard of an old Muslim and forced him to recite Hindu religious incantations. Yet another rumor that made the rounds was that passengers had attacked a mosque in Dahod, and that by the time the train reached Godhra 40 minutes later, a mob was

---

[79] Aiyar, V. S., Mahurkar, U. (March 18, 2002). "Gujarat wasn't a communal riot, it was a mass agitation," *India Today*.

ready to pounce on the train. The enquiry by the government indicated that it was, however, a conspiracy hatched by local Muslims, aided and abetted by forces from across the border in Pakistan.[80]

We can also point out that the carnage at Godhra happened at a time when neighboring Pakistan was trying to cope with international condemnation of the vicious slaying of Daniel Pearl, when the war in Afghanistan began revealing skeletons in Musharraf's cupboard, and pressures began building up in Pakistan to turn the world's gaze away from it. Pakistan's Inter-Services Intelligence (ISI) has been known to have plotted or help plot a variety of violent events to destabilize India, and to upset the Hindu-Muslim equation in India. It was no surprise then that the Gujarat government charged 81 of the 126 arrested for the attack under the Prevention of Terrorism Act (POTA). Those arrested included Bilal Haji, Razak Kurkur, and Maulvi Hussein Umarji, who were later accused of hatching the conspiracy.[81]

Godhra's Troubled History

The most infamous of Mughal rulers, Aurangzeb, was born in Dahod, which adjoins Godhra. The Dahod-Godhra area is predominantly Muslim, and has been witness to many riots. Rioting had become almost a habit in this area since the time of partition in 1947. In the early 1980's a district administrator imposed a day-and-night curfew that lasted nearly a year.[82]

Modi was able to hold on to his job after the Godhra carnage and its aftermath in 2002. Former Indian Prime Minister Morarji Desai was not so lucky in 1927, when he lost his job as a magistrate in Godhra. After his selection in the Bombay Provisional Civil Service, he was posted to Godhra. In his autobiography, Desai describes in detail the 1927 Godhra riots. Gandhi personally intervened with Lord Irwin on Desai's behalf to restore to him his government job.[83]

In 1927, some Godhra Muslims complained that a Hindu procession during the Ganesh festival was provocative. When the procession passed by a mosque in Godhra, Muslims beat up Hindu devotees, and the sponsor of the festival -- Purushottamdas Shah -- was beaten to death. This led to major riots between Hindus and Muslims. The British Collector (chief district administrator) of Panchmahals district ordered Desai to probe the Godhra riots. When he reported that Muslims had attacked an unarmed Hindu religious procession, the British collector was alarmed, and demoted Morarji Desai. The Hindus did not retaliate. It seemed as if Gandhi's call for non-violence was

---

[80] *Rediff on the Net*, August 22, 2002, "Youth's testimony throws new light on Godhra attack".

[81] *India Today*, "Godhra Carnage: On the Fast Track", July 21, 2003.

[82] *India Today*, interview of Modi, March 18, 2002, p. 18, International Edition.

[83] Desai, M. (1974). *The Story of My Life.* New Delhi: Macmillan India

having its effect in some places. The British were playing the communal card, and trying to weaken the *satyagraha* movement, and for this they had to show that the people did not believe in non-violence. The British either ignored or supported Muslim provocation, and used Muslims as political pawns against the Hindu leadership, and to derail India's freedom struggle.

In an essay titled, "Godhra 1928: The story of Muslim war on Hindus as told by Gandhiji"[84] V. P. Bhatia mentions two reports on Godhra that were published in Gandhi's magazine *Young India* in 1928. Even then it was said that Godhra, with a forty percent Muslim population, had a long history of anti-Hindu activity and that Godhra was a bastion of the Muslim League even after 1947. Another essay in *Young India* titled, "What are we to do?" (October 11, 1928) reveals that in the wake of the Khilafat fiasco there was virtually a state of war between the Hindus and the Muslims, and that the Hindus suffered the most in the violence. Gandhi wrote: "Two weeks ago, I wrote in *Navajivan*, a note on the tragedy in Godhra, where Mr. Purushottam Shah (a Hindu) bravely met his death at the hands of his assailants, and gave my note the heading 'Hindu Muslim fight in Godhra'. Several Hindus did not like the heading and addressed angry letters asking me to correct it (for it was a one-sided fight). I found it impossible to accede to their demand. Whether there is one victim or more, whether there is a free fight between two communities, or whether one assumes the offensive and the other simply suffers, I should describe the event as a fight if the whole series of happenings were the result of a state of war between the two communities. Whether in Godhra or in other places there is today a state of war between the two communities. Fortunately, the countryside is still free from the war fever (no longer now), which is mainly confined to towns and cities, where, in some form or other fighting is continually going on. Even the correspondents who have written to me about Godhra do not seem to deny the fact that the happenings arose out of the communal antagonisms that existed there." In the same article, Gandhi wrote: "A Hindu shopkeeper thus complained to me: Mussalmans purchase bags of rice from my shop, often never paying for them. I cannot insist on payment, for fear of their looting my godowns. I have, therefore, to make a voluntary gift of about 50 to 70 maunds (one maund = 82.28 lbs.) of rice every month."

It is in this light we have to analyze the carnage in Godhra on February 27, 2002. However, many in the media, and especially in the English language media, merely targeted "Hindu nationalists" in general, and Narendra Modi in particular for the bloody riots that followed the Godhra train massacre. Rajeev Srinivasan argued that the allegation of some social activists and journalists that the victims on the train provoked the Muslims was akin to blaming a victim of rape for wearing revealing clothes. He

---

[84] Bhatia, V. P. (April 21, 2002). "Godhra 1928: The story of Muslim war on Hindus as told by Gandhiji". *Organiser*.

pointed out to an abhorrent comment by Teesta Setalvad, head of *Communalism Combat*, a group that (selectively) opposes religious extremism in India. She said: "While I condemn today's gruesome attack, you cannot pick up an incident in isolation. Let us not forget the provocation. These people were not going for a benign assembly. They were indulging in blatant and unlawful mobilization to build a temple and deliberately provoke the Muslims in India".[85] That Godhra was being prepared for an assault on the Hindus is revealed in a report in the *Times of India* (March 1, 2002) which pointed out that radical preachers from Kashmir belonging to the extremist *Tableeqi Jamaat* had arrived in Godhra and were making inflammatory speeches, and that there were clashes between some of these outside forces and local Muslims.[86]

Though traditionally the twin towns of Godhra and Dahod are known for Hindu-Muslim divide, it is equally true that there is internecine conflict among the Muslims too in the area. The December 2001 clash between rival Muslim groups should be seen in this light. Islam in India has been "Indianized" over the past millennium. India has its own Islamic schools including the Brelvis, the Deobands, the Sufis, the Bohras, the Ismailis, and the Aga Khanis. The caste system in India transcends the religion barrier. Among Indian Muslims there are "higher" castes and "lower" castes. For example, a "Sayyad" considers himself superior to an "Ansari", and so on. We also note the well-known Shia-Sunni divide.

However, with the increasing influence and power of the Saudi-based Wahhabi sect, advocating a more radical form of Islam, India has been witness to numerous conflicts among Muslims. Though not reported extensively, the Brelvi and Tableeq clash of December 2001 was nothing short of a major riot. People from both groups were injured as they attacked each other with swords, sticks, bricks, and petrol bombs. The police had to resort to tear gas firing to quell the rioting. The Gujarat police had at that time arrested 72 people from both groups after they had registered complaints of loot and plunder against each other. This incident had occurred a month after the local police had warned Muslim boys belonging to the *Tableeq Jamaat* against dressing up like Osama Bin Laden.

During the Muslim holy month of *Ramadan* prior to the Godhra train attack, two Muslim preachers from Kashmir belonging to the *Tableeq Jamaat* came to Godhra's Noor mosque of the Sunnat, and started collecting donations. In the month of *Ramadan* Muslims give alms and donations called "*Zakat*". The actual disagreement began when the duo insisted that they would sleep in the mosque against the instructions of the Sunnat. The Brelvis (Sunnat) had sought to maintain communal harmony in Godhra and Dahod, and had put up notices in the seven mosques of

---

[85] Srinivasan, R. "Blaming the Hindu Victim: Manufacturing Consent for Barbarism", *Rediff on the Net*, March 7, 2002

[86] "Terrified in Godhra", *Times of India*, March 1, 2002.

Dahod mandating that no outsiders should come to the mosques to deliver provocative speeches.

The Brelvis worship in *dargahs* (tombs), celebrate *Urs* (fetes in the memory of Sufi saints), and have faith in the spiritualism of saints, while the puritanical Salafi brand of Islam is propagated by the Tableeqis who deplore any form of deification. Sunnat leaders have participated in Hindu religious festivals. In Mumbai, Hindus also pay homage to the *dargahs* of Sufi saints. But the Tableeqis have been spreading hatred against the Hindus. It was reported that in 2001 the Tableeqis had attacked a *Moharram* procession. The history of this stand-off dates back to 1981, when the Tableeqis objected to Sunnat mullahs from reading and leading the *namaaz* prayers for *Id* at the local prayer ground (*idgah*). This clash compelled the local district collector to step in and barricade the *idgah* to prevent further violence. The Tableeqis are suspected to have carried out the attack on the Sabarmati Express train at Godhra.

Conspiracy Theories

Besides the rumors about what the pilgrims returning from Ayodhya did or did not do at various stops en route, a more bizarre and vicious rumor itself inspired by media reports purportedly analyzing a forensic investigation of the Godhra arson by the police. That rumor or speculation asserted that the Hindus themselves set the train on fire. Since the police investigation suggested that petrol or kerosene was poured from within the train compartment and ignited, some newspapers surmised that the only persons who could have done that were the passengers themselves! The worst of such speculation was published in the *Times of India*, a newspaper that the Western media and academe relies on to provide them "authentic" reporting on India.[87]

An entire slew of such speculation figured on e-mail discussion lists, in symposia and conferences, and those spreading such vicious nonsense seemed to believe that the Hindus were capable of doing anything to instigate rioting against the Muslims, or somehow seemed to suggest that it was all a conspiracy to spread hate against the Muslims and win the next election. Narendra Modi was implicitly accused of masterminding such an election ploy.

Conspiracy theories gained currency and circulation following the September 11 attacks. One such theory that made the rounds, and still seems to guide much Muslim public response to the 9/11 attack against the World Trade Center and the Pentagon, claims that it was a Jewish-Zionist conspiracy to take over the world's finances. A subsequent Gallup poll showed that 61 percent of those surveyed in nine Muslim countries accounting for half the world's Muslim population refused to believe that it

---

[87] "Godhra bogie was burnt from inside: Report" *Times of India*, July 03, 2002

was Arabs who attacked the WTC and the Pentagon.[88]

This mass denial by the majority of the Muslims of barbaric violence by Islam-inspired terrorists is indicative of the persecution mentality that has snared many Muslims and the fantasy world that they live in. It does not mean that conspiracy theories make the rounds only in Muslim communities. They do so in other communities too. Some of these conspiracy theories have been spread by criminals and politicians to achieve their nefarious purposes. However, the belief that the World Trade Center attack was masterminded by Zionists or by the CIA or that the Sabarmati Express was set on fire by VHP members are examples of poor efforts to refute the reality of the hostile attitude of Islamists toward other religionists.[89],[90].

Government Response

When the news of Godhra arson reached Modi, the Gujarat Assembly was in session. The session was immediately terminated, and Modi and his top aides rushed to Godhra to take stock of the situation. Over the phone the then collector of Godhra, Jayanti Ravi, was giving conflicting information of the total number of dead. Further, she was claiming that it was a small incident over a cup of tea that led to this act. The inability of the local administrators to fully comprehend the magnitude of the crime was understandable. It was after all one of the worst mass murders on a train. The site was ghoulish, with burnt bodies still being counted and the charred remains of a mother hugging her child in the burnt down compartment. The public mood was palpably vengeful.

Arrangements were made to identify and cremate the bodies. It was reported then that a suggestion from Modi to cremate the bodies near the hospital where they were brought for post-mortem would have contained the Hindu anger. The Sola Civil Hospital, where the post-mortems were conducted is on the western outskirts of Ahmedabad where the Muslim population is negligible. But the relatives of the dead would have none of it, and were angry that the BJP leadership was "acting in a manner worse than the Congress".[91] It is said that the retaliatory violence against Muslims began as soon as the bodies of the dead reached the homes in different localities in easy reach of Muslim neighborhoods.

The immediate reaction was muted. While TV news channels continued to show footage of the burnt train and charred bodies no leader came forward to unequivocally condemn the crime. As the Collector (Deputy Commissioner) of Gandhinagar, a

---

[88] *USA Today*, February 27, 2002, "Many in Islamic world doubt Arabs behind 9/11".

[89] Lewis, B. (2003). *The Crisis of Islam: Holy War and Unholy Terror*. Modern Library.

[90] Manji, I. (2004). *The Trouble with Islam: A Muslim's call for Reform in her Faith*. Random House.

[91] *India Today*, March 18, 2002, interview of Modi.

The Election That Shaped Gujarat

Muslim IAS officer, told us in an interview on June 9, 2003, "If only the leaders of the Muslim community had unequivocally condemned the Godhra attack, the retaliatory violence would have been less".

CHAPTER VIII -- THE RIOTS

(Note: Since the writing of this chapter ten years ago, various inquiry commissions have weighed in, courts have moved and decided, and the Supreme Court ordered Special Investigative Team – SIT – has cleared Narendra Modi of being complicit in instigating or colluding in the riots. A Metropolitan Magistrate Court in December 2013 upheld an SIT report that cleared Modi in the Gulberg Society massacre in which former Congress Member of Parliament, Ehsan Jafri was among the 68 people burnt alive during the riots.)

According to the Dave Commission, inquiring into the 1985 riots in Ahmedabad, the first reported communal riot in Gujarat was in 1410. Again in 1714, during the Hindu festival of *Holi* there was rioting that forced the Moghul government to replace the Muslim administrator with a Hindu. The 1969 riots were one of the most macabre that Gujarat had ever witnessed. Though the 1985 riots started on an anti- reservation issue, they soon assumed a communal hue. In the 1990s there were again major Hindu-Muslim conflicts. On none of those occasions was there a BJP government or a Narendra Modi to blame. We can therefore surmise that the 2002 Gujarat riots were an immediate reaction to the burning of the Hindus in the Godhra train by the Muslims.

The morning following the Godhra massacre, people were glued to their newspapers and to their television sets. Some editorials perversely criticized the pilgrims for their journey to Ayodhya, and argued that had the Hindus not gone to Ayodhya then the Godhra massacre would not have occurred. They then blamed the Hindus for provoking the Muslims. Interestingly, this logic was never extended to the reaction to the Godhra massacre. If, even if, some of the pilgrims returning from Ayodhya had misbehaved with some stall owners at railway stations, did their act merit the bloody murder of 59 people? And if those actions did indeed lead to retribution by Muslims, as some editors suggested, would it not make sense to say that the torching of a train that led to the fiery deaths of 59 in turn led to the riots in which 600 or 700 Muslims died?

Moreover, as the Nanavati Commission investigating the riots has observed, the accusations against the police for tardy response to the riots were not tenable,[92] and that there was little evidence to suggest that either the VHP or the Bajrang Dal could be held responsible for instigating those riots. As the judge observed, "Yes, there have been instances where people have said the Bajrang Dal and VHP workers at the local level instigated people to riot. But the complaints are primarily of a very general nature. There is no real evidence that has been brought to name individual Bajrang Dal or VHP leaders."[93] The Judge also said that both the Muslims and the Hindus indulged in

---

[92] *Rediff on theNet*, May 18, 2003, "No police lapse in Gujarat riots: Justice Nanavati".

[93] *The Indian Express*, May 20, 2003, "Gujarat Riots Probe: After Modi Justice Nanavati clears VHP, Bajrang

mindless violence following retaliatory attacks by Hindu mobs. These statements by the Commission have been duly criticized by Indian "secularists" and the Muslim leadership and the media.[94]

Tracing back the events of those fateful days, we note that towards the afternoon of February 28, 2002, the bodies of the Hindu pilgrims had begun to arrive in communally sensitive Ahmedabad. The bodies were later taken for cremation. To show solidarity with the families of the dead pilgrims, crowds began swelling the funeral procession. After the cremation, tempers rose high, and the atmosphere was surcharged with anger and hate.

On its part, the government had put the police on alert. At the first signs of trouble breaking out, the Army was requested to intervene. However, after the December 13, 2001, terrorist attack on the Indian Parliament, the Indian Army took positions aggressively along the international border with Pakistan. It was a war-like situation on the border, with the world's largest democracy outraged by the attack on the symbol of its democracy on one side, and an Islamic military dictatorship on the other side. The terrorist attack on the Parliament building was not just an outrage but an attempt to subvert Indian ideals and practices – democracy, freedom of speech, religious diversity, cultural plurality, and an open society. In fact, that attack, as well as several others on the Indian people and institutions are indicative of the "clash of civilizations" – Hindu plurality and accommodation versus Muslim monotheistic exclusivism and intolerance.

More than half a million Indian troops were lined up along the Pakistani border, awaiting signal for action. In the last recognized war with Pakistan in 1971, a surgical strike by India amputated the eastern part of Pakistan, and launched the democratic free nation of Bangladesh. On the western front too, Indian forces reached the outskirts of Lahore, a major Pakistani city.

Pakistan does not stand a chance in conventional warfare with India. But India did not attack in 2002. As Prime Minister Vajpayee would regret a few months later, "not attacking Pakistan after the horrific attack on the Indian Parliament was a mistake". If at all there was an appropriate time to teach Pakistan a lesson it was then, but Indian leaders once again dithered and let matters drift into limbo. There was also pressure from Washington D.C. to not escalate matters.[95]

With Indian troops staring down Pakistani forces, it is no surprise that some have speculated that the Godhra attack was a deliberate plot by Pakistan to ease pressure on

---

Dal".

[94] *The Muslim News*, June 27, 2003, "Gujarat riots Inquiry Commission, a whitewash".

[95] Ganguly, S., "The start of a beautiful friendship? The United States and India", *World Press Journal* Volume 20, Spring 2003.

its soldiers. Pakistani leaders know very well that if a mob of fanatic Muslims attacked and killed Hindus, Indians would be provoked. Public outrage would soon turn to violence beyond the capabilities of civilian authorities to control, and hence the government of India would be left with no option but call its army for civil and police duty.

Moving troops from India's borders is not easy. Nevertheless the mob frenzy that had gripped Ahmedabad prodded the Gujarat government to send an urgent request to the Defense Ministry, and within 16 hours of the first sign of trouble troops were airlifted from the international border and stationed at various sensitive locations in the state. There was some delay, however, because army vehicles could not be immediately airlifted and the soldiers had to wait in garrisons and airports for their transport, including civilian transport that the government rushed in.

The Modi government set up control rooms to regulate the law and order situation. Senior administrative officers and cabinet ministers were on round the clock alert, assessing the situation. Hospitals were geared up to admit casualties and standby forces rushed in wherever needed. Within 72 hours of the eruption of riots, the situation was brought under control. Sporadic violence continued, however, for nearly two months thereafter, instigated by criminal gangs and as some reports suggested, by opposition parties.

When critics accuse the Modi government of not averting mob violence or the police of tardiness in responding to the situation they ignore a number of ground realities. Ahmedabad had a police force of 6,000 and only 1,500 of them were armed. There were just 2120 men in the Rapid Action Force and only 530 could be spared for Ahmedabad. Mobs at times consisted of 2,000 to 10,000 people and police forces were unable to contain them. The police were also expecting the worst riots in Ahmedabad's walled city, where most of the previous riots took place, but that was not the case this time. At Naroda Patiya, where a Muslim Member of Parliament Ehsan Jafri was killed, there were only a few armed guards, and by the time police reinforcement arrived the mob had swelled to 10,000 (see *India Today*, March 18, 2002 for more details).

Hindus wanted to avenge Godhra. When the Defense Minister, George Fernandes, visited some Hindu neighborhoods asking people to remain calm, and warning that the Army would open fire on violent mobs, his vehicle was stoned. When BJP leader Vishnu Patel tried to pacify a Hindu crowd in the little town of Umreth, it turned on him.[96] It seemed no words would quell the anger, and that only time could heal the wounds.

Hindu reaction could also be attributed to the growing sense of frustration at the government's inability to quell the violence and bloodshed in Kashmir, and the concerted attacks elsewhere in the country by Muslim agents and groups. India's secular media ignored the systematic ethnic cleansing of a quarter of a million Hindus of

---

[96] Mahurkar, U., "End of hope", *India Today*, April 15, 2002

Kashmir by Islamic terrorists with considerable help from some Indian Muslims, and the continuing attacks on Indian soldiers and police stationed there, or worse still, attributed them to Indian government policy.

Major incidents of attacks on Muslims, in retaliation for the Godhra arson, took place in the first three days of rioting. Ehsan Jafri, former Lok Sabha member, was brutally murdered at Gulberg Society in the labor dominated Meghaninagar locality. Forty-one others were killed in that attack. The worst carnage took place at Naroda-Patiya, the victims living in a locality bordering the Ahmedabad-Udaipur highway. The mob was furious, and matters turned ugly when a Hindu died in a skirmish. A 15,000-strong mob gathered and butchered 89 Muslims, most of them migrant laborers from the Southern State of Karnataka. In one of the worst attacks in rural Gujarat, 38 people were massacred in Sardarpura in Mehsana district. The Best Bakery Case, in which eleven Muslims and three Hindu workers were killed, was dismissed by a judge because the chief witness turned hostile due to alleged threats against her life.[97] The social structure of Gujarat seemed to collapse as a result of what took place in Godhra. The people of Gujarat were outraged, and sometimes it took inhuman forms, with women being raped and children murdered. Muslim businesses bore the brunt of the retaliatory attacks.

Communal violence cannot be easily rationalized. History plays a significant role and the political and social structures of a society either exacerbate or mitigate the violence. Hindus and Muslims in India are genetically similar. They speak the same regional languages. A Muslim or Hindu of a South Indian state like Tamil Nadu would speak Tamil, whereas a Gujarati Muslim or Hindu speaks Gujarati. Sometimes they share the same last names. For example, in Gujarat, "Patel" is a Hindu last name, but a large number of Muslims also have the last name Patel. It is the caste that is usually denoted by the last name. Thus in India when Hindus converted into Islam they did not leave their caste. Hence caste (*jati*) has transcended religion. For example, the Muslims of Godhra belong to what is called the Ghanchi caste, and they are known as Ghanchi Muslims. It is ironic that Chief Minister Modi, a Hindu, also belongs to the same Ghanchi caste. So, what happened in Godhra and later around Gujarat is not as simple as Modi-baiters theorize.

Poorly equipped Police

The government of Gujarat took unprecedented steps to quell the rioting, but we now know that was not enough. The lower ranks of the police are poorly paid and poorly equipped. Grade III government employees of the government of Gujarat are meagerly paid compared to the employees in neighboring Rajasthan and Madhya Pradesh. A

---

[97] *India Today*, July 21, 2003, "Wanted Justice".

Gujarat grade III employee earns about 2,750 rupees or about $60 per month as basic salary. In addition, they earn a dearness allowance, and house rent allowance all of which amounts to about 4,500 rupees or $100 a month, whereas a grade III employee in the neighboring states earns about 10 dollars more. The ordinary Indian policeman, like the London bobby, is not armed. Even those armed are not equipped with the best and the latest. Heavy, slow-loading, and antiquated guns are not the answer for crowd control. The police have no access to the latest in riot-control technology including water canons and rubber bullets. The low budget for police force, long overdue police modernization, and indifference to significant police reforms have all plagued the Gujarat police force.

In a situation where an infuriated mob of a few hundred men charge at a small posse of policemen equipped with old rifles, the latter tend to quit and run or simply stand and stare rather than shoot at the crowd. They fear being lynched. Regardless of whether a policeman hits the leg or the torso of a rioter or misses, by the time he reloads and aims to fire again the rioters have already pounced on him. For a mere $100 a month, which person would risk his life in this manner? The state employed about 43,000 policemen, and of them 2,000 were armed. On a single day during the riots the Ahmedabad police received 3,500 calls for help, in contrast to the average number of 200 calls received by the police. Ahmedabad Police Commissioner, P.C. Pande said: "In my 32-year career I have never seen something like this. It was an upsurge, unstoppable and unprecedented. A stage came when it became physically impossible for the police to tackle mobs running into thousands".[98]

It was in this situation that Gujarat asked the Indian Army to help. By March 18, soldiers and policemen had fired over 2,000 rounds of ammunition on the rioting crowds, and exploded over 15,000 tear gas shells. The government carried out preventive arrests of over 33,000 people, and over 4,400 cases were registered and under prosecution in courts.

India is a vast country with a billion people. Whatever happens in India assumes mammoth proportions in terms of the number of people involved. Over 200 civilians, both Hindu and Muslim, lost their lives in police firing. An Indian riot situation is too complex for the western world to comprehend and rightly conclude.

The Riot Phases
The rioting pattern manifested itself in two phases: one was the mass spontaneous rioting witnessed in the first three days. This first phase can be linked to the anger and rage following the Godhra attack. Hindus attacked and the Muslims suffered. Mobs targeted Muslim businesses with pinpoint accuracy, and seemed to have planned their attacks on the commercial establishments. People even knew of Muslim businesses under Hindu names. This rioting was limited to cities. However, within 72 hours this

---

[98] Mahurkar, U. (March 18, 2002). "Sins of Modi". *India Today*.

kind of rioting subsided. The riots that followed were systematic, planned, and sporadic. Then, the Muslims took over and began attacking the Hindus.[99]

The methodology rioters adopted in the Muslim areas was the selective targeting of Hindu families living there, or targeting their vehicles, or killing people by slashing their throats to create fear and insecurity. There was also sporadic stone throwing, and the destruction of small Hindu places of worship in retaliation to the Hindus destroying Muslim places of worship. The tomb (*dargah*) of Valli Gujarati, a well-known Muslim poet, was destroyed by the Hindus, and a road built over it. The Muslims in turn destroyed small Hindu temples in their locality. This deadly tit-for-tat continued for about two months. After the first three days, the rioting spread also to certain isolated sections of the tribal belt. Muslims were targeted but this was mainly due to the social ostracism or economic exploitation of the tribal people by the Muslims. This targeting of the Muslims was systematic, and planned, but it was the local people who increasingly ostracized their Muslims neighbors.

One of the most disturbing phenomena the Ahmedabad rioting threw up was the spectacle of well-to-do people driving up in their cars and grabbing expensive clothes and consumer items from shopping malls that had been targeted by rioters. Greed and simple lawlessness displaced the spontaneous rage of the poor, the criminal, and the marginalized.

Pogrom or Lawlessness?

The riots that followed the Godhra massacre cannot be condoned. Reprisal killings of innocent people, or even criminals, are deplorable. The RSS publication *Panchajanya* condemned the riots. It said that those "Who are trying to justify Godhra or Gujarat violence, one way or the other, are doing any good neither to Indian civilization, nor Hindutva, nor society. Whatever the provocation, the Hindu cannot stain his hands with the blood of the innocent.... We have to remember Shivaji had exclaimed on seeing a beautiful Muslim woman won as war booty: 'I wish my mother was as beautiful as you.' Then he restored the woman to her family with honor. This Hindu character is our path."

Eventually the riots played themselves out, but not before many lives had been destroyed and the social fabric of Gujarati society reduced to tatters. Godhra drove a deeper wedge between the Hindus and the Muslims which will take time to heal. Many of the criminals who took part in the Godhra massacre and those who took part in the later riots are now in jail, facing prosecution, and many convicted. However, that process was stymied by a variety of factors, both systemic and individual. Unless the state and its elected leaders step in and make sure that the guilty are punished the

---

[99] *India Today* (April 15, 2002). "End of hope".

civilizational divide will only grow bigger and religion-inspired violence will undermine civil society. But the judiciary in India is independent and beyond the manipulation of any chief minister. The government, however, can provide protection to the witnesses to fearlessly depose to get the guilty punished.

In this regard, Sandhya Jain argued that while 21 persons were arrested for the post-Godhra Best Bakery carnage in Vadodra, all forty-one witnesses turned hostile in court (In Indian judicial parlance, "turning hostile" means committing perjury).[100] The courts do not punish those who lie under oath. The Government of India is trying to bring about a change in the Indian legal system to make perjury punishable.[101] Pretending ignorance of judicial constraints, some in the media complain about "miscarriage of justice". They fail to ask why the key witnesses in the Best Bakery case, Zaheera Sheikh and her mother, declared they were intimidated to commit perjury in court. The media failed to investigate carefully these professed claims of intimidation, while other witnesses, including Zaheera's sister-in-law Yasmin Banu said they were not pressured to say anything by anyone.

Jain wondered how the "aggrieved parties suddenly found the courage to speak the truth (sic) to the media. What was the special protection (or inducement) offered which prompted Zaheera's consummate grandstanding in front of the cameras, when she had only twenty-four hours previously been 'too frightened' to open her mouth in court, where her testimony, once recorded, would have been impossible to shake?" In that event, Narendra Modi's letter (August 05, 2003) to the President of India, requesting him to commission a compilation of information about major group clashes and communal riots since independence made perfect sense. He also suggested that similar information be collected about the number of registered cases of terrorism or extremist attacks, the number of cases in which charge-sheets were filed in court, the number of cases the government of the day had withdrawn even after filing charge-sheets, and the acquittal rate in the cases charge-sheeted and tried by the courts. Modi's idea was to inject some balance into the debate by comparing what he had done in response to the riots with how other governments had responded in the past.

Jain thought it was fair to juxtapose the cases involving Muslim terrorists or communal riots, and their legal aftermath with cases lodged against the Hindus. BJP leader Pramod Mahajan protested the acquittal in Mumbai of seven D-company ("D" stands for Dawood, the notorious smuggler and gangland leader who is supposed to have masterminded the Bombay blasts in 1993 and who is reported to be now in Pakistan) gangsters accused of a criminal conspiracy to assassinate Advani in 2001. Mahajan demanded that Maharashtra Chief Minister Sushil Kumar Shinde ask for a Central Bureau of Intelligence (CBI) enquiry into the "serious lapses" in the

---

[100] Jain, S. "Criminal Law, Secular Yardstick", *The Pioneer*, August 12, 2003.

[101] *Rediff on the Net*, August 11, 2003, "Cabinet clears Bill on Cow Slaughter, CrPC".

investigations of the case, which resulted in the acquittal.

The assassination attempt took place just one year before the outrage at Godhra. In the 1992-93 Mumbai riots the Hindus of Jogeshwari were burnt alive and forgotten, Sandhya Jain points out, and that in the Dabgarwad mass burning case in Ahmedabad, eight Hindus were burnt alive and all accused acquitted. In two cases of Signal Falia and Safi School of Godhra, all the Muslims accused were acquitted. Jain scoffed that no human rights activist was brave hearted to even hint at a re-trial of those cases while they all rushed to the international media, the National Human Rights Commission, and sundry academic symposia to complain about the Best Bakery Case. She bemoaned that the NHRC had ignored the plight of Kashmiri Pandits who have suffered grievously over the past one and a half decades. Not only were the Hindus driven out of Kashmir, but the few remaining in remote villages continue to be subjected to selective murder by Muslim terrorists who wish to see the Kashmir Valley cleansed of all Hindus.

It is unfortunate that the dilemma that plagued India during the painful partition days haunts it even today. This dilemma is about a country – Pakistan -- created specifically for Muslims by dividing the Indian land mass, and a large Muslim population that decided to stay on in India after the creation of Pakistan. Pakistan is still a thorn in the flesh of India, and continues to sow the seeds of hatred between Hindus and Muslims.

The Bombay bomb blasts in 1993 had Pakistan roots; the December 13, 2001 attack on Parliament had Pakistan origins; the Godhra incident had a Pakistan hand behind it; and the Akshardham temple attack too had Pakistani roots. The attacks on Mumbai in 2006, that drew the attention of the world, clearly originated and were plotted in Pakistan. How long can India bear this belligerence, this bleeding by a thousand cuts? How long will secular and democratic India suffer at the hands of an anarchy that has come to symbolize the Islamic military dictatorship and dysfunctional democracy that is Pakistan? How many Godhras will India have to witness?

Instead of asking such questions, most critics maintained that what happened in Gujarat after the Godhra attack was a "pogrom". They referred to "mob leaders" going around Ahmedabad with detailed lists of Muslim households and businesses to be targeted, and to BJP ministers in command of police stations and giving instructions to the police not to arrest rioters. Most communal rioting in India is organized to some extent, and most probably such riots the world over have similar characteristics. To single out the Gujarat riots for this special label therefore amounted to demonizing Modi and his government.

No Remorse

One of the accusations made against Narendra Modi and Gujarati Hindus was that they showed no remorse for the brutal killing and maiming of Muslims in the riots. A number of journalists and social activists have continued to repeat this allegation making it part of modern Indian lore (A decade later, as Indians voted in the 2014 elections, there was the same refrain about apologies not rendered, remorse not expressed. Sankrant Sanu, writing in *The Hoot*, says, "In the Indian culture context we have no easy apology. We don't even have an equivalent to a lightweight word like 'sorry'. We have *prayaschit* and *paschatap*.... The Indian media narrative has followed the Christian script of the West on the apology-redemption track while Modi is responding from an Indian cultural lens").[102]

Some Gujaratis that we met in our ten-day schedule of meetings in Ahmedabad and Gandhinagar in the summer of 2003 were indeed angry and did say that the riots were a reaction to the massacre at Godhra, and that they did not see anything wrong in exacting revenge for such a dastardly crime. They also felt that the media had demonized their Chief Minister, and that it was laughable that they should be damned for exacting revenge. "You can only get a person to reflect carefully and do some introspection if you can provide the space for him to do so", one doctor, who claimed Narendra Modi was his hero, told us. Kenneth Burke's interesting analysis of human reactions when pushed into a corner explores the implications of being driven into a corner.[103] First, "being driven into a corner" results from what Burke terms "dialectical pressure" -- the tendency during conflict for the positions of adversaries to migrate to their polar extremes. Such migration reflects the effort of an adversary to re-cast a position in the most absolute or "final" terms possible and then to attack it as absolute, irrational or untenable. In this case, the adversaries – the media, the NGOs, the social activists, the political opposition to Modi – cast Modi and the rioters in the most absolute of terms. No thought was given to the fact that indeed a person or a people could be goaded to exact revenge. It was as if all Gujaratis were expected to "do a Gandhi" and lie down and surrender or go on a week-long fast to show remorse. The more they were attacked as lacking in "humanity" the more they were determined to show a collective finger at those accusing them of such inhumanity. That the barrage of invective and allegations has gone on now for more than a decade after the riots shows that the Gujaratis and Narendra Modi had little space to rethink what happened in the bloody month of March 2002.

A Gujarati doctor from St. Louis, smitten by Mahatma Gandhi, rued that his native state and his Gujarati brethren seemed to have forgotten their homegrown "saint". The good doctor, full of second-hand remorse, wrote that Gandhi would be considered an

---

[102] Sanu, S. (April 25, 2014). "Modi, media and the theology of apology", *The Hoot*.

[103] Burke, K. (1984, 3rd Edition). "*Attitudes Towards History*". University of California Press.

incarnation of God a few hundred years from now and that Gandhi had a profound insight into the Indian psyche. The response of the Gujarati doctor in St. Louis was very different from the doctor in Ahmedabad who told us why it was difficult to express remorse. The doctor in St. Louis had his facts and his Indian philosophy mixed up. Gandhi's reading of the *Bhagavad Gita* was idiosyncratic, and most did not accept his assertion that the Kurukshetra battlefield represented just the inner struggle in every human being. Gandhi's favorite hero -- Lord Rama -- himself went to battle and killed many while trying to recover his kidnapped wife Sita. And if indeed Gandhi's philosophy of non-violence is so effective why did India see little respite in violence during his own lifetime? How come Gandhi preached non-violence to only one section of humanity?

No doubt Gandhi was a giant among ordinary people. But one can have an extraordinary personality without necessarily being either close to God or to the devil. Gandhi was neither a saint nor a yogi. He was a good man, a wily politician, and someone who wielded power without being elected to any office. Some of his actions were idiosyncratic. He asked his Hindu followers to imitate his lifestyle: in the consumption of food, in the practice of sex, and in beliefs about what is right and wrong. Muslims remained outside the ambit of his influence.

Gandhi's backroom machinations saw Nehru foisted on the Congress Party as president in 1946 when not one of the fourteen Congress Party constituencies chose Nehru for that office. Thirteen chose Vallabhbhai Patel, and one chose Acharya Kripalani. Gandhi intervened and asked Acharya Kripalani -- the choice of the United Provinces Pradesh Congress Committee -- to circulate a note to the Congress Working Committee asking that body to nominate Nehru. Gandhi's stature and personality enabled him to ride roughshod over popular sentiment and choice. He anointed Nehru because, according to him, Nehru was "a Harrow boy, a Cambridge graduate and a barrister" and was "wanted to carry on the negotiations with Englishmen"! Gandhi also believed that Nehru could "make India play a role in international affairs," and more revealingly, that "Jawahar will not take second place". Gandhi's suggestion carried the day, and Sardar Patel, the choice of the people, failed to become prime minister through a palace coup.[104] Gandhi was also instrumental in robbing Subhash Chandra Bose of the presidentship of the Congress Party in 1939. Gandhi worked to undermine Bose's authority, and Bose quit and founded the Forward Bloc.

Some have pointed out that Gandhi was aware of the intrinsic violence in many Islamic injunctions, and through a strange (some might say perverse) argument advocated that the Hindu (and others, such as the Jews) voluntarily succumb to it. This Gandhian formula is what has worked its way through the Indian intellectual

---

[104] Shenoy, T.V.R., "Who will be Prime Minister, Sonia?" *Rediff on the Net*, December 31, 2003

bloodstream in the past nearly sixty years. Therefore, we have the curious "secular" position that the Hindu precept is to be admired but Hindus themselves can be dispensed with. They say that the "truths" of Hinduism will survive the demise of the Hindus. Critics of this argument wonder what happened to Hellenism, Druidism, Taoism, and pre-Christian and pre- Islamic paganisms without practitioners: dead in practice, alive in museums and textbooks, they say.

Gandhiji's critics also point out that he was prepared to restore Muslim rule over India. Gandhiji urged Hindus to die in the face of Muslim violence. This, they argue was an appeal for Hindu exoneration of Muslim violence ("Like a cow into the mouth of a tiger to appease his hunger"). Through Gandhi's chosen successor Nehru, such appeasement was institutionalized as "secularism", says Kak.[105] He argues that the objective of Muslim rule is the conversion of India to a *dar-ul Islam*, just like in Pakistan and in Bangladesh. He points out that Hindus and Hinduism have been all but exterminated from Afghanistan, Pakistan, Bangladesh, and now Kashmir. K. S. Lal has calculated that 80 million Hindus were killed by Muslims between 1000 CE (conquest of Afghanistan) and 1525 CE (end of Delhi Sultanate).[106] Gandhiji ignored much of this, and those who speak on his behalf now seem to wish what he wished for India.

It is difficult to balance the roles of politician and saint together. As we have seen in India, such a mixture does not make for either good politics or a popular religion. But Gandhiji has been so deified that few people, and especially politicians, dared question his life or his politics. It is not as if there are no critics of Gandhiji. As Elst points out, "Gandhi's erratic policies were criticized by his contemporaries like Annie Besant, Sri Aurobindo, Bhimrao Ambedkar, and many others. And none of them tried to kill Gandhi; so there is nothing murderous about these arguments per se. They correctly predicted that under his irrational leadership, the strategy of mass mobilization and 'non- violence' would yield very bitter fruits, as it did during the Khilafat riots circa 1922 and again during partition. Indologists like Alain Daniélou and historians like Paul Johnson have also demythologized the Mahatma. One of the perverse effects of his murder was precisely that criticism of Gandhi suddenly became taboo in India and the myth of his centrality in the achievement of independence became unassailable".[107]

Elst mentions how the conflict dynamic got skewed and how people of Gujarati background began talking about "teaching Muslims a lesson" or giving "Muslims a good beating". As children, these people were brought up on Gandhi's philosophy of extreme non-violence and now in reaction were talking loosely about retaliation and violence. "The psychology behind their evolution is that they have experienced how Gandhian attitudes of appeasing the aggressor and turning the other cheek simply don't

---

[105] Kak, K., "The Bloodstained Halo", *Vigil Online*, Vicharmala 49.

[106] Lal, K. S. (1992). *The Legacy of Muslim Rule in India*. South Asia Books.

[107] Rao, R. (August 19, 2002). "An Interview with Koenraad Elst". Sulekha.com

work", Elst argues, and says that in "dealing with aggression, one should neither appease nor overreact". Thus the canard that Gujaratis have not shown remorse, or that Modi is incapable of showing it should be rejected and the reactions of Gujarati society to events in 2002 be more carefully analyzed to understand the dynamics of religious violence in India.

CHAPTER IX -- MEDIA BIAS AND SELECTIVE OUTRAGE

"Muslims were massacred", asserted Yogendra Yadav, the eminent psephologist (and in 2014 a candidate for the sixteenth Lok Sabha from the Gurgaon Constituency as a member of the Aad Aadmi Party), in a television talk show, but he did not bother to ponder why matters had come to such a pass. Yet others simply put the blame on the RSS or the VHP and the "politics of hatred" allegedly practiced by sections of the "Hindutva brigade". Yet others simply made Narendra Modi the scapegoat, and blamed him for the bloody riots that followed the Godhra massacre.

Few mentioned that it was the killing of Hindu pilgrims in Godhra that led to the multiple rounds of vicious blood-letting. Even if in the interests of minimum credibility, secularists made restrained and muted mention of Godhra, they did not stop baying for the blood of Modi. Lurid headlines,[108] vitriolic editorials, feverish activity by "secular" busybodies to involve international agencies and foreign governments merely hampered the ability of the government to deal quickly and efficiently with the trouble-makers, and led to the polarization of forces – with each group trying to push the other into the corner.

The images of houses that were burned down, shops that were looted, and bodies of hapless victims lying in pools of blood continued to be highlighted on television over and over, hours on end, and for more than a month. The media stoked the communal embers, and visits to Gujarat by self-proclaimed "secularists" merely added fuel to the fire. A rioter, Hindu or Muslim, has no conscience, for otherwise he would not kill innocent people. The Muslims of Godhra who burnt innocent Hindu men, women and children alive in train compartment S-6 were as much demoniac as were the Hindus who killed the Muslims in the aftermath of Godhra. A criminal has no religion, and it is no wonder that the underworld in India, as elsewhere, is one of the most secular institutions in the world!

Many in the media had made up their minds to renounce the "fairness and balance" tenet in journalism since the time Modi took office. Blame had to stick to Narendra Modi, and it suited the plot. Narendra Modi after all was an ex-RSS *pracharak* (activist, grassroots worker) turned Chief Minister. He symbolized "hard-line Hindutva". Stories were spun, and printed. Soon some other newspaper or magazine would carry them, courtesy the original. Then, some eminent "secularist" would speak about it on a television chat show, imparting it greater credibility and circulation. Very soon it became an "accepted truth" because the Human Rights Watch in New York or Amnesty International in London repeated the lies and half-truths in their reports.[109]

---

[108] *The Indian Express*, "Dial M for Modi, Murder" March 24, 2002.

[109] For a passionate denunciation of the role some in the English media played and are continuing to play in Gujarat, see Modi, S.K. (2004). *Godhra – The Missing Rage*, Ocean Books.

Prominent Indian writers who frequently visit the U.S. to give their "secular" versions of Gujarat riots went into a warp mode to blame Modi and his supporters. Egregious and scare-mongering essays were published without the least bit of caution by editors who, of course, had themselves shown in public their political cards. Thus, writing in *Frontline*, Harsh Mander, an IAS officer who had lied about his exit from the IAS in response to Gujarat riots, told readers that the Gujarat of Gandhi was dead, and that "minorities in the India of the future will have to come to terms with second-class citizenship".[110] Mander's tour of the United States was sponsored by Indian-American Muslim organizations and groups claiming to be fighting communalism. Harsh Mander is now on the Haas School of Business, University of California, Berkeley, "Armed Conflict Resolution and People's Rights" program as a working group member.

On a complaint to the Press Council of India that Harsh Mander had violated the Council's guidelines on reporting of communal violence the Press Council found that Mander's article[111] "at several points reiterated rumors that were being circulated at the relevant time. The truthfulness of the facts mentioned therein had not been established at any point of time till then but Shri Mander had chosen to base his views and sentiments on them, and put pen to the opinion thus formed by him." The Council ruled that "it was expected of the author as a responsible serving officer as well as of the respondent paper of repute like the *Times of India*, to be more restrained and circumspect in pronouncing a denouncement of the whole system in a communally surcharged atmosphere." The Council censured the *Times of India* for its "indifferent and irresponsible attitude... in a matter of great public importance" and felt "that a greater responsibility devolved on the editor of the paper in exercising his discretion to select articles for publication in such a situation".[112]

Harsh Mander, Country Director of the British NGO ActionAid India, acquired international fame on the basis of this article and on the basis of his claim to have resigned from the IAS to express his anguish at the alleged role of the State in the Gujarat violence. Subsequent investigation revealed that Mander never resigned but, in fact, had concealed the fact that he had applied for early retirement from the IAS before the Gujarat violence occurred. The Press Council ruling confirms earlier reports that Mander had no evidence to substantiate the statements he made in his article when he wrote it, that his rumors acquired credibility because he had spread them as a serving IAS officer (they have yet to be accepted by any adjudicating authority, even a British

---

[110] Mander, H. (June 11, 2003) "In Search of Gandhi and Godse", *Frontline*.

[111] Mander, H. (March 20, 2002). Hindustan Hamara. *The Times of India*.

[112] Dr. Krishen Kak, IAS [retd] vs. *The Times of India*, Press Council of India decision 14/106/02-03, June 30, 2003).

court) and that, as the Press Council suggests, this was highly irresponsible of him in such a volatile situation and *The Times of India* too erred in publishing this article. Unfortunately, none of the Indian newspapers published this ruling of the Press Council except the online news site *Rediff on the Net*.[113] Harsh Mander's politics and networking enabled him to be included in Sonia Gandhi's National Advisory Council, in which he served from June 2010-12.

Booker Prize winner Arundhati Roy falsified facts when she claimed that Ehsan Jaffri's daughters were raped and murdered when in fact the only daughter of Jaffri was not even in India at that time. Roy subsequently apologized for the error but the damage was done. Balbir Punj argued that Godhra has "been used as a crucible by secular fundamentalists" and that the real villains "in tarring India's image are the Roys in the media and a section of public life, who mix half-truths with fiction to settle their ideological or political scores with the Sangh parivar".[114]

The reports and commentaries were not just erroneous but inflammatory. Editors addressed conferences and symposia where they proclaimed that they were intent on bringing the Modi government down, and that they would "take care" of the BJP. Shekhar Gupta of the *Indian Express* told Pakistani audiences that the media in India "will take care of the BJP," and Vinod Mehta of *Outlook India* expressed a similar willingness to bring the NDA government down while addressing a seminar in Bangalore on the Gujarat events. Ends justified the means, and damaged if not destroyed were rules governing free speech. Twelve million students appearing for their twelfth grade exams was the truth, but "3,000 students did not appear for exams" became headline news.

Modi was accused of saying that for every action there is a reaction, and of implying that the riots that followed the Godhra massacre were justified. The report was published only in *The Times of India*, and no other news outlet corroborated it. Modi even issued a press release asserting that he did not say so, and that he did not countenance the riots.[115] But no one was prepared to listen. Why? The story of Modi as mastermind sold. It fit into the media version of the "grand plot". The media, academics, and political brokers had decided that Narendra Modi would take the blame for everything and anything. People conveniently forgot the communally sensitive nature of Gujarat, where even a cricket match or a kite flying competition can invoke a round of stone throwing and rioting. The history of communal convulsions in Gujarat dates back to 1410, and bloody riots visited Gujarat in 1969, 1980, 1985, 1990, and 1992. The BJP was not in power in 1969, 1980, 1985, 1990, and 1992, which witnessed

---

[113] Lavakare, A. (November 18, 2003), "One Way Street", *Rediff on the Net*.

[114] Punj, B. (May 27, 2002). "The Roys in the Media are Harming India with Half-truths and Worse", *Outlook India*.

[115] Punj, B. (May 27, 2002). "The Roys in the Media are harming India and worse", *Outlook India*.

such savage riots that curfews were imposed for six months at a stretch in some places.

Gujarat riots were not Narendra Modi-instigated phenomena. Why riots take place in some places, and not in others with similar demographic profiles has been studied, and the answers lie in a complex set of factors.[116]

Why did the Indian media adopt a double standard when it came to reporting the murder of innocent civilians, Hindus and Muslims alike, at the hands of Pakistan-trained terrorists? Why does the secular spotlight rest only on the Hindus and not on anyone else? M. V. Kamath blames the media for fanning communal hatred through their biased reporting.[117] V.P. Bhatia points out that the "Secularist media has virtually become a mouthpiece of the Jamaat-e-Islaami and its Pakistani patrons in its misrepresentation of the Hindu counter-offensive post- Godhra."[118] The Gujarat riots are not the only instance of double standards adopted and employed by India's self-proclaimed secularists. They pick and choose the people they wish to demonize, and the events on which they wish to sermonize. Some of the most active in this selective application of concern for human rights were Swami Agnivesh and the Rev. Valson Thampu, both Delhi based, and both veterans of working with an international group intent on anti-BJP propaganda. For an interesting example of their selective outrage, see a letter to the editor written by Surya Narayan Saxena in which he points out that the publicity-seeking duo failed to plead the plight of the Reangs (Bru), members of a tribe driven out of Mizoram by the majority Mizos -- who are Christians -- after large-scale violence in October 1997.[119] Over 30,000 of the Reangs languished in several refugee camps in Kanchanpur subdivision of Tripura. Two years of reminders failed to move these concerned human rights activists, and one can only conjecture that they did not do so because after all Rev. Valson Thampu is Chrisitian. It seems as if every human rights activist's target in India is only the "Hindu fundamentalists", whatever may be the violation of human rights by any other group.

Is it Fact-finding or Grandstanding?

Screen celebrity and Rajya Sabha member Shabana Azmi, Samajwadi Party Member of Parliament Amarsingh, and Communist Party (Marxist) leader Sitaram Yechuri chartered a plane and flew to Gujarat to take stock of the situation. It was an over-worked Gujarat police that did not allow them to visit the riot- hit sections of

---

[116] Varshney, A. (2002). "Ethnic Conflict and Civic Life". Yale University Press.

[117] Kamath, M.V. (May 10, 2002). "Media Hypocrisy and Humbug", *Cybernoon*

[118] Bhatia, V. P. (April 21, 2002), "Godhra 1928: The story of Muslim war on Hindus as told by Gandhiji", *Organiser*.

[119] Saxena, S. N. (December 06, 2003). "Publicity Relations", *The Pioneer*.

Ahmedabad for fear of their safety. One is impressed by the personal involvement of celebrities and the powerful in such troubled times. However, we wonder why they were/are silent when Hindus are routinely killed by Muslim terrorists in Kashmir, and when Hindu pilgrims were burnt alive in Godhra. Why did they not in the name of secularism visit Kashmir nor go to Godhra? However, Shabana Azmi did not lose the opportunity to call Modi a "mass murderer".

Advani termed the selective application of secular values as "pseudo-secularism". Many Hindus, wary and tired of the selective application of secular values and standards, have readily applied the term to the English media in general, and left-leaning academics as represented by the high-flying Jawaharlal Nehru University cadre in particular.

Javed Akhtar, Alyque Padamsee and other well-known Mumbai personalities, vocal in their criticism of the Gujarat government, went to Gujarat and brought the Best Bakery massacre witness Zahira to Mumbai, to provide her "safe haven", but yet none of them raised their voice against the acquittal of the accused in the Radhabhai Chawl massacre during the Mumbai riots of 1993. One crime does not negate another. It is not our intention to rationalize or justify the shoddy trial in the Best Bakery case. However, by drawing attention to the selective outrage of secularists we wish to argue that such bias encourages division and divisiveness, and even radicalization of groups and individuals.[120]

The horror of 9/11 was brought alive by the American media. The American media was very careful in not showing the bodies of the dead. However, the Indian media carried pictures and showed footage of charred bodies and mutilated limbs of victims of Gujarat riots. And they displayed them over and over again. By identifying the religious affiliation of victims and perpetrators the media played an active role in inflaming passions. The constant use of the term "majority of the victims were Muslim" fueled the worldwide condemnation of the Gujarat riots.

A prominent Indian weekly carried Narendra Modi's picture resembling a demon. At a time when the state administration and people need to be motivated in controlling the riots, it is important that they have faith in the chief executive of the state. But many in the media wanted Modi removed, not realizing that in a democracy it is the people who have the right to choose and remove their rulers. There were some who seemed to have embarked on a journalistic vigilante crusade against a constitutionally elected head of government. The Chief Minister sued some of the news magazines and media personalities for defamation but such cases don't find much traction in Indian courts, and decisions arrived at by the courts don't get publicized if it goes against the media.

In this regard, it is interesting to read in the *New York Times* columnist Thomas

---

[120] Note: In February 2006 nine of the 21 accused of murder were convicted and sentenced to life imprisonment. The court acquitted eight others, and issued warrants for the arrest of four missing persons. In July 2012 the Mumbai High Court upheld the sentences of four, and acquitted the other five convicted in 2006.

The Election That Shaped Gujarat

Friedman's question: "Why is that when Hindus in India kill hundreds of Muslims it elicits emotionally muted headlines in the Arab media, but when Israel kills a dozen Muslims, it inflames the entire Muslim world?"[121] In reply to this the eminent Arab journalist, Amir Teheri, wrote in *Arab News*, "The latest round of killings started with the massacre of 60 Hindus by militant Muslims in Gujarat". Taheri added, "The Government (in India or Gujarat) does not conduct the killings in India". He further added that the riots in Gujarat were an internal Indian tragedy.[122]

The Arabs understood the situation in Gujarat, but the self-styled media "knights in shining armor" refused to see the apparent. These protagonists in the "secular media" used each other's reports and analyses to create an echo chamber that repeated the slogan, "Modi is a demon". They used every editorial and reporting trick to defame and humiliate Narendra Modi, so that they could see the BJP in Gujarat weakened and debilitated. V. Sudarshan complained that Arab governments had not even bothered to send demarches *a la* the European Union. That the Europeans changed their tune in 2003 and got off their soap boxes was ignored by these same writers.

There were, however, some fine exceptions in the media who were guided by well-defined and established Indian norms for covering communal strife. They presented balanced and well-researched reports. Some of the reporters risked their lives to capture in vivid detail what happened during the rioting.

To summarize, media's double standards have warped the world's perception of India, and India's religious divide. The application of double standards in the name of secularism was a ubiquitous feature of media reporting and commentary on the Gujarat riots. The ordinary and the indignant Hindu's complaint, not just Narendra Modi's, that "you secularists aren't half as indignant, in fact entirely uninterested, about the quarter million Hindus driven out from Kashmir, a clear case of ethnic cleansing," is not only dismissed out of hand but used as proof of the "Hindu fundamentalists'" rationalization of Gujarat violence.

As Koenraad Elst points out[123], it is all very well for intellectuals to bemoan the impact of either mean- spirited or silly rumors in the genesis of communal riots, but in the case of Gujarat violence, media reports, data and analyses, were just another name for invention, rumor and conspiracy. Elst believes that in this respect, religious extremists such as the Shahi Imam behaved themselves better than secularist campaigners who pose as guardians of modernity. Arundhati Roy, self-proclaimed

---

[121] Friedman, T. (March 06, 2002). "The Core of Muslim Rage". *The New York Times*.

[122] Sudarshan, V. (May 20, 2002). "To Bridge the Gulf". *Outlook India*.

[123] Rao, R. N. & Elst, K. (Ed.) (2002). *Gujarat after Godhra: Real Violence, Selective Outrage*. New Delhi: Har-Anand Publications.

pacifist, used the most violent language in besmirching Gujaratis and risked her international fame she so clearly cherishes by broadcasting blatant lies about atrocities against some Gujarati Muslim women who turned out to be either non-existent or abroad at the time of the riots. Internationally influential media like *The Washington Post* copied from an Islamist website rumors about Hindu provocations behind the Godhra carnage, falsely claiming a Gujarati journalist as source, and never publishing a correction when the journalist himself denied ever having put out such a story.

What the media ignored was that one of the important reasons for riots was that Gujaratis, like other Indians, are frustrated at the state's inability to protect them. Though Indian governments have modernized their security apparatus and intensified their anti- terrorist efforts, the development of technology makes it unlikely that the authorities will win this stand-off with terrorists any time soon. For a determined guerrilla fighter, it becomes ever easier to wreak ever bigger destruction with ever lighter equipment. As Elst points out, while this is no reason to give up the struggle against terrorism, it highlights the need for a more radical solution: either a political agreement which will satisfy the terrorists to the point of making them lay down their arms (as advocated by most secularists, who insist on "dialogue with Kashmiri militants" and the like), or a decisive strike against the political and logistical bases behind the terrorist frontlines, combined with an ideological offensive against their justifying assumptions.

Elst further argues that a large part of the secularists' indignation has been directed against Hindu masses, including Scheduled Castes and Scheduled Tribes, and that it was mainly these layers of Hindu society that had participated in indiscriminate violence against their Muslim neighbors. Whether or not a leadership role is attributed to Hindutva organizations, the overriding fact is that the Hindu masses proved ready to heed calls for "teaching the Muslims a lesson," he says. This readiness cannot be explained as the instant effect of a crash propaganda campaign, but is clearly based on a widespread and firmly entrenched anti-Muslim sentiment.

Once the media had branded Modi as the main culprit for the wave of anti- Muslim retaliation, his popularity only rose. This is what happens in any divided society or where there are historical reasons for suspicion and anger. The Hindu electorate will indeed support a government that shows strength against the perceived threat of Islamic terrorism allegedly lurking in Muslim neighborhoods. This was proven in Mumbai after the riots of early 1993: the electorate rewarded the Shiv Sena for its active role in countering Muslim rioting, even when this included indiscriminate violence against ordinary Muslims. The next elections gave the Shiv Sena a landslide victory, even in constituencies traditionally antagonistic to the Shiv Sena such as Tamil and Gujarati Hindus.

It is fashionable to claim that there is an antagonism between the Hindu masses with their basically secular attitudes and the Hindutva ideologues with their alleged anti-Muslim agenda. No surveys exist to show that this is true. It is merely one of the make- believe theories floated glibly by self-proclaimed secularists.

But suspicion about Muslim agendas is widespread. The reason for this suspicion is that Hindus believe there is collusion between the Muslim masses and their militant vanguard. According to Che Guevara, a guerrilla fighter moves among the masses like a fish in water, and this description fits the understanding that existed between the Muslim masses and the militants regarding expulsion of the Hindus from the Kashmir Valley in 1989-90. It is unlikely that this situation prevails in Gujarat where organized militancy may be a palpable threat but not an everyday reality. At the same time, however, *madrasa* education may slowly increase support for hard-liners among the Muslim masses. In that case, Gujarat and other parts of India may well become tomorrow's Kashmirs. It is necessary to be aware of these possible future scenarios, for the behavior of mobs is not only determined by their experiences of the immediate past but also by their vague apprehensions about the future.

Despite strong and widespread anti-Muslim feelings, Hindus have shown remarkable patience and forbearance in the case of Islamic terrorism in the past. There was no retaliation after the several selective mass killings of Hindu and Sikh villagers or bus passengers in Jammu and Kashmir, or after the attacks on Hindu pilgrims there; nor after the Mumbai bomb blasts (March 1993); or after the bomb attack against a BJP gathering in Coimbatore (February 1998); or after the attacks on the Parliament buildings of Srinagar and Delhi (September and December 2001); or in response to the continued killing and rape of Hindus in Bangladesh. This should be kept in mind when assessing the Hindu loss of self-control after the Godhra massacre.

Elst points out that in spite of secularists' predictions that Gujarat was fast spinning out of control, Hindu self-restraint re-asserted itself after the Akshardham massacre. Given this persistent show of Hindu self-restraint, which proves that violent retaliation against Islamic aggression is more an exception than a general rule, the motives behind the unwarranted secularist alarmism should be questioned, he argues.

Finally, we note that the riots delighted India's secularist circles because they put them back in their business of spreading lies and fancy theories about the BJP and leaders like Modi. Until the riots, the BJP's record in office had, after all, been very disappointing for them. For years they predicted that a BJP Prime Minister would prove to be Hitler and Khomeini in one, and that the Muslims would be thrown into the Arabian Sea if not into gas chambers. In the four years since March 1998, they had to face the embarrassing fact that India's streets remained peaceful. In 1999, they tried to make the most of a spate of incidents between Christians and non-Christian tribe members in which a few Christians were killed. They falsely blamed Hindu activists for some cases of inter-Christian rape and for a series of bomb attacks against churches, which turned out to be the handiwork of a Pakistan-based Muslim group, *Deendar Anjuman*. The bombing of Christian churches in Karnataka, and in Tamil Nadu shocked the nation. The media and some Christian leaders went on a BJP bashing spree, and blamed everything on the "sangh parivar". However, once again the baseless and malicious accusations of these vested interests proved false. Investigations revealed the hand of *Deendar Anjuman* behind these attacks. The Students Islamic Movement of India (SIMI) was also found to have a role in such subversive activities and was banned by the Government of India.

Before ill-informed but consequential international audiences such as the U.S. Commission on International Religious Freedom (USCIRF), the secularists managed to uphold their original story, but in India the campaign to blame Hindu activists for everything has lost its credibility. However, the Gujarat crisis came as a boon to the professional social activists and self-proclaimed secularists. They considered it as godsend for their anti-Hindu and anti-Indian propaganda. Some of them saw no problem in airing their anti-India views from Pakistani propaganda platforms. The Pakistanis, waiting for any opportunity to show India in a poor light, gladly hosted these maverick Indian activists and editors, and highlighted the secularists' line of accusing the state and central governments of complicity in the riots.

In conclusion, the Gujarat crisis has served to throw light on some of the problems of India's opinion climate in relation to the country's communal antagonism. Secularism has become warped and tainted in India, and those flooding the press with their daily statements in the name of secularism are considered by many as some of the most hypocritical and ideologically suspect actors in India.[124] Unfortunately, religious bigotry also remains a real threat to society. "That too is an inescapable, albeit banal, conclusion imposed upon us by the Gujarat riots", says Elst.

---

[124] Dasgupta, S. (February 29, 2004). "Oh, these intellectuals!", *New Indian Express*.

CHAPTER X -- THE DEMAND FOR MODI'S RESIGNATION

"Modi must go, Modi must go, Modi must go" urged an editorial.[125] The media donned the role of judge, jury and hangman, and decided that Modi must pay the price for the bloodletting in Gujarat. The state was unable to protect Muslims and hence Modi must go, Philipose urged. Modi became overnight the villain who masterminded all evil that took place in Gujarat, when in reality the accusers had not one iota of evidence to blame Modi. They misquoted him, they partially quoted him, and they quoted him out of context in a desperate bid to make him the ogre that was responsible for the orgy of violence in Gujarat.

The demonizing of Modi was accomplished very quickly, what with the vast network of media siphoning off lies and half-truths from each other and splashing them across television screens and front pages all over the world. Western journalists, on their perch in Delhi, not knowing any Indian language except English, and reading the *Times of India* to get their daily quota of news and views, simply spun revised versions of these biased reports and passed them on to their readers in the U.S., in Britain, and across the world. And they drew on the only analogies they were familiar with, the ones about Jews and Hitler, and so effortlessly compared Gujarat's Muslims to Jews and Modi to Hitler. The irony of this comparison is that the majority of the Muslims in the world hate Jews.

"Poll can wait, Mr. Modi must go", trumpeted another editorial in *The Hindu*[126] which has become notorious for its anti-Hindu, and anti-BJP stance.[127] It asserted that there were a host of pragmatic or political reasons for asking Modi to quit, and that the Supreme Court judgment de-linking the presidential reference from Gujarat elections presented an even sounder justification for his exit. Modi's ouster would guarantee the Indian media their pound of flesh, and they would feast on it in the name of harmony and on behalf of the Indian Muslim community.

"Narendra Modi Must Go" demanded the People's Union for Civil Liberty (PUCL) giving the "politics of arrogance, and bluster of the majority community" as reasons, in addition to the attack on Medha Patkar by activists of both the BJP and the Congress parties.[128] The roughing up of Medha Patkar was for a totally different reason. Patkar, as we have noted before, has spearheaded the movement against the building of a major dam on the Narmada River. The people of Gujarat wanted the dam, and hence the two major political parties – the BJP and the Congress -- chose to oppose Patkar. Linking

---

[125] Philipose, P. (May 21, 2002). "Imagining a new beginning", *The Indian Express*.

[126] *The Hindu*, "Poll can wait, Mr. Modi must go", September 04, 2002.

[127] Krishnamoorty, D. "The Hindu, Hindus, and Hindutva", *The Hoot.Org*

[128] *The Times of India*, "2002 attack was result of conspiracy: Medha Patkar", September 6, 2013).

the Medha Patkar issue with the "Modi must go" campaign was another example of how vested interests manipulated the political situation to their advantage in their bid to oust Modi. If Modi could be made to abdicate, no doubt a case could be made for the ouster of many other Chief Ministers in India. The only way that the media could justify their demand for Modi's ouster was by holding him responsible for fomenting and orchestrating the Gujarat riots and establishing his culpability.

When BJP leader Haren Pandya was assassinated after the riots in Gujarat, people began to blame Modi. Pandya and Modi did not see eye-to-eye, and when Pandya was killed as he went out for an early morning walk, fingers were pointed at Modi. Pandya's father Vithalbhai Pandya even called Modi a "Ravan" (the "demon" king who abducted Rama's wife Sita in the Hindu epic *Ramayana*). However, investigations revealed that the killers were Muslim assassins from Andhra Pradesh avenging the alleged role of Pandya in instigating the violence against Muslims. The killers were associated with the Muslim underworld with its bases in Pakistan. That did not stop the speculations, insinuations, "investigative reports", and the raking up of the issue in every election since 2003 in Gujarat.[129]

We can compare the assault on Modi and Gujarat by the media and vested interests with situations in other states in India. The examples are neither meant to argue that the post Godhra violence was justified nor to claim that the situation in Gujarat could be compared exactly to anything that has happened or is happening in other states. The examples are meant to provide some context for discussing the problem of apportioning blame, for the recall of elected governments, and for understanding the nature of politics and society in India.

The Andhra Example

The PWG (People's War Group), a Maoist-Leninist organization, was started in 1980 by a teacher turned communist leader Kondapally Seetharamaiah. It has been waging an armed rebellion for the creation of a communist state comprising of tribal areas of the Indian states of Andhra Pradesh, Maharashtra, Orissa, and Madhya Pradesh. This "war" reached a peak recently when its members tried to assassinate the Chief Minister of Andhra Pradesh, Chandrababu Naidu.[130]

The group targets landlords, police, and government ministers and democratically elected representatives, whom it holds responsible as a class for exploiting the poor. Policemen are regularly gunned down, political party activists are murdered, and even members of the State Assembly have been targeted. Former ministers and their kin

---

[129] Note: An *Indian Express* report in January 2014 was headlined, "Haren Pandy killing 'mastermind' was at Pak meeting: IM's Akhtar" confirming that indeed Pandya was assassinated at the behest of Pakistan-based Muslim terrorist organizations.

[130] *Rediff on the Net*, "Andhra CM hurt in Tirumala Bomb Blast", October 01, 2003.

have been killed by the PWG. In March, 2000 the PWG used a landmine explosion to kill a minister of Andhra Pradesh, along with three of his security men. Earlier, the PWG killed a former Speaker of the State Assembly. The atrocities on the poor and the illiterate are untold, and bear mute witness to the jungle law of these extremists. Andhra Pradesh governments have neither been able to put down the violence nor have they worked effectively to mitigate the conditions of the people in the state. But this PWG violence has failed to provoke any drumbeat of protest or demand for a change in government. On the other hand, some human rights activists are agitating against denial of human rights to Naxals.

Karnataka & Tamil Nadu
In the South Indian states of Karnataka and Tamil Nadu, a notorious dacoit named Veerappan played havoc in the Satyamangalam forests, smuggling sandalwood, poaching elephants, kidnapping celebrities and holding them for ransom, and killing policemen. Hiding from the Special Task Force (STF) organized to apprehend him Veerappan not only escaped the dragnet for a long while but continued with his criminal activities until gunned down in October 2004. Yet no one asked for the resignation of the Chief Ministers of these states, even when a senior Karnataka police officer alleged that the Karnataka Chief Minister had paid a huge ransom for the release of a veteran film star whom Veerappan had kidnapped.[131]

The Bihar Example
In the East Indian state of Bihar, the caste system has devolved into a ghoulish man-made artificial segregation that separates one starving illiterate group from another. Bihar has come to symbolize backwardness in India. Today's Bihar is the birthplace of the great Maurya dynasty that ruled India nearly 2000 years ago. Indian Machiavelli -- the great political thinker Kautilya/Chanakya -- and his protégé Emperor Chandra Gupta Maurya ruled Bihar, where Mahatma Gandhi carried on his peasants' movement in the 1920s, and Jayaprakash Narayan inspired students to fight corruption in government offices in the 1970s. The holy river Ganga flows through Patna, the capital of Bihar. After years of penance, and travel, the great Buddha found enlightenment in Bodh Gaya, which is in Bihar.

Bihar at present, though rich in minerals, was rated as one of the most backward states by *India Today*, a leading newsmagazine. A political maverick, part buffoon, part goon ruled the state in the name of his wife, Rabri Devi, and some academics and editorialists continue to label the man, Lalu Prasad Yadav, a secularist. They ignore the fact that Yadav ruled Bihar mafia-style and had run it to the ground. Wolves and jackals

---

[131] Dinkar, C. (2002). *Veerappan's Prize Catch: Rajkumar.* Konark Publisher, Pvt. Ltd.

bayed on the streets of Patna after sundown; industries fled the state; and hired goons high on drugs held court at the Chief Minister's residence. A young, honest civil engineer was murdered for blowing the whistle on corruption and shoddy work in the Bihar section of the interstate highway system being built across the country.[132]

As caste battles raged on, and as infrastructure collapsed, Bihar became the quintessential African-style tin-pot dictatorship. The Maoist Communist Centre (MCC) brutalized people just as much as the upper caste "militias". The MCC ran a parallel government where its courts delivered medieval judgments like cutting off people's ears, nose, hands, and other body parts. From blowing up railway tracks, derailing trains, killing people to disrupting public life, extortion, and laying mines to blow up police and military vehicles, the MCC played a role in rendering Bihar the backwaters of India.

Cases of misgovernance are abundant. When Yadav was indicted on a major corruption charge, he simply anointed his wife Rabri Devi as Chief Minister. She tended to his goats and his kitchen while Yadav held court with his goons and political sidekicks. In spite of such grave abuses the "secular" media did not make too much fuss about the mess in Bihar. Not only that, he also became the darling of the media which reported every word he spoke in Pakistan. It enthusiastically reported his ambition to become the Prime Minister of India. In fact, it showcased Yadav's new circus – a bamboo stick parade organized to take on the VHP in the State! And when the Congress Party cobbled together a coalition in 2004, Lalu Prasad became the Railway Minister and was feted at Harvard University, the Wharton School of Business and others for his "phantom" achievement in turning the Indian Railways around. Faculty who invited and feted him do not have egg on their faces even after Lalu was accused of misusing his position as a Cabinet Minister in allocating land to his relatives, and after his conviction in 2013 in the decades old "fodder scam" case.

The West Bengal Example
West Bengal and Kolkata (Calcutta) have been at the forefront of many cultural, social, and political movements in India. Calcutta, as the capital of British India, was a hub of great intellectual activity and social change. Social reformers like Raja Ram Mohan Roy, visionaries like Swami Vivekananda, and saints like Chaitanya Mahaprabhu, have all called Bengal their home. One of India's foremost religious sects, the Gaudiya Vaishnavas, originated in Bengal. The Hare Krishnas have their world headquarters in the land of Bengal. The founder of ISKCON -- Swami Prabhupada -- was a Bengali born in Calcutta. The great mystic Yoganand Paramhamsa was a Bengali. The Nobel Laureate Gurudev Rabindranath Tagore, and the political activist turned seer Aurobindo Ghosh have epitomized Bengali culture and Indian renaissance.

However, after the coming to power of Communists and their thirty year stranglehold over West Bengal, it is now merely known as the state where Mother

---

[132] *The Indian Express*, "CBI begins probe in Satyendra Dubey murder case", December 13, 2003.

Teresa started her home for the destitute; for destitutes there are aplenty in West Bengal. Once the most industrialized of Indian states, West Bengal became an industrial backwater, despite the initiatives taken late in his tenure by the last CPI-M Chief Minister Buddhadeb Bhattacharjee. The communists finally lost elections in 2011, and the Trinamool Congress Party is now at the helm in Writers Building. Trade unionism, rampant corruption, violence, and political machinations finally made the Communist apparatchik realize that their idea of utopia was hell.

The communists were in power in Bengal for three decades and spared no effort in emasculating the Opposition. The influx of Bangladeshi illegal immigrants has threatened the demographic profile of the area. The communists turned a blind eye to this dangerous influx to appease the Muslims who make a sizeable number of voters, even after the partition of Bengal, into West Bengal (India), and Bangladesh (formerly East Pakistan). On July 21, 2003, at a massive rally held by the Trinamool Congress Party (TMC), a prominent antagonist of the CPI-M, convener of the ruling NDA, and India's defense minister George Fernandes deplored the death of democracy under communist rule in West Bengal. The very same day Sitaram Yechuri, general secretary of the CPI-M, announced that a delegation of Indian communists would go to China (once described by Fernandes as India's No. 1 enemy) to attend the meeting of the Communist Party of China! Yet none in the secular media, or any of the activist academics at Jawaharlal Nehru University, demanded that the Communists quit and that President's rule be imposed in West Bengal.

West Bengal was also in the news for the intensity of violence in the *panchayat* (village level) elections. The elections in 2003 surpassed all state records in violence, killings, coercion, intimidation and terror tactics. Elections were held on May 11, 2003. According to reports, 47 persons lost their lives till May 9 and thereafter another 29 were killed. Of 76 victims, 31 were CPI-M workers, 19 belonged to the Congress, eight from the Trinamool Congress, eight from the BJP and 10 from other parties. The CPI-M was singled out for attack. About 6,300 seats were uncontested and most of them went to the CPI-M and its allies. In Hooghly district alone over 40 per cent in village councils, 42 per cent in village *samitis* (associations/committees) and 25 per cent in regional councils (*zilla panchayat*) went uncontested.

West Bengal was the first state to hold elections to the *panchayats* with official participation of political parties in June 1978. Although there was opposition to the participation of the political parties, the CPI-M and its allies preferred it. Such a situation attracts a sizeable number of lumpen elements to contest and large-scale violence is inevitable. Also, a survey of states showed that West Bengal fared worse in two areas in the past three decades – law and order, and education. Election-related violence and country bomb-making are manifestations of this general deterioration, according to newspaper reports.

The Assam Example

The Northeastern state of Assam is rich in oil and natural gas deposits. Assam lost a part of its territory at the time of partition in 1947 when Sylhet district was donated to East Pakistan (now the independent nation of Bangladesh). Militants have become a security threat to Assam, seeking to secede from the Indian Union. The armed ULFA (United Liberation Front of Assam) movement targeted tea estates and oil and gas installations, and extortion was rampant. The Bangladesh-Assam border areas have seen a tremendous increase in the number of *madarasas*, and have hosted illegal Bangladeshi immigrants. Till recently none of the political parties in Assam or West Bengal considered illegal immigration a security threat ignoring the numerous ethnic and religious conflicts in the area. It was in this context that the brutal Nellie massacre took place – when 1,753 people, mostly Muslims, including children and women, were killed in one day in 1983.

In November 2003 more than 50 Biharis were killed by Assamese, angered that some of their kin had been killed on a train passing through Bihar.[133] Yet no one ever asked for the resignation of the Chief Ministers of Assam on this score. Was it because the BJP was not in power in Assam?

The Jammu & Kashmir Example

Jammu & Kashmir is the only Indian state with a Muslim majority. About one-third of Jammu & Kashmir as shown in maps is with India, the remaining usurped by Pakistan and China. There are three parts to the region: the Hindu-dominated Jammu area, the Muslim-dominated Kashmir Valley, and the Tibetan Buddhist majority Ladakh and Askai-Chin area. In 1947 the princely state of Jammu & Kashmir chose to remain independent. It was a Muslim majority region with a Hindu sovereign.

Since Pakistan was carved out of Muslim majority regions, some argue that logically Kashmir should have gone to Pakistan.[134] According to Akbar two Kashmiris kept Kashmir within India: Jawaharlal Nehru and Sheikh Abdullah. Mountbatten, England's last viceroy to India, and the man who oversaw India's bloody partition, wanted Kashmir to go to Pakistan, and that the Kashmiris themselves did not want to do so. M. J. Akbar paints a benign picture of the Muslims in the Valley and how they had suffered the misgovernance of Maharaja Hari Singh, the last Dogra ruler, and the usury of the Brahmin *pandits*. Sheikh Abdullah founded the Muslim Conference, though he claimed that in the conference, "We stand for the rights of all communities". He changed the name of Muslim Conference to "National Conference" in 1939 but it was and still is predominantly Muslim. He challenged Hari Singh and proclaimed that Kashmiris would never allow the Maharaja to decide the future of Kashmir. Abdullah

---

[133] *Rediff on the Net*, "Five More Biharis Killed in Assam", November 23, 2003.

[134] Akbar, M.J. (1985). *India: The Siege Within: Challenges to a Nation's Unity*. Penguin Books.

was arrested and imprisoned on the charge of sedition but both Gandhi and Nehru supported his cause and brought pressure on Hari Singh to release him.

When Kashmir failed to accede to Pakistan, Jinnah encouraged Pathan tribals to seize Kashmir. Nehru sent Indian troops to Kashmir, and made Hari Singh sign the accession of Kashmir to India. Sheikh Abdullah insisted that the accession was temporary and only the people of Kashmir could decide, and Nehru made that proviso public. Nehru promised that the accession would be confirmed by a referendum under international auspices like the United Nations (Akbar, p. 239). Sheikh Abdullah was sworn is as Prime Minister (not Chief Minister) of Kashmir on October 31, 1947. Pakistan continued the proxy war in Kashmir, but Indian soldiers were able to push back both the regulars of the Pakistani army as well as the Pathan tribals. Nehru, shortsightedly, took the Kashmir case to the United Nations to bring pressure on Pakistan to withdraw from the parts of Kashmir it had occupied. Pakistan now argued that both India and Pakistan should withdraw their troops from Kashmir for an "honest" plebiscite to be possible.

The Indian Constitution, which came into effect on January 26, 1950, provided special status to Kashmir through Article 370. Sheikh Abdullah by then had begun to think of Kashmir as a separate country and wanted it to frame its own Constitution. M. J. Akbar claims that Abdullah had begun to have doubts if India would remain always secular, and if Kashmir would therefore be safe in Indian hands. He asked both India and Pakistan to withdraw their troops from Kashmir but neither would. He proposed a confederation of Pakistan, Kashmir, and India but Nehru would not have it. The ambivalence of Abdullah was all right for Nehru but not for other political parties. The Jana Sangh, newly minted, along with other Hindu groups as well as the Akali Dal of the Sikhs launched an agitation to challenge Sheikh Abdullah. Shyama Prasad Mookerjee, the head of the Jana Sangh, entered Jammu in 1953, courted arrest, and died of a heart attack in jail. There are rumors that he died in mysterious circumstances. Sheikh Abdullah in a speech in July 1953 proclaimed that the time had come for Kashmir to say goodbye to India. The Sheikh was arrested and removed from office, beginning a whole new chapter in Kashmiri history.

The period from 1953 until now is too complicated to capture in a short section of a chapter like this, but it needs to be pointed out that after many stints in jail, and in the wilderness, Sheikh Abdullah became Chief Minister (not Prime Minister) of Kashmir again. Over a period of fifty years India and Pakistan fought two more wars, one in 1965 and the other in 1971. Bangladesh emerged as a new country from what was East Pakistan. The shearing off of its eastern wing gave Pakistan more reason to shear Kashmir off India. China joined hands with Pakistan to play its wily game in the region, and the United States worsened the situation in the sub-continent when it used Pakistan as a conduit for arms to support the Afghani *mujahiddeen* in their fight against the Russians. The Russians lost, reducing Afghanistan into a ramshackle state governed by

The Demand for Modi's resignation

fundamentalist and militant Muslims. Trafficking in guns, heroin, and religious ideology increased in the decade of the 1980s and 1990s following the Russian exit. Pakistan has supported these both overtly and covertly, and its boldest attempt to wrest Kashmir from India came in 1999 when its own regulars and well-supported *mujahiddeen* occupied the icy heights of the Kargil region of Kashmir and threatened to overrun the state. India prevailed both diplomatically and militarily, and the United States now sees the Kashmir problem a little differently because of what militant Islam can do and did in the U.S.

As matters stand, the situation in Kashmir remains unresolved with Pakistan holding on to the captured Kashmiri territory, and naming it Azad Kashmir (Liberated Kashmir). India terms this area as PoK (Pakistan Occupied Kashmir). Thus the inhabitants of this area technically are Indian citizens and should hold Indian passports. But the status is that they have neither Indian nor Pakistani passports. Pakistan has conveniently located and organized training schools for "militants" in POK, where Islamic *madrasas* indoctrinate the students with a militant version of the holy tenets of Islam, urging the poor and the poorly educated to kill non-Muslims considered infidels.

The United States, Israel, and India are the three great enemies of Islam said one Muslim priest of this Pakistani school of hatred. The Al Queda and the cronies of Osama Bin Laden have been active for long in this area.

Hindus have been selectively targeted in Kashmir, and in the late 1980s and early 1990s more than 300,000 Kashmiri Hindus were driven out of Kashmir with the collaboration of some of the local Muslims. This ethnic cleansing of Kashmir and discrimination against the Hindus did not provoke a call for the resignation of the Muslim Chief Minister of Jammu & Kashmir. No one questioned his inability to protect his Hindu citizens. Three hundred thousand Hindus are displaced and the world is silent, while even if 2,000 Muslims are displaced, it becomes not just a national outrage but leads to an outcry by international organizations and discussions in the United Nations.[135]

The Mumbai Riots & Bomb Blasts

The December 6, 1992 demolition of the Babri masjid in Ayodhya led to a number of Hindu-Muslim riots in the country. Muslims were outraged at this destruction as were large sections of the Indian people, and the furor and the controversy over the destruction had not subsided even after a decade of the events. The Ayodhya issue changed Indian politics drastically and spawned a whole industry in academe and publishing that has kept the issue alive.[136]

The Babri Masjid was built on a ground considered holy by the Hindus, and where

---

[135] Pandita, R. (2013). *Our Moon has Blood Clots*. Random House India.

[136] Elst, K. (1991). *Ayodhya and After: Issues before Hindu Society*. New Delhi: Voice of India.

originally a temple for Lord Rama stood. Just as Mecca, Medina, Karbala and the Al-Aqsa mosque in Israel are the most holy sites of Islam, in India there are many sites 800 million Hindus consider holy. Kashi, Mathura, Ayodhya are but only three of them where Muslim rulers have demolished temples and built mosques on holy Hindu ground.

Any mosque built on a destroyed Hindu temple site is an abomination, even if it happened five hundred years ago. We cannot reverse history, however, and modern civic ethos demand that conflicts be resolved through legal processes or carefully considered inter-community resolutions. The destruction of the Babri mosque paralyzed life in many parts of India, including Mumbai (Bombay) where there was rioting on an unparalleled scale. A Congress Party led government was in power in Maharashtra. The Srikrishna Commission named to probe the riots severely reprimanded the Mumbai Police for its partisan role in the riots, and about 16 police personnel including very senior officers have been indicted on rioting charges. The Muslims targeted the lowly constables as also the officers of the Mumbai Police, and stabbed to death many policemen in broad daylight. At that time no one asked for the resignation of the Chief Minister Sudhakar Rao Naik. There was a total law and order failure in the state. In 1992 both the state and central governments were under Congress Party rule.

Following the Mumbai riots, the Mumbai underworld orchestrated multiple bomb blasts on a Friday in order to take revenge and teach Hindus a lesson. Over 250 Hindus lost their lives, and over 1,000 were injured. The Mumbai underworld is dominated by one main gang -- the Dawood Ibrahim gang. Dawood Ibrahim, a Muslim, is the son of an ex-Mumbai police constable. He is a Konkani Muslim, i.e., his roots are from the coastal Konkan area of Maharashtra. The bomb blasts were the handiwork of the members of the Dawood gang, who were trained in Pakistan. It has been widely reported in the media that Dawood and his men are on the payroll of the Pakistani intelligence agencies. Considering this severe breakdown in law and order, and the serious intelligence failure in preventing the Mumbai riots and bombs blasts, the government of Maharashtra should have taken moral responsibility and resigned. However, none of the "secularists" demanded it. If Maharashtra had a BJP government at that time, there is no doubt that media headlines and editorials would have screamed for its resignation if not for the International Court of Justice to step in.

There were more bomb blasts in Mumbai on August 25, 2003, in which 48 people were killed.[137] The "secularists" rationalized that this was pay-back for the Gujarat violence of 2002. No one asked for the head of anyone for lax intelligence and failure to stop the massacre.

---

[137] *Rediff on the Net*, "At least 48 Die in Mumbai Blasts", August 25, 2003.

The Assassination of Indira Gandhi

Two Sikh bodyguards who assassinated Indira Gandhi on October 31, 1984, were driven by their anger over the Golden Temple episode. In the wake of Indira Gandhi's assassination, mobs overran the streets of New Delhi and other parts of India over the next few days, killing at least two thousand Sikhs. The New Delhi police was accused of being partisan observers and not doing much to stop or apprehend the rioters. Only after the deployment of the army, almost three days after the onset of the riots, was order fully restored. More important, some top Congress Party leaders were accused of instigating the riots and bloodletting. Congress Party leader H. K. L. Bhagat was accused of masterminding the retaliation against Sikhs.[138]

Rajiv Gandhi, Indira's elder son, was sworn in as Prime Minister. He was said to have remarked that "When a big tree falls, the ground is bound to shake."[139] No one asked for Rajiv Gandhi's resignation. In fact in that polarized atmosphere general elections on a nationwide scale were held within 45 days of Indira Gandhi's death. The Election Commission of India chose to conduct elections then when the whole nation was emotionally charged, but interestingly enough when Modi called for elections in Gujarat, the EC chose to grandstand because a few thousand Muslims (and Hindus) were displaced.

Gujarat riots 1969, 1985

In 1969 and 1985 when riots rocked Gujarat it was a Congress government in power, and yet no one asked the Chief Ministers to step down. In 1969 the riots lasted for 12 days, and spread to 11 districts of the State. About 519 deaths were reported, 1,028 injuries, and registered offences neared 990, with more than 25,000 people rendered homeless.

The examples and analogies we have provided above point out that there was never an instance when a Chief Minister or a Prime Minister was asked to quit because of a law and order problem (since 2003 there have been more communal riots and killing but there has been no call for the scalp of any head of a state government). But the drumbeat of hate mounted against Modi, not just in India but around the world, is a clear indication of the double standards and ulterior motives of sections of the Indian elite who have made ruination and demonization of the BJP a crusade. The methodology adopted by the "secularists" is to demonize Modi as a "Muslim killer" and a "Muslim hater".

It is true that many Muslims as well as Hindus died in the riots which engulfed Gujarat after Godhra. But Modi did not lead the rioters like H. K. L. Bhagat did, nor was he found guilty by the Nanavati Commission looking into the matter. It is true that

---

[138] Kaur, N. (September 1, 2001). "Waiting for Justice", *Frontline*.

[139] *The Hindu*, "The Original Sin of 1984", November 1, 2012.

there was failure on the part of the Home Department in preventing the Godhra attack, and the ensuing riots. With its billion dollar budgets, and advanced technology, the CIA still could not in time predict India going nuclear either in 1974 or during Pokhran-II in 1998, nor could the CIA prevent the WTC attacks on 9/11. Similarly, the Israeli Mossad could not predict and prevent the assassination of Yitzhak Rabin at the hands of a fellow Jew. To hold Modi responsible therefore for the Godhra massacre or the ensuing fratricide is merely an act of cussedness of self-proclaimed secularists.

The media's demand for Modi's resignation was uncalled for, unprecedented, and undemocratic. It did not help bring normalcy to Gujarat, nor did it help in the reconciliation of Hindus and Muslims. The more the media painted Modi as an ogre the greater the support he won, and the more the anger and animosity against the Muslims.

In the December 2002 elections, the media's campaign proved to be a blessing in disguise for Modi. He gathered more than 55 percent of the votes polled, and about 70 percent majority in the State Assembly. His government came back to power ever stronger and more resilient. An interesting fallout of his victory was that Modi simply did away with the free transportation provided to journalists from Ahmedabad to the State Secretariat in Gandhinagar. If they were to caricature him, they would have to do so riding their own vehicles!

We note that the demand for Modi's resignation came mostly from the English-language media. The local Gujarati Press and a large section of the Hindi media analyzed the situation differently. The demand for Modi's scalp came especially shrilly from the Delhi-based English media. Their ire seems to have been stoked by the repeated airing of TV footage showing burning houses and dead children and women. At one time, a prominent Indian English news channel was banned in Gujarat because it showed the same scene daily, thereby adding to the already prevailing tense situation.[140]

This "Delhi Syndrome" even swayed many in the BJP who began to ask for Modi's resignation. They had not visited Godhra or other parts of Gujarat to ascertain the facts for themselves, but based their views purely on media reports. Even Prime Minister Vajpayee admonished Modi saying that a ruler must follow "*Raj Dharma*" (duty of a king). According to Hindu tradition a king or a ruler does not discriminate among his subjects, for the king or the ruler does not discriminate between children and his subjects. Only after Modi's government prepared a fact-filled dossier and circulated it widely did the demand for Modi's resignation disappear.

Modi and the media have always had a special love-hate relationship since his days at the party head office in New Delhi. Modi took on Rafiq Zakaria, the veteran Muslim politician, in a verbal duel on national television. This verbal skirmish in September

---

[140] Modi, S. K. (2004). *Godhra: The Missing Rage*. Ocean Books.

2001, a few days before Modi became the Chief Minister, prompted Suhel Seth to write a column in the Indian Express titled "Narendra Modi's passion for hatred".[141] An outraged Modi expressed his displeasure on the phone to Suhel Seth, his one time friend who had stooped to the secular Indian's habit of running down the Hindus to curry favors with fellow secularists.

Is Modi misunderstood? Probably yes. Is it because of how he responds to the media and the way he presents himself in public? He usually comes across as a stern man. He rarely smiles in public, and his voice is a rather heavy baritone. His image is that of an ultra-hardliner, but he is not. Once he said to one of the co-authors that his image does not reflect his true self. His human and sensitive side is ignored and every gesture of his analyzed for identifying some "demonic" trait in him. Ashis Nandy, one of India's well-known social scientists, had the gall to proclaim that Modi had the personality of a mass murderer. That one can get away with such nonsense in India is indicative of the mindless deification or demonization of leaders in the country.

Modi of course is unhappy and concerned about his negative image in the media. He is a poet and a writer, and aspired once upon a time to be a copy-writer or a journalist. He spent two years wandering the hills and mountains of India and seeking the counsel of sages, when he was young. It is unfortunate that the Sabarmati Express was burned down in Godhra by Muslims, and riots ensued, but the demand for Modi's resignation, though well coordinated and vicious, boomeranged on his opponents.

---

[141] *The Indian Express*, "What the BJP leader said on TV reveals BJP's hidden agenda", September 26, 2001.

CHAPTER XI – A "SUPER COP" TO ADVISE MODI

With Parliament in session, Opposition parties demanded invoking Article 356 of the Indian Constitution to dismiss the state government, and impose President's Rule in Gujarat through the office of the Governor. Article 356 can be promulgated in case of failure of constitutional machinery in the states. On the written report of the governor of a state, the President of India can use Article 356 to impose Central Rule in that state. If the president's action is ratified by both houses of parliament, then the duration of president's rule is for a period of six months, this period extendable to a further six months, but not beyond that, unless a proclamation of a state of "Emergency" is in force in the whole of India or a part of it. However, Article 356 (5b) empowers the Election Commission of India to extend this proclamation beyond the first one-year period, if it can prove that there are problems in holding general elections to the legislative body of the state.

The governor is the head of a state, but the chief minister is the head of the government. However, when president's rule is imposed the chief minister is dismissed and all executive powers then rest with the governor of the state. Law and order had failed in Gujarat, the state police were unable to protect the Hindus from Muslim activists and gangs in Godhra, and later could not prevent riots when Hindu zealots took revenge on Muslims. Thus it was a double failure on the law and order front. The media demanded the ouster of Modi, and the opposition parties too aggressively sought the imposition of President's rule. Some believed that if Modi was replaced by another BJP leader, possibly Haren Pandya, then maybe the opposition parties and the media would scale down their attack. Others argued that in an election year it would mean that the BJP would have to accept the responsibility for not being able to protect the Hindus in Godhra, and Muslims in Ahmedabad, and thus would lose on both fronts. If Modi was removed, it would have meant a change of guard two times within a span of six months.

No chief minister ever resigned in the history of independent India on a law and order issue, and certainly the BJP did not like its man to be the first to do so. After the demolition of the Babri mosque in 1992, the Congress government in power in Delhi dismissed BJP governments in four states, invoking Article 356. The BJP lost power in Uttar Pradesh, Rajasthan, Madhya Pradesh, and Himachal Pradesh, and the Congress Party grossly abused Article 356.[142]

There was no constitutional breakdown following the Ayodhya episode in Rajasthan, Himachal Pradesh, and Madhya Pradesh. Even in Uttar Pradesh, other than rioting, the constitutional mechanism was functioning. When a state government is

---

[142] *Frontline*, "It must be retained, but its abuse prevented", July 04, 1998.

dismissed under Article 356, the central government has to seek ratification of its move in both houses of parliament. Even if one of them rejects it, the imposition is revoked, and the state government is put back in place.

When the BJP came to power, it dismissed the Lalu Prasad-Rabri Devi government in Bihar citing misrule, and grave law and order situation. The BJP and its allies did not have a majority in the Rajya Sabha (Upper House of Parliament). They needed the support of the Congress Party in the Rajya Sabha to ratify the dismissal of the Bihar Government. The Congress backed out at the last moment after promising support to the BJP. The ratification though passed in the lower house, could not pass in the upper house. The Congress did not find it incongruous to protest the BJP's move. The imposition of Article 356 was revoked and Lalu Prasad Yadav government was back in business. The BJP did not forget the truancy of the Congress Party, and when the Opposition and the Congress Party demanded the dismissal of the Modi government, it rightly rejected this "insane" demand.

Vajpayee was, however, under growing pressure from his allies like the Telegu Desam Party, the Bihar-based Samata Party, and the Janata Dal (United). Only Maharashtra's Shiv-Sena, BJP's alter-ego, and closest ideological ally, supported the BJP in rejecting the demand for the imposition of President's Rule in Gujarat. The Shiv-Sena leader Bal Thackeray came out openly in support of Modi. The government then decided to take steps to save Modi, and yet pacify its allies.

The Constitution of India provides a way out. Article 355 allows the Central Government to take control of the law and order machinery of a state, without dismissing the state government. Article 355 deals with the duty of the center to protect states against external aggression and internal disturbance. It states that, "It shall be the duty of the Union to protect every State against external aggression and internal disturbance and to ensure that the government of every State is carried on in accordance with the provisions of the Constitution."

Narendra Modi was against conceding even an inch to the opposition demand, as it would amount to accepting a mistake or weakness, but finally gave in. The Central Government then imposed Article 355, taking charge of the law and order situation in Gujarat. In May, the Government of India, in an unprecedented move, appointed K.P.S. Gill, the retired Director General of Punjab Police, as the Security Advisor to the Chief Minister, with Gill reporting to Advani, the Home Minister in Delhi.[143] He was given the rank of Minister of State in the Gujarat Government. This was a strategic move by Advani aimed at getting Gujarat back to normalcy, and simultaneously meeting the demands of the allies, the opposition, and the media.

Gill was a retired IPS (Indian Police Service) officer. He was a former Chief of Police in Punjab and in Assam. The IPS is an elite police service corps of the central government. Over six feet tall, Gill is an imposing Sikh who proudly sports a beard and

---

[143] Gupta, S., & Mahurkar, U. (May 20, 2002). "What can Gill do?" *India Today*.

turban. He is one of the few retired/serving police officers who have earned the nickname "Super Cop". It was K.P.S. Gill's stern and "take-no-prisoners" actions against the Pakistan-based terrorists in Punjab that ended the terrorist menace there. Gill achieved "notoriety" in the late-1970s for taking new initiatives in crushing the insurgency in Assam.

Gill did not come untarnished though. He was fined $ 5,500 by a court that upheld a complaint by a woman bureaucrat who accused Gill of pinching her bottom. Gill was also accused of arranging a helicopter for five policemen who flew to Calcutta and killed suspected terrorists. A West Bengal court later sentenced the five policemen to life imprisonment when it was found that the "terrorists" were just a fellow policeman Lachi Singh and his wife Rani who had converted to Islam and had taken the names of Bashir Ahmad and Sakina. The court charged them with killing the duo and of disposing of their bodies. The High Court observed that it was Gill who had allowed the requisition of the Dolphin helicopter to fly the five Punjab policemen to Calcutta. The helicopter was meant for the privileged use of the Chief Minister.

Though it was many years since Gill had retired, it was believed that his presence would reinvigorate the Gujarat police, add a new element to the chain of command, and motivate the officers. Gill was given an office in the Secretariat, on the same floor as the Chief Minister, and a detailed map of Ahmedabad was posted on the wall of his office, with areas of violence marked in red. There was some resentment among senior officers of the Gujarat Police when they learnt that Gill was coming to Gujarat. Gill was of the Punjab State cadre of the IPS, and his colleagues in Gujarat were not in a mood to welcome an "outsider". He was given the rank of an Inspector General of Police, and a senior Muslim police officer was appointed as his O.S.D. (Officer on Special Duty).

Gill held daily meetings with the Chief Minister, senior ministers, senior bureaucrats, and the Gujarat's Director General of Police. Like the Gujarat officers and ministers who did not like outside interference in the affairs of their state, Gujarati language press was also not happy with Gill's appointment. They accused Gill of not interacting with them, and restricting himself to entertaining the English press. Thus when Gill's term ended the Gujarati press did not attend his farewell. He did not visit the secretariat that often, but preferred to hold meetings at the CRPF (Central Reserve Police Force) guest house where he was staying. Gujarat is a "dry" state. The sale and consumption of alcohol is prohibited by state law. One cannot help but wonder how the whiskey-quaffing Punjabi survived in staid Gujarat!

Gill often made extensive field trips to affected regions, and also visited relief camps, met with the Muslim community leaders, and also Hindu leaders. He held discussions with all concerned groups. However, the riots subsided within 72 hours, and there were only random and sporadic incidents that really did not need the oversight of a Central Government officer. Gill's presence had marginal effect on the ground situation in Gujarat but served as some kind of a morale booster for Modi's detractors as well as Gujarat's Muslim population.

During his tenure in Gujarat, Gill was an advocate of early elections. He felt that early elections would force all political parties to concentrate on restoring peace and normalcy. Gill's appointment helped assuage some Muslim sentiment as well as divert media attention. It relieved the pressure on the State Government to some extent.

Rehabilitation of the Riot-affected

The post-Godhra riots displaced people of both Hindu and Muslim communities. Hindus living in Muslim areas were targeted as were Muslims living in Hindu areas. Places of worship of both religions bore the brunt of the rioters. Deities in Hindu temples were damaged by Muslim rioters, while Hindus burnt copies of the *Koran*, and damaged mosques.

The media was unduly interested in knowing which community suffered most damage. How many Hindus were arrested versus how many Muslims? How many Hindus were displaced versus how many Muslims? At a time when Gujarat was licking its wounds, a select group of activists and their media instigators began gathering statistics of this nature to prove to the world that post-Godhra riots were equivalent to a pogrom, and that the Modi government had meticulously planned it. Unfortunately, this quest for facts and figures did not translate into objective reporting. It is still the fuzzy and inaccurate phrase "nearly 2,000, mostly Muslims, were killed in Gujarat" that is used in the media and by activists seeking to dredge out the last bit of hatred against Modi.

What were the actual numbers of those killed and displaced? In a *Times of India* report, the toll, one week after the bloodiest of riots, stood at 677. The riots were controlled within 72 hours.[144] The report said that nearly a hundred people were killed by the police trying to control the riots. A report dated April 28, 2002[145] gave more figures of dead and injured and businesses burnt down. Of the 726 people killed, 552 were Muslims and 168 Hindus, including the 58 on the Sabarmati Express. Of the people killed in the first month of police firings, 60 were Hindus and 40 Muslims. In the second month, when 70 more succumbed to police firings, 53 were Muslims and 17 Hindus. A July 28, 2002 report in the *India Times*, cites the Chief Rehabilitation Officer of the Gujarat government, a Muslim official, as saying that he had disbursed compensation to the kin of all 925 victims (including Hindus) in the riots. When such precise figures were available and easily accessible by anyone who could spend an hour searching the Internet, one wondered why the media and some human rights organizations were keen on inflating the toll.

---

[144] Desai, B. (March 7, 2002), "Toll now 677 due to recovery of more bodies", *The Times of India*.

[145] Pandey, S. (April 28, 2002). "More fall prey to police firings in Gujarat", *The Times of India*.

The Election That Shaped Gujarat

For the first time in the history of Gujarat, Narendra Modi formed an all-party core committee for relief distribution that ensured the equitable distribution of relief material and allayed fears that the government would give more relief to the displaced Hindus than to the displaced Muslims. The transparency shown by the government in relief distribution was commendable, and unprecedented. There were many relief camps in the riot-hit areas, with the largest being at Shah Alam and Shahibaug areas in Ahmedabad. Modi did visit some relief camps, but there was information that his visit would certainly embarrass Muslim inhabitants in Shah Alam and Shahibaug camps. Therefore, he chose to visit them only with the Prime Minister. However, the information proved right because when Modi visited these relief camps, residents chanted anti-Modi slogans in front of the Prime Minister. It was only as a mark of respect for the Prime Minister that Modi sat and listened to all the slogans from the people.

On previous occasions, Modi spoke of the plight of thousands of violence- affected people, and expressed his desire and determination to improve their condition. People were staying in miserable conditions, but the cash strapped government, also burdened by many overdrafts, could only provide relief in a phased manner. It was thus strange that certain foreign charities that gave money openly for the building of *madrasas*, shrunk back when it came to donating money for the relief of affected people. Even if these foreign charities had given money for the relief of only Muslims, the government of Gujarat would have readily accepted it. People spoke of loans but not assistance!

Before the Prime Minister's visit, the Gujarat government put in extra effort to sanitize the relief camps, giving them a face lift and spraying DDT powder to disinfect the perimeter. The government also erected a *shamiana* (a cloth canopy), replenished the water-tanks at Shah Alam and Shahibaug camps and disbursed cash doles worth Rs. 1,000 to each riot-hit family to take care of their immediate needs. One can criticize these measures as last minute, face-saving tactics because it is in the nature of people and institutions to "pretty up" a place for a VIP's visit.

In view of governmental delay in giving economic assistance to both Hindus and Muslims, the VHP (World Hindu Council) came to the aid of Hindu victims of rioting promising to reimburse medical bills of members of the Hindu community injured in the violence and to provide financial aid to those who lost their homes. Gujarat's VHP secretary Jaideep Patel declared that this was a "local decision" and that the money would come from funds locally raised. Similarly, some Muslim organizations and charities came to the aid of Muslim victims. It was unfortunate that the VHP and the Muslim organizations made religion the basis for offering help. It would have helped assuage some of the bitterness and anger if they had disbursed aid irrespective of the faith of the victims and thus made amends for their own culpability in the violence. However, one could argue that any such attempts at providing succor by these organizations to the "other" community would have led to accusations of hypocrisy.

At a relief camp named Daryakhan Ghummat, the Gujarat police received one thousand complaints and registered FIRs (First Information Reports). The Additional Commissioner of Police Keshav Kumar then randomly examined a slew of complaints to help ascertain which were repetitive, which were bogus, and which could in the end be converted into FIRs or criminal indictments. The police attributed the delay in registering the complaints to the sheer magnitude of violence and shortage of staff. They then waited for the situation to return to some degree of normality before completing the inquiries, and filing charge-sheets in courts of law to bring the rioters to book. At the Naroda police station, under whose jurisdiction the infamous Naroda-Patiya massacre took place the police converted 707 complaints into 103 FIRs (or criminal indictments).

On May 13, the Gujarat government announced that it would provide riot victims with the opportunity to file individual FIRs naming culprits, set up special committees to record statements of women who had suffered, and take steps for the reconstruction of damaged religious structures of both religions. Narendra Modi announced these steps after a meeting with about forty Muslims leaders and a team from the National Commission for Minorities. Modi assured the Muslims that the Hindus would not take over Muslim shrines. He further assured that a three-member committee, comprising of local women social workers, would be set up in each affected district to record complaints relating to attacks on women. This committee would submit its report to the police for registering FIRs and prosecuting the guilty.

On the issue of missing persons, Modi announced that the government would form a committee to ensure the kin of those reported missing in the riots received compensation. This had to be done because under the existing rules the government had to wait for six years to provide posthumous compensation. In the present instance the rule was waived for both the Hindus and the Muslims. Modi then announced the names of two Muslim administrators, Shamim Kazim, member of the National Commission for Minorities, and Kari Mohammad Mazhari, Chairman of the National Minorities Finance and Development Corporation, to coordinate with the government for speedy and effective implementation of the rehabilitation package announced by the Prime Minister. This package was worth 1500 million rupees ($33 million). He also announced that two NGO representatives would monitor the re-survey of damaged properties of both Hindus and Muslims, and submit a report to the government. Modi allayed the fears of displaced people and said that the relief camps would not be shut down until the inmates were rehabilitated properly.

By the middle of June 2002, the Modi government won praise from Home Minister Advani for quick and effective rehabilitation work. Advani said that he was satisfied by the state's rehabilitation efforts as many riot victims, both Hindus and Muslims were returning to their homes. At one time, there were over 150,000 displaced people, but by the middle of June only about 18,500 people were in the nineteen remaining camps. Advani mentioned that an end to the riots and return of the people to their homes was not the end of governmental involvement. The Modi administration would take steps towards social, economic and cultural rehabilitation too.

By July 4, 2002, more than four months after the Godhra incident, relief camps were shut down as the administration found that the situation had become normal, and it was desirable to discontinue incurring additional expenditure on providing free food, shelter, and other facilities. Some NGOs were opposed to the closing of the relief camps as more than ten thousand people still lived in them. But the government felt that if others could return to their homes these people too could follow suit. Relief camps could not have a permanent existence, and because the situation had normalized the camps were to be closed down.

Before they were closed, people staying in the relief camps gave written statements to the administrators that they were ready for the closure if certain help was given and arrangements made for their safe return. After all this, some people and the NGOs complained that the camp inmates had been tricked into signing such statements. When they wanted twenty-four hour CRPF protection, government said that personalized protection was not possible but area policing would be increased by drafting paramilitary forces to avoid any untoward incidents. After the closure of the relief camps, governmental responsibility ceased and so did governmental financial assistance. Those who wanted to keep these camps running would have to generate private funding. Some people complained that the government was closing down smaller relief camps and forcing people to shift to bigger camps in Darikhan Gummat, and Shah Alam areas. People were unwilling to leave the smaller relief camps as these were near their residential localities, whereas the bigger relief camps were some distance away.

The Modi government even set-up a two-member judicial enquiry commission consisting of two retired judges, one from the Supreme Court and the other from a High Court to look into riot related grievances. On the rehabilitation front, within three months of the riots, ex-gratia compensation payments were paid in 745 cases of death and in 1,532 injury-related cases. Cash doles amounting to $130,000 (6.6 million rupees) were handed out to 40,256 people within two months of the riots. $930,000 (45 million rupees) was disbursed in the form of household kits to 28,756 families. An amount of $2.64 million (130 million rupees) was spent on essential food items in relief camps, and an additional miscellaneous expenditure of $890,000 (42 million rupees) towards relief camps was incurred. Housing assistance for partially and fully damaged houses was given in 21,089 cases. Special maternity and childcare arrangements were made at relief camps. Nearly $1.3 million (65 million rupees) was given to 9,890 beneficiaries who had lost their earning assets for livelihood. The Government spent $12.25 million (600 million rupees) on rehabilitation.

All these steps taken by the Modi government made the then Union Law Minister, Arun Jaitley, assert that the manner in which Narendra Modi handled the riots was the best ever. Jaitley flayed Modi's critics and commended Modi on his handling of the carnage as better than any government did in the past. He challenged Modi's critics by asking them to point out which government had acted in more alacrity than the Modi government in bringing the massive riots under control. The police quickly had arrested nearly 4,000 people, fired over 10,000 rounds of ammunition, and over 200 people were killed by the police firing to quell mob violence. He gave the example of how in one case there were 20- odd policemen and a mob of 15,000 rioters. Yet the police managed to control them. He urged the media to highlight such positive incidents, rather than continue their Modi-bashing spree.

In a broadside against Arundhati Roy, Jaitley said, "We also had one of the country's leading novelists using entirely fictional events for her writing on Gujarat. It became part of the false rhetoric people were swayed by, and nobody seems bothered about truth." On the question of Modi's government being soft on the rioting masses, Jaitley said: "I don't understand this argument…We live in a society governed by the rule of law. A lot of those who had been arrested under preventive measures had to be released because the judges gave them bail." Jaitley summarized his evaluation saying that on the whole the state administration deserved to be commended for the way it came to grips with the tragic situation. He gave the example of how in one case there were 20- odd policemen and a mob of 15,000 rioters. Yet the police managed to control them. He urged the media to highlight such positive incidents, rather than continue their Modi-bashing spree.

At a later date even the U.S. Assistant Secretary of State, Christina Rocca, issued a statement that the Gujarat Government had indeed done much towards rehabilitation of the riot victims, while at the same time expressing "horror" at the events in Gujarat. On March 22, 2003, she was called to testify at a U.S. Senate hearing on South Asia. When asked about the situation of minorities in Gujarat, India, Rocca said "much action" has been taken by the Indian Government against those behind the Gujarat massacres. "The legal system in India is agonizingly slow and that gives the impression that nothing is happening. But the fact of the matter is that they did take action and they are continuing to take action" she said.

In contrast, the European Union likened the Gujarat situation to apartheid and said that it had similarities with Nazi Germany of the 1930s.[146] It would seem strange that the worst perpetrators of genocide, mass ethnic cleansing, religious bigotry, and colonialism in human history, not just in recent human history but in all of human history, would don the mantle of saviors of humanity. Some of these European leaders and activists no doubt are full of guilt and shame at what their immediate ancestors – their fathers and grandfathers, their mothers and grandmothers – did in the name of nationality, ideology, and ethnicity. But for them now to claim the role of "moral police", many felt, was an overreach, however well-intentioned the effort. It was, once again, the West seeking to carry the rest of the world's burden. Instead of spending

---

[146] Pal, A. (July 2003). "Bush ignores India's Pogrom". *The Progressive*

more time introspecting on the horrors they inflicted on humankind they were extra keen on sitting in judgment on criminality elsewhere.

There was also no dearth of Indian activists, NGOs, and academics who lauded the European attempt to meddle in India's affairs. Some of these activists did not consider it amiss to take their grievances abroad: a Jawaharlal Nehru University (JNU) professor of international relations, Kamal Mitra Chenoy, a Catholic Christian editor turned activist, Father Cedric Prakash, and a Muslim activist, Teesta Setalvad, traveled all the way to the U.S. and deposed before an American government commission of inquiry on India's religious conflict. No American would deign to travel to depose before a foreign government's official commission inquiring into events in the U.S. Americans would think it as suspect if not traitorous. In India, such activists and self-anointed moral police are rarely called to question about such activities. As the well-known Indian feminist, academic, and activist, Madhu Kishwar, said at the South Asia conference in Madison, Wisconsin in 2003, "There are some Indians who would spit on their mother for $50,000!"

Unfortunately, certain elements in the Indian media judged the Gujarat government on a scale humanly impossible to reach and achieve, and inferred the opposite. This disconnect between the real world and the ideal world caused these reporters and commentators in the media to publish reports that not only presented a skewed picture of Gujarat but also damaged the national interests of India overseas. Had these powerful media elements compared the government's performance with other governments during whose tenure riots had broken out, they would have realized that the incumbent Gujarat government under Narendra Modi indeed did much better than other governments caught in similar predicaments.

CHAPTER XII -- THE HISTORIC GOA MEETING

It was amidst the controversy surrounding Gujarat and the media onslaught on the BJP that the party held its National Executive meeting (April 12-14, 2002). The venue was Goa, the famous tourist attraction. With all the heat Gujarat generated in the country, Goa seemed the right place to hold the important conclave and to soothe frayed nerves. Goa, with its beautiful beaches and famed churches, was under Portuguese rule until 1965, when Nehru sent the Indian Army to drive the colonial power out. Goa's old name was Gomantak, and some indigenous people still refer to it by that name.

In the days prior to the meeting, BJP delegates called Gandhinagar to convey their messages of support to Modi. They were vigorous in their denouncement of the media assault directed against the Chief Minister. The stench of media reports and editorials crucifying Modi enveloped the atmosphere at the five-star Marriott Hotel in Goa, where the inaugural session was held. The BJP leadership came under pressure to sacrifice Modi.

The leadership was split on the course of action. One school of thought was that it would be wise to replace Modi by reinstating the old patriarch Keshubhai Patel, who by that time had claimed he was fit to rule. Undaunted by advancing years, the septuagenarian said he was ready to wear the crown, once again. Some felt that the young Modi baiter, Haren Pandya, should be given the opportunity. A sizeable number of delegates backed Modi. Heading the BJP was Jana Krishnamurti, a party veteran. Every important leader in the BJP was present at this historic meeting. In its importance, the 2002 Goa meeting was compared to the 1989 Nagpur meeting.

In 1989, Rajiv Gandhi was the Prime Minister, and the Congress party enjoyed a two-thirds majority in parliament. This gave Rajiv Gandhi the enviable strength to amend the Constitution of India, and the power to impeach any High Court or Supreme Court judge, or even the President of India. No other Indian party had been able to achieve the coveted two-thirds majority earlier or later.

Such a majority could lead to misuse of power and it did. One instance is that of the infamous case of Shah Bano, a Muslim woman divorcee denied maintenance by her husband. India does not have a uniform civil code. Separate laws apply to different religious groups regarding marriage, divorce, inheritance, and such other civil matters. A Muslim woman in India does not get alimony after divorce. Shah Bano's appeal went up to the Supreme Court of India. The Court termed the treatment meted out to Shah Bano as exploitation of women, and allowed her to appeal. It delivered its verdict in 1985.

The decision, based on a section of the Criminal Penal Code, went against the legal precedent of treating such Muslim family disputes under the special provisions of the Muslim Personal Law Application Act. As could be expected, the Muslim clergy and the Muslim political leadership rejected the verdict as an infringement of the cultural autonomy of Muslims. Public protests followed, and the conservative clergy and even

Muslim journalists whipped up enough frenzy among the mostly conservative Indian Muslim population to compel Rajiv Gandhi government to undo the court verdict. The government, with its two-thirds majority, was able to pass a bill annulling the Supreme Court verdict. It was in consonance with the time-tested appeasement policy of the Congress to retain influence with its Muslim vote bank.

The absolute two-thirds majority the Congress Party won in the 1984-1985 general elections held after the assassination of Indira Gandhi reduced the BJP to a mere two-member nonentity in Parliament. BJP stalwarts like Vajpayee and Advani were all out of Parliament. The BJP's survival as a national party was at stake.

At its National Executive Meeting in 1989, the BJP took the historic decision to pursue the Ram Temple issue. This decision irreversibly changed Indian politics, and weakened the position of the Congress Party as the only viable national party in the country. It ushered in a new era of coalition politics. After 40 years of Nehruvian socialism and Indira Gandhi's populism, India opened up its economy in the early 1990s, and the BJP came to power riding the crest of a coalition collage called the NDA (National Democratic Alliance).

The 2002 BJP National Executive meeting also took place at a similar seminal moment, and generated an intense debate whether to continue to advocate Hindu nationalism or suffer a Congress-type Nehruvian secularism that advocated minority appeasement. The BJP was going the Congress Party way, many feared. However, the ranks threw up a new and young generation of BJP politicians, including Narendra Modi, the articulate and media-savvy Arun Jaitley, and the BJP's man Friday, Pramod Mahajan. There were also the likes of the fiery Uma Bharati, Venkaiah Naidu, Gopinath Munde, and others among the second rung of BJP leadership who commanded attention and sizeable support among the people. Uma Bharati became the Chief Minister of Madhya Pradesh, after the BJP captured power in three states – Rajasthan, Madhya Pradesh, and Chattisgarh in the assembly elections held in November 2003.

The Goa conclave began on April 12, 2002 at 4:30, Friday afternoon. After Jana Krishnamurti finished speaking, Modi stood up and said he was placing his resignation before the delegates. Termed histrionic by the media, Modi's move was to challenge his party colleagues: to see whether they would succumb to media and external pressures, or whether they would stand united and fight. Modi's words were heard in hushed silence. Krishnamurti adjourned the meeting for a short period to consult senior party leaders.

The National Executive Committee meeting was scheduled to begin on Saturday, but with Modi announcing his resignation, was advanced to Friday night. When Krishnamurti addressed a press conference later, he disclosed what Modi had said. "Modi gives in" the headlines said the next day.[147] Some constitutional experts debated

---

[147] Bhatt, S., & Prabhudesai, S. (April 12, 2002). "Modi gives in, submits his resignation." *Rediff on the Net*.

whether a party's National Executive Committee meeting was the right venue for submitting a chief minister's resignation, and if so, whether it was valid. The forum to submit his resignation would be the floor of the state assembly in the presence of the elected representatives of the people, and not a party meeting, they argued. Yes, the resignation would be valid only when it was announced on the floor of the assembly but there is no rule that bars a person from announcing his resignation elsewhere.

BJP vice-president, and ex-Deputy Chief Minister of Maharashtra, Gopinath Munde declared that no ally of the BJP-led NDA government should part ways with the BJP, especially at a time when the Congress Party was growing in strength. Supporting Modi, Munde said, "Whatever may be the feeling of the people in the rest of the country, Gujarat has gained a lot from Modi. It is thus not easy to remove him. It is a time to remain united, and not go to the extremes." Munde urged the BJP and the NDA to counter the anti-BJP propaganda vigorously.

Modi later revealed that he had made up his mind to resign and seek a fresh mandate of the people of Gujarat five days before he had submitted his resignation to the National Executive Committee. He also thanked Vajpayee and Advani for their continued support. One of the reasons mentioned by Modi for resigning was that he did not want to appear responsible for the negative assessment and image of Gujarat – locally or internationally.

The BJP National Executive Committee delegates reassembled and decided to reject Modi's resignation. Thus a consensus emerged for the strategy to be adopted by the BJP for the coming Gujarat elections. Modi, in one master stroke, quelled all opposition within the party, and emerged a leader "chosen" by the National Executive. His detractors in the Gujarat BJP were silenced. Jana Krishamurti criticized the attacks on Modi, and said the nation had to be saved from forces whose only aim was to destabilize the BJP government, even when the situation demanded the cooperation of everyone to restore normalcy in the riot-torn state. The BJP president accused the Congress of fostering an attitude that was not conducive for the healthy growth of democracy in India.

Few at that time knew how divided the BJP was over the issue of Modi. Narendra Modi single-handedly persuaded the BJP into drawing a strategy for the future. It was very important for Modi and the BJP to decide whether assertive Hindutva was to be pursued or whether caste-based and minority appeasement politics would once again be the recourse. As a source from the Prime Minister's office later disclosed, Vajpayee was open to suggestions from all quarters, and that replacing Modi was not dismissed out of hand. But the RSS was vehemently against the removal of Modi. The RSS through its senior leader Kushabhau Thakre conveyed to the BJP leadership that it was in the Central Government's long term interests not to cave in to the pressure tactics of either the coalition partners or the Opposition parties.[148] In fact, whenever the BJP leaders

---

[148] *Rediff on the Net*, "RSS forces Vajpayee to change tack on Modi issue", April 13, 2002.

met to discuss Gujarat it was Kushabhau Thakre who put his foot down on the matter of Modi's replacement. According to a widely reported view in the media, Thakre was the most influential among the RSS leaders who spread the word in the RSS that Modi would have to be defended even at the cost of the BJP-led NDA government.

So strong was the opposition from the RSS quarters that Vajpayee had no choice but to back Modi. According to media reports, Law Minister Arun Jaitley was the author of the strategy to submit the resignation at the National Executive Committee meeting. The reports also claimed that Jaitley, in consultation with the RSS, asked Modi to submit his resignation. It was a "heads-I-win-tails-you-lose" situation. There would be no defeat for Narendra Modi. Modi satisfied the media too. He did resign after all, didn't he? But now it was the party that had once again entrusted to him the job to rebuild Gujarat, and win the elections that were looming on the horizon.

Modi's resignation offer also indicated that he did not care for hanging on to power. He was a party worker, and only the good of the party and his state were paramount to him. His strategy worked, and this one move was multi-dimensional in its scope and effects. The RSS in turn issued a statement that the security of the minority lay in the goodwill of the majority, and that certain members of the minority community could no longer go on provoking the majority community and still complain of discrimination. In a more muted version of this statement, the BJP president said, "If the message can go to everyone in society that whosoever provokes another, and whoever takes initiative in provoking or attacking another, whatever religion he may belong to the state as well as society will come down on him heavily to punish him. Everyone in society will remain assured that justice will be rendered to all with no appeasement of anyone.[149] Modi traveled to Goa a hunted man, but returned stronger, and ready to take on the Congress Party. He was no longer alone, and the decision of the National Executive Committee meant that the BJP and RSS affiliates were behind him.

The Congress Party, along with other "secular" parties and agencies that were salivating and eagerly waiting for Modi's "slaughter", were disappointed when the BJP National Executive Committee rejected Modi's resignation. The Congress termed the rejection a "negative development for Indian democracy". Party spokesperson Anand Sharma termed it an indication of BJP's bankruptcy, and insensitivity to public anguish over the Gujarat carnage, adding that the "oust Modi" campaign would continue. The Congress leadership believed that the BJP would wilt under public pressure and remove Modi. They forgot that never in the history of Indian democracy, a Congress Prime Minister or Chief Minister had resigned following riots, whether it was the post-Babri demolition riots, or the anti-Sikh riots after the assassination of Indira Gandhi.

---

[149] *Rediff on the Net*, "Jana echoes RSS line on Minority Welfare", April 13, 2002

There were a few barely noticeable ripples in the political arena when the BJP rejected Modi's resignation. Shambhu Srivastava, the spokesperson of a BJP ally, the Samata Party, resigned from his party for its support to the BJP led NDA government. He even criticized Vajpayee's speech in which he asked Muslims to do some introspection and find out why there was conflict in the world. Srivastava termed Vajpayee's call for introspection as unfortunate. Later, when things cooled down, Srivastava joined the Samata Party once again, only to resign at a later date and join the Congress Party.

The battle for Gujarat was just beginning.

CHAPTER XIII -- VAGHELA BECOMES GUJARAT CONGRESS PARTY PRESIDENT

Godhra and its aftermath made the Congress Party's quest to regain power in Gujarat an uphill task. Party leaders were confused about the strategies to adopt and the path to pursue. On the one side was its time-tested 50 year-old policy of minority appeasement, and on the other was the option to fight the BJP on its own turf by adopting a policy of soft Hindutva. The Congress party, under the leadership of Nehru, and in its later years driven by a desire to be secular and to appeal to minorities, adopted a "wink and nod" approach to supporting minority religions, and an aggressive public posture against Hindu groups and religious demands.

India nursed a unique culture and civilization for millennia, anchored in its native variegated forms and practices of Hinduism (often referred to as *sanatana dharma*), until the advent of Islam and Christianity which disrupted this ancient inclusive and catholic culture. For all its apparent diversity and variety, Indian culture was homogenous. The renowned demographer Kingsley Davis perceptively observed in 1951 that, "Indian ideas and institutions... resemble those of no other people. They have a peculiar shape and flavour of their own.... This peculiar culture has to some degree penetrated and pervaded nearly every part of what is geographically India. It has everywhere been affected by local, indigenous variations... But neither the geographical nor the social barriers inside the subcontinent have been sufficient to prevent the widespread diffusion of a common, basic culture, which despite great variation is peculiar to India".[150] As Jain notes, this common basic culture received its first serious blow when Islam reached the heartland of India towards the end of the twelfth century, with the defeat of Prithviraj Chauhan. Islamic rulers were unswerving in their commitment to maintain a distinct Islamic identity. Acculturation into the spiritual milieu of India was stubbornly resisted by Islamic rulers. Moreover, they sponsored the growth of a community that was at variance with the native cultural ethos.

The British added a chapter to this religious heterogeneity by their systematic patronage and propagation of Christianity. Jain says that the far more dangerous legacy of the British was the negation of India's civilizational homogeneity and the de-legitimization of its ancient civilizational principles. Christian evangelization continued to be extremely aggressive and unapologetic even in the post-independence period, especially in the North-east states. Observers believe that there is a design behind conversions in sensitive border regions as well as in other parts of the country. Pope John Paul II's acerbic remarks against the Tamil Nadu government's legislation preventing change of faith through force, fraud or inducement are indicative of the

---

[150] Jain, S. (August 26, 2003), "Political lesson of Demography", *The Pioneer*.

Church's aggressive designs on India.[151]

Indian culture has spanned millennia, and unlike the grand edifices that stand in mute testimony to "dead cultures" like that of the ancient Egyptians, the Greeks, and the Romans, Indian culture has survived the ravages of time and aggressive monotheistic creeds. The Indian way of life is synchronous with nature, and postulates the ideology of "live and let live". It is not fundamentalist in its outlook, but has an accommodating worldview. This way of life accepts other religions also as authentic, and hence does not proclaim superiority over other paths to the divine.

The Congress Party, however, overlooked a very important aspect of Hinduism. It equated the need of the Semitic religions to proselytize, with the fears of the Muslims in a non-Muslim majority country that has a non-Muslim government. Over the past millennium, Muslim kings ruled most parts of India before the advent of the British, but with the prospect of an independent India, Muslim society faced the possibility of rule by a government dominated by Hindus. The inherent secular nature of the Hindu way of life was not acceptable to some of the Muslim intelligentsia, who saw reason in the two- nation theory of Jinnah, the founder of the Islamic Republic of Pakistan. To assuage Muslim fears, the Congress Party was over-zealous in its interpretation of secularism. This over-zealousness resulted in a policy of appeasement towards the Muslims, and a consequent denial of Hindu rights.

Since time immemorial, traditional education in India included studies of Sanskrit scriptures along with mathematics and other subjects. The Vedic texts of India taught people about the need to be in harmony with nature. The role of a human being was that of a caretaker, to supplement nature, and not exploit it. Traditional schooling was seriously undermined during the period of British colonization and even more so, ironically, after India gained independence. In the name of secularism even the teaching of yoga and meditation was discouraged in India's schools, and elite universities like Jawaharlal Nehru University (which is home to most of the well-known Indian academics) refused to offer Sanskrit to its students even as it presented a smorgasbord of foreign languages including Persian and German. Thus, and tragically, most India-trained scholars know very little about Hinduism because the study of Sanskrit was limited or ignored in top Indian liberal arts colleges. We, therefore, now have become reliant on foreign scholars and universities for exegesis and interpretation of Hinduism. *Outlook India* magazine reported a Supreme Court decision in which the Court quoted from the Encyclopedia Britannica for a definition of Hinduism.

This is the state of Hinduism in India, and no doubt there is both a willful and a mischievous attempt by those who call themselves "secularists" to label any effort to support or encourage the study of Hinduism as acts of "fundamentalism", "Hindu chauvinism" or "Brahminism". Or they assert that they are not against Hinduism as much as they are against Hindutva. Then follows a litany of abuse against or

---

[151] *The Economic Times* (June 14, 2003). "Jaya blasts Pope for views on anti-conversion laws".

mischievous characterizations of Savarkar and Golwalkar, the RSS and the VHP, and the BJP as a mask and cover for the RSS and the VHP.

But what happens when the voters begin to realize that these are false claims and that this has done serious harm to their interests? The outcome of the 2014 general elections shows that voters cannot be fooled all of the time, and that they respond both with their feet and their votes. The burning of the Sabarmati Express at Godhra angered the Hindus but the Congress Party did not condemn the actions of the Muslim-led mob nor seek to work with Modi to quickly quell the riots that ensued. Instead, the party spokespersons were vocal in condemning the riots, without addressing the primary cause for it.

With Gujarat elections in mind, Congress Party stalwarts began to rethink their strategies. They realized that Gujarat had become a BJP stronghold, with the Vishwa Hindu Parishad and the concept of Hindutva enjoying vast appeal. The party reluctantly decided to tread a new path that the media labeled "soft-Hindutva". Though the party was not as vocal as the BJP in supporting the rights of the Hindu community, party leaders issued statements fashioned to appeal to the Hindu majority. However, their inability to articulate a clear stance on communal issues affected its campaign strategy.

The Vaghela Factor

Shankersinh Laxmansinh Vaghela, a Kshatriya, once with the RSS and BJP, turned their *bête noire*. In the late 1990's, Vaghela's open revolt against the BJP was spurred by the Narendra Modi-Keshubhai Patel domination. Vaghela felt they had nudged him into a corner. Vaghela struck back, taking 60 MLAs with him and flying off to Khajuraho to keep them from being seduced back by the BJP. He was able to pull down the Keshubhai Patel government, the first BJP regime in Gujarat. This was a major shock to the BJP as Vaghela was an RSS man at that time.

Vaghela was known to be a belligerent fighter, almost to the point of being reckless, and he supposedly did not care about the consequences of his actions. The day he got his expulsion letter from the BJP, he publicly tore it, cheered on by hundreds of his supporters. Angry with the BJP leadership for deciding to support the Modi-Patel duo, he launched his Rashtriya Janata Party (RJP), announcing, "My high command will be the people of Gujarat." He became the Chief Minister of Gujarat with the Congress Party's support in 1996.

As Chief Minister in 1997, Vaghela ordered the arrest of the VHP leader Pravin Togadia. He had been warned that Togadia's arrest would create a major law and order problem. Gujarat watched in shock as Pravin Togadia was arrested. Eventually, the Congress Party withdrew support citing rampant corruption in the Vaghela government. It was ironic that the same Vaghela was president of the Gujarat Congress Party in 2002. Such are/were the dynamics that shape politics in India where there are not only no permanent friends nor permanent foes but not even a modicum of principles. Most alliances originate in the whim of a political leader or in the pursuit of power. The BJP is not averse to making such opportunistic pacts and has paid dearly at various times for joining hands with incompatible groups.

In the 1998 state elections, the regional party of Vaghela suffered a jolt when it won only four seats out of the 182 assembly seats. However, the RJP and the Congress Party together polled more votes than the BJP. However, the BJP formed the government with a nearly two-thirds majority. The RJP was finished as a viable political party, and so Vaghela merged his party with the Congress Party. In his brief tenure as Chief Minister, however, Vaghela made some attempts to cut bureaucratic red-tape, and took some quick and effective decisions aimed at rejuvenating the economy. Fulfilling some old demands, he created six new districts, doing what the BJP and the Congress Party governments had not done.

The day Modi became the Chief Minister the Congress Party's think tank went into a huddle to evaluate the effect of Modi on their future prospects. After Godhra and its aftermath, public opinion in Gujarat was quite polarized. The demonization of Modi by large sections of the English-language media turned to be a blessing in disguise, and the image of Modi as a hardliner and strong leader gained much traction among the voters in view of the give-and-take arrangements that had come to characterize the Gujarat political scene. People wanted something different, and Modi was the answer.

In April-May 2002, the BJP conducted a massive state-wide survey of over 20,000 people. Every assembly constituency was sampled. Modi, well-informed about political campaigns, wanted data about the public's reaction to the many questions raised by the media about Gujarat politics and society. The survey showed a huge and favorable shift in public opinion toward Modi. Over 90 percent of the people wanted him as Chief Minister. Such a polarization was unheard of in India since the time Rajiv Gandhi swept the imagination of voters in 1984-85, when the Congress Party won a two-thirds majority in Parliament after Indira Gandhi's assassination.

Due to the Catch-22 situation in the Congress Party about continuing to appease the minorities or adopting a softer version of Hindutva, the BJP succeeded in emphasizing its Hindutva credentials. The Congress Party was not able to counter this campaign that Sonia Gandhi described as "venomous". Right or wrong, there was a section of the Hindus who believed that the Congress Party viewed the minorities as more equal than the others. This feeling had been building up over the years, and the BJP was able to exploit the Hindu community's siege mentality. This happened first in 1990 during Lal Kishen Advani's *rath yatra*, and then it was in the wake of the Godhra train burning.

The Congress Party had its ideology to defend, but could not come across as just a pro-minority party. This had more to do with perception than reality. In the Nehruvian period, immediately after India became independent, it was all right to take the view that minority fundamentalism could not be equated with majority communalism, and that

Muslims needed special protection after the country's partition. But times had changed. Years of such minority appeasement set off a reaction that manifested particularly when the Congress Party or others like the Samajwadi Party failed to condemn Muslim communalism for fear of losing Muslim votes, and when politicians sought the support of the Shahi Imam of Delhi for votes, or when "fatwas" were issued to Muslims to vote *en bloc*. The Congress Party needed to find a person who could address the "soft Hindutva" agenda, and simultaneously take up the challenge of defeating the BJP.

Former Gujarat Congress president Amarsinh Chaudhary was a tribal leader. The party traditionally performed well in the areas of tribal dominance. The importance of Amarsinh Chaudhary to the party's Gujarat unit was unchallenged. Uncomfortable at the erosion of its position overall in the state, the party bosses wanted some change. They wanted someone who could win over the media, take on the tech-savvy Modi, and woo the Hindus of the state.

Vaghela fit the bill. He and Modi were similar in temperament, and so probably ended up as foes. The Congress had no one like Vaghela, and needed him to counter Modi's rising popularity. Post Godhra, the Congress Party cadre was in a sort of coma, very different from the exhilarating times of the victory at Sabarmati just a few months before.

Sonia Gandhi quickly decided to appoint Vaghela as State Congress Party President, sending alarm bells in the BJP camp. Vaghela did not waste a single moment in taking the attack into the BJP camp. He began his term by placing a bouquet at the martyrs' memorial in Ahmedabad, and by organizing a massive rally. Suddenly, taunting slogans began to make the rounds of the Congress Party camps. Slogans like "*Dekho, dekho kaun aaya? Modi, tera baap aaya*" ("Look, who has come? Modi, your father has come") appeared to challenge and discomfit Modi. Vaghela finally got the platform to vent his feeling of betrayal against the BJP, and Modi became his hated foe.

The arrival of Vaghela was not without internal consequences. Rumblings within the Congress Party that Vaghela was after all an ex-RSS man made party spokesmen uncomfortable in the defense of his choice. The Congress Party had characterized the RSS as a hardcore Hindu organization. The definition of the word "Hindu" for the RSS is not religion-based, but more culture-based. For the RSS, everyone living in India, irrespective of caste, creed, religion, or social strata is a Hindu. Accepting an ex-RSS man at the helm of affairs of the Congress Party was unthinkable for some party leaders. Party halls echoed with grumblings, and some argued that only "true" Congress Party workers should be given top posts.

CHAPTER XIV – STATE ASSEMBLY DISSOLVED

Members of state assemblies in India are elected for a term of five years. The previous assembly elections in Gujarat were held in February 1998, and elections were due again in February 2003. Before the Godhra massacre, the BJP government suffered a period of "incumbency disease" and was at the receiving end of the people's ire. With the events of 9/11, the attack on the Indian Parliament in December 2001 by terrorists trained in Pakistan, and the massacre at Godhra followed by its tragic aftermath, led to a polarization of the electorate. Hindus began to respond to their feelings of anger and their sense of siege by Muslim fundamentalists, while Muslims felt ever more insecure and restive at the growing Hindu resurgence.

Instead of unanimous condemnation of the Godhra massacre we had the unfortunate and eerily muted response from a large section of the English media, the entrenched intelligentsia, Muslim leaders, and the "secular" political leadership. Modi became the target of the media, which broadcast a daily chant of "Modi should go", and publishing outrageous editorials and reports mauling him. Such an orchestrated demonization campaign against a state Chief Minister was unheard of in the history of independent India.

Modi endured the onslaught grimly. His demeanor was termed arrogant, but that was to be expected from a man who had been subjected to a vicious vilification campaign. While he publicly conveyed a, "I don't give-a-damn" image, he seethed at the abuse showered on him. Was it really worth his while to be in the hot seat at that point? Neither a masochist nor a sage but a man with strong convictions, he withstood as well as anyone could the barbs and the bullets aimed at him.

Finally, he made up his mind to resign. It was a stunned BJP National Executive Committee that then had to deal with his decision. It turned down Modi's resignation, and instead advised him to dissolve the State Assembly and seek a fresh mandate. It was felt, that if the people of Gujarat gave Modi a clean bill of health and re-elected him, it would enable him to regain and reclaim power.

The National Executive Committee of the BJP adopted a resolution titled "Godhra and its Aftermath" stating, "Instead of accepting his (Modi's) resignation, the National Executive advises him to seek dissolution of the assembly, go to the people and seek their verdict," adding, "In a democracy there is only one way to put the issue and the calumny to rest. The people are the one who can and must decide."

The BJP declared that the need of the hour was a national consensus aimed at calming both Hindus and Muslims in Gujarat. This resolution was quite extraordinary for it enumerated the steps taken by the Modi government to curb rioting. In earlier Hindu- Muslim riots in India, few state governments had taken such quick and harsh measures against rioters, both Hindu and Muslim, as the Modi government had taken, but the media gave him no quarter, and his political opponents reaped the benefit.

The Election That Shaped Gujarat

The BJP resolution stated that Modi had called in the Indian Army 16 hours after the first signs of trouble breaking out. The Indian Army was in a state of high alert, in a war-like situation on the border with Pakistan. A Congress Party government in Gujarat, under similar circumstances, took five days to call the army. Up to the time of the National Executive Committee meeting, the Modi government arrested 27,000 people, and launched 3,400 criminal cases. Police firing against rioters killed 139 people. But not only was this police action ignored it was alleged that the police were complicit in the riots.

The BJP president Jana Krishnamurti was critical of the negative reaction from the Opposition and some of the BJP allies over Modi's handling of the violence in Gujarat. He said, "I must mention here that the role of opposition and our critics was not exactly commendable, but on the other hand condemnable. Every time Gujarat faced severe situations, our opponents and critics mounted a severe attack on the state government with an orchestrated voice demanding the head of the chief minister. When the people are facing a calamity and when the government is struggling to calm down the situation, the role of opposition should be to strengthen the efforts of all those who are strenuously exerting themselves to contain the situation." Krishnamurti added: "But their efforts were directed towards demoralizing and discrediting those who were carrying out their responsibilities sincerely." On April 15, 2003, the General Secretary of the BJP's Gujarat unit, Nalin Bhatt, told the media that Modi had been authorized by the party to take an appropriate decision on dissolving the State Assembly and calling for fresh elections.

On April 17, 2003 the Gujarat Cabinet met, and after an hour-long discussion, deferred a decision on the dissolution of the State Assembly, and seeking a fresh mandate from the people. As twelfth grade school examinations were scheduled, Modi did not want the Assembly dissolved then. There were calls by some to persuade Muslim students not to appear for their annual school examinations but Modi was emphatic in his advice to students to complete the exams. He provided security for children, stationing police officers at the examination centers. Assured that there would not be violence about 12 million students appeared for the exams. Exams were held a second time for those who could not attend, and a third time for those still left out, till every child wanting to appear for the exams had an opportunity to do so. Modi made it clear that he would not allow riots, politics, and personal grudges with the media to play havoc with the academic life of the children of Gujarat. The dissolution of the State Assembly was thus deferred. After this decision of deferral, the Gujarat unit of the Congress Party made provocative statements claiming that the Modi government was afraid of seeking a mandate.[152]

---

[152] *Rediff on the Net*, "Modi is scared of going to the polls: Congress", April 17, 2002.

State Assembly Dissolved

Following the BJP meeting in Goa, the Central Parliament met. Opposition party members, along with some alliance partners of the BJP, raised a ruckus in the Lok Sabha and proceedings were stalled time and again. Valuable legislative days were lost. In Parliament, even a solitary MP can hold it hostage refusing to heed the Speaker or the Chairman, and deny an opportunity for other members to speak. Though the house marshals can on the orders of the Speaker or the Chairman remove the errant member from the floor of the House, such disciplinary action is rarely taken. A method of persuasion is adopted, and if there are enough members supporting it then the entire House gets adjourned. Each legislative day lost due to stalled proceedings is expensive to the Indian tax payer. It is said that unnecessary walk-outs, intemperate exchanges, disorderly scenes, noisy uproars cost the nation in 2002 about 5,000 rupees ($100) per minute, 300,000 rupees ($6,000) per hour, 2,100,000 rupees ($42,000) per day and 147,000,000 rupees ($294,000) per week.

It is the right of every Member of Parliament to get an opportunity to express his or her views even when they routinely flout House rules. The Gujarat issue set off a similar uproar. The Opposition wanted a discussion on Gujarat under Rule 184 that would lead to a vote, while the government wanted discussion under Rule 193 that did not require voting. A stalemate ensued as Opposition members held the house to ransom, with more than a week's legislative time lost in the commotion. Opposition members kept shouting "*Modi hatao, desh bachao*" ("remove Modi and save the country"), while BJP members retaliated by saying "*Sonia Gandhi maafi mango*" ("Sonia Gandhi, apologize") for her attack on Prime Minister Vajpayee, and "*Desh ke gaddaron ko POTA mein giraftar karo*" ("Arrest the traitors under the Prevention of Terrorism Act").

At this juncture Modi hinted at the possibility of early elections in Gujarat. On June 17, 2002 he said that elections would be held before March 2003 when the assembly completed its term. Modi submitted his resignation to the Governor, and the state assembly was dissolved on July 19, 2002. The House still had nine months of tenure left, and this led to criticism by the Communist Party of India (Marxist) and the Congress Party which viewed it as an attempt to force the Election Commission's hand in view of the constitutional restriction that there should not be more than a six-month gap between successive sessions of the assembly. The last assembly session was held in April 2002, and therefore, by law, the next session would have to be held in October 2002.

It was not just the Opposition demanding Modi's head. Ram Vilas Paswan, the Janata Dal Party leader, and an NDA-alliance partner, asked for imposition of President's Rule in Gujarat after the dissolution of the State Assembly. Paswan was a member of a faction of the Janata Dal (JD) party that has suffered "multiple fractures" over the years. Paswan was in the opposition before and voted against the BJP in the one-vote defeat of 1998. Later, when the BJP won the general elections, and formed the National Democratic Alliance government in 1999, Paswan joined the BJP-led alliance, and was made a minister in the Union Government.

The Election That Shaped Gujarat

After expressing opposition to Modi, Paswan quit the NDA on April 29, 2002. He is a "backward community" leader, born into a Dusadh family, and when the BJP aligned with another backward community leader (the Bahujan Samajwadi Party leader, Mayawati) in the North Indian state of Uttar Pradesh, Paswan feared that his power base was threatened. Modi's removal became a convenient excuse for him to quit the NDA government.[153] The day the state assembly was dissolved Paswan said that he would tour Gujarat for five days from July 20 to July 25, 2002 to spread the message of communal harmony. It is the nature of Indian politics that Paswan's support was sought and given during the campaign in the 2014 elections, and he is now the Cabinet Minister in the Modi government heading the Department of Consumer Affairs, Food and Public Distribution

When Indira Gandhi was assassinated in 1984, there were violent anti-Sikh riots in the country. At that time the ruling Congress Party took advantage of the polarized atmosphere in the country and called general elections within forty-five days after Indira Gandhi's assassination. The same party now claimed that the situation in Gujarat was different, and sought deferment of elections. Elections were held in December 2002, about nine months after the burning of the train in Godhra, and the ensuing riots that sputtered on for about two months. Modi dissolved the assembly four and a half months after the first instance of trouble, and after bearing the heat from a combination of opposition from the media, international censure, and the drumbeat of vilification from opposition parties. He then offered the people of Gujarat a chance to re-elect him or to choose a new government.

---

[153] *The Hindu*, "Paswan quits, to vote against Government", April 30, 2002.

CHAPTER XV -- GUJARATI HONOR

Mahatma Gandhi said that if one wanted the shortest possible course in understanding Indianness, he would have to undertake a train journey across the length and breadth of the country at least three times! From Champaran in Bihar to Dandi in Gujarat, Gandhi undertook many journeys, some on foot to mobilize the Indian people for India's freedom struggle. The weapon of Gandhi was non-violent opposition. It catapulted the lawyer who left the shores of South Africa to a position of immense power and influence, and despite his lack of party affiliation, made him the Congress Party's "unofficial" leader. Ironically, the apostle of non-violence and his assailant Nathuram Godse, a Brahmin, shared some interesting traits. They both led an ascetic life, and swore by the Bhagavad-Gita. However, their interpretation of the Gita was quite different, with Godse adhering to the more traditional interpretation (that a man should follow his dharma, do battle, and not be concerned with the fruits of his action) and Mahatma Gandhi reading the Mahabharata war as analogous to the conflict within a person that one has to prevail and overcome – the battle being over one's own desires and weaknesses rather than conquering an external foe.

It was Gandhi again who made popular the idea of "*yatra*" or pilgrimage by marrying traditional pilgrimage to political ends. While people all over the world have undertaken journeys to spread their message, Gandhi's strategy to win people was unique at that time. After India gained independence, political parties co-opted Gandhi's strategy for a variety of political ends, most of them short-term and narrow.

These *yatras* gained new momentum in the late 1980s with Advani's *rath yatra*, coordinated by Narendra Modi. Hugely successful, it enabled Advani to gauge the enthusiasm of the people of different regions, directly interact with the poorest of the poor, eat with the locals, and be among them. From a political angle, the *yatras* enabled party leaders to evaluate the organizational abilities of party members as well. Grass-roots party workers got to meet their political bosses. This invigorated them into action and boosted their morale. It was one way of lubricating the political machine of the party. Prospective and incumbent candidates, through whose constituency the *yatra* traveled spared no efforts to make it a success. For a prospective candidate it was an opportunity to exhibit his influence, and for an incumbent a way to prove his re-election possibilities. At select junctions and towns big rallies were held, and the top political leaders addressed the people. In short, they were like the train journeys that presidential candidates used to undertake in the U.S. The Indian media gives extensive coverage to such *yatras*, and the power and presence of the tour is felt in each home tuned into the nine o'clock evening news bulletin.

Ever since the days of Advani's *yatra* to mobilize support for the Ram temple in Ayodhya, these political tours have become a routine for the BJP. After Advani, it was Murli Manohar Joshi's *Swaran Jayanti yatra* on the occasion of India's 50 years of independence, which culminated with the hoisting of the Indian flag in Srinagar, the

The Election That Shaped Gujarat

beleaguered capital of Kashmir. The BJP's youth wing (Bharatiya Janata Yuva Morcha) organized a similar *yatra* that passed through all the border areas of India, under the leadership of Ram Ashish Rai, a youth leader from Uttar Pradesh. It was called the *Seema suraksha jagran yatra* (Border Areas Security tour). Rai was later expelled from the BJP for alleged anti-party activities.

As we wrote this chapter in 2004, the Congress Party and the BJP were taking out more such *yatras*. In Maharashtra, which was expected to go to the polls in 2004, the BJP leader Gopinath Munde was taking out a *yatra* titled *Sangharsh Yatra* to bring to light the "bad governance" of the Congress Party in the state. In the elections in Rajasthan and Madhya Pradesh in November 2003, the Congress Party, under the leadership of film star-turned-politician, and Member of Parliament, Sunil Dutt, conducted a tour called the *Sadbhawna Yatra* or the "journey for peace and harmony" among Hindus and Muslims. It is ironic, however, that Sanjay Dutt, son of Sunil Dutt, had been an accused in the Bombay Bomb Blast case of 1993. The worst terrorist attack in India was carried out in Mumbai (Bombay) in 1993 by Muslim criminal gangs trained and abetted by Pakistan. The underworld don, Dawood Ibrahim, and the Memon brothers engineered multiple bomb blasts killing more than two hundred people, and injuring a thousand more. The constituency that returned Sunil Dutt to Parliament had a large number of Muslim voters. It was for these reasons that a section of the Hindus viewed such *Sadbhawna Yatras* as the obvious extension of the Congress Party's old policy of Muslim appeasement. The slogan of this *yatra* was "*Desh jodo*" (unite the nation). Hindus complained that the demand for a separate and independent Kashmir state is popular only among certain sections of Muslims.

When Narendra Modi began planning a *yatra* just as Gujarat was just recovering from a serious spell of violence, sections of the Indian media condemned it. Modi claimed that it was time to re-emphasize the glory of Gujarat, and its entrepreneurial and social culture, especially when Gujaratis and their leaders were being vilified everywhere. Modi desired to travel to each and every part of Gujarat. The *Gujarat Gaurav Rath Yatra* (GGY) or the *yatra* for the honor of Gujarat was launched, according to Modi, to boost the sagging morale of the state and its people. The new Congress Party state president Vaghela labeled Modi's *gaurav yatra* as a *kalank yatra* or embarrassment (*kalank* is defined as a "blot" or "stigma").

At a time when Godhra and its aftermath seared the soul of Gujarat, Modi said he was trying to revive the glory of the state by easing tensions between the two communities, and enabling the people to get on with their lives. On the other hand, he said, the Congress Party desired to inflict on Gujarat self-defeating pangs of guilt and shame attached to the riots. Some in the media asserted that such a *yatra* would further polarize Hindus and Muslims. The media challenged this right of Modi by characterizing his initiative as divisive, and capable of creating further fear in the minds of the Muslim minority. The Congress Party did not want the GGY at all for they feared that a *yatra* of this kind would definitely endear Modi to the masses, and strengthen the BJP at the hustings.

Modi wanted the GGY to start from July 4, 2002, that being the American independence day. He wished to commemorate American democratic ideals and lend support to the U.S. in its battles against terrorists, post 9/11. He wished to make connections both symbolic and real with democracies around the world fighting religious fundamentalism and terrorism. India has suffered a thousand cuts from the Pakistan sponsored cross-border terrorism for more than a decade, but very few in the international media were willing to connect the dots and tell the world that the attacks against India were very much part of the Islamic fundamentalist attempts at challenging the world order.

It was this fundamentalist mindset that authored the gruesome attack on Hindu pilgrims at Godhra. The GGY, planned by Modi, sought to spread the idea of Gujarati unity and preserve the famed Gujarati culture. However, under pressure from opposition parties and the media, Modi postponed his *yatra*. The riots that followed Godhra arson on February 27 were controlled within seventy-two hours, with sporadic retaliatory rioting continuing for about two months. By the end of April, however, things had more or less returned to normal, which strengthened Modi's belief that a July 4 start of the *yatra* would augur well for a return to normalcy in the state.

The opposition realized the new power of Modi, and felt threatened by his emergence as a Hindu icon. Motels and snack joints along the highways garlanded photos of Modi. The *yatra* would consolidate his position even further. The July 4 *yatra* was to take off from the famous Gujarati cultural site of the temple of "Ambaji". The word "Amba" denotes the Divine Mother, or Mother Nature. According to Sanskrit texts, the Goddess Amba is a form of the mother of the Universe, being the wife of Shambhu or Shiva. People from all over Gujarat undertake pilgrimage to her temple, which is a historic monument. Pilgrims walk barefoot for days to the temple as penance. The devotees believe that the penance of walking barefoot to the temple of the Divine Mother would rid them of all their miseries. One can read a similar story in *The New York Times*.[154]

The Ambaji temple is ancient indeed, dating back to the days when fire sacrifices used to take place, and mystics used to wander the length and breadth of India. The faith of fifty million Gujaratis in the Divine Mother Amba is unparalleled. Women, old people, and children all walk the long road to the temple to seek Amba's blessings. The road to the Ambaji temple passes by the office of the Chief Minister. It also passes by the great Akshardham Temple in Gandhinagar.

The GGY was also aimed at reviving the socio-cultural legacies of Gujarat. Seeking to remind people that the pain of the dreadful events of Godhra and the stigma of the

---

[154] Waldman, A. (September 8, 2003). "Shoes, and Religious Ire, Fall Away at a Saint's Feet", *The New York Times*.

ensuing riots should lead to a catharsis, Modi wanted to urge Gujaratis to overcome religious divisions, and emerge once again strong and accommodating.

Narendra Modi is also a devotee of the Divine Mother. During the "Nav-Durga" religious days, or the "nine days of the Divine Mother", Modi does not eat a single grain of solid food. As penance, he sustains himself for these nine days only on liquids. In his room Modi has adorned the walls and alcoves with symbols and pictures depicting the Divine Mother. He practices yoga and meditates every morning seeking the blessings of Ambaji. Modi, caricatured as a cold and calculating man, is a deeply spiritual person, according to those who have observed him closely. As part of his spiritual quest Modi has undertaken extensive pilgrimages to traditional Hindu holy places. According to the newly published biographies, he even journeyed to the remote Himalayan region of Manasarovar, and Mount Kailash in Tibet that have immense spiritual import for Hindus. It is in this context that Modi chose the Ambaji temple to start the *gaurav yatra*.

After the July 4 start was postponed, the *yatra* was re-scheduled for late July or early August, but once again, under pressure postponed. On August 21, 2002 the Congress Party sought Vajpayee's intervention to prevent Modi from taking out the *yatra*. Sonia Gandhi, in a letter to the Prime Minister, reminded him again about the riots that followed Godhra. Sonia Gandhi wrote: "I am sure you will keep in mind the overarching aim of maintaining and consolidating peace and amity among the people of Gujarat while advising the chief minister [Narendra Modi] in this matter of importance and urgency".[155]

Keen on maintaining democratic traditions, Modi respected the letter of the Leader of the Opposition, and postponed his *yatra* once again. It was a moral stance Modi always took, and he wanted to defeat the Congress Party and his opponents not only through the ballot box but also on ethical and moral grounds. The man, branded and taunted as a mass killer of Muslims, and a murderer of democracy, in reality is a faithful supporter and protector of democratic traditions. Modi knew that more the Opposition and the media cried "wolf", the more their credibility and their influence were sagging.

Even Lalu Prasad Yadav, the doyen of India's criminal politicians (convicted and jailed in the multi-million rupee "fodder scam"), jumped on to the anti-Modi bandwagon and the media dutifully reported his opposition to the *yatra*. True to his wonted "rustic" wisdom and playing to the gallery he made the unusual demand for the arrest of Modi under POTA for planning the *yatra*. Yadav's government in Bihar depended on the support of the Congress Party, and to return the favor he made the most absurd of statements that the media duly reported. He claimed that the proposed

---

[155] *Rediff on the Net*, "Sonia asks Vajpayee to stop Gaurav Yatra," August 22, 2002.

yatra would "terrorize" Muslims in Gujarat. In his brazen and crude style he termed the *Gujarat Gaurav Yatra* as a *Danga Rath Yatra* (arson rally). He even toed the Congress Party line in demanding the imposition of President's rule in Gujarat. He also promised to launch a countrywide agitation against the *yatra* in the first week of September 2002. The media, however, recorded no such agitation, and the threats and verbiage were for media consumption only.[156]

It was not the first time that Yadav demanded the arrest of Modi. A veteran jailbird, implicated in a number of scams and criminal matters, and the "joker and crook" who reduced Bihar to a wasteland, Yadav frequently led the "secularist" charge against the BJP and the RSS. So, his suggestion in November 2002 that Modi be arrested and be debarred from contesting elections was absurd theater at its worst.[157]

The *yatra* was now re-re-scheduled for September 3, 2002 and was planned to begin from the remote village of Phagvel, in Gujarat's Kheda district. Phagvel is home to the temple of Bhati Maharaj, a nineteenth century campaigner against cow slaughter. The cow occupies a very special place in Hindu life. The protection of the cow is not of course unique to the Hindus and Hinduism. Even among certain Muslim communities the slaughter of milk-giving cows is prohibited. In India the protection of the cow is a very sensitive issue. People are willing to give up their lives for the protection of the cow. When McDonalds opened their franchise in India, one of the first things they did was to proclaim that no beef would be used in any of their products in India.

Bhati Maharaj is respected as a saint in Gujarat because he died while protecting cows. The legend of Bhati Maharaj says that he was newly married when news came that some Muslims were killing cows. Immediately leaving his new bride, Bhati Maharaj, of the Kshatriya caste, went to protect the cows and was killed in the ensuing fight. Legend claims that he saved the cows only by making the supreme sacrifice. Gujaratis consider him a saint, and the villagers believe that the spirit of Bhati Maharaj still protects the cows of the area, and that anyone who takes an oath of protecting the cow emerges victorious in his other battles. The bond of faith is very strong among the people of Phagvel, and surrounding areas. Modi's choice of Phagvel as the starting point of his much re-scheduled GGY was another stroke of political genius that associated him with the legend of Bhati Maharaj.

Besides socio-cultural reasons, there was a subtler political message that Modi wanted to convey to Vaghela who belongs to the same (Kshatriya) caste as Bhati Maharaj. The village of Phagvel lies in the Kapadvanj parliamentary constituency that Vaghela represents. Modi thus started his *yatra* from the capital of his opponent. This bold "in your face" strategy is the hallmark of Modi, one that replenished his strong man image. However, Vaghela spared no effort at spoiling Modi's game plan.

---

[156] *Rediff on the Net*, "Arrest Modi for planning Gaurav Yatra: Laloo," August 30, 2002.

[157] *Rediff on the Net*, "Laloo accuses Modi of inciting communal tension," November 12, 2002.

The Election That Shaped Gujarat

The re-scheduled GGY was proposed to start from September 3, 2002. The same day the Congress Party planned a parallel event at the very point of the launch of the GGY. A hitherto unknown group calling itself "Bhati Sena" threatened to disrupt the BJP *yatra*. Confrontation over the *yatra* had been building up ever since Vaghela announced that members of his Kshatriya community would honor him on September 3 at the Bhatiji temple. Though the local administration issued prohibitory orders, Vaghela was determined to go to Phagvel making it clear that if anyone tried to stop him and his supporters, they would not flinch from giving a fitting reply. Vaghela cleverly sought even the intervention of Lok Sabha Speaker Manohar Joshi to ensure his protection. He also threatened a day's fast to protest the alleged "misuse of official machinery" by the BJP for the *yatra*.

With so many VIPs planning to stage events, Phagvel became a fortress. With the Congress Party-backed Bhati Sena threatening to disrupt Modi's *yatra*, slated to be flagged off by former Uttar Pradesh Chief Minister Rajnath Singh, the government was not taking any chances. At the *dharamshala* of the Bhatiji Maharaj temple, from where Modi was to kick off his *yatra*, police set up a 24-hour control room. From 6 a.m. on September 1 to 6 p.m. on September 3, a congregation of more than five persons at the temple premises was banned. There were 40 policemen around the area, reinforced by a company of 120 troops of the State Reserve Police. On the day the *yatra* was to be inaugurated, Vaghela chose to hoist the traditional 52-yard flag in Bhatiji Maharaj's honor. Jagdish Thakore, a leader of the Thakore community to which the Maharaj belonged, said that from September 2 onwards they would sing bhajans (religious songs) at the temple, because they had vowed to felicitate Vaghela, if he became the president of the Congress Party's Gujarat unit.

Modi had bigger plans. He could not allow himself to be intimidated by such strategies. Phagvel was a symbol, not the entirety of Modi's plan. Modi, like a clever military general, made a strategic withdrawal. It is said that the brave and the foolish die on the battlefield, while the wise live on to fight another day. Modi wrote a letter to Vaghela stating that in the interest of Gujarat and the interest of unity among the people of the state he was once again re-scheduling the GGY.

The Gujarat BJP president Rajendrasinh Rana, also of the Kshatriya caste, cited appeals for peace made by Pramukh Swami, the religious head of the Swami Narayan sect and of Acharya Mahapragyaji, a Jain sadhu with a vast following, as the reasons for the BJP to postpone its *yatra* and once again re-schedule it, this time for the *yatra* to begin on September 7, 2002. By doing so the BJP indicated that it would listen to religious leaders, thereby creating goodwill among various sections of Gujaratis.

Modi's public withdrawal gained him more popularity and stature while Vaghela could not withdraw and re-schedule his program, as doing it would reveal a plan to disrupt peace in a sensitive state. Modi thus took the fizz out of the opposition scheme. On September 3, after Vaghela's event, the BJP once again postponed the GGY. The *yatra* was now to begin a day later on September 8, 2002. The BJP general secretary Bhupendrasinh Chudasama said that September 7 coincided with the Hindu observance of *Shravani Amavasya*, or the day of the New Moon in the Hindu lunar calendar month of Shravan. He said, "On Shravani Amavasya people throng temples in the state and the many fairs that spring around them. Therefore, the BJP has decided to put off the launch of the *yatra*."

After many postponements, and nearly six months after the Godhra massacre, Modi had his way, and the *yatra* received the green signal. It was to be a momentous mobilization of people and resources for the BJP. The GGY was expected to generate unprecedented public support for Modi, and to set the tone for the BJP's campaign to rule Gujarat again.

CHAPTER XVI – THE ELECTION COMMISSION VISITS

The Election Commission (EC) is the agency that conducts elections in India. The EC is a permanent constitutional body and was established in accordance with the Constitution on January 25, 1950. Originally, the EC had only a Chief Election Commissioner (CEC). It now consists of a CEC and two Election Commissioners. The President appoints the CEC and the election commissioners. They enjoy a tenure of six years, or up to the age of 65 years, whichever is earlier. They enjoy the same status and receive salary and perks as available to judges of the Supreme Court of India. The CEC can be removed from office only through impeachment by Parliament.

The pro-active role played by the EC in the Gujarat 2002 assembly elections was controversial, and drew criticism and also applause for its role in chastising the state government – the elected office-bearers as well as the bureaucracy – for perceived lapses in the run-up to the elections.[158] The CEC, J. M. Lyngdoh, won the 2003 Magsaysay Award for his role in conducting the elections. Lyngdoh received the government service award for "his convincing validation of free and fair elections as the foundation and best hope of secular democracy in India."

In a display of contempt for the state government, the EC approached the Supreme Court for a clarification on the convening of a new assembly within six months after the dissolution of the old.[159] It won the Supreme Court approval for delaying the elections, which at last were held in December 2002. Free and fair elections did take place, but not without causing a lot of ill-feeling among BJP members that felt the EC had adopted a posture that favored the Congress Party.

T. N. Seshan, the former CEC who became a legend in taking political bosses to task, opined that "The question whether the situation on the ground is consistent with holding of a free and fair election is entirely within the powers and ambit of the Election Commission. It is not with the political parties in the state or at the Centre. It is not at the courts. The Constitution has devised the Election Commission as the mechanism to decide whether elections can be held free and fair".[160] Seshan, like Lyngdoh, belonged to the Indian Administrative Service (IAS).

The IAS is an elite administrative group that traces its roots to the Indian Civil Service of the British era. The institution is unique, though it needs revamping. Bitter critics of the IAS accuse the cadre of a feudal and archaic approach to governance and governing. Instead of serving the public, they are accused of lording over their turf like

---

[158] *The Tribune*, "Gujarat situation quite delicate: CEC". August 12, 2002.

[159] *Rediff on the Net*, "Only Musharraf's men will compare Gujarat with Kashmir". August 23, 2002.

[160] *Rediff on the Net*, "Only Musharraf's men will compare Gujarat with Kashmir". August 23, 2002.

feudal kings of yore.[161] However, occasionally it produces officers who leave their marks on the sands of governance that are difficult to be erased even after much passage of time. T. N. Seshan was one such. In a famous confrontation with Lalu Prasad Yadav on the question of issuing voter identity cards, Seshan refused to give in to the tantrums of Yadav. Seshan was firm on bringing in electoral reforms and made life uncomfortable for political parties.[162] The changes he brought were salutary, and without the persistence and courage of this IAS officer, the Indian election campaigns and processes would still be captive to ugly political machinations and the vandalizing of public buildings and private property by election graffiti. To cut Seshan to size, political parties conspired to dilute his authority by increasing the number of election commissioners. They promoted Seshan as the Chief Election Commissioner, with two Election Commissioners to assist him. The commission now became a three-member committee, and it was this committee that was jointly supreme now, and not anyone of the individual members of the committee.

Lyngdoh belonged to the Bihar cadre of the IAS. Known as an upright officer, he was appointed Chief Election Commissioner by the incumbent BJP government, which also named retired Judge J. S. Verma as the Chairman of the National Human Rights Commission (NHRC). Later on, both of them chose to oppose the BJP on crucial issues. In the past, government appointees to important constitutional posts toed the government's official line. However, the BJP struggled and battled with a hostile set of bureaucrats, even those it chose for high office: it speaks either for BJP's naivety or lack of political experience, or the elite administrators' unwillingness to promote the BJP's political agenda.

It is the job of the government chosen by the people, and not the bureaucracy, to set the direction of its performance. The bureaucracy simply carries out the orders of the elected officials. However, the bureaucracy is the "permanent" government whereas politicians get into and out of office. If elected officials lack a clear understanding of administrative processes, they can be nose-led by bureaucrats who are much more knowledgeable about government machinery. The CEC is also no ordinary "babu" (bureaucrat) who kowtows to any Chief Minister of any state, or even to the Prime Minister. S/he can be impeached only with a two-thirds majority of the Lok Sabha. The BJP in Gujarat had itself to blame for antagonizing the CEC. Modi and others were reported to have made acerbic and imprudent remarks about the CEC, even alluding sarcastically to the religious affiliation of Lyngdoh. Winning votes is important, nay necessary, to govern a people, but that cannot be at the cost of undermining government institutions. In the heat of political battles, however, politicians play to the gallery, and Modi, embattled as he was, succumbed to grandstanding as he faced a whole

---

[161] Gupta, G. V. (October 10, 1999). "IAS: God with feet of Clay", *The Tribune*.

[162] Seshan, T.N. et al. (1995). *Degeneration of India*. Viking/Allen Lane.

phalanx of opposition: political parties, the media, the intelligentsia, and as he may have realized, even the EC and the CEC.

Considering the role traditionally attached to the EC, one would be astounded to see how much more pro-active the EC was in Gujarat. As T.V.R. Shenoy wrote, "As long anticipated, the Election Commission has set itself on a collision course with the Government of India... but I cannot help feeling that it is a no-win situation for all concerned. Either Gujarat shall be denied its democratic rights to be administered by a government of its own choosing, or the Chief Election Commissioner -- the man charged with conducting 'free and fair' elections in Jammu and Kashmir -- will be condemned as a bit of an ass".[163] For more on Lyngdoh, see "Lyngdoh's Vigilantism".[164]

The tug-of-war between Modi and the EC probably started early in June-July 2002, when there were talks of Modi resigning and calling for early elections. It was reported on July 17, 2002 that Modi would make use of a technicality and compel the EC to call for early elections. The state assembly had to be reconvened in six months, and as the last session was in April, the next session would have to be in October. At that time it was felt that the EC was constitutionally bound to hold elections to assure that the assembly reconvened in time. Prior to this the EC had ruled out early elections.

On July 19, 2002, the Gujarat Assembly was dissolved, which threw the ball into the court of the EC. However, some argued that if President's Rule was imposed in Gujarat under Article 356 of the Constitution, the six- month requirement would be waived. Since a BJP-led government was in power in New Delhi, and no party had ever removed its own government from power, it was difficult to fathom how Vajpayee would recommend to the President that the Modi government be dismissed. Another rather improbable argument was that the six-month deadline was applicable only to an existing assembly and not to a dissolved assembly. The simple six-month requirement was interpreted in different ways by vested interests to delay the elections under one pretext or another. People feared that a refusal by the EC for early elections in Gujarat and an equal reluctance by the Center to impose President's rule could lead to a confrontation between the two constitutional organs, the EC and the government.

A week after the Gujarat assembly was dissolved the EC deputed a nine-member team to visit the riot- hit areas of Gujarat to assess whether the law and order situation was conducive to the conduct of early elections. The EC team rejected the claim of the Gujarat government and the state police that the situation was under control. Under the supervision of Deputy Election Commissioners A.N. Jha and S. Mendiratta, a team of EC officials began working, and had six days to ready their preliminary report. The

---

[163] *Rediff on the Net*, "EC versus Govt of India," August 20, 2002.

[164] Dasgupta, S. (December 30, 2003). "Lyngdoh's Vigilantism". *Rediff on the Net.*

The Election Commission Visits

EC was expected to take a decision based on the report. The nine-member team divided itself into three groups, so that as many riot-hit areas as possible could be visited for situation assessment. A member of the team said that their brief was to visit places, talk to the people who were affected, and find out what needed to be done. Only after that would they be able to estimate how long it would take for full poll preparedness. It was a fact-finding mission. Even before the inspection was complete, the members seemed convinced, as most opposition political parties were, of the impossibility of early polls. The opposition parties, activists, and others complained that a large number of people had been displaced in the violence. This was, however, debatable as the term "large" is relative. Out of fifty million Gujaratis, if fifty thousand people were displaced temporarily, would it be a problem to hold elections? Yes, said the EC. A quarter of a million Hindus, constituting more than 50 percent of the Hindu population of Jammu and Kashmir are displaced as a result of the ethnic cleansing by Islamic terrorists trained by Pakistan. However, the EC chose to hold elections in Kashmir in September 2002. The BJP leadership complained about these dual standards.

Before beginning their work, members of the commission again maintained that many people had not returned to their homes, and some were not confident enough to go out and vote. The statements of the EC made an interesting point. Their reliance on words such as "large", "many", "some" indicated a speculative mindset bent upon justifying a predetermined stance. That is exactly what the EC did. What they failed to note was that S.M.F. Bukhari, Gujarat's Chief Coordinator of Relief, a Muslim, had stated that of the 133,000 refugees who had taken shelter in the 110 camps across the state, 12,229 were still living in the camps in July 2002, indicating that the vast majority of the refugees had already been rehabilitated. He stated that the kin of the dead and injured had received 680 million rupees as compensation. Bukhari also said, "We could achieve 100 per cent success in rural areas where we involved the local leaders and made them convince the refugees to return home. The state machinery behaved as a catalyst", according to *India Times*, July 22, 2002. This was three days after the State Assembly was dissolved. This was three days before the EC investigators arrived in Gujarat. Yet, the commission as well as the media seemed to have ignored this very specific and factual information.

The nine-member team completed its field work, and sent a report to the CEC. It was then decided to send another team to Gujarat. The EC declared that the entire election commission was to visit Gujarat along with CEC Lyngdoh, and the two Election Commissioners, T.S. Krishnamurthy and B.S. Tandon. This was an extraordinary decision, as it was the first time that all the members of the EC were visiting a state for the sole purpose of evaluating the situation before taking a decision on the election. The EC thus chose not to rely solely on the report of its nine-member team. Why the EC chose to make another visit, almost immediately after its own team had reported, is not known. If the EC was to visit Gujarat, then what did the first team accomplish? Was it not waste of public money? What did such multiple visits achieve? The BJP was not wrong in believing that the EC had prejudged the issue and was intent on delaying elections. The EC once again held meetings with the police and the riot victims in order to "…know the people's mindset, especially those affected by the riots."

Lyngdoh, Tandon, and Krishnamurthy visited the cities of Ahmedabad, Vadodara, and other areas for two to three days. In Vadodara, Lyngdoh questioned the Collector of Vadodara, Mr. Jha, and obviously irritated at Jha's answers, asked him if he was a "joker". Such public insult of a serving IAS officer by the CEC was not taken lightly by the Gujarat IAS Officer's Association. They expressed displeasure at this public humiliation of a junior IAS officer by a senior officer. Whether it was Jha or Police Commissioner Tuteja, who was standing next to Jha, the CEC called a "joker" is not known. Each claimed that it was directed at the other officer! What was clear, however, was the attitude of the CEC. We don't know if the jury that decided to give Lyngdoh the Magsaysay Award took this particular episode into account when they short-listed him for the honor.

What is also a matter of concern is that the EC, on its various visits to the State, chose merely to meet with the victims of Godhra's aftermath, but not the victims of the carnage at Godhra itself. We don't know if the EC was influenced by media reports of the post-Godhra riots or by the alleged remarks of Modi, but it seemed clear that the EC was not the detached institution that it needs to be to conduct fair and free elections.

After visiting the riot hit areas, Lyngdoh told the media that the situation in Gujarat was "muddy". With this episode of visits over, the EC got down to what everyone was waiting for -- writing its report, and taking a decision on the schedule for the next elections to the state assembly.

CHAPTER XVII -- CONGRESS' "SOFT HINDUTVA"

The BJP was riding the Hindutva wave, and after the gloom of repeated defeats, the party was on a comeback trail. Party leaders aggressively projected Hindutva in their speeches, and Narendra Modi made it clear that he would not continue with the policy of "minority appeasement," the hallmark of Congress Party governments.

Gujarat has a rich and long history, and its contribution to Indian culture and tradition is impressive. The VHP has very strong roots in Gujarat, and has incorporated Gujarati pride in their Hindu identity. Highly prosperous merchant communities from Gujarat have settled all over the world, yet retained their culture and traditions. The BJP leadership realized that it was important that this Gujarati pride be nurtured and their sense of grievance assuaged.

To even attempt to challenge the BJP, the Congress Party would have to rethink its strategy. The minority appeasement ploy in the name of engaging Muslims in a constructive dialogue angered many Gujaratis. In their public pronouncements, the BJP leaders pointed out that they were not against any religion or religious group, but that they were against the Congress Party's appeasement policy that short-changed the majority, and in turn had led to the minority nursing a sense of siege or demonization.

Such a policy of divide and rule by India's most powerful political party had a number of consequences, one of which is the periodic conflagration between the Hindus and the Muslims for reasons that could be petty or serious. These religious riots and communal clashes have frayed the secular fabric of India. Communities have set up impregnable emotional walls, and there is fear and mistrust in many parts of Gujarat, if not all over India. Knowing that past policies would not work, the Congress Party stole a page from the BJP book to formulate what the media has labeled the "Soft Hindutva" strategy.

The Maha Gujarat Sant Sammelan (the conference of holy men of Gujarat) at Mahudi, a small town of religious significance in Gandhinagar district, was widely believed to be the work of the Congress Party. With Vaghela, an ex-BJP-RSS man as its State unit president, the Congress Party was soon learning how caste-religion based conventions could be used to spread political messages. The Congress Party "sponsored" function was attended by small time holy men from across the region, but the party claimed that each of those holy men had their pockets of influence in their respective villages amongst the Other Backward Castes (OBCs), whom the Congress was eyeing as a potential vote bank.

Murari Bapu is a well-known holy man of Gujarat. His conventions are always full, and he has thousands of followers. There is an imitation of Murari Bapu who is called "Chhote" Murari Bapu or Murari Bapu Jr. He was one of the speakers at the convention. He said that his followers were not satisfied with the performance of the BJP, and that the BJP leaders had broken their promises. "They have not done anything to build the Ram temple at Ayodhya. They have ditched the *sadhu samaj* (ascetic community). We will ask the Hindus not to vote for the BJP this time. The *sadhu samaj* will support the Congress Party," he proclaimed.

Chhote Murari Bapu was seen as the "poor man's sadhu" in this part of Gujarat. In Gujarat, quite a few religious networks hold sway over voters, and political parties cash in on these networks of off-the-shelf holy men who are in the "market". The Congress Party officially denied its involvement with the event at Mahudi. But the vice-president of its state unit Shaktisinh Gohil said, "We have not sponsored it.... But it's a fact that the sadhus of Gujarat are displeased with the BJP.... All of us know that the BJP won the last election by exploiting people with 'Hindu' sentiment. They captured power through the vote of the people they exploited. Now many Hindus with genuine devotion for Hinduism in their hearts are questioning them." It seemed that overnight the Congress Party had become a party representing aggrieved Hindus.

Holy men of North and Central Gujarat with influence over the Rabari and Bharwad communities also attended the Mahudi congregation. One month prior to the Mahudi meeting, the holy men had met at Vaghela's village, Vasania. The Mahudi plan seems to have been drawn at that time. The Rabari, the Bharwads, and the Thakore communities were to be their targets for wooing.

A participant in the congregation disclosed that one ritual for consolidating the votes of a community is to get its leader to accept *paan* (betel leaf). He said, "In north Gujarat they distribute *paan* to unite the community in favor of one party or the other. A community leader's acceptance of *paan* means that he and his followers have accepted the invitation to vote for a particular candidate." The Thakore community has a different method. They have a tradition called *jalo*, a community lunch where electoral choices are negotiated – in a kind of dinner diplomacy.

Even witch-hunters of the Sabarkantha district were roped in. The convention adopted several resolutions, which in practical terms did not have much impact on the Gujarat elections. One such resolution favored amendments to the Devasthan (temple) Abolition Act.[165]

The "soft Hindutva" line in Gujarat was not something new or creative. It can be seen either as a charade or as a desperate move to win back the confidence of the Hindu voter. In 1999, the Congress Party was said to have adopted it in Bihar.[166] Even before that, Rajiv Gandhi sought to woo Hindu voters by reopening the Ayodhya temple debate after the Shah Bano fiasco. So, political parties such as the Congress Party, touting secularism, found it imperative to actively court the Hindus. Following the BJP's massive win in Gujarat, in neighboring Madhya Pradesh, which was preparing for assembly elections in November 2003, veteran Congress Chief Minister Digvijay Singh

---

[165] *Rediff on the Net*, "Congress moves to counter BJP's Hindu card in Gujarat," August 22, 2002.

[166] Singh, A. (February 17, 1999), "Congress' soft Hindutva and Muslims", *Times of India*.

began to profess reverence for cows and proposed a law banning cow slaughter. Similarly, the VHP insistence on their cadres carrying *trishuls* (tridents) in Rajasthan and elsewhere, which would have evoked the ire of the media and "secular" groups, was respected as part of political theater and ignored for fear of hurting Hindu sentiments.

CHAPTER XVIII -- THE FORTY PAGE COMMANDMENT: THOU SHALL NOT HOLD ELECTIONS

The forty-page report of the Election Commission can be summarized in one sentence: elections should be deferred indefinitely as the situation is not conducive for free and fair elections.

What is conducive or not conducive for free and fair elections are debatable propositions. There is no hard and fast rule or a particular set of criteria to judge whether a situation is conducive. It is thus the sole discretion of the EC to define what is conducive. Apparently, the situation in Kashmir where every day militants spill blood was conducive for the conduct of free and fair elections, but not in Gujarat. Similarly, the situation just forty-five days after the assassination of Indira Gandhi, and the subsequent pogrom against the Sikhs, was conducive for elections, but even six months after Godhra the EC thought that the situation in Gujarat was not right for elections. Such vastly differing standards for conducting elections challenge the neutrality and objectivity of the EC, and this time its especially aggressive CEC, Lyngdoh.

Article 174 of the Constitution of India is relatively simple to decipher. Titled "Sessions of the State legislature, prorogation and dissolution," its essence is that "six months shall not intervene between its last session and the date appointed for its sitting in the next session." The EC as the protector and conductor of "free and fair" elections in India interpreted Article 324 to be more important than Article 174, and subsequently did not accept the logic that Article 174 was a constitutional command devoid of exceptions.

In the 40-page report on the perceived conditions in Gujarat the EC listed the circumstances for such an exception. Indulging in linguistic gymnastics, the EC added a new dimension to the interpretation of Article 174. And what gave the EC the authority to do that? The EC cited Article 324 as the basis of its decision. Article 324 states that, "The superintendence, direction and control of the preparation of the electoral rolls for, and conduct of, all elections to Parliament and to the Legislature of every State and of elections to the posts of President and Vice-President held under this Constitution shall be vested in a Commission (referred to in this Constitution as the Election Commission)." It is thus "the preparation of the electoral rolls for… all elections" over which the EC has supreme dominion. Hence it is the "conduct of all elections" that is vested in the EC, and not "whether to hold elections." As L. K. Advani later put it, "The EC is to hold elections, and not withhold elections."

Arvind Lavkare pointed out some previous pronouncements of the Supreme Court concerning the Election Commission:[167]

---

[167] Lavakare, A. (August 27, 2002), "The EC's Gujarat Order". *Rediff on the Net*.

1. "However wide the powers of the Election Commission relating to direction and control may be, its orders must be traceable to some existing law and cannot violate the provisions of any law including State Acts" (Dhanoa vs. Union of India, AIR 1991 SC 1745);

2. "Article 324 does not enable the Election Commission to exercise untrammeled powers. The Election Commission must trace its power either to the Constitution or the law made under Article 327 or Article 328. Otherwise, it would become *imperium in imperio* which no one is under our constitutional order" (State Bank of India vs. Election Commission AIR 1995 SC 1078);

3. "We assume that the powers of the Election Commission under Article 324 are plenary. But the question is, in the garb of conduct of elections, can the Election Commission usurp the power not vested in it?" (Ibid);

4. "We direct that the Election Commission shall not withhold the elections to the legislative assemblies of Bihar and Orissa on the ground that the said Governments had failed to complete the process of issuance of photo identity cards by the deadline prescribed by it" (Ram Dev Bhandari vs. Election Commission AIR 1995 SC 852);

5. "The court construed Article 324 as conferring only executive, but not legislative, powers on the Election Commission. The court disagreed with the contention that the Constitution gave complete power to the commission under Article 324 for the conduct of elections. The Constitution could never have intended to make the commission an apex body in respect of matters relating to elections…when the commission submits a particular direction to the Government for approval (as required by rules), it is not open to the commission to go ahead with the implementation of that direction at 'its own sweet will', even though government approval is not given" (Elucidation of judgment on A. C. Jose vs. Sivam Pillai, AIR 1984 SC 921). [168]

Thus the EC's fiat of postponing elections was both arbitrary and prejudicial. For more discussion of the legality and the Constitutionality of the order, one can read Lavakare's

---

[168] Jain, M.P. (2002, 4th Ed.). *"Indian Constitutional Law"*.

careful analyses.[169,170]

Another reason for deferral of the election was the displacement of "many" people. The EC did not define what the "many" meant. Even in "normal" elections in India, the percentage of people voting is about 50 to 60 percent. The population of Gujarat is fifty million, and even one percent equals five hundred thousand people, 0.1 percent means fifty thousand people, and a mere 0.01 percent would equal five thousand people. So, if the EC was referring to the permanent displacement of five thousand voters, they still would constitute only 0.01 percent of the population. Compare this, again, with the state of Jammu and Kashmir where over two hundred and fifty thousand displaced Hindus are living like refugees due to the selective targeting of the Hindus by Muslim terrorists. The population of Jammu & Kashmir is about seven and a half million. Two hundred and fifty thousand displaced people constitute 3.3 percent of the Jammu and Kashmir population. Yet elections have been conducted in that state since the Pandits were driven out (or as some say, "ethnically cleansed") from Kashmir in the mid to late 1980s.

A third point was the fear of Muslims being selectively removed from electoral lists, or that those who were living in relief camps would not be included in the electoral list. The EC cited the 0.01 percent to 0.1 percent error of displacement as a reason for the reinterpretation of Article 174. It overruled the norm that "elections should be held in six months", created an exception selectively applied, and made multiple visits to provide authenticity to its activist role. Under the directions of the EC, the Gujarat's Chief Electoral Officer asked district collectors to begin the process of a "special revision of the electoral rolls in the riot-affected cities, towns and villages", to accommodate the "many" that were displaced.

Revision of electoral rolls is an annual event, and revised electoral rolls were published in May 2002. Yet in August 2002, the EC wanted the process repeated. Local government officials at the district level are in charge of the revision process. During this process, other administrative work takes a back seat, and practically all governance comes to a standstill. Money, time, effort, and manpower are required for revising the electoral rolls for a population of fifty million. At a time when the state government could have spent the time better in the cause of infrastructural development, the EC chose it fit to demand of the government its time and resources to revise electoral lists.

The EC announced that from August 28 it would invite claims and objections. This

---

[169] Lavakare, A. (September 4, 2002), "The Gujarat Impasse". *Rediff on the Net*.

[170] Lavakare, A. (February 13, 2003). "We need a CEC not a CEO". *Rediff on the Net*.

primary process was over in three weeks. Official enumerators also undertook house-to-house surveys in cities, towns and villages of the riot-hit districts. The CEO, in consultation with the District Election Officers, drew the list of areas. After such surveys, the enumerators prepared three separate lists of deletions, inclusions, and corrections in the existing rolls. The final revised rolls were published on October 15. To further justify the delay, the EC also directed the Chief Election Officer to issue photo identity cards.

The EC order exceeded its constitutional jurisdiction when it suggested to the government that in order to protect the sanctity of Article 174 President's rule could be imposed in Gujarat so that the six- month deadline would no longer be required. The EC's 40-page order created a gray area in the interpretation of Article 174, thereby paving the way for future misuse by a selective and absolute interpretation of the "situation conducive for free and fair elections" clause which in turn could be interpreted to warrant an indefinite suspension of the democratic process.

The Government of India could not be a mute witness to such unconventional and arbitrary interpretation of the Constitution. Prime Minister Vajpayee called his Cabinet for an extraordinary meeting attended by Solicitor General Harish Salve, and Additional Solicitor General Kirit Rawal, as special invitees. The Cabinet decided to make a Presidential reference under Article 143 of the Constitution, as the EC's order raised "far- reaching constitutional questions" and "contradictions". The matter was referred to the Supreme Court through a Presidential Reference. Deputy Prime Minister Advani said that if the CEC had confined his observation to simply his opinion that the law and order situation in Gujarat was not favorable for an election, it would be within his limits to say so, but when the EC puts in a paragraph which says that not holding the election before October 6, 2002 would mean a constitutional crisis the EC was extending its authority. At the Cabinet meeting, there was a very strong demand by many ministers to challenge EC's ruling in the Supreme Court, but Vajpayee vetoed it and pleaded for a "restrained and dignified" approach rather than a confrontation. The EC, after all, was a constitutional body. The Cabinet's decision immediately came under fire from Opposition parties, which said it displayed contempt for the EC and undermined the prestige of this constitutional body.

Information and Broadcast Minister Sushma Swaraj said that the breakdown of the constitutional machinery was a pre-requisite for the imposition of President's rule and the EC's stand that Article 174(1) (which specifies the six-month upper limit for the gap between two assembly sittings) was mandatory, but should yield to Article 356 (central rule) was contradictory and would lead to a constitutional crisis if Parliament failed to ratify it. Therefore, the Government of India through the President asked the Supreme Court three questions:

> 1. Does Article 174 yield to Article 324, meaning thereby that the timeframe provided under Article 174 is subject to Election Commission's order under Article 324?

2. Can the Election Commission under Article 324 frame an election schedule on the premise that if the timeframe provided under Article 174 is not complied with then the President will step in under Article 356?

3. Is the Election Commission bound by the mandate of Article 174 and therefore bound to conduct election within the timeframe, drawing the forces and resources as required from the central government for conducting free and fair election?

This Presidential Reference was signed by President Abdul Kalam, and issued to Solicitor General Harish Salve, as Attorney General Soli Sorabjee was not available. The Registrar General of the Supreme Court said that the reference was placed before a five- judge constitutional bench headed by the Chief Justice of India, B.N. Kirpal. It sought the Supreme Court's opinion on questions relating to the legality of the EC's recommendation that President's Rule be imposed in Gujarat as assembly polls could not be held within a stipulated timeframe.

The five-member constitutional bench of the Supreme Court of India on October 28, 2002 said that Article 174 applied only to an existing assembly and not to a dissolved one. Therefore, in its opinion, there was no time limit for holding elections for an assembly dissolved prematurely. The bench further added that there was no conflict between Article 174 and Article 324, as the latter gave the EC exclusive power for conducting polls. It said that, "Article 174 and Article 324 operate upon different planes and neither of them is subject to the other." It thus rejected the EC's arguments that Article 174 will yield to Article 324 in matters of conducting elections.

On the point of the EC's recommendation that President's Rule be imposed under Article 356, the Court observed that President's rule could be imposed six months after the last sitting of the assembly, if elections could not be held before that. The Court opined that there was no infraction of mandate to hold elections within six months of such a last sitting of the elected assembly, and hence the application of Article 356 did not arise.

Solicitor General Salve was of the opinion that while the EC's power to hold free and fair polls was unquestionable, it could not make recommendations for imposition of President's Rule and the dismissal of a state government, as it was beyond its purview and jurisdiction. The Court asked Salve about the situation if the gap between two sittings of the assembly stretched beyond six months. Salve said that a council of ministers could, in such a situation, continue in office for six months from the date of dissolution as per Article 164.

The justices then opined that Article 324 cast a responsibility and duty on the EC to hold polls at the earliest. It added that timely elections were the essence of democracy, and that temporary law and order problems could not be construed to be grounds for deferring the holding of elections. The Court reminded the EC that it was under a constitutional duty to conduct polls at an early date and for that purpose could draw all resources to ensure free and fair elections.

Almost everyone welcomed such a balanced and quick decision by the Supreme Court. Lyngdoh claimed it to be a vindication of the EC's stance, while the Opposition parties claimed that the Supreme Court decision had vindicated their stance too, and that BJP's conspiracy to play the communal card in the aftermath of Gujarat riots had been exposed. The BJP too described the Supreme Court decision as a victory for its stance, that there was no need for the imposition of President's rule in Gujarat, and that the Supreme Court had made the EC aware of its constitutional responsibility to conduct free and fair polls, and hold early elections.

The five-judge constitutional bench comprising Chief Justice Kirpal, Justice Khare, Justice Balakrishnan, Justice Bhan, and Justice Pasayat must thus be thanked for protecting the democratic process of the country, and bringing into line over-zealous constitutional institutions that cross their jurisdiction. But the order of the Apex Court was especially praiseworthy since it did not publicly chide such authorities but reminded them of their grave constitutional duty and responsibility.

It was now certain that elections in Gujarat would be delayed, and the six-month requirement was waived as the assembly was dissolved. Modi turned his attention to the GGY, and traveled through the state addressing large rallies. The GGY was Modi's tactical answer to the delays. The delays in fact proved to be a blessing in disguise. He earned more time to tour the state and visit more villages and towns, and interact with people. The GGY -- a socio-cultural "bulldozer" was set in motion, and people of Gujarat were exposed to what got labeled as "Moditva".

We have argued that for democracies to work and succeed, their institutions will have to be in place and work according to the constitutional structures that created them and defined their roles. In this instance, we have seen how the attempt by one institution, the Election Commission, to exceed its authority was foiled by the intervention of another institution for putting democratic processes back on track. Unfortunately, we have seen that politicians and weak-kneed or sanguine officers of those constitutional bodies undermining institutions the Constitution created.

CHAPTER XIX -- THE GGY: *NA BHUTO, NA BHAVISHYATI*

Na bhuto (not like this before), na bhavishyati (not again after this). The *Gujarat Gaurav Yatra* was considered an event that the country had not witnessed before, and one which would most probably not be repeated. It was September 8, 2002, a week before Modi's birthday, when former Chief Minister of Uttar Pradesh Rajnath Singh inaugurated the 5,000 kilometer-long Gujarat Gaurav Rath Yatra. Senior national leaders of the BJP were conspicuous by their absence. Though Vajpayee and Advani were not expected to be present at the inauguration, observers interpreted their absence as an implicit rejection of the GGY.

Over 50,000 people came to flag Modi off on his journey. Would the *yatra* evoke and shore up Gujarati pride or was it an affront to good sense? Indian politics are mostly theater, and Modi cannot be blamed for resorting to a strategy that many before him had used effectively. Modi is known to be a master at staging these events, and he once again proved that he could launch yet another "play" in the face of opprobrium and political challenges. He proved that it was not only the "progressives" who could plan and enact "street theater" but a self-proclaimed Hindu nationalist too could do it, and do it better.

"An affront to Muslims" some charged, but even the Muslims of Modi's own village rejected the criticism that Modi was anti-Muslim. They knew their village boy could not be the demon that the Congress Party was portraying him as. Modi became the chief and sole whipping boy for the events in Gujarat following the massacre in Godhra. If at all Modi was guilty, then he was guilty to being the Chief Minister of a state whose police force had no modern equipment for riot control. If at all he was guilty, then he was guilty of trying to control a situation when literally whole neighborhoods poured out on to the streets and went berserk. Modi was no super hero who could have controlled and managed the huge public outcry against the Godhra massacre. Would anyone else have been able to? Even the great apostle of peace, Mahatma Gandhi, could not control the violent Hindu-Muslim riots in India. When Mohammad Ali Jinnah demanded the creation of a Muslim nation, and called for a Day of Direct Action (August 16, 1946), the country was witness to bloodshed not seen before in the history of modern India.

It is said that Modi used rhetoric that prodded Gujaratis to violence. Modi had been Chief Minister for five months when Gujarat burst into flames. In those five months he was mostly busy trying to ward off internal threats from disgruntled BJP leaders. He was also learning the administrative ropes in that period. He had to contend with various pressure groups, including the VHP that sought to shape policies for their own benefit. Thus, the demand that Modi be held accountable or even the expectation that Modi would know how to assuage the anger and the hurt of Gujaratis after the Godhra massacre discounted the power and influence of ground realities.

Modi was now trying to revive in his people a sense of honor in Gujarat which had taken a severe drubbing. He was trying to cope with powerful media interests and political opposition. In the 1997 James Bond movie "Tomorrow Never Dies", Elliot Carter, the media baron is portrayed as the most powerful man in the world because he has the power to communicate with the people. Elliot Carter says that the emperors of the modern world would no longer be the Julius Caesars, or the political bosses, but they would be the people who have control over the media. The media can set agendas and control news flows, and exercise tremendous power in modern society. Modi was portrayed as the villain of Gujarat, and there was little he could do to counter that except to go directly to the people.

In the Gujarat context, the GGY was the best way for Modi to communicate with the people, lubricate the BJP political machine, and campaign for the elections -- all in one campaign. No wonder the Congress Party tried all the tricks up its sleeve to prevent the GGY from taking off, and once it took off, to counter it.

Both Hindus and Muslims thronged the inauguration of the GGY in Phagvel village. It was a journey that Modi said would help people recover pride in their state and in their culture. Modi's constant reference to *"paanch karod Gujarati"* or "fifty million Gujaratis" was an effective slogan of appeal to all Gujaratis – the Hindus and the Muslims, and of all castes and classes. The appeal was symbolic and strategic, seeking to overcome the previous appeals to caste, religion, and region.

Modi reserved his most caustic criticism for the Congress Party, accusing it of trying to capitalize on Godhra in its attempt to come to power. "The Congress (Party) is trying to reach Gandhinagar through Godhra, a dream which will never be realized", he reminded the crowds that thronged his meetings.

Sonia Gandhi had at an earlier rally blamed the BJP and Modi for turning "Gandhi's Gujarat" into "Godse's Gujarat" alluding to Nathuram Godse who assassinated Gandhi. Modi considered Sonia Gandhi's charge insulting. He pointed out that when Sonia Gandhi had visited Porbandar, the birthplace of Gandhi (no relation to Sonia Gandhi, or the Nehru dynasty) she had invoked the name of Mahatma Gandhi only three times, while she mentioned Godse thirteen times in her speech. Continuing to take pot-shots at Sonia Gandhi, whose foreigner status had split the Congress Party, he charged that "Sonia is a daughter of Italy who does not have proper knowledge of India's history".[171]

From September 8 onwards, the *yatra* was organized in phases. Every Saturday, Sunday and some Mondays, Modi traveled and returned to Gandhinagar to take care of his official duties. The first phase of the journey was the launch of the *yatra*.

---

[171] *Rediff on the Net*, "Modi begins yatra with swipe at Congress," September 8, 2002.

The Election That Shaped Gujarat

The Second Phase

From September 14 to 16, 2002 Modi traveled to Jhanjharka, a religious town in Ahmedabad district, Zanzarka, Dhandhuka, Barvala, Lathi, Botad, Gadhada, Dhasa, Chavand Amreli, Savar Kundala, Chalala, Dhari, Visavadar, Mendarda, Vanthali, Junagadh, Dhoraji, Upleta, Jamjodhpur, Bhanvad, Khambhaliya, Kalyanpur and Dwaraka. The three day journey covered 603 kilometers (377 miles). He addressed crowds in seventeen assembly constituencies that encompassed twenty-one sub-regions (talukas), and five administrative districts (zilla). The journey began in Jhanjharka. The cultural significance of this village is the presence of the famous temple of Sant Baldevdasji Maharaj who spent his whole life advocating social unification. A crowd of more than 30,000 people assembled to greet and listen to Modi. In his speech, Modi rejected the notion that his *yatra* would divide society, and instead blamed the Congress Party for the division of the country and for driving a wedge between Hindus and Muslims. Modi said, "In 1857, Hindus and Muslims had put up a united front against the British, but by the time 1947 arrived not only the society got divided but even the country got divided. The division of the country is the sin committed by the Congress Party. Congressmen are guilty of the division of India. At that time Bharatiya Janata Party was not even born."

Modi described this second phase of his *yatra* as the *Dalit Yatra*. This *yatra* would be through the *Dalit* (lower caste) areas in the Saurashtra region. To appeal to the *Dalit* community, Modi reminded people that the BJP had the largest number of *Dalit* members in Parliament, and the largest number of *Dalit* women members in Parliament. He added that even in Gujarat, it was the BJP that had more *Dalit m*embers in the Legislative Assembly compared to those of the Congress. He reasoned that since the BJP was making inroads into *Dalit* strongholds, the Congress Party was obviously getting nervous.

Modi also raised the issue of General Musharaff's September 11, 2002 speech at the U.N. General Assembly, where he chose to criticize India's human rights record by referring to the Gujarat riots. The U.N. was not the right forum to bring up this internal matter, but Musharraf thought that he would be able to seduce representatives of Muslim nations to condemn the Gujarat events.

The Saurashtra region is the stronghold of the Patel community to which Keshubhai Patel belongs. Still nursing the hurt of being ousted by Modi, Keshubhai did not participate in the second phase of the GGY passing through Saurashtra, citing ill-health. Ministers of the central government Ashok Pradhan and Satya Narain Jatiya were present. It was at this time that Advani gave Modi a "pat on the back," praising his much-criticized GGY saying that it was the "need of the hour" and that the popular response to it had unnerved the Opposition. He observed that of late there was a new sense of confidence in the party, saying, "The party's activities, its zonal conferences, the political programs, have made the opposition jittery. The hostility of the opposition is the result of the successful programs of the BJP."

Addressing a party office bearers' meeting in New Delhi, Advani said, "When the opposition parties denigrate Gujarat as Godse's Gujarat, the need for restoring Gujarat's Gaurav (honor) is all the more important." He added that that the GGY was "highly successful".[172]

Phase Three

From September 21 to September 23 Modi traveled to Navsari, Unai, Dharampur, Nana Pondha, Vapi, Pardi, Valsad, Khergauv, Chikhli, Bilimora, Gandevi, Amalsad, Abrama, Navsari, Vasar, Mahuva, Bardoli, Vyara, Songadh, Mandvi, Zankhvav, Mangrol, Kim, Olpad and Kamrej. This phase of the *yatra* covered 530 kilometers (325 miles). He addressed meetings in seventeen assembly constituencies in the seventeen *talukas* and three *zillas*.

After he traveled through the *Dalit* areas of Saurashtra, the third phase began with prayers at the temple in Unnai village in Navsari district. This phase of the GGY covered tribal areas. Jayanti Barot, the convenor of the GGY, said that BJP leaders highlighted the measures taken by the government for the welfare of tribals. At the inauguration, BJP's Gujarat unit president Rajesndrasinh Rana, and Union Minister for Textiles, Kashiram Rana were present.

Modi traveled to Vapi, called the "Houston of India", a large industrial city. He visited Valsad, the birthplace of India's former Prime Minister Morarji Desai. Also visited was the fruit export town of Amalsad, famous for exporting *chickoos* and mangoes. At Amalsad is Gujarat's fine arts university, the Kala Mahavidyalay.

The town of Navsari has a special place in India's epic struggle for independence. Madam Cama, who for the very first time hoisted India's flag in London, thereby pledging her support for India's Freedom Movement, hailed from this place. Navsari is also famous for being the stop before Dandi, the end point for Gandhi's famous Dandi march. Gandhi undertook the Dandi march to protest the British ban on salt production without license. Gandhi argued that salt was a basic necessity for every human being, and the British government ban on its production by Indians without license was a draconian administrative move, and had to be opposed. Mahatma Gandhi stayed overnight in the town of Navsari before proceeding to the now historic town of Dandi, about 20 kilometers away, and performed the "Salt Satyagraha". The great poet Narmad, famous for his songs of Gujarati pride, wrote, *"ya hom karine pado fateh chhe aage"* (plunge in, for there is success ahead in Navsari). The town of Navsari is predominantly a Gayakwadi town -- a town famous for poets and singers.

---

[172] *The Telegraph*, "Advani pats Modi on Gaurav Yatra", September 16, 2002.

Phase Four

On October 5 and 6 Modi traveled to Ambaji, Hadad, Kheroj, Khedbrahma, Vadali, Idar, Dharoi, Kheralu, Siddhapur, Patan, Shihori, Thara, Radhanpur, Sami, Shankeshwar, Dasada, Patadi, and Surendranagar. The town of Ambaji is a famous for the historic temple of Amba Mata. Ambaji is also the center of marble industry in Gujarat. The original place of Ambaji temple is Khedbrahma, which in various myths, is considered a very holy place. There is a seven-storied step well along with other temples, which were built by King Vikram.

The town of Siddhapur, on the banks of the now lost river Saraswati, is a holy place for "Matru Shraddha" or devotees of the Mother Goddess. The historical Rudra-mahalay (associated with Lord Shiva) is also an attraction in Siddhpur. Included in the itinerary was Patan, founded by Siddharaj. Patan is a place of immense historical importance. It was once the capital of Gujarat. "Patola" saris and fabric of Patan are known for their unique design. The special quality of the fabric emerges from the intricate tie-dyeing or "knot dyeing" known locally as the "bandhani" process. The Sahastraling lake of Patan is a famous tourist attraction.

This phase of the journey covered 432 kilometers (270 miles). Modi addressed meetings in 12 assembly constituencies in 12 *talukas* and two *zillas*. It started from the historic temple site of Ambaji in North Gujarat. Modi had just completed one year in office and the BJP celebrated this event with a meeting on October 8.

Phase Five

On October 16 and 17 Modi traveled to Porbandar, Madhavpur, Mangrol, Keshod, Gadu, Veraval, Talala, Prachi, Kodinar, Una, Jafarabad, Rajula, Mahuva, Talaja and Palitana. This phase covered 435 kilometers (272 miles). The Chief Minister addressed the people in 12 assembly constituencies in 13 *talukas* and two *zillas*.

Porbandar is known all over the world as the birthplace of Mohandas Karamchand Gandhi. But apart from being Mahatma Gandhiji's birthplace, Porbandar is also known as the holy town of Sudama, the indigent friend of Lord Krishna. Situated on the shores of the Arabian Sea, the town of Porbandar is a natural, all-weather port, and an important fishing town as well. Modi also traveled to Palitana – a holy place for the followers of Jainism.

Phase Six

From October 19 to 21 Modi travelled to Shamalaji, Modasa, Meghraj, Malpur, Lunawada, Santrampur, Zalod, Limdi, Dahod, Limkheda, Bandibar, Baria, Chhotaudepur, Pavi – Jetpur, Bodeli, Naswadi, Rajpipla, Kevadia, Tilakwada, Dabhoi, Vaghodia, Savli, Bhadarva, Sankalda, Vansad, Sarsa, Umreth and Nadiad. In this three-day schedule he covered 627 kilometers (392 miles) addressing people in 22 assembly constituencies spread over 24 *talukas* and five *zillas*.

The town of Shamlaji is an ancient place of pilgrimage with temples to Lord Shiva, Goddess Sumangala alongwith Devgadadhar Shamlaji. Every year, on the special full-moon day of Kartik Purnima, when the lunar body enters a particular constellation, a big fair is held. This fair is of particular importance to women who come in large numbers to worship the deities, and seek blessings for their family and husbands. The "Damodar-astakas" are ancient Sanskrit incantations and are recited with great vigor during this time.

Phase Seven
From October 26 to 28 the *yatra* traveled through Kutch (Mandvi), Matano Madh, Nakhatrana, Mandvi, Bhuj, Mundra, Anjar, Adipur, Gandhidham, Nandgam, Chirai, Bhachau, Samakhiyali, Malia and Morbi, Tankara, Dhrol, Padadhari, Lodhika, Kalawad, Jamkandorna and Jetpur.

This three-day journey covered 683 kilometers (427 miles), with Modi addressing gatherings in 11 assembly constituencies in 17 *talukas* and one *zilla*. At the starting point, according to legend, about fifteen centuries ago, the mother goddess appeared before Vanik Devchand of Marwad and blessed him. Guru Viraraja, the grandfather of Mekandada, the Chief Priest of this temple, was a famous mystic.

Phase Eight
On October 31 the Chief Minister traveled through Karamsad, Vadtal, Chaklasi, Mahudha, Mahemadabad, Kheda, Matar, Dholka, Bavla and Sanand, covering 154 kilometers (96 miles), and with events in seven assembly constituencies within seven *talukas*, and three *zillas*.

October 31 is the birth anniversary of Sardar Vallabhbhai Patel. It also happens to be the day Indira Gandhi was assassinated by her Sikh bodyguards in 1984. Vallabhbhai Patel was the second-most important man in the Indian National Congress after Mahatma Gandhi. He was from Gujarat, and a very close confidant of Gandhi. On the question of who would be free India's first Prime Minister, it is said that all but one of the various state Congress Committees favored Patel. The one other sought Acharya Kripalani. None wanted Nehru.

Mahatma Gandhi desired that after India's independence the Indian National Congress, which spearheaded the country's freedom struggle, break up into groups and contest elections, thereby giving rise to a healthy multi-party democracy. But Gandhi was keen that Nehru be the head of the government. If Gandhi had indeed chosen to stay away from day-to-day politics, and desired to live an apolitical life, then he should have refrained from imposing upon the country his choice of Prime Minister. It was upon Gandhi's request that Patel, much senior to Nehru in years and experience, stepped back, and Nehru became the first Prime Minister of free India. After India achieved freedom, there were still many princely states that had not joined the dominion of India. Patel, as Home Minister, is credited with accomplishing the accession of all

The Election That Shaped Gujarat

princely states to the Union of India. Nehru volunteered to get one princely state accede to India -- his native state of Jammu and Kashmir. History is witness to the blunder that Nehru made in this effort, a price India is paying even today.

Immediately after Gandhi's assassination, Nehru and Patel worked closer together. However, their ideological inclinations and personality traits were such that they began to drift apart. By the end of 1948, Patel was thoroughly disenchanted with Nehru's handling of the national issues facing the country. He also felt that he no longer enjoyed Nehru's confidence. Patel wrote to Nehru that no self-respecting man could work with him in the Cabinet.[173] According to Datta, Patel was convinced that Nehru was misguided on the Kashmir policy. Patel reportedly told Bakshi Ghulam Mohammad on April 8, 1948 that if he were given a free hand as in Hyderabad, he would solve the Kashmir problem in no time. He also disliked Nehru's signing the pact with Liaquat Ali because he believed that the appeasement policy towards Pakistan would not yield any fruitful results. Datta points out that Patel had a gloomy view of the future of the Congress Party. He felt that self-seeking individuals were destroying the Congress. He also felt deeply upset over Nehru's mode of governance.

It is not as if only "Hindutva" supporters point to the Nehru-Patel rift. Writing in the *Hindustan Times* (April 12, 1997), Khushwant Singh says, "Sardar Patel's principal contender for Prime Ministership of the country was Pandit Nehru who was Gindhiji's first choice for the post. But the Sardar had his supporters and his reputation as a man of iron will, an able administrator and one who single-handedly brought ruling princes to heel were points in his favor. It served Nehru's ambitions to have the stigma of anti-Muslim prejudice stick to the Sardar. It was common knowledge that if you wanted Pandit Nehru to turn against any politician or civil servant all you had to do was to call him a 'Patellite'". However, "progressive" historians and intellectuals continue to whitewash the serious differences that Patel and Nehru had, and the serious misgivings Patel had about Nehru.[174]

Nehru's dislike for Patel was thus well-known. Quite a bit of gloss has been put on Nehru's authoritarian tendencies and his *prima donna* personality. "He was a democrat, he was forward looking, he kept the Hindu fundmentalists under control, he made India modern", his biographers and supporters claim. What they do not highlight is the fact that Nehru was no mean hand at manipulating people in general and Congressmen in particular. He tried to make sure that Patel's candidates and choices were overlooked. When Patel supported Purushottamdas Tandon for the presidentship of the Congress Party, and Tandon won, Nehru deliberately weakened Tandon's position, and then took on the mantle of the president of the party himself while retaining the prime

---

[173] Datta, V. N. (September 30, 2001). "Patel's Legacy", *The Tribune*.

[174] Gandhi, R. (September 16, 2001). "Not History". *The Hindu*.

ministership. This authoritarian tendency was also evident in his daughter Indira Gandhi. India's "secular/progressive" brigade is comfortable justifying and rationalizing the machinations of Nehru because for them he was the bulwark against "Hindu fundamentalists". It was only Patel's discipline that allowed him to work with someone like Nehru, and Patel died without leaving even a house or any property to his family, whereas the Nehru/Gandhi family has become one of the richest and most powerful families in India.

Sardar Patel thus is a bone of contention between the Congress/secular brigade and the BJP/Hindutva brigade. What and whom Patel represented and what he stood for is vigorously debated, and Narendra Modi, who was born just around the time Sardar Patel died, and who believes he has the same indomitable will of Sardar Patel, has sought to fashion himself after the "iron man", as Patel was known. Many of Modi's supporters see the persona of Patel reflected in Modi, and have begun to call him "Chotte Sardar" (the younger Sardar), which rankles the secularists no end. Several of them have written strongly asserting that Sardar Patel would have nothing to do with the likes of Modi.

The appropriation of symbols is part of the battle of ideas and for intellectual and moral space. All along, the Congress, Nehru, and his cohorts appropriated Gandhi's legacy and name, and all that is considered good and modern in India. Not only have they appropriated for themselves these symbols, but have also vigorously and single-mindedly sought to demonize the Hindutva groups and leaders. The no-holds-barred campaigns were successful in transforming India into a Nehruvian state. There have been innumerable paeans to Nehru by a virtual army of international academics and intellectuals. Someone like Sardar Patel has been banished into the nether regions of the "also ran". It was the BJP's push and perseverance that finally led the Indian government to honor Sardar Patel posthumously with the Bharat Ratna award (the highest civilian award). But that it came forty years after Patel died shows the influence of Nehru on Indian politics and society. Despite his biographers' claims, Nehru loved, desired, and accumulated power at the cost of those who were superior to him in administrative capabilities and moral character.

Modi began the eighth leg of the GGY from Karamsad, the birthplace of Patel, on his 127th birth anniversary. The event was hosted by the youth wing of the BJP. At the event, Modi reminded Gujaratis of how the Congress Party had shown utter disrespect for Sardar Patel, and how Nehru had "sabotaged" Patel's prospects of taking over as the country's first prime minister even though "13 out of the 14 states supported Patel's candidature". It was not just Nehru who was to blame for playing politics, but more importantly it was Gandhi who proved himself an autocrat, ignoring the democratic principles of majority will and desire. In these times, when Gandhi has been canonized saint, it is hard to point out the weaknesses of an admirable man but very much a man with many frailties. Without ever running for office, Gandhi was kingmaker, spoiler, and manipulator. Whether he did so for what he thought was the highest good is not important. That he did so through undemocratic means is what many have ignored, especially when it came to invoking Gandhi to upbraid "Hindu nationalists".

In the course of his speech, Narendra Modi disclosed how deep was the hatred of Nehru-Gandhi family for Sardar Patel that even after so many years of his death no member of that family had visited the place of his birth in Karamsad, and that he (Modi) would not rest until the members of the Nehru-Gandhi family came to Karamsad. As a mark of respect, and to associate Sardar Patel – the "iron man" of India -- with his campaign, he touched the feet of Sardar Patel's granddaughter-in-law and sought her blessings in front of the over 100,000 people that had gathered.

Modi referred to the 1984 anti-Sikh pogrom that was organized and abetted by the Congress Party, and said that Congress leaders had no moral right to criticize the BJP for the Gujarat riots as the BJP government had taken all possible steps to minimize the violence.

Just prior to the Karamsad leg, the Election Commission announced the dates for the elections and the code of conduct for the elections. Modi, not given to be a shrinking violet, sarcastically thanked Lyngdoh for the choice of election dates and attributed the same to "divine will" since the announcement came when he was at Karamsad. Invoking Hindu numerology, he claimed that number eight was the number of planet Saturn

(*Shani*) that governed destiny, and thus the eighth leg starting from Karamsad had special significance for him. It enabled him to turn the GGY into a poll campaign. This political theater rankled the media and the Modi opposition no end. The more it irritated and angered them, the more they wrote in cynical terms of Modi's campaign, his personality, and his vision. The more they did so, the more Modi's popularity increased.

At Karamsad, Modi warned once again about Islam-inspired terrorism that threatened India. The warning proved prescient because a month later (September 24, 2002) Pakistan-trained terrorists struck the Hindu temple at Akshardham, in the capital of Gujarat, where thirty people were killed and more than 100 injured.

Modi of course did not have a smooth ride and full acceptance from even within his party. Keshubhai Patel organized a parallel program on the same day at Lodhika in Saurashtra, when his supporters weighed him on a scale with a load of blood opposite in a bizarre *"rakta tula"* (blood scale) ritual.[175] The BJP's central leadership sought to downplay Keshubhai Patel's absence saying that all BJP programs were organized under his direction as he was chairman of the party's campaign committee. However, elections would be fought under the leadership of Modi.

The BJP general secretary in charge of Gujarat, Arun Jaitley, said at the Karamsad

---

[175] *Times of India,* "Keshubhai to be weighed in blood," June 10, 2002.

meeting that had Sardar Patel been alive, he would have opposed the idea of those born in foreign countries serving as India's President, Vice-President, Prime Minister or Army Chief. As the campaign was in full swing, and Sonia Gandhi, of Italian descent and Congress Party president who aspired to be Prime Minister of India, was easy target.

Phase Nine
On November 11 and 12 the *yatra* took Modi through Dakor, Thasara, Balasinor, Shahera, Godhara, Kalol, Ghoghamba, Halol, Baroda, Padara, Karajan, Sarbhan, Cross Roads, Jambusar, Amod, Vagara, Bharuch, Zagadia, Ankleshwar, Hansol and Surat.

This phase covered 505 kilometers (316 miles), and Modi addressed meetings in the 15 assembly constituencies of 18 *talukas* and four *zillas*. The journey began in Dakor where the temple of "Ranchhod Rai" is located on the banks of the river Gomti. Gujaratis of all faiths visit this town.

Numerology, astrology, palmistry, and every other kind of fortune-telling become popular during election time in India. Everyone running for office consults the most famous and the most expensive of astrologers. A variety of celestial signs are searched and found to indicate the best of tidings in the campaigns and in the results. The BJP's numerologists are no mean contenders in this field. So, the ninth phase of the GGY was interpreted for such signs, and they were promptly found. Nine is considered a magical number. The sum of all the individual digits of the resultant of any single digit number multiplied by nine equals nine. For example, if eight is multiplied by nine, the resultant is seventy-two. If its individual digits 7 and 2 are added they equal nine. This is true of all positive single digit integers. Vedic mathematics, mocked by India's modernists, but found scientific by many, contains many such formulae and the Modi campaign used them to good effect.

The ninth leg of the GGY was inaugurated on November 11 from the religious town of Dakor, and covered the constituencies of Thasra, Balasinor, Shera, and Godhra. Godhra was, of course, Ground Zero, where it all began. The seismic impact of the massacre will continue to be felt for years to come. The *yatra* also covered Kalol, Goghambha, and Halol before it halted for the night at Vadodara. The next day it passed through Vada, Padra, Karjan, Jambusar, Amod, Vhagara, Bharuch, Jagadia, Ankleshwar, and Hasto before reaching Surat City in South Gujarat. In this phase the GGY covered the two municipal corporations of Vadodara City, and Surat City.

Security arrangements for this leg were special since it was to pass through the historically troubled town of Godhra. Even in Godhra, the *yatra* did not cover any Muslim dominated areas. It was a testing time for the State police. Godhra Superintendent of Police Narsimha Komar said that additional forces were sought from Gandhinagar and that adequate security arrangements had been made all along the route.

The Election That Shaped Gujarat

After this leg, about 35 assembly constituencies still remained, of which 12 were in Ahmedabad city. Hence, the convenor of the *yatra* Jayanti Barot felt that two more phases were required. The tenth phase was to cover Bhavnagar, Rajkot and Jamnagar municipal corporations, while in its last leg the GGY would cover Ahmedabad municipal corporation and nearby areas.

Phase Ten
On November 29 and 30 Modi traveled through Deodar, Bhabhar, Vav, Tharad, Dhanera, Deesa, Iqbal Gadh, Palanpur, Vadgam, Unjha, Visnagar, Mehsana, Jotana, Kadi, Vamaj, Sheratha, Adalaj and Gandhinagar. In these two days, he covered 381 kilometers (238 miles), and addressed people in 14 assembly constituencies within 11 *talukas* and three *zillas*.

Phase Eleven and Twelve
Covering Dhrangadhra, Halavad, Sara, Than, Chotila, Jasadan, Atkot and Rajkot on December 2 and Khambhat, Tarapur, Sojitra, Petlad, Bhadaran, Borsad and Anand on December 3, the journey of the last phase started from Khambhat and ended in Anand where the world renowned co-operative "AMUL" dairy (Anand Milk Union Limited) is located. Modi traveled 306 kilometers (191 miles), and spoke to people in 11 assembly constituencies encompassing 10 *talukas* and three *zillas*.

In four months, Narendra Modi traveled about 5,000 kilometers (3,125 miles) crisscrossing the length and breadth of Gujarat, taking his case to the people of Gujarat, right down to the villages, for it was the people whose vote would decide BJP's fate. The *Gujarat Gaurav Yatra* was extremely popular. Even the hostile media could not but acknowledge the vast crowds that lined the streets and gathered in public spaces to just see Modi. Women held up their children to seek the Chief Minister's blessings. The elderly came to bless him in turn. It is not unique in India to see such scenes repeated in election times. Popular leaders like Indira Gandhi or even Rajiv Gandhi were garlanded, hugged, kissed, and people fell at their feet. India is both a spiritual space and a feudal place, and in a mix of both the divine and the despotic, people continue to re-enact primordial urges and desperate desires. However, what was unique in Modi's travels across Gujarat was that he acquired his persona so quickly and his magic spread so fast. Someone, who continued to be demonized as a fascist, an Indian Milosevic, as even a Hitler, received ovation as a figure of liberation and a leader of substance. The large majority of Indian voters still vote based on emotional and local considerations, the latter of which includes caste affiliations, but Modi's popularity seemed to transcend such barriers, or at least the caste barrier.

The people of Gujarat made up their mind even before casting the first vote. Modi was their "deity", and they were now "worshipping" him. More often than not, the *yatra* would be stopped in the middle of the road by groups of people who refused to let it go forward before they had a glimpse of Modi. Such unscheduled stops were the people's way of telling him that he was their undisputed leader. Such interruptions threw the *yatra* behind schedule, compelling it to go on till late at night as much as 1:00 a.m. before the election code of conduct restricting open public gatherings after 10:00 p.m came into effect.

Even when the *yatra* was hours behind schedule, and even late at night, people waited patiently for Modi to turn up. They refused to leave before having a glimpse of Modi and hearing him speak. In one instance, during the *yatra* of the Karamsad leg, Modi saw an old woman with a stick in hand trying to make her way through the crowd. He stopped his convoy, waited for her to approach the convoy, and bowed his head to take her blessings. Such encounters, not stage managed, but very much part of the Indian civilizational scene, made Narendra Modi the hero of Gujarat, and this surely must have been the reason why the people voted so overwhelmingly for the BJP.

There have been many *yatras* in the past, and many will take place in the future too, but the GGY of Narendra Modi was an operation par excellence. It came at a time when every one of his opponents wanted it stopped. Both Modi and the opposition knew that if the *yatra* succeeded, the elections were a mere formality to reinstall him as Chief Minister.

Modi's speeches in Gujarati were always popular. People laughed, smiled and shouted in appreciation. Bursts of laughter reverberated when Modi referred to Musharaff as "Miyan Misharaff". The Pakistani dictator was iconized as a comic figure who had raised the issue of Gujarat in the U.N. General Assembly but who conveniently chose to forget the massacre at Godhra. Then Modi would remind people of self- sacrifice. He showed himself master of the public mood and taste, and pressed all the right emotional buttons. Of course, this rankled the media and the opposition, but Modi could not be blamed for challenging those who demonized him.

In "Modispeak" no one was spared. From Sonia's Italian descent to Musharaff's character, from Vaghela's trip to the United States to Godhra and the riots, from media attacks to Opposition calls for his resignation, Modi spared nothing and no one. He referred to false propaganda by sections of the media, specially mentioning the lies of Arundhati Roy, and raised questions about national security and the need to revive Gujarati honor, as well as the importance of the Narmada dam project. A well-informed and talented speaker, and a charismatic leader, Modi was the chief author and lead man in the play called "Moditva".

Modi traveled in a van that had a hydraulic lift that emerged from under a lotus umbrella equipped with speakerphones and lamps. Former Punjab Chief Minister Prakash Singh Badal had earlier used this van in his election campaign. Badal lost his election bid but the vehicle augured well for Modi who won handsomely.

Modi's GGY was not all talk and travel. There were many teams working in tandem for its success. One team supervised, coordinated and provided logistical support; and another team was monitoring feedback from the people at the local level about the effects of the *yatra*, evaluating the number of people at each meeting, and correlating it with the demographic make-up of the area or constituency. The number of people for each and every meeting was calculated and the same then pressed into a scale judging the effect of the GGY. Psychological evaluations were made. Another team comprising psychologists and psephologists surveyed people to judge the "Modi Effect" or "Moditva". Modi had asked one of his young confidants from the BJP youth wing about the need to undertake a mini GGY in areas where the "effect" was not assured. Hence there was also a mini GGY that toured areas where the magnitude of the "correct" effect was not up to the mark. Modi received detailed data and evaluations regularly.

General Secretary of the BJP Arun Jaitley set up his base in Gujarat for the elections, and was a hands-on leader in charge of the day-to-day operations as well as overall election strategy. The support provided by Arun Jaitley to Modi was extraordinary.

A young team from an advertising agency worked late nights and distributed special "Modi cards" similar to baseball cards, with Modi's photo and popular one-liners. This team would arrive at a place a night before the scheduled arrival of the *yatra* and distribute publicity material. Photographs specially selected by Modi, portraying his various emotions -- from a smiling face to a stern look -- were printed in thousands and distributed. Each photograph, pamphlet, or card was region-specific. Political propaganda was sophisticated, and it was left to the Opposition to try and figure out the response. Modi succeeded in creating an aura of power around him with his team of hand-picked youngsters working full time for him. His young supporters provided necessary and vital technical and computer expertise, crunching out poll numbers, rating the response to the GGY in various areas, and rating Members of the Legislative Assembly (MLAs) on a scale of one to ten, and utilizing feedback reports on their re-election prospects.

Careful surveys yielded rich dividends, but many in the media continued to play down the popular support for Modi. Most media commentators either ignored the response to the *yatra* or merely expressed their virulent opposition to it. Many even went to the extent of contradicting their own surveys and deliberately publishing reports and analyses that claimed the BJP would lose. Some of them confided to local BJP leaders that it was their strategy to try and skew the political reality and the election outcome in Gujarat. That the media played a part in the political battle in Gujarat is one story that went unreported. History writing became the handmaid of partisan politics despite the lofty claims of "official" and "expert" historians about their art, science and expertise. Journalism, as practiced in India, also became a no-holds-barred game of political gamesmanship and one-upmanship. In the name of fighting for democratic ideals and secular principles, the most powerful and articulate of historians and media commentators threw overboard the basic tenets of journalism and academic integrity.

Modi chose to start each leg of the GGY from points of historical or religious importance. It was Gujarat's honor that he was fighting for, and it was Gujarat's honor that he sought to restore. People say that Modi single-handedly won Gujarat for the BJP. If one were witness to the *yatra* winding its way through Gujarat, it would be hard to deny that assessment. Of course, no individual can accomplish goals of that magnitude without capacity to attract devoted workers and colleagues. That Modi did so effectively once again accrues to his credit. Critics, of course, are aghast that this particular political theater was so successful. But isolating Modi's drive for derision and accepting others' campaigns as part of political life in India was both hypocritical and dangerous. That the same is being repeated in the 2014 General Election should therefore not come as a surprise.

CHAPTER XX -- WAITING FOR THE POLLS

The suggestions of the Election Commission transgressed the constitutional limits and jurisdiction of the body. But in their haste to project themselves as the protectors of Indian democracy, the election commissioners advocated a certain view, and dared to undertake a fishing expedition and sought to interpret the Constitution in their own idiosyncratic manner. Without the backing of powerful forces, the EC would not have dared to attempt what it did. Unfortunately, we are not privy to the consultations and confabulations among concerned parties in New Delhi that encouraged the EC to don the particular activist role that it did. The Supreme Court rightly rejected the assertion of the EC that Article 174 regarding the six-month deadline would yield to Article 324.

The EC also dared to suggest that President's rule be imposed in Gujarat. To suggest the imposition of President's Rule not only causes alarm but also reveals a misplaced courage to openly challenge the constitutional guidelines defining the role of the EC. On this count too, a five-judge Constitutional Bench of the Supreme Court struck down observations of the EC, adding that as there was no infraction of the mandate to hold elections within six months of such a last sitting of the elected assembly the application of Article 356 did not arise. Solicitor General Harish Salve argued that it was beyond the purview and jurisdiction of the EC to make recommendations for the imposition of President's Rule. The Constitutional Bench elaborated on Article 324 and stated that timely elections were an essential part of democracy and thus temporary law and order situations could not be construed as grounds for deferring the elections.

Considering that there were no instances in the past of such daring and overzealous recommendations by the EC, people in the BJP felt that the EC was not neutral in this instance. The election commissioners were carried away by their own sense of righteousness and were willing to bring down a government or to play spoilsport in the elections. It is important that administrators, politicians, and the media fight for what is right. However, to usurp roles and powers that are not theirs, and at a time and in a context where there are other agencies that have a jurisdiction over such matters, it was an act of insolence if not hubris for the EC to charge into this particular arena.

The inherent desire of some people to subvert a particular political ideology, and their frustration when the ideology is accepted by the people, is one reason why they become overzealous in certain cases, and not in others. The desire to promote a particular ideology in India has made some of her intellectuals and administrators willful and willing provocateurs, prevaricators, and obstructers. Secularism has become their religious faith, ironically, and they are willing to claim for themselves powers not provided either by the Constitution or by a democratic dispensation. This is nothing but the expression of gall by self-chosen guardians of morality.

For these "secularists" a controlled version of liberal democracy is acceptable, nay desirable, while they get apoplectic when others seek to curtail some freedoms in other contexts, for example in the case of promulgating a law like the Prevention of Terrorism Act (POTA). They appease a certain section of society, at the same berating appeasement of other groups. This selective umbrage is merely an indication of the impatience of some groups who want to achieve *their* vision for India, democratic practices be damned selectively.

The ultimate choice lies with the people of India, and not any institution that is there to assist the strengthening of India's democratic fabric. Institutions need to be bounded not just by self-restraining ethics, but also by ensuring that their sharp teeth do not get blunted by biting into issues that are not theirs to bite into.[176]

After the deferral of the elections in Gujarat, the EC asked for a special revision of electoral rolls, hardly three months after their annual publication. It then issued instructions for identification of voters who had moved, with January 1, 2002 as the qualifying date. Even though the identification process was over much before, the EC wanted the process to be repeated. It was a monumental waste of administrative time and loss of thousands of dollars of the tax-payers' money.

On August 9, 2002 the BJP set up a poll committee, compelled by signs of growing indiscipline in the party. To give a clear message to the disgruntled or already identified dissenters, the party formed this committee under the chairmanship of Keshubhai Patel. After the refusal of dissident Haren Pandya to apologize for the comments he made, and his choosing to resign instead, it became necessary to form such a committee. The decision to do so was taken at the residence of BJP president Venkaiah Naidu. The meeting lasted two and a half hours, and was attended by Advani, Modi, Keshubhai Patel, and BJP Gujarat Unit's president Rajendrasinh Rana. The elections were fought, however, under the leadership of Modi.

The President of India visited Gujarat for two days -- August 12/13 -- to evaluate the situation in the state. The press claimed that it rattled the BJP since the President is a Muslim. It was the President's first official visit, and he had sought a briefing on the relief and rehabilitation measures undertaken. Asked whether the Gujarat government had invited the President, the Chief Secretary G. Subba Rao said, "The President is visiting Ahmedabad for he has an old association with the city. Being the President, he doesn't need any invitation from the government."

Rashtrapati Bhavan sources downplayed the political implications of the President's visit by saying that he wanted to provide "a healing touch" to a state ravaged by two disasters one after another -- the earthquake of 2001, and Godhra and its aftermath in 2002. Another reason that was cited was the President's desire to pay tribute to Mahatma Gandhi. He visited Mahatma Gandhi's ashram on the banks of the Sabarmati and met intellectuals, political leaders, technologists and industrialists. He visited the

---

[176] Sharma, V. (August 14, 2003). "Human Rights Commissions – Trials, Retrials, or Satires," *Free Press Journal*.

relief camps, and made a courtesy call at the house of noted scientist Vikram Sarabhai. The President described Vikram Sarabhai as his guru and a great visionary.

Former President K.R. Narayanan did not visit Gujarat, even though it was towards the end of his tenure that Gujarat witnessed the Godhra massacre and its aftermath. Political circles were surprised at Dr. Kalam's visit because there was no precedent of a President visiting areas affected by communal riots. Nor was there a precedent of a President asking for a personal briefing from a state government on the details of the relief and rehabilitation work. The only memory of such a pro-active initiative taken by a President was in 1987, when President Venkataraman toured some drought-hit areas. It is strange that some people believe that Presidential interest in such matters constitutes "activism". Since the office of the President of India is similar to the office of a titular head in other countries, it is assumed that all that the President can do and should do is perform "ceremonial" duties. President Kalam was fortunately not one to be hemmed in by overly strict interpretations of the role of President and therefore engaged himself more actively in transforming his office to a bully pulpit, albeit a stately one.

The President's agenda included not just the victims of the riots. After his visit to Ahmedabad, he traveled to Bhuj – the epicenter of the 2001 earthquake. He saw a "roofless" school, and asked for details of relief and rehabilitation measures that the State had taken in the devastated area.

When the Presidential reference reached the Supreme Court, the EC took another step indirectly challenging the reference. After the President had made a reference, it was no business of the EC to ask the Supreme Court what to do, and what not to do. Once again the EC transgressed into a territory that was not its jurisdiction. There is no parallel to the audacity that the EC displayed. On August 18, the EC requested the Supreme Court to decline giving an opinion on the Presidential reference on Gujarat elections since the questions framed by the EC in its 40-page report were "hypothetical". The Commission's advocate Venugopal stated that, "The court should refrain to answer the presidential reference on the matter of Article 174 of the Constitution under which time limit of six months (between two sittings of a state assembly) applies only to two sessions of the House from the last sitting to the next one and not from the date of dissolution of the House.... The question is if the court believes that the President has assumed that Article 174 applies to dissolution of the House, then it is subject to Article 324 which gives power to the Election Commission to hold election".[177]

To further buttress his argument, Venugopal cited over half a dozen examples of the Supreme Court declining to answer Presidential References in which questions were

---

[177] *Rediff on the Net*, "SC should not answer Presidential reference on Gujarat Poll: EC," August 18, 2002.

either not clear or were beyond the subject matter of the reference. However, in this case the Supreme Court declined to oblige the EC, and issued summons to the concerned parties -- the EC, all the State Governments, and the six recognized parties (BJP, Congress Party, Bahujan Samaj Party, Communist Party of India - Marxist, Communist Party of India, and the Nationalist Congress Party).

Modi was piqued at the stance taken by the EC, and saw a sinister similarity between the stances of the Congress Party and the EC. He made the mistake of thinking that the religious affiliation of the CEC and that of the Congress President had something to do with the EC's dilatory and obstructionist tactics. It is hard to prove such a surmise even if there was one. For Modi to have referred to Lyngdoh's religious affiliation was one of his mistakes that came back to bite him rather quickly. For someone, whose every word and posture was endlessly analyzed, to make an issue of Lyngdoh's Christian faith bordered on the demagogic and the stupid. This is one of several instances where Modi's playing to the gallery deserved to be criticized unequivocally.

People pointed out that Sonia Gandhi, after marriage to Rajiv, did not adopt the religion of her family, but remained a Roman Catholic. But this kind of analysis is faulty at best and crude at worst. Rajiv Gandhi was the son of a Hindu mother and a Parsi father. He was not a Hindu. Nor did he follow the Parsi religion. So, the conspiracy theories Modi gave public expression to did him more harm than good.

Lyngdoh is a Roman Catholic, as is Sonia Gandhi. Modi began expanding Lyngdoh's initials J. M. in his public rallies as James Michael, to tell the voters that since the CEC was a Roman Catholic he was the person behind the delay in holding the elections. The media rightly deplored such tactics, and Rajiv Shah of the *Times of India* then wrote an article addressing the Chief Minister of Gujarat not just by his last name "Modi" but typing his full name as Narendra Damodardass Modi, along with other full names of Modi's ministers.

Lyngdoh was incensed at Modi's tactics but he should have known that the EC's tactics, though more sophisticated, were blatantly political. Lyngdoh claimed he was an atheist, and that it was religion that was responsible for a lot of social conflict. Instead of doing his work the CEC struck a high public profile, joined issue with Modi, and the media played to the hilt this rivalry, for rivalry it had become. Both parties to the conflict had transgressed political and social bounds, and it was another incident that highlighted the still tenuous nature of the democratic processes in India. We do note, however, that in the United States, there is much more skullduggery committed in the name of politics, and the only difference is that American politicians wear suits and ties, and Indians don't!

Human Resources Minister Murli Manohar Joshi tried to rein in Modi by criticizing his remarks, but Modi unfortunately seemed to have fallen in love with his "discovery" of what "J. M." stood for. This derision of the CEC invited criticism from all quarters. By August 24, 2002 Vajpayee had to intervene. He said that no one should use "improper language or make indecorous insinuations". He also tried to douse the anger within the BJP over Lyngdoh's decision to recommend President's Rule in Gujarat. He observed, "One may have differences over the decision or the attendant observations of the Election Commission with regard to the assembly polls in Gujarat. There are constitutional means to deal with such matters."

If Modi was afraid there was a conspiracy to defeat him and his party, he chose a rather crude tactic to hit back. Such tactics can come to haunt both an individual and a party later on, and it is no wonder that not only India's Muslims but a fair majority of Christians too do not trust the BJP.

Modi was, however, right in pointing out that the EC was keen on delaying elections only in the case of Gujarat. He noted that never in the history of independent India had elections, recommended by a popular government, been postponed for reasons of law and order situation. Elections were held within 40 days of the anti-Sikh carnage in Delhi in 1984 and also the infamous Nelli violence in Assam, he pointed out.

By August 28, the EC launched a special drive that took its personnel door-to-door in the riot-affected areas to check the names of the existing voters to see if the registered voter was living there or had moved elsewhere. This drive went on till September 18 in all the districts of Gujarat, except Dangs and Jamnagar. Those desirous of making or reporting changes in the electoral rolls were asked to inform the local collectorate.

While the EC and the BJP were busy with their verbal duels, the Congress Party got busy with some behind the scenes work. Scouting for political allies, it kept itself open to alliances with its break-away faction -- the Nationalist Congress Party of Sharad Pawar -- the pro-Muslim Samajwadi Party of Mulayam Singh Yadav and Amar Singh, the CPI (M), and any other party that opposed the BJP. Before addressing a rally at Bharuch, the party's general secretary Kamal Nath said that it was necessary "to keep communal forces out of power for which strategies need to be drawn." The pro-Muslim Samajwadi Party is an Uttar Pradesh-based party. After the demolition of the Babri Masjid in Ayodhya, the Muslim community in Uttar Pradesh was disillusioned with the Congress Party and sought someone who was equidistant from both the BJP as well as the Congress.

The Congress Party's traditional vote banks were Muslims and the backward castes. However, by the late 1990s the rise of Mayawati's Bahujan Samaj Party (BSP) saw the *Dalits* moving away from the Congress Party and closer to the BSP's orbit. The Muslims of Uttar Pradesh, already disillusioned with the Congress Party, saw Mulayam Singh's Samajwadi Party as one that catered to their needs. Deprived of the votes of both the Muslims and the backward castes, the Congress Party began losing influence and power drastically. The upper caste and middle class votes traditionally went to the BJP. However, the BSP made in-roads into the BJP's vote bank too and emerged stronger than ever in the 2002 state elections. The BJP and the BSP aligned to form a government in Uttar Pradesh, for even though the Samajwadi Party bagged the largest number of seats it fell short of a majority. In return for the support in Gujarat, the Samajwadi Party wanted the Congress Party to help it topple the coalition government of the BJP-BSP in Uttar Pradesh. The BJP-BSP combo collapsed, though only after Gujarat elections. Such is the state and fate of politics in India. The BJP, once known as a more disciplined party, succumbed, in the name of realism, to forging short-term coalitions and partnerships based not on any principle or policy but on the compulsion to remain in office.

Strangely, the Congress Party was the one that stuck to discipline by going it alone in the general elections in 1999. However, it realized that the dynamics had changed in India, and for the 2004 elections it sought alliances, right and left, with the DMK, the NCP and other regional and national parties.

Muslim votes are an essential part of non-BJP calculations in any election. Muslims make up about 13-14 percent of India's population. It is a "minority" totaling anywhere between 170 and 180 million people, with the world's second or third largest Muslim population after Indonesia (205 million) and Pakistan (178 million). With vast numbers of Muslim illegal immigrants in the border districts of West Bengal and Assam, India's Muslim population, according to some researchers, is more than that of Pakistan's. Muslim dominated areas traditionally witnessed either a large percentage of voting, or a very low voter turnout. Hence, parties like the Samajwadi Party seem to have clung zealously to their monopoly of Muslim votes in Uttar Pradesh. In view of the tremendous success that Modi's GGY met with, the Congress relied more and more on a large Muslim turnout. The entry of Samajwadi Party would have further divided the Muslim vote, giving the BJP an easy run to the post. A BJP leader acknowledged that the BJP stood to gain if the Samajwadi Party and the Nationalist Congress Party cut into the Congress vote.

Final Preparations

The EC provided special facilities for those voters displaced after the riots. People who had moved, or whose houses had been destroyed were told that they could also vote. The EC took steps to ensure that the State government complied with law and order obligations, and censured what it perceived as communally oriented campaigns. The EC also banned a Hindu religious *yatra* organized by the Vishwa Hindu Parishad. Display of what the EC considered as provocative posters and hoardings was prohibited.

Considering the influx into Gujarat of a large number of Congress Chief Ministers and other dignitaries from both the BJP as well as the Congress Party for the poll campaigns, the EC asked the State Government to cut down on courtesies extended to such dignitaries under the election code of conduct. The EC also passed orders regarding government expenditure on advertisements and hoardings. Many of these advertisements and hoardings appealed to the people to cast their vote and also to educate them on how to use the electronic voting machines.

By October, people became restive waiting for the EC to announce the election dates. On October 9, 2002 the BJP president Venkaiah Naidu urged the EC to immediately announce the schedule. How long could democracy wait? The riots had stopped, relief camps were closed, people had returned to their homes, albeit somewhat reluctantly, revision of electoral rolls and other procedural formalities were nearing completion, and the process was waiting for its consummation. There were no reasons to further delay the polls. Naidu pointed out that in the past, elections were conducted under more difficult circumstances in Assam where insurgency and separatist movements were rampant. Even in Punjab and Mizoram, racked by separatist violence, polls were held. The situation in Gujarat was not any worse than in those states. Indefinite postponement of elections was a negation of democracy, Naidu said.

In the third week of October, Lyngdoh began meeting with Gujarat electoral officers indicating that the announcement of dates was on the cards. The EC, delaying the elections on one pretext or the other, was now keen on showing that it would hold elections soon. According to the new guidelines the Supreme Court prescribed, the deadline for the meeting of the newly elected state assembly was January 19, 2003. If the assembly was not constituted by that time, then President's rule would have to be invoked to prevent a constitutional vacuum. Many constitutional experts expressed in no uncertain terms the view that a temporary law and order problem could not be a justification for postponing the democratic process, and the EC's job was to hold elections, and not withhold them. When the Supreme Court seemed to have made up its mind, and was ready to pass an order, the EC proposed on October 22 that elections be held in two phases on December 16 and 19. At that time it was rumored that a formal announcement would be made on October 31 or November 1 after a full-fledged meeting of the EC. The very next day on October 23 the CEC reviewed poll arrangements with State's Chief Election Officer Gurucharan Singh and Union Home Secretary N. Gopalswami in New Delhi. An hour after the constitutional bench passed its order on the Presidential reference, the CEC called a press conference where he declared that the polls would take place in a single phase, and not in two phases, as previously planned. November 25 was declared as the last day for filing nominations, elections would be held on December 12, and the counting would begin on December 15. Also, December 12 was scheduled as the day of elections for three parliamentary constituencies and five state assembly constituencies in other states. Lyngdoh announced the imposition of the model code of conduct with immediate effect.

Regarding law and order scenario and requirement of personnel, Lyngdoh considered that since elections were to be held in a single phase, a large force of security personnel was required to ensure that there was no violence and that there would be free and fair elections. The EC asked for four hundred companies of paramilitary units to be deployed. Nearly one hundred thousand security personnel were needed to ensure elections free from violence or intimidation. Of these about seventy thousand would come from Gujarat state police, while the rest would be supplied by the State Reserve Police Force (SRP), the Central Reserve Police Force (CRPF), and the Rapid Action Force (RAF).

The EC calculated that for the thirty-three million-strong Gujarat electorate there would be one security office for every 329 people in the state. The CEC directed the State Election Office to increase security during polls. The cost of Gujarat Elections, along with the by-election of the Mehsana parliamentary constituency, was estimated at about four hundred million rupees or about ten million dollars.

The administrative machinery of the state government was used in the conduct of elections. Teachers were put on election duty thereby disrupting school schedule of students. Local district level administrative officers were deputed almost routinely for census, for updating electoral rolls, and for election duty. This often affected their work in the local district.

There are numerous proposals to see that such a situation does not repeat. However, there is no consensus among political parties if indeed they think that elections are a drain on the resources of the country. One suggestion is that the terms of governments in India could be extended to seven years like the term of the French President, and remain fixed. Another idea, based on the German model, is that a government should not be sacked unless another one was sworn in as an alternative in the Lok Sabha. All elections in India right from the village level, to the urban and town councils, to state legislatures, up to Parliament should be held in one stage over a period of twenty to thirty days. This process should be held once every seven years. Such a scenario would give uninterrupted time for the elected representatives to govern, and not get diverted by elections frequently. Parties would then behave more as agencies that assist governance rather than agencies that are geared full time for fighting and winning elections. The question of by-elections (special election held to fill a vacant seat) could also be answered. If a candidate dies in office then the party to which he belonged could nominate some other candidate to complete the tenure, but new elections would not be held till the tenure was over. If a candidate defects or resigns, then too his party would nominate another one in his place.

The goal of democracy certainly cannot be a repeated reiteration of people's verdict through frequent elections. India could well use the time, money and energy spent on elections for infrastructural development, poverty alleviation, and other serious projects if it wants to become a developed country by the year 2020, a goal set by President Abdul Kalam. These changes would ensure that the EC's authority and autonomy are well-defined, and that the CEC does not make changes which are legitimately the domain of the elected representatives. The EC just holds elections and announces the results. To inject transparency into Gujarat elections, Lyngdoh said he would invite foreign media and diplomatic missions as observers, a plan he extended to the successful elections in Jammu & Kashmir.

The Election That Shaped Gujarat

Lyngdoh disclosed at the press conference that 400,000 voters were found not residing at places where they were registered earlier. Out of these about 174,000 people wanted to vote and had been identified and registered. Out of fifty million Gujaratis, about thirty-three million were registered voters. After this mammoth exercise by the EC, the subsequent five months' delay and after the dissolution of the assembly, Lyngdoh's statistics showed that only half of one percent of the electorate had changed its registered address, and wanted to re-register in order to vote.[178]

Elections in Gujarat were a mammoth task. The EC required forty-five thousand Electronic Voting Machines (EVMs), and these had to be brought from Uttar Pradesh. As many as 35,052 polling booths had to be set up. The voting was scheduled from eight in the morning to five in the evening.

The allegation that there was mass persecution, "Bosnia-like" migration, and ethnic cleansing of Muslims in Gujarat was proved to be baseless. Statistics released by the EC after nearly two months of painstaking field work were a slap in the face of the authors of the hate campaigns against Modi. Nowhere in the world, much less in the world's largest democracy, were elections delayed and postponed for the sake of one-half of one percent of the entire electorate. Modi should have been exonerated, and dignity restored to his name vilified by the "protectors" of secularism. Anyway, such statistics usually never found space in the columns of newspapers or academic seminars. These statistics revealed themselves only to diligent and patient investigators.

Within a week of announcing the elections, the EC directed transfer of police personnel. The directive ensured that no police official operated in his home district for more than four years. The Modi government called this directive as routine and transferred four hundred and seventy-eight officers of the ranks of inspector and sub-inspector across Gujarat. The transfers were based on their place of origin and service record.

With battle-lines drawn, and the call for war given, parties started intensive campaigning. The BJP was already on the fast track with Modi traveling from one district to another for the previous month and a half. With only forty-four days before election, the BJP machine shifted into a higher gear. The next forty-four days would define and decide the fate of the BJP and Modi, and also put their indelible mark on democratic process in the country. The forty-four day wait would end on December 12, and show whether the people of Gujarat wanted a continuation of the appeasement policy of the Congress Party, or would opt for the Modi plank of "development and Gujarati pride".[179]

---

[178] *Rediff on the Net*, "Gujarat election on December 12: Election Commission," October 28, 2002.

[179] Sharma, V. (August 7, 2003). "Strategic Interests v/s Superpower Seductions," Vishal Sharma, *Free Press Journal*.

Waiting for the polls

A BJP defeat would mean the Hindutva agenda coming under severe scrutiny, and a rethink by the likes of Advani, Jaitley, and Modi of their philosophy of life and politics. With general elections two years away, there would be pressure on the coalition allies to reconsider their ties with the BJP, and to consider if continuing with the BJP would not adversely affect them too. With the exception of Shiv-Sena and possibly a few allies, the others would sever their ties with the ruling NDA. The fall of the NDA government could scare the BJP allies. A decade of hard work by the BJP would be wiped out. The growth of the BJP post-1984 would suffer reverses. Losing Gujarat, even after Godhra, would be worse than even the 1984 debacle. It could leave the BJP cadre emotionally shattered, and the confidence in their political/social ideology weakened. To regain its strength would probably take the BJP another election or decade, and certainly many *yatras*. Narendra Modi as a political entity would be finished.

However, if the BJP won it would be attributed to Modi's modus operandi, which was characterized as polarizing the masses on communal lines. "Pseudo-secular" arm-chair critics would denounce the election. The Left/Marxists would reinterpret the result as a victory not for Modi but for a polarized society. No one would agree that the hard work Modi had put in by visiting each and every one of the 182 constituencies and taking the fight directly to the people had anything to do with his victory. The Westernized intellectual class would not digest a BJP victory, blinded as they were by a myopic worldview. They would give little or no credit to the choice of the Gujarati people.

The victory would inject the BJP cadre with vigor and new confidence. It would propel the dynamic Hindutva theme onto a new dimension. The VHP would then probably ask for its share and seek governmental intervention in the Ayodhya issue. The party's political allies would feel secure, and as a party the BJP would gain in size and stature. Modi would emerge stronger, and may be his position in Gujarat would be undisputed. The likes of Keshubhai Patel and Haren Pandya would be relegated, their discontent quashed.

The democratic process can fell the high and mighty as well as make the weak and the little-known powerful heroes. It is the verdict of the people that is supreme, and it favored Modi. In a manner of speaking, the Gujarati people's choice defined the path that the world's largest democracy would take in the coming decade. The battle for Gujarat ended in a strategic victory for the BJP on the eve of the national election for Parliament. But as we now know, the BJP-led coalition suffered a major blow in the 2004 general elections, and had been in the wilderness till 2014, when "Moditva" set to sweep the nation.

CHAPTER XXI – THE RATH YATRA OF LORD JAGANNATH

"Jagannath Swami nayan pat gaami, nayan pat gaami, namo Vasudev" -- Lord Jagannath, the Lord of the Universe, it is believed, never closes his eyes. Legend has it that when the great mystic Narada, son of Brahma, went to see Lord Krishna in Dwarka (present day Gujarat), he saw Krishna with his brother Baladeva (Balarama), and Subadhra his sister. The image of all three deities together stayed in the mind of Narada. Lord Krishna then prophesied to Narada that in *Treta-yuga* (second of the four ages of humankind – *Satya yuga*, *Treta yuga*, *Dvapara yuga*, and *Kali yuga*) he was a resident of Dwaraka, but in *Kali-yuga* (present time) he would appear on the east coast of India, the present day Orissa/Odisha. Jagannath Puri in Odisha houses one of the most famous of all deities of Lord Krishna along with Balarama and Subhadra.

According to sacred/ancient texts of India, more than five thousand years ago Krishna appeared towards the end of *Treta-yuga*. One of his most important tasks was the ultimate surrender of the soul to the super-soul. Radhika (*Haraa-shakti*) or the internal potency of Krishna also appeared with Him. The Supreme Lord and His internal potency along with their associates displayed the pastimes that they eternally engaged in the spiritual world.[180]

The age of *Treta* preceded the birth of Moses, and it was believed that people lived a lot longer than they live in the age of *Kali*. A thousand cycles of the Earth around the Sun, to be exact, was the estimated duration of human life! Subala, a friend of Krishna, had prophesied that Krishna would have to live away from Radhika for ninety- years. The words of Subala came true, and Krishna did leave Radhika. According to Vedic texts, there are two kinds of happiness: when a couple is together there is a feeling of togetherness (*sambhoga*), and when a couple is separated then it is said that the love inside grows even stronger. There is a feeling of longing (*vipra-lambha*).

Vrindavan was supposed to have been the most beautiful of all woods. Its presiding deity is Vrinda Devi, and it is the personal garden of God. Ninety years had passed, Krishna was no longer the cowherd boy of Vrindavan; he was "Dwarkadheesha" the king of Dwarka, yet for the denizens of Vrindavan, he was always their Gopal (cowherd). When the *gopis* or the milk-maids of Vrindavan came to know that Krishna was near Kurukshetra, they all went there, and Radhika met Krishna there after a gap of ninety years. The Supreme Lord was covered by the energy of his own longing. The *gopis* then pulled the chariot (*rath*) of Krishna from Kurukshetra to Vrindavan. It was the meeting of the soul (*gopis*) with the "super soul" (Krishna).

The *Jagannath Rath Yatra* is an annual event in India. Nearly five million people participate in the festivities and chariot- pulling. The deities of Lord Jagannath, another name for Krishna, along with Balarama and Subhadra are taken out, and placed on huge magnificent wooden chariots, forty-five feet high, and with sixteen wheels. The

---

[180] Prabhupada, A. C. (1970). *Krsna – The Supreme Personality of Godhead*. Bhaktivedanta Book Trust.

diameter of each wheel is about seven feet. The chariots are then pulled by devotees, akin to the *gopis* pulling the chariot of Krishna from Kurukshetra to Vrindavan. From Lord Jagannath's temple, the chariots are taken to Gundika temple, dedicated to the consort of King Indradyumna, who is believed to have built the first Jagannath temple in the country. The King of Orissa is entrusted with the work of sweeping the path in front of the Lord's chariot. The king is the monarch of men, but in front of the Lord of the Universe he is but a humble servant. This ritual symbolizes the destruction of man's false ego and surrender in the service of the Supreme Lord.

The secular nature of the *Jagannath rath yatra* is evident as the trio of Jagannath, Balabhadra and Subhadra are worshipped by different sects and by members of different religions. When the temple administration came under the Bhaumas of Assam, of the Buddhist faith, they named the deity as Nilanchal after the Kamakhya temple in Guwahati. The Shaivaites worship Balabhadra, as Shiva, whereas the followers of the Shakti cult worship Subhadra as Mahakali. Lord Jagannath is also worshipped by Jains.

The festival of this chariot-pulling or the *Jagannath Rath Yatra* takes place in the Hindu lunar month of *Aashaad* in monsoon, and it is a ritual dating back to epic times. Some even attribute this auspicious day in the month of *Aashaad* to be the day, when the Rig Veda, the earliest of the Vedic scriptures was revealed. About five hundred years ago, Chaitanya Mahaprabhu (1486-1534) – one of the greatest of Krishna bhaktas -- is said to have participated in the pulling of the chariot of Lord Jagannath.

Jagannath *rath yatras* are taken out in New York City, San Francisco, London, and in many other major cities of the world, wherever there are large enough Indian communities, or where there is a Hare Krishna (ISKCON) center. These *yatras*, in various parts of the world, symbolizing the surrender of the soul (*atman*) to the super soul (*paramatman*) and yet maintaining its individuality, were inspired by one of India's foremost spiritual ambassadors, Swami Prabhupada (1896-1977).

In Orissa, the centuries old *rath yatra* at Jagannath Puri takes a detour to halt at the tomb of a 17th century Muslim saint, Salbeg. The high priests of the Jagannath temple do not allow non-Hindus to enter the temple. Hence the Muslim saint Salbeg, who had spent his lifetime singing the praises of Lord Jagannath, was also not allowed to enter the temple. However, the Lord himself went out to meet his devotee. Legend says that the chariot carrying the deities of Jagannath, Balabhadra (Balaram) and Subhadra refused to move at the auspicious hour till Salbeg, the Muslim saint was sent for. Earlier he was externed from the city on the eve of the *yatra* by the high priests. Since then the *yatra* has halted every year at his tomb.

In the city of Ahmedabad too the *Jagannath Rath Yatra* has become an annual event. However, in 2002, there were objections to the *yatra* being taken out in the interests of preserving the fragile peace in the city. Petitions reached Prime Minister Vajpayee urging him to cancel the *yatra*. *Rath yatras* are associated with the BJP, and people thought that if the *Jagannath Rath Yatra* was allowed in Ahmedabad in an election year it would polarize the masses and strengthen the BJP. This was also the time when the *Gujarat Gaurav Yatra* was postponed, and hence people thought that even the *Jagannath yatra* should be scrapped.

Some in the media argued that in Ahmedabad *rath yatras* always guaranteed discord. The VHP was adamant that the *yatra* would continue as it was a symbol of unity and not division. Elaborate security arrangements were made to prevent any untoward incidents. Police raided a Muslim's house and found a huge cache of explosives. Timely action by the police prevented what could have been a major disaster. His interrogation revealed that the arrested man wanted to take revenge for the riots that followed Godhra.

However, the *yatra* passed off peacefully but for some minor incidents.[181] Yet, Modi continued to be the target as fingers were pointed at him prior to the *yatra*, and later. At any sign of trouble, whether real or imagined, the Opposition cried "Modi". They questioned Modi's commitment to secularism, and he was branded as anti-Muslim. Modi complained that there was a deliberate campaign to weaken the morale of the people and the democratic institutions by forces keen on ousting him. He accused his opponents of spreading rumor "to demoralize police forces, divide the administration and create an atmosphere of mistrust". Even in the month of March, when Hindu-Muslim riots were at their peak, Hindu festivals like Holi, Shivratri, Dakor Mela, and the Muslim festival of Muharram passed off peacefully. So, Modi wondered why there was such opposition to the *Jagannath rath yatra*.

Speaking at Shivaji Park, Mumbai, in January 2003, Modi disclosed that the Congress Party was so divided on the issue of opposition to the *yatra* that they took the matter to Sonia Gandhi, who quite innocently asked to which party Jagannath belonged! If Modi's anecdote has any iota of truth, then the obvious mistake was due to the foreign origin of Sonia Gandhi, who obviously is not well-informed on India's culture, customs, and mores. Modi sarcastically said that Lord Jagannath did not belong to any political party, but we all belonged to Lord Jagannath's party.

---

[181] *Times of India*, "Gujarat tense after *rath yatra* related riots", July 13, 2002.

CHAPTER XXII – SURVEYS

A professional polling agency carried out a survey in April and May 2002, predicting that the BJP would win 153 seats in the Gujarat Assembly if elections were held then. Ninety percent of the people surveyed across the state were in favor of Modi continuing as Chief Minister. This was at a time when media barons and their tribe sitting a thousand kilometers away in New Delhi were busy firing salvos at Modi, and at the BJP. They chose to overlook the desire of the people and turned astrologers forecasting Modi's and his party's "inevitable" defeat. They were not only removed by physical distance but were also light years away from public perception and ground realities.

The survey showed that there was a huge and unprecedented surge in support for BJP under Modi. The media either deliberately chose to ignore this surge, or interpreted it as a short-lived phenomenon. They calculated that Modi's popularity would decay exponentially as time passed, and if elections were delayed, the BJP even under Modi would not win. Armed with such reasoning, the media went to town seeking to undermine the goodwill and support Modi enjoyed. Media barrage was concerted, coordinated, and breached the fundamental norms of media ethics and journalistic principles of fairness and balance.

Tackling the Media
How did the BJP manage to hold its own against media pressure? Media attack on Modi probably started the very next day after Godhra, when the *Indian Express* in its editorial charged Hindus of provoking Muslims.

Traditionally, some powerful sections of the media derided everything the BJP stood for. When Vajpayee, soon after taking office in 1998, gave the go-ahead for nuclear testing at Pokhran-II, they condemned it. While the majority of Indians basked in the pride of a technological achievement and what was claimed as a major security bulwark against Pakistan, these editorialists and academics warned direly of the end of India and a nuclear holocaust.[182] When the arson took place in Godhra, instead of condemning the attackers, journalists began rationalizing the massacre saying the victims were VHP provocateurs who somehow deserved what they got because they had gone to Ayodhya. There were rare exceptions, like Vir Sanghvi of the *Hindustan Times* who condemned not only the Godhra arson but also the theory that the *kar sevaks* (devotees of Lord Ram who had gone to Ayodhya to perform *puja*) had it coming. As foreign media correspondents are based in New Delhi, they reproduced the Ayodhya refrain of the Indian "secularists". The image of India was thus sullied, as twisted interpretations of the events blamed the "Hindu nationalist" BJP for everything that was wrong in India.

---

[182] Bidwai, P., & Vanaik, A. (2000). *New Nukes: India, Pakistan and Global Nuclear Disarmament*. Olive Branch Press.

The Election That Shaped Gujarat

The media have never been charitable to the BJP, and have dwelled in the illusion that deriding the Hindus was the only correct way to uphold secular values. Since secularism is the most coveted of all virtues in India, a politician may be corrupt but he will be condoned if he makes a show of secularism by openly praising Islam or promotes Muslim interests. Ashis Nandy, no supporter of the BJP, argues that those Indians who claim to be secularists are in fact authoritarian. He says that Indian secularists are an emblem of "a person or group willing to accept two corollaries of the ideology of the Indian state: the assumption that those who do not speak the language of secularism are unfit for full citizenship, and the belief that those who speak it have the sole right to determine what true democratic principles, governance and religious tolerance are".[183]

Similarly, *India Today*, in an editorial on the outcome of Gujarat elections, said, "Truly, this election was held in the backdrop of two riots, one bloody, the other pure sophistry. In the latter, professional secularists and the conscience-keeping industry sought out the darkest entries from the glossary of hate to describe the crime of the Hindu – Holocaust, fascism, Hitler.... They rhapsodized the ghettos of victimhood, and, forever scavenging for a cause, they found a self-serving monster in Modi. The election exposed their pretence".[184]

A politician like Lalu Prasad Yadav may be downright offensive, destroy the economy of a state, encourage mafias to overrun society, adopt the combined image of a village moron and a lumpen buffoon, disrupt parliamentary proceedings by shouting, and terrorize businesses to fund the expenses for his daughter's wedding, but the media will dismiss all these as mere frivolousness, because Yadav has wrapped himself in the robe of the secularist, and proclaims repeatedly that he is a leader in the battle against the "Hindu fundamentalist BJP".

It was a predicament within the BJP too. Would the party continue to believe in its ideology and support Modi or give in to the demands and pressures of the media? The choice was obvious. Being at the receiving end of unforgiving, belligerent elements in the media, the BJP chose to support Modi.

The Congress Party seemed to have gotten wind of the BJP survey results, and successfully attempted to delay the elections. BJP's April-May survey was carried out so quickly and at a time when people were still scared by the events following the Godhra massacre. The polling agency had to insure its field surveyors for safety as they ventured into each and every assembly constituency. Modi, endowed with scientific temperament, wanted things in black and white. MLAs were evaluated by the people they represented, Modi's popularity index was charted, and careful analyses of various

---

[183] Nandy, A. (2003). *The Romance of the State and the Fate of Dissent in the Tropics*. Oxford India Press.

[184] *India Today* "More than Modi". December 30, 2002.

sociological indices were made.

A rumor was floated in August 2002 that the BJP-sponsored survey showed it would get only a simple majority. The party immediately scotched the rumor as false. The Congress Party sought to capitalize on the rumor by claiming that hopes of a BJP win were fading with the passage of time, and that the BJP could only win in a polarized environment. Modi was growing impatient, since he knew that the GGY would prove the Congress Party's claims wrong.

In November, with the GGY in full swing, an *India-Today-Aaj Tak-* commissioned opinion poll predicted a two-thirds majority for the BJP in the elections to be held in a month. The poll carried out by ORG-MARG forecast a fifty-five percent vote for the BJP. The survey showed that the party had a 10.2 percent swing of votes in its favor and this would help the party get between 120 and 130 out of the total 182 seats. The poll further revealed that polarization of the public on religious lines after Godhra was staggering. Over nine thousand voters were interviewed, with nearly three thousand in urban areas, and six thousand in the rural sector, spread across fifty-two constituencies. It predicted that the Congress Party would get between 45 and 55 seats with a vote share of 42 percent, and that other parties did not stand much of a chance in the bi-polar environment. They would get only between two and seven seats, with a mere three percent of the votes.

The survey inferred that there was a sharp divide between how outsiders saw the events in Gujarat and how Gujaratis viewed them. Many commentators missed this vital point and either erroneously or deliberately spun a different tale or predicted a different outcome. Demonized by the media, Modi became the average Gujarati's demigod. People hung photos of Modi in their homes, and garlanded them. During the GGY, women held up their babies to Modi so that he could bless them. Never in the history of India had a single tragic event, as in Godhra, created such outrage and anger in the public. Hindus increasingly were concerned and angry about Pakistan-based terrorists, and Godhra was the igniting point for their pent up frustration and wrath.

The *India-Today* group survey claimed that the aftermath of the riots had successfully nullified the anti-incumbency mood visible in the last days of the Keshubhai Patel government. It seemed that the people of Gujarat had already made up their mind as to who would be their Chief Minister, and naturally voted for him. In a month's time, results proved the survey accurate. The BJP won 126 seats with fifty-five percent of the polled votes.

There were other polls that did not predict such an outcome. *The Week* magazine survey portended a close fight. It gave BJP only ninety-five seats, and the Congress eighty-five. The survey conducted by TN Sofres Mode said that BJP's swing from the last Lok Sabha elections was negative, more so among the Muslims and forward castes, and in urban Gujarat. It gave the BJP a vote percentage of 49.9, and Congress a close 48 points. The surveyors claimed to have interviewed over three thousand voters, across twenty-four constituencies. It monitored reactions from eight constituencies of

The Election That Shaped Gujarat

Bhuj, Godhra, the Dangs, Ellisbridge, Sabarmati, Bharuch, Rajkot-II, and Vadodara. The survey said that over one-third of the electorate was not affected by the GGY, while an equal number affirmed that Modi's GGY had rekindled pride among a large percentage of Gujaratis. Fifty-two percent of the electorate wanted Modi to be the Chief Minister. Even though the survey "chose" to reduce the number of seats BJP would win, it affirmed the popularity of Narendra Modi.

India-Today conducted another survey giving BJP only between 100 and 110 seats, and Congress Party between 70 and 80 seats. These surveys began to create an impression that the Congress Party was increasing its strength, and the gap between the two main contending parties was decreasing very rapidly as the election-day neared.

The surveys quantified BJP's advantages in terms of three factors -- the primary one being the personal popularity of Narendra Modi. Other factors were the ideological agenda set by Modi in the backdrop of Godhra and the Akshardham attacks, and a feeble anti-incumbency factor. In fact Modi's popularity even exceeded the popularity of Vajpayee.

Exit polls carried out by *Aaj-Tak*, a leading television news channel, gave the BJP between 93 and 109 seats. To form a government the party would need only ninety-two seats in the 182-seat house. The Congress Party was expected to get between 72 and 88 seats.

Aaj-Tak's rival channel *Zee-News* too conducted its own exit polls. The *Zee News-Taleem* exit polls gave the BJP 101 seats, and the Congress 69. Independent candidates were believed to get about eleven seats. It claimed to have interviewed 9,000 voters across 31 constituencies, and inferred that BJP would get 57 percent of the votes and the Congress Party 34 percent.

Region-wise too, the BJP's superiority over the Congress Party was evident from these polls. In North Gujarat, it expected BJP to get 54 percent of the vote share, and the Congress Party 37 percent. In the Patel community stronghold of Saurashtra, it gave BJP about 48 percent of the vote share, and Congress Party about 40 percent. In Central Gujarat, it predicted BJP would get 60 percent of the votes, and Congress Party about 34 percent. Finally, in South Gujarat it forecast BJP getting 50 percent of the votes, and Congress 24 percent.

The Congress Party issued a statement urging people to ignore the exit poll forecasts. Party spokesman Satyavrat Chaturvedi said, "We do not want to cast aspersions on anyone.... We acknowledge that all media organizations are well within their right to conduct such polls. But we want to make it clear that the people of Gujarat braved the threat of terrorism to vote for safety and security and for the development of the state. They voted against the communal and divisive rule of the present government of Narendra Modi". Even when the battle was over it seemed that light had still not dawned on the opposition camp.

On the day of counting, one television channel sought to delay or deny the inevitable, claiming the count showed a neck-and-neck race. Counting had begun early morning, and by noon, a high profile English news channel was proclaiming as if the Congress had indeed done the impossible. A few hours later this illusion-haunted media house of cards crashed under its own flimsy weight. When the day ended not only did the BJP win, but it won by winning more than the phenomenal two-thirds majority.

The Congress Party's media management under its leader Kamal Nath was much better than BJP's media management. This has nothing to do with any extraordinary skills the Congress Party used. A certain section of the media has traditionally been hostile to the BJP. It is therefore easy for the Congress Party to capitalize on this factor. Its spokesmen always get more mileage even if they have nothing insightful to say. The BJP has to work extra hard and spend more money to get its word out with little assurance of even neutral coverage.

Like the then-new Labor Party of Tony Blair, the BJP needed its own Alistair Campbell, and a whole army of its own spin doctors. It had become necessary for the BJP to train more media-savvy and tech-savvy people to project itself as the political party of choice for Indians in the twenty-first century. A vast majority of people in India does not trust the English press. However, the Indian language press does depend upon the English media for much of its news coverage. Therefore, the BJP's weakness in handling the English press will continue to be a major hurdle in reaching out to the public more successfully. A more successful and articulate management and handling of the English as well as the foreign press in New Delhi would greatly help the party fight its political rivals. However, even that might not ensure fair coverage and balanced reporting because as Kissinger pointed out that just as policy is not made "in an emotional vacuum by 'objective' people,"[185] (p. 143) news is also not reported by "objective" reporters and scholars in a sterile office or newsroom.

Times are changing, and with regional parties gaining strength, the mantle of a national party will be shared both by the BJP and the Congress Party. The battle between these two giants of Indian politics will be the battle for the soul of India.

---

[185] Kaplan, R. (2000). *The Coming Anarchy:Shattering the Dreams of the Post Cold War.* Vintage Books.

CHAPTER XXIII -- AKSHARDHAM

The attack on the Akshardham Templein September 2002, in Gandhinagar, leading to the deaths of thirty-seven people and injuries to more than eighty,[186] needs to be understood in the background of Islam-inspired terrorism and worldview. It has become fashionable to characterize the attack as a fall-out of the Gujarat riots. The immediate cause may indeed be that. But the real reason of the influence of extremist Islam whose practitioners want the world made Muslim (*ummah*) is rarely alluded to in the mainstream media or in academic works.

The question of who is more evil, the person who in the name of religion kills people of other religious faiths, or is it the person who trains, motivates, and inspires young men to carry on such activities? Killing of innocent and unarmed civilians in a place of worship is certainly heinous, and motivation for such acts comes from those who wear the garb of religious teachers but who through their words encourage such violent, even demoniac actions. The Islamic Republic of Pakistan is the breeding ground for religious extremists, and the government of Pakistan and military agencies support materially and otherwise these extremists.[187] Terrorists trained in Pakistan routinely carry out deadly attacks in the name of religion.[188]

Just as Lord Chamberlain, Prime Minister of Britain, followed a policy of appeasement and gave time to Hitler to plan and become a menace to humanity, India too followed a similar policy of appeasement of Pakistan due to strategic lobbying in Washington and in London by pro-Pakistani groups, and American and British investment in Pakistan over the decades. Pakistan became a dangerously unstable country with the demise of its democratic institutions, and its military and religious leaders taking over the control of a strategically located nation. Compounding this deterioration were Pakistan's tribal regions where the laws of Pakistan are seldom adhered to. Tribal justice frequently targets women as a means to humiliate a family. Gang-rapes are prescribed as punishment, and honor killings of women by their own family members are a tragic reality in Pakistan. Christians are particularly targeted, and the Hindu population in Pakistan, about fifteen percent in 1947, is now down to an abysmal 1.4 percent. Bombs are lobbed into churches, temples destroyed and taken over, Hindu businessmen and families targeted, and armed Islamic terrorists with automatic weapons open fire on devotees. It has become a lawless land armed with

---

[186] *The Times of India* (September 25, 2002). "Temple siege ends, commandos kill 2 militants".

[187] Gall, C. (2014). *The Wrong Enemy: America in Afghanistan 2001-2014.* Mariner Books.

[188] Coll, S. (2005). *Ghost Wars: The Secret History of the CIA, Afghanistan, and Bin Laden, from the Soviet Invasion to September 10, 2001.* Penguin Books.

nuclear weapons. Events leading to the confession by Pakistan's hero, Abdul Qadeer Khan, of nuclear weapons trafficking,[189] and the two attempts at assassinating General Pervez Musharraf, and later the assassination of Benazir Bhutto, show that the Pakistani snake had begun to bite itself. The United States was under pressure to make sure that Pakistan did not implode and that its nuclear arms did not fall into the hands of Muslim extremists, while at the same time pumping billions of dollars into the Pakistani society and military to keep the Pakistani ship of state afloat.

The Americans used Pakistan as a frontline state to train guerilla fighters called "*mujahideens*" and to use them to attack the Soviet Army in Afghanistan. American taxpayers' money funded the training and supply of modern weapons to the *mujahideens*. Also, billions of dollars flowed from Washington for propping up a failing state. With the Soviet withdrawal from Afghanistan, anarchy dawned. The infamous Taliban, who practiced an ultra-radical form of Islam, enslaved Afghan society. The *mujahideens* employed against the Soviets were now directed to carry out a "*jihad*" against India, with Kashmir as the prime target.

Kashmiri Muslims practice *Sufism*, a more tolerant version of Islam that promotes mutual co-existence. It is an Indianized if not Hinduized form of Islam. However, Pakistani sponsored cross-border terrorism scarred and changed the culture of Kashmir forever. The last decade of the twentieth century saw an unprecedented attack unleashed by Islamic zealots on the indigenous Hindu population of Kashmir. With a vision to make Kashmir an Islamic state, the agents of Pakistan executed a policy of killing any non-Muslim who dared to remain in Kashmir. Westerners were particularly targeted and killed in the most gruesome manner. The most common methods of execution used by these terrorists, euphemistically labeled as "militants" were decapitation and mutilation. The Pakistani obsession for Kashmir has less to do with love for the people of Kashmir, and more with the urge to harass India, whom Pakistan views as an object of perpetual enmity. The *mujahideen* trained in Pakistan and used against the Soviets are the same people who became "freedom fighters" in Kashmir targeting India. They were the ones seduced by Osama bin Laden and the ones who trained the fanatics who carried out the September 11 attacks on U.S. targets. Only the names of the terrorist organizations have been changing, but the people, the sources of money, and the training facilities have all remained the same. The guardian and not-so-secret supporter of all these groups has invariably been the Pakistani military and religious establishment.

The Making of the "Islamic Bomb"

India's nuclear aspirations began the day communist China, with its imperial ambitions, attacked an unprepared India. In that attack in 1962, India lost a substantial amount of

---

[189] Broad, W.J., Sanger, D.E., & Bonner, R. (February 12, 2004). "A Tale of Nuclear Proliferation: How Pakistani built his Network". *The New York Times*.

her land. After the 1962 India-China war, Pakistan chose to ally closely with China, and became its "all-weather ally". China went nuclear in the 1960s, and India detonated a nuclear device in 1974, but at that time chose voluntarily not to exercise the nuclear option. Over the years the close nuclear ties between Pakistan, China and North Korea forced India to reconsider the nuclear option in 1998, and to induct nuclear weapons. Though India went nuclear, it adopted a doctrine of "no first use". It was an opportune moment that brought into the open the clandestine Pakistani nuclear program. Two weeks after India tested its nuclear weapons, Pakistan too detonated a nuclear device calling it the "Islamic Bomb", to give it a pan-Islamic color.[190] It was true that Pakistan became the first Islamic country to possess a thermo-nuclear device. At that time there was a popular joke in India as to why it took Pakistan so long to detonate a nuclear device. The answer: because the instruction manuals were in Korean and Chinese languages!

The insidious and dangerous actions of the Chinese and the North Koreans now pose a direct threat to the security of nations, not just in South Asia but all over the world. In the past the *mujahideen* on becoming *jihadis*, turned against India first and then against the United States, Israel, and the West. There is no guarantee that Pakistan's Islamic bomb would not, in a similar manner, fall into the hands of Islamic terrorists or the Hizbullah. Reports from Iran and Libya indicated that those countries received substantial aid from Pakistan to augment their nuclear programs. Pakistan remains a threat to global security.[191] As Hoagland writes, "Pakistani help has been instrumental to the ambitions of Libya and Iran to acquire such weapons and in North Korea's development of them. Washington has long known this but has been reluctant to confront Islamabad. When I wrote in 1995 about the evidence that U.S. intelligence had gathered of Pakistan's help to Iran, a State Department spokesman denied that account. As recently as a few months ago, Pakistani spokesmen were denouncing columns here spotlighting the North Korean connection. The blanket denials have stopped, and U.S. officials speaking on background are now spelling out details of Pakistan's involvement in Iran, North Korea and Libya".

Islamic terrorism may one day end; Saudi involvement with *Wahabism* may give way to reformation; radical Islam may metamorphose into a more tolerant and accommodating version; but the Pakistani hatred of India may never end despite the recent "breakthrough" in talks between the two nations.[192] It would be too naïve to think otherwise. The *raison d'etre* of the Islamic Republic of Pakistan has been a

---

[190] Raja Mohan, C. (2003). *Crossing the Rubicon: The Shaping of India's new Foreign Policy*. Penguin Books

[191] Hoagland, J. (January 8, 2004). "Nuclear Resolution", *The Washington Post*.

[192] Dasgupta, S. (January 05, 2004). "Lessons from Islamabad", *Rediff on the Net*

sectarian world vision -- wherein Muslims will not live peacefully with non-Muslim majorities unless Muslims wield the power. The founding fathers of Pakistan assumed that if India did not return to pre-British Muslim rule, it would have to be divided. It is difficult to come to terms with such a myopic and sectarian world vision. Pakistan knows well that its dreams were only partly realized because a large percentage of Muslims stayed back in Hindu majority India. Hence the myth propagated by Jinnah and his coterie for a land of the pious (Pakistan) turned out to be a barren land of lies and terror. Pakistan of today is anything but the land of the pious, with the likes of Osama Bin Laden, the criminal drug syndicate, killers of Daniel Pearl, smugglers of guns and gold, and every other kin of this underworld fraternity finding extraordinary synergy with the Generals of its army, its tribal leaders in the North-West Frontier Provinces, and the gangsters of Karachi (Bin Laden having been discovered a resident of Abbotabad, near Pakistan's Military Academy, and killed by American Navy Seals in May, 2011). They say that three A's run Pakistan: Allah, Army, and America. But we can add another -- the "addicts" of the huge drug cartel that is next only in operational size and economics to the Columbia drug cartel.

While a variety of ingredients went into the making of India's freedom struggle, yet the one that mobilized most Indians was the non-violent theory and practice of Gandhi's *satyagraha*. Pakistan was founded through backdoor negotiations, public riots, and the massacre of innocents. These have been Pakistan's antecedents and its legacy. While India built up self-restraint, Pakistan spewed hatred and violence. To expect Pakistan to give up the very reason of its birth and become a version of India is too much to ask for, even though India's "Wagah-border candle holders" keep trying. Pakistan was born out of sectarianism, fed on hatred, and nurtured on violence. Now that it has become a global menace, reforming it is not just in India's interests alone but those of other global communities too. May be, it is with this in mind, that the United States, abettor of Pakistan's many unseemly activities, sought to make it a major non-North Atlantic Treaty Organization ally "for the purposes of our future military-to-military relations".[193]

Pakistan and its people are of Indian origin and were a part of India till 1947. So where did Pakistan go wrong? To answer the question one needs to go back seven years before India's independence. Jinnah persuaded the participants at the annual Muslim League session in Lahore in 1940 to adopt what later came to be known as the Pakistan Resolution, demanding the division of India into two separate sovereign states, one Muslim, the other Hindu. To press his demand for a separate land carved out exclusively for Muslims, Jinnah and his Muslim League called for a "Direct Action Day" on August 16, 1946. There was large scale rioting and massacre of thousands of innocent Hindus at the hands of Jinnah's goons. Alas! There was no Amnesty International, Human Rights Watch, the International Court of Justice and the coterie

---

[193] *Rediff on the Net*. "US to make Pakistan non-NATO ally". March 18, 2004.

of global human rights brigades to record the violence and seeking punishment for the perpetrators.

Pakistan therefore is the perfect breeding ground for religious extremism. The attack on the twin towers of the World Trade Center in 2001, the Bali bombings in 2002, the suicide bombings in Israel, or the attack on the famous Akshardham temple in Gujarat, are the work of people who graduate from Islamic hatred-producing factories operating non-stop in Pakistan and to some extent, in Palestine.

The Beauty of Akshardham

The Akshardham Temple in Gandhinagar, capital of Gujarat, belongs to the Swaminarayan sect. This sect is founded on the teachings of Lord Swaminarayan, and is a typical Hindu sect focusing on prayer, non-violence, community service, and tolerance. The monks of this sect practice strict celibacy, and live a life of simplicity. The Swaminarayans have constructed temples all over the world. The Swaminarayan sect temples are some of the most beautifully constructed and decorated temples in modern India. They showcase the art, culture, and quality of Indian craftsmanship.

The Akshardham temple is located directly opposite the Governor's residence. According to news reports, those who attacked the temple made reconnaissance trips two or three times with the help of local Muslim guides before carrying out the attack. At first it was reported that the terrorists had planned to attack high profile government buildings like the Secretariat. However, because of the heavy security protecting these complexes they chose the Akshardham Temple. The temple was a softer target because of the large crowd of devotees visiting it every day, and because of the easy access it offered.

The temple complex is spread over 23 acres and is crowded with visitors and worshippers in the evenings. At the center of this spacious complex, an imposing architectural masterpiece -- the Akshardham Monument -- enshrines the golden *murti* (representation) of Lord Swaminarayan, the founder of the Swaminarayan faith. It is an imposing three-storied building, and is an architectural marvel. Its 6,000 tons of pink sandstone, from Rajasthan, have been pieced together with incredible accuracy. It took more than 12 million man-hours of 900 skilled craftsmen to create this magnificent monument of 93 sculpted pillars, 40 windows carved from both sides, and a feast of forms and filigrees. No steel or cement has been used to ensure that the monument will last for a thousand years. It is 108 feet high (32.92 meters), 240 feet (73.15 meters) long and 131 feet (39.93 meters) wide.

The Akshardham Temple was designed and crafted according to ancient Indian architectural treatises called *Sthaapatya shastras*. The monument rests in the lap of silence and tranquility. There are three floors, the *Hari Mandapam* -- the main floor, the *Vibhuti Mandapam* -- the upper floor, and the *Prasadi Mandapam* -- the ground floor. Akshardham is more than an architectural masterpiece: it is the embodiment of love of the devotees of Lord Swaminarayan.

The temple has the tallest structural stone pillars in India -- four delicately sculpted pillars that rise to 33 feet and the longest stone support beams in stone architecture -- 22 feet, and long single-piece beams, each weighing five tons. No iron or steel has been used: only stone to ensure that the temple beckons generations of devotees. There are 73 richly patterned and 63 partially carved pillars. Sixteen pillars have profuse *roopakam* -- sculptures and figures. There are 64 large traditional sculptures with spiritual meanings and 192 small figurines of gods and goddesses adorn the pillars.

The temple complex has 25 domes of varying sizes and depths. There are grandly ornate porches and three exclusively decorated porticos. Intricately carved from both sides are 30 large windows and 24 small grills. There are 220 stone beams for structural support. Fifty-seven stone screens filter the light streaming in. Nearly 160,000 cubic feet of pink sandstone has been carved and assembled to make this modern day marvel. To build this amazing monument, five types of stones were used: pink sandstone from Bansipahadpur, yellow stone from Jaisalmer, white marble from Makrana, maroon granite from Jhansi, and white marble from Ambaji.[194]

Attack on the Temple

September 24, 2002, a fourth Tuesday, will be long remembered as the day when terrorists stormed into the temple and killed 37 people -- unarmed men, women and children. Most of the killed were Hindus, but two Muslims -- Anwar Mir and Abdul Mir -- also perished in the attack.

At about five in the evening, at prayer time, terrorists armed with grenades and automatic weapons entered the complex from the eastern side by climbing over the low wall near the gate facing the Governor's bungalow. After entering the complex the terrorists headed for the main building where the main deities are kept for worship.

However, one volunteer at the gate saw the gunmen going towards the main building and called security to shut the doors to prevent access to the deities. It is in this main building that devotees congregate to have *darshan* of (observe) the deities. The maximum number of people could also be taken hostage in this area. Strange as it may seem, even after meticulous planning and being armed to the teeth, the gunmen could not gain entry into the main building. The volunteer had warned just in time, and the doors were shut. The gunmen fired on them, even threw a grenade but of no avail. The heavy doors of the main building would not budge.

Frustrated, the gunmen then went towards the exhibition hall, where too a large number of people lined up for tickets to see the exhibitions. Here the largest number of causalities took place, as people were inside a closed room, and the gunmen threw grenades and opened fire indiscriminately. A couple of eyewitnesses narrated gory

---

[194] Information on the Akshardham Temple in Gandhinagar was culled from a variety of sources on the Internet.

accounts of how they saw bleeding bodies scattered in the temple premises and spent bullets all over the place.[195] As Akshardham is a sprawling lush green area, it became all the more difficult for the scores of commandos to secure the area in phases from any further detection as they slowly zeroed in on the main precincts of the temple.

Local Police Contain the Terrorists

The local Gandhinagar police led by Superintendent of Police Brahmabhatt were the first to arrive at the temple. The gunmen hiding in thick bushes showered the police team with heavy automatic fire. Six policemen were hurt, and two killed. One of the police personnel who died in the line of duty was a Muslim. Superintendent of Police Brahmabhatt was injured in the shoot-out with a bullet piercing his hand. But the undaunted officer went to the hospital, had the bullet removed, got the wound stitched, and was back in action at the temple in his blood stained uniform. The government rewarded him for his exemplary show of bravery, strength and courage in the discharge of duty.

The local police and commandos of the state reserve police participated in the first round of action against the terrorists. Their initial role was to see that there were no further civilian casualties, remove the injured and the dead from the scene, and secure the area to prevent the escape of the terrorists. Local commandos took up vantage positions.

The National Security Guard Called In

After units of the Gujarat police secured the perimeter, the National Security Guard (NSG) units from New Delhi were called. The NSG units are elite commando squads trained in anti-terrorist operations. At about 1810 Indian Standard Time, just over an hour after the terrorists stormed the Akshardham temple, the Director General (DG) of the elite National Security Guard summoned Brigadier Raj Seethapathy and asked him to carry out the anti-terrorist operation. Reports were already trickling in of several unarmed, civilian devotees being killed in the indiscriminate firing by the terrorists. There was no time to lose.

Immediately after getting the go-ahead for the operation, forty commandos of the NSG, led by Brigadier Seethapathy, left their base in New Delhi and headed for the airport from where they would go to Gujarat, a thousands kilometers to the south. However, the NSG units were caught in a traffic jam, and reached the airport at about 1940, an hour after leaving the base. These are the ironies of life in modern India.

The city of Gandhinagar has no airport, hence the NSG commandos landed at Ahmedabad airport, and traveled by road to Gandhinagar, a distance that took over

---

[195] See *Rediff on the Net* archives containing reports about the attack on the temple.

twenty additional minutes to cover. By the time the NSG commandos reached the site, it was dark. Nightfall further compounded the task of security forces trying to rescue people trapped in the temple complex and to locate the terrorists.

The NSG units were briefed by the local police and Akshardham temple volunteers who showed them an exact model replica of the temple and explained the entire architecture of the temple to show possible places of advantage that the NSG units could use to carry out their operations. The NSG then got down to doing reconnaissance. The entire complex was well lit up, but there were several dark spots.

The state police told the NSG that there were two terrorists participating in the attack and one of them had been killed. Brigadier Seethapathy, with one of his team, then walked across the lawn in the middle of the complex to inspect a body, which the state police said, was of the terrorist killed, but later identified as that of a police officer. His walking across also had another purpose. For sometime there was no firing and the NSG had no clue where the terrorists were hiding. As soon as they went near the body, the terrorists began firing from the right hand side of the main entrance to the central complex. The rest, according to Brigadier Seethapathy, was easy to plan.

The Flushing-out Operation

One of the NSG aims was to avoid collateral damage to the beautiful complex and any further bloodshed. The terrorists were well-trained and had over 130 rounds of ammunition with them and used between 20 and 25 grenades. They had come prepared for a very long haul. According to Seethapathy, the attack on Akshardham was very similar to the December 13, 2001 attack on the Indian Parliament. It seemed to the NSG that the terrorists were keen on taking some people hostage and bargain with the authorities.

After being briefed at about 0130 IST the NSG units began to take their positions. Their task was to locate and eliminate the terrorist threat. In order to locate their position the NSG units carried out a surveillance operation in which two of its personnel were injured and one killed. One of the injured, Surjan Singh was in coma a year and a half after the attack with a bullet still embedded in his brain stem.

At 0130 IST, the terrorists came out of their hiding and resumed firing. An NSG team was placed at the rear, while another team kept up pressure from the front. There was a small fence but the two terrorists jumped over the fence in order to escape the dragnet, but the NSG kept engaging them.

The operation to flush out the terrorists continued the whole night, with the NSG unable to make any headway. The terrorists were heavily armed, and well stocked with ammunition. Around 0300 IST, the NSG got really close to the terrorists. It was around this time that NSG commando Suresh Yadav fell. It was pitch dark in the rear part of the temple, and very difficult to carry out operations. Subedar Suresh Yadav, who laid down his life, was an experienced fighter. He was killed during the final assault. Yadav had taken cover behind a tree, which had two branches splitting away. A bullet scraped the split and killed him. After Yadav fell, the NSG commandos waited for dawn to break.

The final assault was over in a few minutes. Once the NSG spotted the terrorists, the latter sneaked into a bathroom at the rear of the right wing and locked themselves in. It took just a few bullets fired from precision weapons to eliminate the threat. They had been hiding in the toilets, and the low-lying camouflaged areas. They were well-trained in guerilla warfare and combat operations. The two terrorists who mowed down thirty- seven and injured over 80 did not fit the stereotypical image of terrorists. One of them was a teenager, while his companion was slightly older. They were a little over five feet tall and could not have weighed more than 60 kilos. They were well stocked with food, water, and ammunition indicating again that their plan was to take people hostage and negotiate.

A strip search of the bodies of the terrorists revealed a letter written in Urdu. A hitherto unknown group calling itself the *"Tehreek-e-Kasas"* claimed responsibility for the attack. The Urdu letter claimed that the temple attack was in retaliation to the killings that followed the Godhra carnage. In this operation about seven commandos were injured -- four from the NSG, and three from the state police -- while three commandos lost their lives, one from the NSG, and two from the state police.

Former security advisor to the Chief Minister of Gujarat K.P.S. Gill felt that there was no need for the intervention of the NSG to "neutralize" the two terrorists. He said, "The task should have been accomplished by the commandos of the Gujarat police." Gill was also not very happy about the time it took to mobilize and order the operations. He added that formal orders for the operations to flush out the terrorists were given hours later, and it was important therefore to reduce bureaucratic hurdles, and facilitate immediate action by the security forces to save time in situations where even seconds mattered. Gill blamed also those agencies that were keen on delaying elections in Gujarat. Advocating early elections in Gujarat to bring back normalcy in the state, he felt that all those who colluded to postpone election in the state were in some way responsible for instability in the state.

The body of Subedar Suresh Chand Yadav, the hero of Gujarat's Akshardham anti-terrorist operation, was brought to Delhi, and Deputy Prime Minister Advani placing a wreath on his body, said Yadav made the supreme sacrifice to save innocent lives. Hailing from Khankhera village in Alwar district in Rajasthan, forty-one years old, Yadav is survived by his wife and two children. He had joined the army in 1979 and was a part of the 13th Mahar Regiment after which he moved to the Central Reserve Police Force. He was on deputation to the NSG where he was part of the 51st Special Action Group. His body was taken to the NSG headquarters at Manesar, Haryana and cremated with full military honors, while the bodies of the terrorists lay unclaimed in cold storage of a mortuary.

The Anti-Terrorist Squad handed over the bodies to the Civil Hospital to keep them for a month, awaiting claimants. After the bodies remained in the cold storage for about a month, the Government of India, and the Government of Gujarat handed them to a local Muslim organization that buried the terrorists' bodies according to Islamic rites at the Musa Soher ground in Shahibagh area of Ahmedabad city amidst tight security. Members of State's Muslim WAKF Board took the bodies from the Ahmedabad Civil Hospital and performed the last rites in the presence of locals. The burial had twice been previously postponed for security reasons.

Panel to Probe Attack
The Modi government set up a panel to probe the attack on the temple. Addressing a press conference in Ahmedabad, Modi said that the attack was a conspiracy by an "enemy" country. He said whether it was the December 13, 2001 attack on the Indian Parliament or the temple, the motive behind it was only one -- to destabilize India. The probe committee was headed by Director General of Police K. Chakravarthy, and asked to look into all aspects of the attack, including the logistical support provided to the two terrorists who carried it out. The terrorists, who were killed by security forces, did not appear to be locals. Modi further said that there were two identical letters in Urdu placed in the pockets of the slain terrorists, and that they were aimed at misleading the investigations. He complimented the security personnel for their swift and courageous action.

Modi announced a reward of a hundred thousand rupees ($2,200) for anyone providing information about the terrorists, and a compensation of one million rupees ($22,000) to the next of kin of each of the three security personnel killed in the operation. The twenty-three security personnel injured in the attack would get fifty thousand rupees each ($1,100). Compensation for the civilians killed would be according to government norms.

Within three days of the attack, investigators identified the slain militants as Mohammad Amjad Bhai from Lahore (Pakistan), and Hafiz Yasir from Attock (Pakistan). The two had hired a private taxi from Kalupur railway station in Ahmedabad. After hearing of the attacks in Akshardham, the taxi driver Raju Thakur voluntarily approached the police and told about the two passengers that he had dropped off at the temple.

Thakur and the owner of the taxi identified the terrorists from photographs, and they were later taken to the hospital cold room where they saw and identified the bodies of the terrorists. The terrorists paid a fare of 120 rupees ($3) to cover the twenty kilometers from the railway station to the temple. On September 28, 2002, four days after the attacks, Deputy Prime Minister Advani said that going by the signs and pattern of the attacks -- the arms used, and the dry fruits in the possession of the terrorists -- the Akshardham attack appeared to be the handiwork of Pakistan-based *Lashkar-e-Toiba*, an internationally banned terrorist outfit.

The Election That Shaped Gujarat

Seven days after the attacks, the probe was making good but gradual progress. The police interrogated Hira Solanki, brother of Gujarat Minister of State for Fisheries Purushottam Solanki, who was present at the temple, and had fired at the terrorists from his licensed .9mm pistol, but could not kill them. Hira Solanki, a BJP MLA in the dissolved assembly, had kept presence of mind, and in an act of extreme bravery was the first armed man to confront the militants. As they were heavily armed, and he only had a pistol, Solanki could not be very effective. Had he managed to kill one or both of the militants, certainly the number of casualties would have been considerably fewer. During his two-hour long meeting with police personnel Solanki gave a detailed description of how on hearing gunshots, he rushed into the temple complex through Gate 6 and opened fire on the terrorists with his pistol.

The investigators also recorded more statements, including those of the police personnel and SRP commandos who were among the first to reach the spot. As dry fruits were found on the body of the militants, and as they were the primary food stuff found in the stomachs of the militants during post-mortem, it was clear that they had purchased them in a planned manner for a long haul.

Protests Mark Attack

There were two *bandhs* (general strike) -- one called by the Congress in much haste on the very next day of the attack -- and the other an All India Bandh called by the VHP, and the Shiv-Sena. During both the *bandhs*, life came to a standstill, as people showed solidarity with the victims of the Akshardham attack. The Congress Party *bandh* was primarily limited to Ahmedabad. In the Muslim-stronghold Shahpur area of Ahmedabad, shops and business establishments remained closed, with people preferring to stay indoors.

The next day was the *Bharat bandh* or an All-India general strike. The previous day's Congress *bandh* was localized, while the VHP-sponsored *bandh* brought life to a standstill all over Gujarat, even as police, paramilitary forces and army units maintained tight surveillance in sensitive urban areas of Ahmedabad, Surat and Vadodara. Though the ruling BJP did not support the VHP-sponsored *bandh*, its cadres were active in ensuring the success of the protest. Public buses stayed off the roads. Vehicular movement was minimal. Communally- sensitive localities of Dariapur, Mirzapur, Shahpur, Astodia and Kalupur in Ahmedabad, and the main bazaars were closed. People preferred to live out the *bandh* staying indoors.

BJP's Anti-Terrorism Day

To denounce the gruesome attack on the Akshardham temple, the BJP decided to organize a nation-wide "Anti-Terrorist Day" on October 1, 2002. BJP president Venkaiah Naidu, addressing the media, appealed to the people to "speak in one voice against the menace of terrorism". He also appealed to the international community to take "serious cognizance of the diabolical designs of Pakistan" and realize that the Islamic Republic of Pakistan was an "established headquarters of terrorism".

Naidu added, "It is ironical that Pakistan on the one hand claims to be a member of the international coalition against terrorism, while on the other it unabashedly patronizes terrorism… It is time now to take further steps for totally eliminating and wiping out the terrorist menace from the country". Naidu claimed that the Government of India had succeeded on the diplomatic front by isolating Pakistan in the international arena, and that the world was increasingly realizing the threat to global peace and security from Pakistan-based terrorists.

Musharraf's Provocative Statement at the UN

The attack on Akshardham was aimed at disturbing the fragile peace in Gujarat. It seems ironic that the attack on Akshardham took place just a few days after General Musharraf spoke of Godhra in the U.N. General Assembly. While the Godhra train attack may have been the handiwork of local Muslims instigated by agencies across the border, the Akshardham attack was clearly not the work of local Muslims. One of the reasons that the attack on Akshardham did not result in large scale anti-Muslim riots was due to this perception.

On September 27, 2002, in an attempt to further provoke India, Musharraf claimed that the Akshardham attack was a revenge attack by local Muslims. Asked if he thought that India would invade Pakistan to destroy terrorist training facilities there, Musharraf as usual denied the presence of such facilities in his country, and said that anything was possible, but if India invaded, Pakistan was prepared to respond.

Calls for Peace

Indian leaders appealed to the citizens of Gandhinagar and Gujarat to maintain peace and communal harmony. Advani rushed to Gandhinagar, his parliamentary constituency. He said that the attack on Akshardham temple was to divert attention from the outcome of assembly elections in Jammu and Kashmir, which had gone in India's favor. Adding, "I see a deliberate design in it," he said that terrorists wanted to divide Indians along religious lines, and appealed to the people of Gujarat to maintain peace. Terming it as a continuing war in which there will be battle after battle, Advani said that India had no option but to wage this war against terrorism.

Prime Minister Vajpayee, then on a visit to the Maldives, said that his government was strong enough to tackle the scourge of terrorism. He cut short his visit to the Maldives and returned to India a few hours ahead of schedule, flying directly to Ahmedabad from Male, the capital of Maldives.

The BJP described the terrorist attack on the Swaminarayan temple as a "frustrated reaction" of Pakistan following the successful assembly polls in Jammu and Kashmir. It urged the people of Gujarat to exercise restraint and defeat Islamabad's conspiracy to disrupt communal harmony in the country.

The National Commission for Minorities strongly condemned the terrorist attack on Akshardham temple. In a written note, the NCM appealed to people of Gujarat to maintain unity and harmony "in this hour of crisis". Several Indian Muslim leaders also expressed outrage at the incident. The Movement for Empowerment of Muslim Indians said that the "attack on innocent devotees cannot be justified under any circumstances". Muslim organizations demanded that the government take all necessary steps to safeguard innocent lives and appealed to people not to play into the hands of evil forces, and thereby promote Pakistani designs. The outrage that followed Godhra sent a very strong message that people in India expected their Muslim brethren to stand besides them in an hour of crisis. The quick response of the Muslim leaders in condemning the Akshardham temple attack and standing side-by-side with Hindus was one reason that no riots broke out after the temple attack.

President Kalam termed the attack a cowardly act intended to destroy India's secular fabric. A statement added that the President prayed that all strength be given to the suffering devotees and also to the Swamijis (monks) of the temple. In this moment of anguish, Dr. Kalam said, he would appeal to the people of India, especially those of Gujarat, to maintain peace. He said, "We should unitedly defeat all the evil designs against our great country which lives and shines through the civilizational heritage of our nation and the tolerance of our people".

There was international condemnation of this barbaric act. The United States and Britain condemned the attack. New Jersey Governor McGreevey in a statement said that he was personally saddened by the attack, since it took place at the world renowned Akshardham temple that he had visited during his trip to India in 2000. Governor McGreevey requested New Jerseyans to remember the victims and families in their prayers. New Jersey has the third largest number of people of Indian origin, and that is reflected in the significant political presence of Indians at various levels of government. Kiran Desai, Deputy Vice Chair of the state's Democratic Committee, met with McGreevey immediately after the news of the terrorist strike reached the U.S. Desai said that the attack was a scar not only on Gujarat but on the entire nation.

The Hindu Swayamsevak Sangh, having 50 chapters throughout the U.S., asked Indians to "refrain from any acts of retribution" while calling upon legal authorities to identify the terrorists and "investigate their connections, if any, to international terrorist organizations and nations that support them."

Former security advisor Gill asked Gujarat government to provide security to minorities in the wake of the attack on Akshardham temple. Gill said that an important task of the state government at that juncture was to ensure protection of the minorities. Keeping in view the sensitive communal situation, Gill further suggested that curfew should be imposed around the temple complex to prevent any kind of slogan-shouting, as it could take a "dangerous turn". The people of Gujarat responded to their government's call, and refrained from any communally violent actions. As a precautionary measure an army brigade was deployed in sensitive areas of Gujarat.

The leader of the pro-Hindu Shiv-Sena party issued a statement from Mumbai calling the attack on the Akshardham temple "one that crossed all limits". The VHP urged military action against Pakistan to destroy its terror network. On the eve of the VHP-sponsored *bandh*, Dr Pravin Togadiya, VHP's international general secretary, added that failure to declare war on Pakistan made the public wonder if India was serious about tackling terrorist menace.

The head of the Swaminarayan sect, Pramukh Swami Maharaj Shastri Narayan Swarupdas, appealed to people for peace and unity in the wake of the terrorist attack, calling the attack a national tragedy. After the Akshardham attack places of worship all over India were put on alert. Metal detectors and baggage scanners were installed in various places. Security was also tightened at the famous Mahabodhi temple at Bodh Gaya, where Lord Buddha attained enlightenment around 2,500 years ago.

Was it Intelligence Failure?

Was the attack on Akshardham an intelligence failure? It is always difficult for state agencies to have exact details and time of terrorist attacks, especially when these plans were hatched outside Indian borders in well protected complexes of the Pakistani establishment. Even the CIA with all its facilities, and money could not foresee the 9/11 attacks. India is densely populated, there are numerous ethnic/religious enclaves, police forces are limited, and it is impossible therefore to foresee each and every attack planned and carried out against a variety of targets.

Politicizing the Akshardham attack

On September 27, 2002 (a Friday), the Congress Party demanded that Article 356 be invoked and President's rule be imposed on Gujarat for "failing to prevent" the terrorist attack on Akshardham. Congress spokesman Abhishek Singhvi described the attack as a grave security lapse on part of the Gujarat government, which, he said, was so busy making arrangements for Modi's Gujarat Gaurav Yatra that it had not paid enough attention to other priorities. The BJP in turn accused Sonia Gandhi of soft-pedaling on the issue. Yet another Congress Party spokesman, Anand Sharma added that the Gujarat government "cannot put a veil on its misdeeds by repeatedly shifting and changing its stances and statements." When asked whether the Congress Party that had earlier tried to distance itself from what their Gujarat chief Shankar Sinh Vaghela was saying and his call for a state *bandh*, was now endorsing his stand, Anand Sharma said, "We had conveyed our anger. The *bandh* was to pre-empt the designs of the VHP". He added that the Congress Party had always treated the issue of cross-border terrorism from Pakistan as a national challenge.

While President Musharraf claimed that it was riots that triggered the attacks, Shankersinh Vaghela blamed Modi. Vaghela claimed that Modi's controversial utterances during his election campaign were responsible for the attack on the temple and charged the BJP government with plunging the prosperous state of Gujarat into an unprecedented communal mess. Addressing a meeting in Ahmedabad, Vaghela said, "The message found with the two slain militants made it clear that it was a reaction to the nonsense you (Modi) keep uttering."

Vaghela showed signs of typical Congress weakness, when he said, "Religion would have no meaning if the common people's survival was in question. Stop talking about religion; we are more interested in our survival." Apparently such statements were not to the liking of the people nor did they reflect the prevalent mood in Gujarat.

Akshardham Temple Reopens

Five days after the gruesome assault that shocked the nation the gates of Akshardham temple were thrown open to devotees for a special prayer session to pay homage to those killed by terrorists. The event, presided by Pramukh Swamiji, was attended by Modi, his predecessor Keshubhai Patel, and other VIPs. Hundreds of eager devotees, including relatives of the victims, sat cross-legged on the sprawling green lawns as security force personnel took strategic positions.

The Swaminarayan sect is a prayer sect, and does not believe in violence, and does not allow weapons inside its temples, but perhaps, for the first time in its history, uniformed gunmen were seen inside the temple complex during a prayer. Within a month closed circuit TV was installed in the temple, and the management decided to double the height of the compound walls from five to ten feet to make scaling it all the more difficult. The Government of Gujarat also increased its security cover, even as CRPF personnel camped outside the temple premises, along with temple volunteers.

Investigating the Akshardham Temple Attack

On August 30, 2003, the Guajrat police said it had arrested five persons hailing from the Muslim dominated Dariapur and Shahpur areas of Ahmedabad in connection with the terrorist attack. Interrogations revealed that the banned Pakistan based terrorist outfits *Jaish-e-Mohammed* (JeM) and *Lashkar-e-Toiba* (LeT) had masterminded the strike. The conspiracy was hatched sometime during the post-Godhra riots, and the five accused had provided logistical support to the two terrorists. The arrested were identified as Altaf Malek, Salim Sheikh, Abdul Miyan Sayyed (from Dariapur), Mufti Abdul Kayoom Mansuri, and Suleman Aadam Ajmeri (from Shahpur). Gujarat police had information about some local Muslim youths working in various parts of Saudi Arabia and closely collaborating with Pakistan's Inter-Services Intelligence, the JeM and LeT. They had visited Ahmedabad recently. Salim Sheikh revealed during interrogation that JeM and LeT terrorists involved him and a Riyadh-based person from Ahmedabad, Rashid Ajmeri.

Rashid Ajmeri in turn directed his brother Aadam, who was in Ahmedabad, to help the two terrorists. Police immediately nabbed Aadam Ajmeri from his home.

Interrogation revealed that Aadam Ajmeri was called to Hyderabad a week before the attack and briefed about the conspiracy by two men – Abu Talha and Ayub Khan, who told Ajmeri that two persons would come for the Akshardham operation from Pakistan. The Ahmedabad police commissioner said Aadam Ajmeri then contacted Mufti Abdul Kayoom Mansuri and Maulana Abdullah, who were then running a relief camp in Bawahir Hall in Dariapur area of Ahmedabad.

A week prior to the attack, Aadam Ajmeri received the two terrorists, identified as Hafiz Yasir from Lahore (previously thought to be from Attock) and Mohammed Farooq (previously thought to be Mohammad Amjadbhai from Lahore) from Rawalpindi, at the city railway station. Police also disclosed that the terrorists were shown the secretariat building as well the state assembly building, but considering the huge crowd and less resistance at Akshardham, they decided to target the temple instead.

To plan and carry out their attack they visited the temple twice for reconnaissance. On the day of the attack, they were four of them including Aadam Ajmeri and Ayub Khan, who went ahead of the terrorists, in an auto-rickshaw. The four had also surveyed other crowded places like the BJP office in Khanpur, VHP office in Paldi, the Bhadrakali Temple in Karanj and the Mahakali Temple in Dudheshwar.

The two locals, Ayub Khan and Aadam Ajmeri, positioned themselves near the temple before the terrorists arrived in a taxi. Police said that a few hours before launching the gruesome attack, Mufti Abdul Kayoom Mansoori administered the *namaz-e-shahadat* (prayer for martyrdom) to the two terrorists at a mosque in Kalupur. As previously planned, the terrorists stormed the temple through Gate number 3 at 1630 IST and seeing that the attack had started, Aadam Ajmeri and Ayub Khan fled the spot. Aadam Ajmeri then dropped Ayub Khan at a railway station in Kalupur area, from where he rented a taxi and fled south towards Vadodara City.

A local court in Gandhinagar remanded the five accused to fourteen days in police custody. They were produced in the court of Chief Judicial Magistrate S. H. Oza. Two of those arrested, Mufti Abdul Kayoom Mansuri and Maulana Abdullah are Muslim clerics who ran relief camps in Ahmedabad. The others were Salim Shaikh, Altaf Malek (both worked in Riyadh and allegedly hatched the conspiracy there) and Suleman Aadam Ajmeri.

Just three days after Gujarat police broke the news of the conspiracy, Jammu & Kashmir (J&K) police gave a different version. Rejecting the claims of the Gujarat police about the involvement of the terrorist group JeM in the Akshardham attacks, the J&K police on September 2, 2003 said that the attack was carried out solely by the LeT. Based on the interrogations of an illiterate Muslim mechanic Chand Khan from Bareilly in Uttar Pradesh, J&K police claimed that two LeT men from Pakistan, named Shakeel and Abdullah, had executed the entire operation. Mechanic Chand Khan had migrated from his hometown in Uttar Pradesh to Anantnag district in Kashmir in search of a job. In the Kashmiri town of Anantnag, he found work as a motor mechanic. While he was there, Khan came in contact with the two LeT operatives and agreed to assist them in their travel within India.

On September 19, 2002 Chand Khan left for Bareilly in U.P., with the two terrorists and his family in a LeT vehicle. After dropping his family home, he and the two terrorists traveled by bus to New Delhi and via Jaipur, they reached Ahmedabad, hiding their weapons in their bedding. The temple was attacked on September 24, 2002. Kashmir police insisted that their information was correct. Top officers of the intelligence establishment in Kashmir interrogated Chand Khan. The motor mechanic reaffirmed that the two terrorists killed in the Akshardham complex by security forces were Pakistanis.

Gujarat police were extremely cautious in accepting the confession of an illiterate, jobless mechanic, when it had evidence of a criminal conspiracy. Without local support it would have been extremely difficult to carry out such a complex operation. However, J&K police stuck to their guns, and on September 10, 2003 disclosed further that the conspiracy for carrying out the temple attack was hatched in the house of J&K Minister for Food and Shelter Abdul Aziz Zargar. According to the Press Trust of India, the report of the J&K police was based on the confessions of an alleged accomplice in the attack and the diary of a Pakistani militant.

The report disclosed that Chand Khan had claimed during interrogation that all the planning was done at the residence of Abdul Aziz Zargar and that the two suicide attackers of Lashkar-e-Toiba, including himself, started their journey for Gujarat from Abdul Aziz Zargar's residence. The residence of Abdul Aziz Zargar, who was elected a member of the state legislature from Noorabad constituency in Kulgam Tehsil, is located at Manzgam near Shopian in south Kashmir. The minister vehemently denied the accusation and any knowledge about the planning.

State police too denied any link between Abdul Aziz Zargar and LeT militants personally but added that militants used to frequent the minister's village. The report also cited a request by the minister after winning the elections, asking the police to withdraw the guard at his residence. The request was, however, cancelled after militants gunned down a PDP legislator Abdul Aziz Mir in Pampore.

The report quoted notes from a diary of a Pakistani militant, Zahoor Manzoor Chowdhury, which mentioned specific dates of meetings at the home of Abdul Aziz Zargar. Initially, it was this diary that led J&K security agencies to arrest Khan, who corroborated the diary entries. Developing leads on the Akshardham attack provided by the Intelligence Bureau, J&K police zeroed in on Chand Khan.

Chand Khan told interrogators that he had escorted the two LeT militants from Srinagar to Bareilly from where they boarded a train to Jaipur and later a bus to Ahmedabad. Khan also said that the two terrorists, who were killed by NSG commandos, had also planned to carry out an attack on the Gaurav Yatra. Chand Khan denied any role of the five persons arrested by Gujarat Police, and told the interrogators that there was no local support.

On September 11, 2003, Jammu &Kashmir Minister for Agriculture Abdul Aziz Zargar resigned on moral grounds as his name was linked to the Akshardham attack. Earlier, Zargar denied the allegations that he had anything to do with the terrorists. He said, "I decided to submit my resignation to the Chief Minister of J&K as a campaign has been launched against me. I don't know of any conspiracy and the charges are baseless."

On September 24, 2003 the first anniversary of the Akshardham attacks, Gujarat police reiterated its claim that the sensational attack was carried out at the behest of Pakistan's Inter Services Intelligence jointly by the Jaish-e-Mohammad (JeT) and Lashkar-e-Toiba (LeT). Joint Commissioner of Police C. P. Pandey said LeT terrorist Chand Khan had lied to the J&K police about his guiding the two terrorists. Arrested in J&K, Chand Khan concocted the story of his involvement, but on the basis of documentary evidence available to them and information revealed during the interrogation of Chand Khan, Gujarat police concluded that their version of the plot was more credible.

Concept of *Shahada*

To understand the attack on the Akshardham temple and the terrorist attacks worldwide by those proclaiming their Islamic faith, we need to study closely the Koranic concept of "*Shahada*" or martyrdom. This, scholars of Islam and terrorism experts claim, is the reason why certain Muslims kill themselves fighting for a cause that they think is based upon the tenets of Islam.[196] Data indicate that about two-thirds of the Palestinian "suicide bombers" were devout Muslims.

"We love death, as much as you love life", is a famous statement of a Khalifa who attacked the Byzantine empire, and defeated an army more than three times the size of his own army. This love for death and the "wonders" of the after-life are psychological methods that are used to convince people to die. That the "*shaheed*" (martyr) will get seventy-two black-eyed virgins, and piles of rice in Heaven, are commonly used scenarios in the psychological factory of suicide bombers.

The motivation may be different for different people, but a human being needs to be strengthened psychologically to face his own death, or bravely withstand the horrors of war, or kill another human being whom he does not even know. The bosses of terror, who cleverly use religious dogma to further their own objectives, misinterpret the tenets of religion. Hence more important than the psychology of the suicide bomber is the psychology of the organization to which he belongs. No suicide bomber operates alone. No one just cherishes to become a suicide bomber, and carries out the operation all by himself. It is the organization that recruits, trains, mentally brainwashes the

---

[196] Cook, D., & Allison, O. (2007). *Understanding and Addressing Suicide Attacks: The Faith and Politics of Martyrdom Operations*. Praeger SecurityInternational.

susceptible youths, gives them money, manufactures the explosives, chooses the target, and escorts the suicide-bomber to the target. The organization also takes care of the family of the suicide bomber. It is well-oiled machinery that produces suicide-bombers either in Palestine or in Pakistan.[197]

Some have argued that the Israeli handling of the Palestinian issue has aggravated the situation in that region and driven numerous Palestinian Muslim youth towards suicide bombings. However, studies indicate that only a very small fraction of suicide bombers had spent some time in an Israeli jail, or had a member of their immediate or extended family killed or hurt by the Israeli forces. Hence personal grudge or revenge could certainly not be a major motivation for suicide bombings. Motivation at times is religion, at times nationalism, and at times augmentation in one's social status. We should also not ignore the role that media plays in all these matters.

A Palestinian youth, who joins a martyr organization, almost instantly finds his status in the Palestinian society going up. His family gets more respect. The young in his village adore him. Some drift into the terrorist organization and find warmth, friendship and esteem there. His social standing undergoes a complete illusionary metamorphosis. Suddenly, he is an important person in his village, for he is going to die for a cause – the cause of Palestine or the cause of Islam. Once the young man joins the organization there is no way of coming out of it without losing his self-respect and public dignity.

Palestinian television chat-shows eulogize suicide bombers. Their pictures are pasted on city walls and buses. Chat-show experts mystify the last moments of the suicide bomber by explaining how he feels the presence of Allah, and does not feel any pain. Young children in Palestine play a game called "*Shahid-Shahid*". The Palestinian children are groomed early in the concept of "*Shahada*". These strategies and schemes used by the leaders and clerics effectively convert normal, ordinary human beings into human bombs.[198]

The Nazis indoctrinated an entire generation through the art of effective propaganda, and now certain elements in the name of Islam are doing the same. It does not matter whether it is Palestine or Pakistan, the methodology is similar, and the results almost identical. Organizations producing suicide bombers may be Arabic or Tamil like the LTTE, but are determined to challenge or even obliterate civilized human existence. These organizations take away the childhood and youth of innocent Muslims and kill innocent Jews, Hindus and Christians all in the name of a perverted understanding of religion. Monotheistic faiths claiming monopolistic domain over human spiritual matters make it easy for extremist elements to pervert these faiths. It is high time that

---

[197] Hoffman, B. (June 2003). "The Logic of Suicide Terrorism". *The Atlantic*.

[198] Weiner, J. R. (2003). "Palestinian Children and the New Cult of Martyrdom". Harvard Israel Review.

the moderates and the learned in the Islamic world come out vocally and aggressively against these organizations that have hijacked their religion.

Countermeasures against suicide bombings will succeed if there is a change in public attitude. The terrorist factories in Pakistan and Palestine must be shut down, and their instigators put behind bars if civilized human existence has to endure, and to ensure that no more Akshardham like attacks occur in future. Terrorism is a global threat, and the blurry logic used by "progressives" to draw false analogies about various struggles for independence and freedom should not lead to confusion about religion-inspired violence.

That the Akshardham Temple attack took place in the context of and close to the elections planned for the State Assembly showed the willingness of India's religion-inspired neighbor to push Indians to the brink, and to engender further strife in the sub- continent.

CHAPTER XXIV -- TICKET DISTRIBUTION

India is the largest democracy and the United States the most powerful democracy in the world. These two countries situated on the opposite sides of the planet are unique in their own ways, and yet in many ways similar. Both are multi-cultural, multi-ethnic nations. The United States is a nation of many nations, while India is a single nation with many social traditions, a thousand languages, and infinite diversity that has been attracting the attention of people since the past five thousand years and more.

Though both India and the United States are democracies their forms of government and election processes are quite different. The Indian election exercise is based upon the Westminster model of the United Kingdom. India is a bicameral prime ministerial system at the center, and a chief ministerial system in the states, while the United States is a governor-based system of an active and executive President heading the federal government, and governors heading the state governments.

In the United States, citizens who are not convicted of felony can contest and register to vote for elections (with some variation across states). Electioneering process consists of two main parts -- the primary and the general election. Any person contesting a primary has to get votes either from the voters registered as Republicans, or from those registered as Democrats, or third party registered voters, say the Green party. The primary is a unique U.S. institution, born in the era of political reform at the beginning of the 20th century.

Primaries give the opportunity to political parties to see which of the candidates is most favored by their registered voters. Winner of the primaries from each party then contests the general election as the particular party's candidate. Hence the American system gives freedom to all, whether well-known and powerful, or a new entrant, to contest the primaries and prove their worth or following and win, and then contest the general elections.

Not all citizens of the political constituency can vote, however. Only those who have registered themselves as voters have the right to vote. At the time of registration voters have to declare their affiliation, i.e. whether they are Democrat, Republican, independent or favor a third party (in states with "closed primaries"). Once their affiliation is registered, they can vote only for the candidate of their party in the primaries (with some exceptions). Thus if a person is registered as a Democrat, then he or she is entitled to vote for a Democrat candidate only in the primaries, unless it is an "open primary" state, like Georgia or Mississippi, where a registered Democrat can vote in the Republican primary and vice versa.

Prior to the elections, each party tries to get as many voters registered as it can owing allegiance to it. Then in the primaries each party's voters vote for candidates from that particular party, and the winner of the party's primary then contests the main election. Thus primaries are not a contest between two rival parties, but a contest

Ticket Distribution

between rivals within the same party. On the day of election, each party tries to get the maximum number of its voters to vote, with the winner becoming the public representative. The general election is a contest between rival parties.

In the U.S., if you are a citizen 18 years of age or older, you do not necessarily have the right to vote for presidential candidates in the national election. When citizens punch their ballots for President, they actually vote for a slate of electors. Electors then cast the votes that decide who becomes the President of the United States. Usually, electoral votes align with the popular vote in an election. American founding fathers thought that the use of electors would give the country a representative president, and avoid a corruptible national election.

In India, the process is very different. There are no primaries. People come out to vote only once for each election. Most people do not have to register themselves. The Election Commission of India does the laborious work of compiling the lists of voters through the office of the district collectors, the administrative chiefs of areas akin to a group of counties in the U.S. Counties in the U.S. can be compared to *talukas* in India. A group of *talukas* makes a district. And a group of districts makes a state. There are over five hundred such district collector offices spread across the country. Electoral rolls are revised every year. Additions, subtractions, and objections are noted and the voters' list revised. If one does not find his/her name in the voters' list before the deadline for revision, then he/she will have to register as a voter.

Any citizen of India can contest elections. There is no hindrance. Even felons are permitted to contest elections, provided their sentence is not imprisonment for more than two years. Nevertheless, your franchise can never be taken away. It is a fundamental right given by the Constitution of India, and hence even felons have a right to vote.

People usually contest elections as candidates of well-known political parties. There is no limit at present on the number of political parties in India. Some estimate there are over 1,500 political parties in India. There are parties, as also their breakaway factions, and break away factions of these factions, and so on. Hence, if there was the Janata Dal Party (JD) once, now we have several factions named Rashtriya Janata Dal Party (RJD), Janata Dal (United) Party (JD-U), Janata Dal (Secular) Party (JD-S), Biju Janata Dal (JD-Biju), and the Samajwadi Janata Dal Party (SJP).

It may seem strange to a foreign observer but democracy in India is truly complex. It is possible that while Janata Dal (United) Party may be a part of the coalition government and therefore in power, Janata Dal (Secular) Party may be in the opposition. The Janata Dal emerged as a strong third option opposed to BJP's nationalist views, and the Congress Party's Nehruvian view of state atheism. The strongest versions of the Janata Dal in 2003 were the Samata Party of George Fernandes (India's Defense Minister in the NDA Government) and Nitish Kumar (the Railway Minister in the NDA Government who is now, in 2014, the Chief Minister of Bihar, and a strong and vocal opponent of the BJP, after he broke up with the BJP in

June 2013). The Samata Party was primarily a Bihar based party. The Janata Dal (United) of Sharad Yadav was also an alliance partner of the ruling coalition, while the RJD of Lalu Prasad Yadav was the ruling party in Bihar. Due to various corruption cases slapped against Laloo Prasad Yadav, he maneuvered to make his wife the Chief Minister of Bihar. Power after all is harnessed to remain within the family. If this makes the reader's head spin, it is no more complex than the American system that allows for primaries, caucuses, electoral colleges, and such other "experiments" in democracy.[199]

Two other surviving versions of the Janata Dal family are the Samajwadi Party (SP), primarily a party that attracts Muslim voters and provides voice to their needs. The SP continues to be headed by Mulayam Singh Yadav. Finally, there is the Bahujan Samaj Party (BSP). , a *Dalit* leader, is the chief of BSP. It is a party that regards the lower castes to be its main voters. The BSP-BJP coalition was a formidable force, and was in power till 2012, heading the government of India's most populous state of Uttar Pradesh.

Similarly, the breakaway factions of the Congress Party are the Nationalist Congress Party (NCP) headed by the Maratha strongman Sharad Pawar from Maharashtra, who walked out of the Congress on the issue of the foreign origin of Sonia Gandhi, the Trinamool Congress Party (headed by Mamta Banerjee from West Bengal), the Goa Rajiv Congress Party (which later merged with the NCP), and Moopanar's South India based Tamil Maanila Congress. P. Chidambaram, finance minister in the UPA-led Central Government, is one of its members. Parties of Congress origin subscribe to an ideology popularly known as Nehruvian secularism.

Indian Communists also have break away factions like the Communist Party of India – Leninist (CPI-L), the Communist Party of India – Marxist (CPI-M), the Communist Party of India – both Leninist and Marxist (CPI-ML). These parties subscribe to Communism and its many versions.

The Tamil Nadu based Dravidian parties are also many like the Dravida Munnetra Kazhagam (DMK), All India Anna Dravida Munnetra Kazhagam (AIADMK), Marumalarchi Dravida Munnetra Kazhagam (MDMK), and the Pattali Makkal Kachi (PMK), to name a few.

The Bharatiya Janata Party is also the child of a breakaway group of the 1980s. The Janata Party emerged as the main opposition party to the Congress Party in 1977 after Indira Gandhi revoked the state of internal emergency she had imposed on the country between 1975 and 1977. The Janata Party, basically cobbled together from a variety of parties opposing the Congress Party, romped home to victory in the 1977 elections, and

---

[199] Note: The Janata Dal [United] was formed with the merger of the Sharad Yadav faction of the Janata Dal, the Lokshakti Party and the Samata Party on October 30, 2003.

Ticket Distribution

Morarji Desai became its first Prime Minister. Atal Bihari Vajpayee was the Foreign Minister at that time. The Janata Party broke apart while the BJP took birth on April 6, 1980. The BJP itself split in Gujarat, leading to the formation of the Rashtriya Janata Party (RJP).

The Election Commission of India has specified norms for recognition of parties and their symbols. Hence parties garnering a specified number of votes on a national basis are categorized as a national party, and those getting a specified number of votes at the state level are recognized as a state party, while the remaining parties are known as unrecognized parties. People not owing any affiliation to any party can also contest elections as "Independents". To get a ticket to contest elections from a national or state party effectively means winning the right to contest the election using the election symbols of that party. To get a party's symbol, you need a letter from the president of that particular party. Usually, it is a symbol that the illiterate and the old readily recognize. The symbols thus make the difference between victory and defeat. No two candidates can contest on the same symbol in the same elections at the same time, and from the same constituency. The symbol of the Congress party is a hand/palm, while that of the BJP is the lotus. Use of religious symbols is prohibited, and candidates are not permitted to canvass for votes on religious grounds.

To get a party's ticket means to become that party's official candidate for elections from a particular constituency. But getting a ticket is no easy task. One has to prove one's worth to the party, or have a "god-father" on whose recommendation one could get a ticket to contest from a winnable constituency. It is more difficult to get an election ticket for a constituency that is a sure win than a constituency that brings defeat. Political parties are always on the lookout for star performers and campaigners who can win seats. For this reason film stars and television actors are hot commodities that every party scouts for in elections. Actors and actresses like in America are popular in India too. If it is no wonder that Arnold Schwarzenegger could become the governor and Ronald Reagan the president for two terms, it is not surprising that several actors have entered the political arena in India, with a couple of them becoming Chief Ministers of powerful states. The only time when a prominent super-star lost a direct parliamentary election from an urban constituency was when Rajesh Khanna contested against BJP stalwart L.K. Advani from South Delhi constituency, and lost by a narrow margin of 1,500 votes. Rajesh Khanna was a "super star" and if it were not for the experience and popularity of Advani, Khanna would have easily won.

As victory and defeat are dependent on party symbols and tickets, and party bosses have tremendous clout over ticket distribution. Their words are final. Sometimes more than the candidate's qualifications his or her potential to cause damage is weighed. Candidates who have a greater damage potential are pampered and pacified. Docile and new candidates seldom get the opportunity to prove their mettle.

Once a person gets the party's ticket, it becomes his or her job to win the election. The party may provide some limited funding in certain cases, but most of the time the candidates have to fend for themselves. Candidates at local level and for state elections usually win on local and developmental issues, while candidates for federal elections win on nationalistic appeal or through personal charisma. Political ideology rarely comes into play except to make specific promises to specific sectarian interests.

In the 2002 state elections in Gujarat, the issue was only one: Narendra Modi. In a few months, from being a new and the youngest Chief Minister of Gujarat, Modi was relegated to the "hall of shame", and portrayed as secular India's "enemy number one". Godhra and its aftermath shook the conscience of the nation and scared the Muslims. Of course, Modi happened to be the Chief Minister at that time: if Godhra could not have been prevented, its aftermath too could not have been prevented. Just as Clinton or anyone else could not have stopped the 9/11 attacks if they were in office instead of George W. Bush, similarly the Godhra attack could not have been thwarted if someone else was the Chief Minister of Gujarat. Just like blaming President Bush for 9/11 does not make sense, blaming Modi for the Godhra tragedy and the post-Godhra anti-Muslim riots too does not make sense.

Election Antics and Accusations

In July 2002, Congress Party's Gujarat president Shankersinh Vaghela announced he would not contest the elections. Vaghela was already a Member of Parliament, and so did not want to lose his parliamentary seat fearing that the magic of Modi would take that seat also from him. This, however, was not the official reason given for his not contesting the elections. He portrayed himself as a self-sacrificing politician, and urged Congress Party's state leaders to sink their differences to take on the ruling BJP in the ensuing polls.

In August 2002, it was alleged that Haren Pandya told the "Concerned Citizens' Tribunal", a group consisting of retired judges and administrators as well as other activists, that Modi had asked the police not to apprehend people who wanted to avenge the Godhra massacre. The BJP denounced this allegation immediately as mischievous and false. State BJP president Rana asked Pandya for clarification. Pandya's reply conveyed through the media said that he had not deposed before the Concerned Citizens' Tribunal, claiming that "I don't understand your reason to seek my clarification about reports which have not even named me.... Somebody insisting on my explanation on the basis of baseless information is harmful for the party. And this is why I send this clarification through the media."

Modi and his party did not like Pandya publicly denouncing Modi. He was asked to apologize or resign from the ministry. Pandya chose the latter. The Pandya-Modi quarrel reached a finale when the party denied him ticket, which went to someone else contesting in his place. Pandya chose to be spiteful, and Modi responded by putting his foot down. Such intra-party conflict and personality politics have been major reasons for unstable governments, poor governance, and frequent elections in India. Add to the mix a government machinery that can be easily manipulated by elected representatives – transfers of police officers, IAS officers, and others heading government institutions immediately after a new government takes office is both accepted and expected – and then you have the ugly combination of personality politics and a subservient bureaucracy. Modi had to brave and stave off threats to his power and position more from within his party than from the opposition in the initial stages. After all, it was only five months after he became the Chief Minister that the Godhra massacre took place, and he therefore had little time to consolidate his position, clean up the house, and get administrators of his choice.

Meanwhile, early in November 2002, George Fernandes' Samata Party, and Sharad Yadav's Janata Dal (United), both BJP's coalition partners in the federal government, announced that they would contest Gujarat elections on their own and not as NDA partners. For 182 seats in the state legislature, the Samata Party would field 50 candidates in the Saurashtra, Kutch, Central and South Gujarat regions, while JD (U) would field 20 to 25 candidates. Shambhu Shrivastava, Samata's spokesperson, said, "We will have no alliance with BJP in Gujarat. There will be no common manifesto or program. We will have our own manifesto and they will have their own." Union Minister Sharad Yadav of JD (U) said that his party had contested the previous assembly election in Gujarat on its own and four of its candidates had won.

About a month and a half before the election, the BJP got its act together and held a series of meetings with state leaders to know their views about possible candidates. Prior to these meetings Modi asked one of his young lieutenants to make a comprehensive report on each and every constituency, the number of possible candidates, their strengths and weaknesses, and extrapolate their "winnability" index to give him a better micro-picture of local politics. This was extremely confidential and laborious work. His lieutenants planned a quadruple approach: first, they would gather views of the local electorates, actual people who were going to vote. A previous survey had summarized people's views on each and every possible candidate. Second, views of local party leaders were also sought. Third, interaction with government officials at the district level generated a different collage of views. Lastly, the police machinery at the local level was informally asked for its views. Thus, from this unique quadruple-level survey, Modi's assistants were able to weave together a complex but extremely realistic picture of the political reality. The report was considered so confidential that only one copy of it was made and given personally to the Chief Minister. The hard-disk of the computer was later formatted so that under no circumstance could the report be replicated.

Modi's desire to govern, his supporters say, is guided by his pragmatic and practical approach to situations. He was now well-armed with detailed reports about each prospective candidate. Modi thus knew more than what the candidates knew about their prospects.

BJP spokesman Arun Jaitley announced that the meetings were a part of the exercise to distribute tickets and that state leaders would discuss the report of district units for this purpose. He also said that the state election committee would meet on November 10, 2002 in Gandhinagar to begin selection of candidates. Officially, the selection would be based on reports given by the state's local leaders at the conclusion of the three-day meeting.

About the same time, the Congress Party also held meetings at Mount Abu. The two-day Congress conclave was aimed not only at Gujarat but also to evaluate prospects of coming back to power in New Delhi. But in reality the Congress Party was much disturbed by the huge success and public support that Modi and his *Gujarat Gaurav Yatra* (GGY) were receiving. The people of Gujarat were coming out in huge numbers to see the man the opposition hated and blamed.

Modi's first public meeting after the announcement of elections, and the enforcement of the model code of conduct, was at Karamsad, the birth place of Vallabhbhai Patel. The Congress Party and its apologists were caught on the wrong foot. Sardar Patel, notwithstanding his differences with Nehru, was after all a leader of the Congress Party, and here was Modi capitalizing on Patel's name. To counter Modi's salvo, the Congress Party too decided to launch its election campaign from Karamsad lest Gujaratis conclude that the Congress Party did not respect Sardar Patel or his memory.

The alleged decline in support for the BJP in the powerful Patel community due to the Modi-Keshubhai Patel feud made the Gujarat unit of the Congress Party happy. Attributing this alienation of the powerful Patels to the sidelining of Keshubhai Patel in the BJP, the Congress described Modi's recent claim to Sardar Patel's legacy as a gimmick to win back the Patel community's sympathy.

Immediately following the Mount Abu conclave, the Congress decided to drop at least 10 to 12 of its incumbent legislators in the state assembly. The central election committee of the Congress party then finalized candidates for 75 out of 182 seats for the December 12 elections. The election committee met again on November 16 to finalize names for the remaining seats but preferred to wait for strategic reasons for the BJP to name its candidates for at least 35 of the 182 seats.

The BJP too had problems of its own. The tussle between Keshubhai Patel and Narendra Modi began to delay BJP's candidate list. As a fall-out of this tussle, Modi announced that it was possible for him to prepare a tentative list of prospective candidates by the November 16 deadline set by BJP's central leadership. This contradicted the statement issued by BJP president Venkaiah Naidu who had earlier announced in Delhi that a list of candidates would be finalized at a meeting on November 16 of the party's election committee headed by Vajpayee. After Modi's announcement, the proposed meeting was postponed.

On his part, Modi attributed the delay in finalizing the list to the India-West Indies one-day international cricket match scheduled in Ahmedabad, and his preoccupation

Ticket Distribution

with the *Gujarat Gaurav Yatra*. Modi, however, clarified that he had taken into consideration others' views, and had extensive meetings with partymen at the district level. He assured that the lists would be ready well before the last date for filing nominations.

An unofficial version indicated that Keshubhai Patel demanded a large share of seats for his own supporters. The RSS and its affiliates that had played a key role in building Modi's image as a "Hindu icon" now demanded their share of the spoils and were lobbying for candidates of their choice in several key constituencies. Without a consensus, Modi was unable to make an announcement. He heard everyone, got detailed reports prepared, and presented them to the concerned people, and wanted to be fair in ticket distribution, without accommodating the over-sized baggage of Keshubhai's supporters.

Notwithstanding the tussle within the BJP, the Congress Party declared names of its candidates for 140 out of 182 seats. It announced that the Central Election Committee had authorized Sonia Gandhi to choose candidates for the remaining 42 seats. The Congress Party too had its share of party in-fighting, with state party leaders alleging nepotism in the nomination process. Disgruntled party workers complained that people with connections to senior leaders but with scant grass-roots support got tickets. Senior party leaders tried for tickets for their own kin and clan. Shankersinh Vaghela recommended his son Mahendrasinh for the Sami-Harij constituency. While the deceased chief minister Chimanbhai Patel's son Siddharth, a member of the dissolved assembly, sought a ticket from the Dabhoi constituency, former chief minister Madhavsinh Solanki's son Bharat was equally keen on getting a re-nomination from the Borsad constituency. To be fair, both Bharat and Siddharth were capable of winning, and were asking for tickets not just because their fathers were senior Congress leaders. Congress party's former chief minister and tribal leader Amarsinh Chaudhary too wanted his son Tushar Chaudhary be given nomination, helping him launch his political career in the upcoming elections. Narsinh Makvana, a Congress leader from the backward castes sought nomination for his son from Bavla constituency in the Saurashtra region of Gujarat.

A *Koli* (fisherman community) leader of the Congress, Savashi Makvana, and his relatives tried to get nominated from Chotila assembly constituency in Saurashtra. The *Koli* community forms substantial sections of the electorate in twelve to fifteen constituencies, and so their votes are deemed extremely important considering caste equations. From the town of Bhavnagar, the *Kshatriya* leader Kiritsinh Gohil lobbied ferociously for his son Mahavirsinh for the Ghogha seat. Congress leader B.K. Gadhvi's son Mukesh Gadhvi sought nomination from Banaskantha region. Poll equations in India have become complex by the day, and it takes a courageous, clever, and canny leadership to steer the party towards something like a consensus on these issues.

The "all in the family" dynastic concept is not new to the Congress Party Jawaharlal

The Election That Shaped Gujarat

Nehru became the first Prime Minister of independent India; his daughter Indira Gandhi (no relation of Mahatma Gandhi) followed suit; her son Rajiv Gandhi grabbed the mantle of leadership after Indira Gandhi's assassination, and later his wife Sonia Maino-Gandhi (of Italian descent) became president of the Congress Party, and was projected as the party's choice for Prime Minister in the event of the Congress Party winning and heading the government in 2004. The sacrifices made by the Nehru-Gandhi family are indeed tremendous but the dynastic rule continues, with Priyanka and Rahul Gandhi, children of Sonia Gandhi, being "groomed" to succeed her. How then can the ordinary Congressman remain behind? When everyone is all for himself, why should the father not lobby for the son? Even the BJP has embraced this grand tradition. So, there was the instance of Keshubhai Patel's son seeking a BJP ticket from Visavadar constituency in Saurashtra.

Seeing that the BJP meetings in Gujarat did not produce a consensus, the party leaders met in New Delhi at the residence of the Prime Minister, with the party president Venkaiah Naidu chairing the meeting. All the BJP stalwarts were present, including Modi, Keshubhai Patel, Advani, Parliamentary Affairs Minister Pramod Mahajan, External Affairs Minister Jaswant Singh, former BJP president Kushbhau Thakre, Gujarat state unit president Rajendersinh Rana and his predecessor and former finance minister Vajubhai Vala.

After a long wait, and extended discussions between state leaders that went well into the early hours of the morning, Modi and Keshubhai reached an agreement, and in the end the BJP announced its first list of 144 candidates for the 182 seats. This list included two former MPs, three former MLAs, ten who belonged to the Scheduled Castes category, twenty-six to the Scheduled Tribes category, and eight women. To pacify Keshubhai Patel, the BJP acceded to most of his demands and a large number of candidates belonging to the Patel caste were accommodated.

The most dramatic outcome was Modi getting the party nomination from Maninagar constituency in Ahmedabad. He had previously contested from Rajkot-II constituency. Rajkot is a Patel stronghold, and Modi did not want to take any chances. During his early days in the RSS, Modi had lived and worked extensively in Maninagar. If at all any place was Modi's home in his early days, then it was surely Maninagar. Seven people filed nominations from this assembly constituency. The place had witnessed communal riots in the aftermath of the Godhra massacre, and had over 20,000 voters from the minority Muslim community. Maninagar was severely hit during the devastating earthquake that struck Gujarat in 2001. A school building had collapsed killing many children.

However, even the high profile meeting at the Prime Minister's residence could not make Modi agree to give a ticket to Haren Pandya. Hence the former Home Minister's name, a known detractor of Modi, did not figure in BJP's first list. The party kept the nomination to Pandya's Ellisbridge assembly constituency open, and also did not name its candidate for the Visavadar constituency in Junagadh district held by Keshubhai Patel. Patel had refused to accept a ticket for his son to contest the elections following a row with Modi. The clash of the BJP titans continued.

It was the prevalent view at the party that Keshubhai Patel was capable of inflicting considerable damage to the party's chances. Hence, the party tried to woo the estranged Patel leader. To pacify him, the BJP offered a ticket to his son, but Keshubhai angrily turned it down. It was expected that Patel's son would be declared as party nominee in the second list.

Somehow, decision makers in the BJP were not ready to accept the truth of the tremendous popularity of Narendra Modi. With the luxury of hindsight, Modi, with or without Keshubhai Patel, would have won. He had become the icon of Gujarati pride and had played his cards right. Yet Modi needed the party machinery to function at the grass-roots level without hindrance, and so the BJP tried to pacify Keshubhai Patel. By November 20 the BJP released its second list with an additional eleven names, bringing the total number of nominations to 155 for the 182 assembly seats. Haren Pandya's name did not figure even in this second list. Speculation ran high, and all eyes were focused on the Modi-Pandya issue. If Modi won, it would mean that New Delhi accepted Modi as the undisputed BJP leader in Gujarat. If Pandya won, then it would cloud matters and diffuse power in Gujarat. Modi's move to deny a ticket to Pandya was psychological. Pandya could be accommodated in the central government, or even made a minister later, but for the moment the battle for Gujarat was in question, and hence the party did not overrule Modi's demand to take charge of the Gujarat BJP.

Haren Pandya claimed that in Gujarat the BJP contested only 181 of the 182 assembly seats. This was because the result of the Ellisbridge contest always went in his favor. Pandya had always been a clever manipulator of the complex equations within the Sangh Parivar, and hence was a shrewd politician that Modi wanted to sideline. Several senior BJP leaders, including Keshubhai Patel, sympathized with Pandya, who was perceived as Patel's proxy in those days. The rivalry against Modi brought Pandya and Patel closer.

It was widely reported that in the eleven days that Gujarat's BJP leaders discussed in detail potential candidates for each seat, Modi kept mum on the Pandya issue. If Modi had mooted the Pandya issue or opposed him in the beginning, there would have been arguments for deciding each seat, and the Pandya factor would have weakened Modi's position. Modi therefore waited for the right time to make his move. After days of deliberation, when candidates for most of the seats had been finalized, Modi raised the Pandya issue and opposed his candidacy from Ellisbridge. Modi claimed that Pandya was behind the media's hate campaign against him. Modi is believed to have told the party's senior leadership that if Pandya were given a ticket, he would quit. The threat was real. Modi was the man of the hour, and the party had to rally behind him. After the Godhra riots, Modi had borne the brunt of the media onslaught and the entire Gujarat elections were focused on him. Hence if the BJP were to win, then Modi would have to emerge as the uncontested leader of the BJP. In Pandya, Modi found a detractor of some power and influence.

A day later the BJP released its third list of an additional twelve candidates bringing the total number of nominations to 167. Pandya's fate still hung in the balance. It was reported that to resolve the Haren Pandya conundrum, the party offered him a position in the central government, but he refused it on Keshubhai Patel's advice. Even senior party leader Arun Jaitley rushed to Gujarat to defuse the tension between various BJP factions. Factionalism was damaging the party. However, factionalism was equally rampant in the Congress Party, and this canceling effect cushioned the trauma for both parties. In fact, the Congress Party's infighting in Gujarat prevented the central leadership from announcing its own second list of nominations.

All these discussions, late night and early morning meetings, and the *Gujarat Gaurav Yatra* demands took their toll on Modi. RSS strongman Madandas Devi was scheduled to arrive in Gujarat to meet with Modi and to persuade him to compromise. The night before, walking with Modi in the garden, his young confidant found Modi particularly pale and tired. The very next day Modi was hospitalized complaining of chest pain. The meeting with Madandas Devi was cancelled.

Meanwhile, the Congress Party came out with its second list of 56 additional candidates, but did not announce who it would nominate to challenge Modi in Maninagar. It also did not announce who would contest from Ellisbridge. The Congress party thus announced 164 candidates keeping the candidature for the remaining 17 constituencies in suspense.

As a gesture of opposition unity the Congress Party left the Bhavnagar (North) assembly constituency for the CPI-M party to contest. To work to defeat BJP, the Communists announced their whole-hearted support for the Congress Party. Defence Minister George Fernandes' Samata Party put up 60 candidates in Gujarat and released the first list of 14 candidates in Ahmedabad. None of the candidates of the Samata Party won.

The BJP then announced its fourth and fifth lists, taking the total of nominations to 181 of the 182 seats. However, the party was still to settle the Haren Pandya issue, and did not announce the nomination for Ellisbridge. On November 24, with three weeks to go for the elections, the Congress party nominated dissident ex-BJP leader and Modi- baiter Yatin Oza to challenge Modi. Yatin Oza, a dynamic young BJP leader, and a practicing lawyer in the High Court of Gujarat, and president of Gujarat High Court Lawyers' Bar Association, represented the Sabarmati assembly constituency twice, but resigned in 2001 from the BJP and joined the Congress Party. This led to by-elections, which the BJP lost, and paved the way for Keshubhai Patel's removal, and Modi becoming the Chief Minister. With just one day left for the last day for filing of nominations, and in a gesture to gain sympathy and oblige senior party leaders, Haren Pandya announced that he had decided not to contest the election to avoid embarrassment to the party. With Pandya backing out, the BJP nominated Pandya's protégé Bhavin Sheth as the Ellisbridge candidate. With the nomination of Bhavin Sheth in place of Pandya, the BJP announced its complete list for all 182 assembly seats.

Angry with the withdrawal of Haren Pandya from the electoral race, his supporters attacked Amit Shah, a BJP municipal councilman from Ellisbridge area, at a party event. They hurled chairs at him and attacked him with sharp-edged weapons. Police indicted three Pandya supporters for the attack, but they made no arrests. Following the resolution of the Haren Pandya-Narendra Modi tussle, and the nomination of Bhavin Sheth as BJP's candidate from the Ellisbridge constituency, the Congress Party released its list of seven candidates. It nominated Pradeep Ruwala to contest the Ellisbridge seat. With the declaration of this list, both the Congress Party and BJP finished the nomination processes for their candidates. The BJP fielded candidates for all the 182 assembly seats, while the Congress fielded candidates for 181 seats, leaving one seat for the Communist Party.

The complex exercise of electoral nominations was over, and the parties got down to serious election campaigning. The fate of the candidates would be decided in less than a month. Tempers were running high, and election fever was catching on throughout Gujarat. People enjoy election times for it is like a huge *mela* (fair). It is one time, when the high and mighty rulers of India have to disembark from their air-conditioned coaches and helicopters and come to the villages and *mohallas* with folded hands to seek votes.

CHAPTER XXV -- NARENDRA MODI IN HOSPITAL

(Note: Many of the details of Narendra Modi's hospitalization and the efforts of his staff and others come from the recollections of co-author V. Sharma). For two months, the Chief Minister of Gujarat spent every weekend and Mondays on the road, traveling over 15,000 kilometers, taking his cause to the 50 million people of the state. When Modi took office in October 2001, in his inaugural speech he said that his effort would be to contact each and every person of Gujarat. A mammoth task indeed! Even as the media and the Congress Party blamed Modi for everything under the Sun, he made his way among the people telling them about his efforts to improve their lives as well as how some people were portraying a false image of Gujarat. For Modi, the *Gujarat Gaurav Yatra* was the vehicle to communicate with the people of Gujarat. He went to each and every one of the 182 assembly constituencies, spoke at hundreds of public meetings, and literally touched hundreds of thousands of people.

The GGY would start early in the morning, and end late at night. It traveled continuously for three months. Modi kept his spirits and his energy up by taking medicines and vitamins, and healing his injured vocal chords by drinking warm medicated water. The endless public speeches took a toll on the man. The heat of October, coupled with the dust in the air, turned him dark, and exhausted his body and limbs. The stress of the ticket distribution meetings that ran till the early morning hours added to the strain of the GGY. While other leaders could take a nap and a break, Modi was committed to resuming the GGY road trip. Constant travel, discussions, evaluations, and trips to Delhi in order to brief party bosses, and efforts to pacify the likes of Keshubhai Patel were too demanding for one man to handle. The stress and strain of such politics and politicking can take a heavy toll. No longer was Modi a young RSS *pracharak*, or merely one of the general secretaries of the BJP. He was a fifty-two year old man, burdened by office, and without an immediate family that could have cared for him. Dinners were late at night, sometimes as late as one o'clock in the morning, or whenever the meetings ended, or when he came back from the GGY. Irregular meal times led to further decline in his health.

After one late night walk with Modi, his young confidant awoke the next morning to hear that the Chief Minister was admitted to the intensive care unit of a hospital.[200] There was fear that Modi suffered a heart attack. Some had spread the rumor that hospitalization was a convenient way to avoid meeting with Madandas Devi.

Modi lay in the intensive care unit, with his medical parameters monitored by Dr. Dholakia, physician to the Governor of Gujarat. His ECG readings were normal in the morning but by evening became slightly abnormal, technically called a "T-wave"

---

[200] *The Times of India* (November 22, 2002). "Narendra Modi hospitalised, advised rest".

inversion. Not wanting to take any chances the doctors prescribed special clot-dissolving medicines. These expensive medicines are technically called TPA (Tissue Plasminogen Activator), or Thrombolytic agents. These were expensive medicines, and not many had them in Ahmedabad, and certainly no chemist kept them in Gandhinagar. Each vial cost about 75,000 rupees ($1,500). Modi personally did not have this kind of money to buy the medicine. His personal staff began collecting money so that medicines could be purchased. His personal assistant Om Prakash took the little money he had in a plastic bag, and brought it to the hospital just in case money was needed. Modi's young confidant told Additional Principal Secretary Anil Mukim that medicines could be ordered from Mumbai, but money would have to be paid to the chemists there. Mukim, in turn asked Gujarat's liaison officer in Mumbai if he had enough money. He did not. Hence the young confidant called up a friend and asked for a loan of 75,000 rupees.

Cardiologist Dr. Manoj Swami was asked to fly from Mumbai immediately and since there were no flights at that hour the District Collector of Gandhinagar made arrangements for Dr.Swami to travel by the Gujarat Mail train.

According to government rules the expenses of a serving Governor's treatment would be met by the government, as also the Health Secretary's medical treatment. But nobody was sure about rules concerning a serving Chief Minister's treatment. The confusion was cleared when Chief Secretary G.S. Subba Rao arrived at the hospital and said that the Chief Minister's medical costs would be borne by the government.

It was thus ironic that one of the richest states of India had one of India's poorest chief ministers, if not the poorest. Modi remained an RSS *pracharak* throughout his life. A *pracharak* is one who volunteers to dedicate his life for the upliftment of society; it is a vow of poverty. It is a hard life of celibacy and simplicity. Narendra Modi has no house to call his own. In Ahmedabad he stayed in quarters provided by Sanskardham, a children's school run by the RSS. His mother, Hira Ba, aged 94, still lives in their family home, a medium sized house in Modi's native village. Modi's brother is a lower rank officer in the Information Department of the Gujarat Government, and keeps a low profile.

Narendra Modi does not entertain any of his relatives. Modi is thus a unique man, his aides and close observers say, free from the attraction for money that most politicians have. He is a loner, for whom work and his spiritual quest seem to be the two main driving forces.[201] He is fond of technology, wears an expensive watch and spectacles. He is also fond of dressing smartly in traditional Indian clothes. However, the media squeezes mileage even from the kind of clothes he wears. For example, in a hateful profile of Modi, the BBC says, "the 52-year-old minister is not given to spartan tastes -- he is widely known instead for his love of expensive clothes and designer

---

[201] Marino, A. (2014). Narendra Modi: A Political Biography. New Delhi: Harper Collins.

accessories".[202] Yet another commentator snidely claimed that Modi bought himself a new wardrobe after he became Chief Minister but did not leave his communal attitudes behind.[203] That India is being robbed by criminal politicians and corrupt bureaucrats matters little to the cynical and angry commentators. However, a Modi has to be castigated for wearing an expensive watch! Over the past ten years since this manuscript was first completed, Narendra Modi has a healthier bank balance. According to a report in The Times of India, April 25, 2014, on April 9, when Modi filed his nomination in Vadodara, he had Rs 11.74 lakh – about $20,000 in his bank accounts, with his total investments, including gold rings and tax refunds, estimated at Rs 51.57 lakh – or about $90,000. Compared to Modi's assets, the leader of the Aam Aadmi Party, Arvind Kejriwal declared that his assets amounted to Rs 2.14 crore or about $360,000 and the leader of the Congress Party, Sonia Gandhi, claimed that she had assets worth Rs 9.28 crores or about $1.5 million. Sonia Gandhi has been accused by Subramanian Swamy, a politician of long standing, of having billions of dollars stacked away in Swiss bank accounts, and she was listed as one of the richest political leaders in the world by *The Huffington Post*, which calculated her wealth to be about $2 billion, though the news aggregator later withdrew that report.[204]

Modi's personal staff acted as his family and kept vigil round the clock at the hospital. The warm and sensitive side of Narendra Modi is rarely visible to the media and the outside world. This has made him the "Hindu hardliner", someone to be scorned, castigated, and demonized. In the crassly speculative media, and the ideologically-biased academe, he has been even characterized as having the demeanor of a mass murderer.

Haren Pandya and Keshubhai Patel were among the first ones to visit Modi in the hospital. On seeing Keshubhai Patel, Modi jokingly told him "*Hoon jindaa choon*" ("I am still alive"). Keshubhai Patel replied, "May you live a hundred years!" Arun Jaitley, along with BJP spokesperson Amitabh Mishra, also arrived from Delhi. Vajpayee called to know about his health, and so did Advani. Modi's brother Somabhai arrived and sat outside the room waiting on his younger brother.

The doctors later said that Narendra Modi had been admitted to Gandhinagar Civil Hospital following a complaint of body ache, throat pain, and extreme fatigue. He was advised complete rest. Doctors clarified that there did not seem to be any cardiac problem. However, to be doubly sure, they wanted Modi to be shifted to the

---

[202] Rao, R. (December 30, 2002). "Profile: Narendra Modi", *BBC*.

[203] Kapoor, C. (March 17, 2002). "Old Wine, New Bottle", *Indian Express*.

[204] Rebello, M. (December 02, 2013). "Sonia Gandhi is richer than Queen Elizabeth and the Sultan of Oman, claims 'Huffington Post' Report". *DNA India*.

Government Hospital in Ahmedabad that had better facilities than the Government Hospital in Gandhinagar.

In the morning, when he was informed that he would be moved to the Ahmedabad hospital, Modi said he did not want the press to broadcast pictures showing he was ill. He wanted the strong man image to remain. A convoy of about fifty cars, both government and private, blocked photographers trying to take photographs of Modi lying on a stretcher. His staff was afraid that photos of Modi carried on a stretcher would be telecast all over Gujarat and India, and feared that it would dampen the morale of the party just before the elections. It was important not to allow the press to take such pictures. The entire hospital complex was cordoned off and all media personnel asked to stay at some distance. A cloth screen was erected to prevent any pictures being taken. A view of the ambulance leaving the hospital was blocked by people who stood in front of press cameras with their hands held up. This way Modi was brought into the ambulance, and the convoy left for Ahmedabad. No one knew which hospital Modi was being taken to. People thought it would be some expensive private hospital. No one thought that Modi was headed for the government hospital. In the hospital, security arrangements were tight. No media or press personnel were permitted inside the perimeter. His staff and security personnel ensured a media-sterile environment.

In the Ahmedabad hospital Modi underwent angiography that showed that there was no blockage in his heart. He then rested for two more days before leaving the hospital. Doctors told the media that Modi did not have any cardiac problem, and that they conducted all necessary clinical tests. They declared him to be perfectly all right, but stated that he needed rest. After discharge from the hospital, Modi appeared well rested, but he waited a little more before resuming active electioneering. (Note: As the long, nine-phase electioneering entered the final phases in the elections to the sixteenth Lok Sabha, at the end of April 2014, it was reported that Modi appeared tired and with a "puffy" face. His ability to hold large audiences enthralled, and his hectic travel across the country, had begun to take a toll.)

CHAPTER XXVI -- VHP IN THE FOREFRONT

The Vishwa Hindu Parishad (VHP) declared that elections in Gujarat would be a "vote for the *Ram bhakts* (followers of Lord Ram)", and the Hindu martyrs of Godhra. After all, those innocent, unarmed Hindu men, women and children who had gone on an Ayodhya pilgrimage had gone in response to a VHP call, and were burnt alive at Godhra on their return journey. Everything that happened later started with the massacre of these Hindu pilgrims.

The VHP announced a massive religious awareness campaign to ensure the victory of those who, according to the VHP, respected Hindu sentiments. It announced that 500,000 of its volunteers who lived in 10,000 villages would not campaign for any particular political party. Pravin Togadia, VHP's International General Secretary, said that in the elections the choice would not be between Narendra Modi and Shankarsinh Vaghela. Instead, the vote would be in memory of "Godhra martyrs and Ram devotees". The VHP planned a village to village tour to meet the eye witnesses of the Godhra incident in batches of two and three as part of a Hindu awareness program. The Parishad was particularly caustic in criticizing the National Human Rights Commission (NHRC), charging it with bias. The VHP said that NHRC Chairman J. S. Verma's comparison of the Gujarat violence with "war" was mischievous and improper.

The Election Commission of India (EC) mounted pressure on the Gujarat government and asked for a detailed report on the planned Vishwa Hindu Parishad *yatra* starting from Godhra on November 17. The VHP was furious, as it asserted that it was not a political organization but a religious one. It was not contesting any elections, and hence did not come under the purview of the EC. The Gujarat-wide program of the VHP was scheduled to start from Godhra on November 17, 2002 and end at Akshardham in Gandhinagar on December 6, 2002. The EC said that a final decision in this regard would be taken only after getting a complete report from the Gujarat government.[205]

Certain NGOs, the Congress Party, and others expressed apprehension that the VHP program could disturb the fragile peace in Gujarat. The VHP declared that it was going to carry out prayer meetings, and certainly Hindu prayers could not be construed to disturb the peace of Gujarat, or lead to fresh violence. The EC said that it received complaints that the VHP was displaying replicas of the burnt Sabarmati Express at public events. The VHP countered by stating that what it was showing was the truth, and the reality of how Hindu pilgrims were burnt alive by Muslims in Godhra, and how certain people and elements in the media had blamed the pilgrims for inviting this death sentence. Labeling Godhra as the *"Somnath of Gujarat"* (in an analogy to the Somnath

---

[205] *Rediff on the Net*. "Togadia barred from entering Godhra". November 16, 2002.

VHP in the Forefront

temple of India that was raided and destroyed many times by Islamic invaders, and rebuilt by the Hindus over and over again), Togadia said, "I want to tell the entire nation that there will be no violence at all during our *yatra*. It is a *yatra* of saints and the freedom of religious expression should not be curbed." He also showed the written permission for the program that VHP got from the Panchmahals District Magistrate. Togadia further made it clear that nearly 2,000 religious leaders from all over the country would join the *yatra* from various places.

Togadia accused CEC Lyngdoh of misleading the nation and attempting to impose his own will on the masses. He said Lyngdoh was acting as if he was the Chief Minister and Chief Secretary of Gujarat as well as the Collector of Panchmahals district. He said that the CEC was terrorizing the Gujarat bureaucracy, and called his actions "fascist". He called Lyngdoh the third party in Gujarat after the BJP and the Congress, and said that the Congress Party did not have just fourteen chief ministers in the country but fifteen, and Lyngdoh was the fifteenth.

Togadia expressed surprise that Lyngdoh did not ask the VHP for details of its proposed program but chose to believe certain media reports, and ordered the ban. He challenged the CEC to prove that the event would incite communal passions. VHP leader Acharya Dharmendra disclosed that he would lead the VHP program and spread the message of *Hindupat Padshahi* (Hindu sovereignty). A *rath* (chariot) named *Bhavani* (after the Hindu goddess) with the *paduka* (sandals) of Swami Ramdas and the statue of Shivaji would be part of the program, and the message of Hindu awakening was to be preached.

The VHP was not at all pleased with the demands from the EC. It termed these actions of the EC as double standards. VHP's Giriraj Kishore said, "He (CEC) is going too far to prove his secular credentials, which have come to be identified with Hindu bashing. Lyngdoh gave the green signal to elections in Jammu & Kashmir despite widespread terrorist activities, but here (in Gujarat) he is objecting to a mere *yatra* of Hindu religious leaders.... The VHP is a non-political organization and everyone has a right to create awareness among their communities."

Giriraj Kishore made a lot of sense when he questioned as to why Lyngdoh was not taking note of the political *fatwas* (Islamic edicts) issued from mosques. The silence of the EC on such obvious discrimination gave further credence to the accusations. After getting the report from the State Government, the Election Commission banned religious rallies in Gujarat.

The VHP labeled the CEC as anti-Hindu, and his actions an infringement on the fundamental right to practice one's religion, and that its activists would defy the ban and risk arrest, but carry out their religious activity. The VHP announced that December 6, 2002 would be celebrated as *Vijay Diwas* (Victory Day). It was the day when Hindus pulled down the Babri mosque in Ayodhya in 1992. In an act of defiance the VHP planned to organize *Ramdhun* (prayers to Lord Ram) in the 18,000 villages of Gujarat.

The main contention of the EC was that it had acted upon the report sent by the

Gujarat Government. The report spoke of possible trouble if the VHP sponsored such events. The EC tried to turn the tables on the BJP government by banning the VHP program citing the report as the reason. The BJP was furious. The Gujarat Government later, in typical bureaucratic style, issued a statement that its report was ambiguous in nature and did not explicitly say that the VHP's program would be detrimental to the law and order situation and result in riots. The conclusion was that the report was used by the EC, and it extrapolated an interpretation to ban the religious events sponsored by the VHP.

The ban on all religious rallies by the EC was unprecedented. It provoked many debates. Would the EC ban Muslim rallies at the time of *Muharram* if that coincided with the holding of elections? Or if there is the *Jagannath Rath Yatra* during election time, how would the EC react? If there is *Kumbh Mela* – the largest gathering of pilgrims in the world -- would the EC ban it too? Law is reason if it is free from prejudice. It cannot have arbitrary application. For a society to deserve the "civilized" label, it should resolve all problems, free from prejudice and malice, which can have enduring consequences.

In a rebuff to the VHP, the Prime Minister's Office strongly criticized its program. In an interview with a leading television news channel Prime Minister Vajpayee said that the EC's ban on the proposed rally by the VHP was justifiable in view of the prevailing conditions in Gujarat. Asked about the criticism that the ban was biased, Vajpayee said that a superficial view could justify that statement but a deeper understanding of the issues would leave one with no choice but to support the ban. He supported the Government of Gujarat by saying that it had done the right thing by respecting the directive of the EC to prohibit religious processions in the state ahead of the assembly election. Vajpayee appealed to all organizations to honor the EC's directive, as it was a constitutional authority, and to help the state administration in discharging its duty. The BJP issued a statement supporting the Prime Minister's view, and reiterated that the party's priority would be to ensure that all the political and social activities and election processes in the state were conducted in a peaceful, harmonious and fearless atmosphere.

The VHP rejected the Prime Minister's appeal not to go ahead with its program and to make Godhra a poll issue. On the contrary, it reaffirmed its stance that it was the fundamental duty of the organization to tell people of the atrocities Muslims committed on Hindus, just as certain NGOs and media elements were focusing only on the violence Hindus inflicted on Muslims in the post-Godhra riots. Hence, the VHP affirmed that it would go ahead with the march with a replica of the S-6 coach of the Sabarmati Express. In a clear sign of defiance Togadia said, "We will go ahead with the *yatra* to uphold the fundamental rights of the Hindu society and are ready to face the consequences... I expect the prime minister to safeguard the fundamental rights of the

Hindus and not succumb to pressure from secular forces... Godhra is at the heart of Hindutva. It is impossible to forget the gruesome Godhra carnage."

Each step that the government took in trying to prevent the VHP carrying out its program, only hardened the resolve of the VHP. Its leaders described Vajpayee's endorsement of the EC ban on its Gujarat program as most unfortunate. It affirmed that its program was irreversible. Acharya Dharmendra accused Lyngdoh of hijacking the Gujarat administration, and added that free and fair poll was Lyngdoh's responsibility, but no society had ever given a bureaucrat the right to object to anything that saints do.

The very next day Manoj Agarwal, the District Magistrate of Panchmahals District, barred Togadia from entering Godhra. Agarwal also denied the VHP permission to carry out its program. Agrawal said the administration had sealed all entry points into Godhra, and the administration was in constant touch with Gujarat government in view of VHP's threat to continue with its program from the science college grounds in Godhra. The district administration deployed one company of the Rapid Action Force, eight companies of State Reserve Police, 700 local policemen, and police reinforcements from adjoining districts to manage any possible deterioration of the law and order situation, even though the VHP had promised it would not take the law in its hands, nor would it create any trouble, but just carry out religious prayers for the dead. The district administration on its part made preventive arrests and took all possible steps to maintain peace in Godhra. Strict vigil was kept at the railway station, bus stations and security personnel were deployed in sensitive areas of the town.

These strong measures the Modi government took against the VHP program eluded media appreciation. As a compromise the VHP proposed a prayer chanting program. It hoped the EC would permit this. But no one had time to debate, the elections were around the corner, and a major confrontation with the EC at this juncture would be unproductive. The RSS held a meeting to discuss the ramifications of the unprecedented steps the EC had taken. It was certainly an infringement of the right to practice one's religion. However, under the ambiguous concept of "free and fair" elections, the EC exercised powers to decide what was free and fair. The Supreme Court earlier had said that the conduct of elections is the sole prerogative of the EC. Till such time there is a clear understanding and adjudication of what constitutes "free and fair" elections, the EC continued to use this clause as it considered best. Hence, it augurs well for democracy that the powers of the EC be re-evaluated so as to clearly define its role but within the boundaries of logic and reason and not the CEC's idiosyncratic interpretations.

On November 17, to comply with the EC's directive, Gujarat police arrested VHP leaders Pravin Togadia and Acharya Dharmendra when they tried to defy the ban and proceed to Godhra. Twenty other VHP activists were arrested. Togadia's wife and daughter were also taken into preventive custody as a precautionary measure. However, by afternoon all of them were released.

In a separate incident, about 100 VHP and Bajrang Dal activists were arrested when they tried to enter the venue of the VHP's proposed program at the Science College in Godhra. At the time of arrest, the activists raised anti-Lyngdoh, and anti-Muslim slogans. They were all released after the tension abated. This handling of the situation by the Modi government received praise from the RSS which said that the VHP had every right to explain its stand on Godhra, and place before the people facts regarding the sufferings of the Hindus, and carry out their religious prayers. RSS spokesman Ram Madhav said that, "The VHP had carried out its program in a peaceful and democratic manner."

Undaunted by the lack of support from the government for its programs, the VHP announced another set of events, saying that the *yatra* would take the shape of public meetings.[206] During election time the EC had banned religious rallies but there were no restrictions on the holding of public meetings. The VHP chose to label its events differently in view of the arrest of Togadia and Acharya Dharmendra. VHP leader Giriraj Kishore mentioned that the VHP had other planned events including a public meeting in Ahmedabad on December 6 to mark the tenth anniversary of the demolition of Babri mosque in Ayodhya. The *Vijay Diwas* (victory day) meeting would also be addressed by VHP chief Ashok Singhal. He said the event would be peaceful. The VHP chose not to confront the Gujarat government, and did not blame it for the arrest of its leaders, as the state government had to comply with the EC directive.

On December 3, 2002, nine days before the election, VHP's General Secretary Dr. Jaideep Patel was shot at in the town of Naroda by two unidentified men riding a motor-cycle. Dr. Patel was operated upon in a local private hospital in Ahmedabad, and there was no danger to his life. The bullet had struck the base of his skull and was removed through multiple surgeries. The police announced a reward of fifty thousand rupees ($1,200) to anyone providing clues about the assailants. Only a day earlier the Intelligence Bureau claimed to have informed Dr. Patel about a threat to his life, but he was not provided any security. Dr. Patel was one of those blamed for instigating the mobs that ran amuck and killed Muslims following the Godhra carnage.

At a meeting held in Ayodhya, the president of the Ram Janmabhoomi Nyas, Mahant Ram Chandra Paramhans said the main event of "*Shaurya Diwas*" would be organized at the Akshardham temple in Gujarat on December 6. The revered monk told reporters at Ayodhya that the VHP would organize the event in Gandhinagar to avoid unnecessary security checks at Ayodhya. The EC allowed the VHP to hold the "*Shaurya Diwas*" rally but imposed curbs on the speeches of the leaders during the rally. The program was to be low-key to avoid any confrontation. The actions of the EC triggered some welcome debate on issues such as freedom of religion, and freedom of

---

[206] *Rediff on the Net*. "Yatra to take shape of public meetings: VHP", November 17, 2002.

expression. Would Indian democracy allow the free exercise of such activities or could freedom be infringed upon in certain predetermined circumstances? Would the granting of absolute powers to interpret constitutional guarantees help or hinder democracy? Is the electoral process more important than the personal liberty to pray or speak?

The duel between the EC and the VHP seemed destined to continue even on the day of elections when there were media reports that Togadia's name was missing from the electoral rolls, even though the rolls had been revised. It was an embarrassing moment for the EC. Absence of Togadia's name would certainly have resulted in lengthy inquiries later, and hence it was imperative that the EC clarify the situation. Togadia was registered to vote in the Sarkhej constituency. He claimed that the names of residents of an entire housing society in his area were missing from the voters' list. An embarrassed EC asked all district collectors to look into complaints of missing names from voters' list.

After searching through its database, the EC said that Togadia's name was registered in the Naroda Patiya assembly constituency in Ahmedabad and not in Sarkhej. With the discovery of the names in a different constituency the matter was closed. However, there were many other registered voters, even in Modi's own Maninagar constituency who could not find their names on the voters list. Addressing his supporters in the Maninagar assembly constituency soon after the conclusion of the polling, Modi said, "The EC is answerable to what has happened. It ordered the revision of electoral rolls thrice in ten months, costing the state exchequer crores of rupees."

Lyngdoh claimed that people had been given a lot of time to respond if they found mistakes in the electoral rolls, and if they had not responded then the EC could not be blamed. Lyngdoh shrugged off complaints by stating that the electoral rolls were available to political parties as well as to individuals. It was déjà vu all over again, in 2014, when thousands of voters' names disappeared from lists.[207]

After the elections Togadia was said to have declared that India would become a Hindu country in two years' time. The BJP immediately expressed its disapproval of Togadia's remarks. These dynamics within the "Sangh Parivar" are indicative of the nature of politics in India. There are "moderate" elements within the RSS and the BJP and there are those who hold extremist views. To merely cast the whole "parivar" as extremist is therefore simplistic. Unfortunately, Praveen Togadia was up to his old tricks, after being completely marginalized by Narendra Modi, when he made a provocative speech in Bhavnagar, Gujarat, on April 20, 2014, and Modi had to step in to shut him up.

---

[207] *Times of India*, "Thousands of voters' names go missing in Mumbai", April 25, 2014.

CHAPTER XXVII -- *HUM PAANCH, HUMARE PACHEES*

The media has widely commented on one of Modi's election speeches wherein he made a snide remark about Muslim population and fertility rate. In the speech on September 9, 2002 he said referring to the Muslim male's right to wed four wives: *"Hum paanch, humare pachees, aur unke che sau pachees"* ("We five, our twenty-five, and their six hundred and twenty-five"). There was a hue and cry over this speech, and the National Commission for Minorities (NCM) asked for a text of the speech to evaluate its alleged inflammatory contents.

Modi said that his remarks were misinterpreted. In his speech, Modi spoke about the extraordinary progress made by China in economic development and population control. He asked if religion played a role in China when it came to economic development. He asked the people who could possibly benefit from the lingering poverty and joblessness that came with population explosion. However, in India whenever anyone sought to devise a comprehensive strategy for population control, people who claimed to be progressive immediately attacked it as anti-Islamic. Modi stressed in his speech that Indians must get over their narrow mindset and that there was an urgent need to control population that pushed the nation's per capita income among the lowest in the world, even though India's GDP was one of the highest in the world. Modi said that religion should not be brought into the debate on population control. If India had to progress, and offer its young men and women jobs, then it had to control its population. An economic system had to be developed in which every child born, regardless of whether he was a Hindu or Muslim could get education and employment.

Modi went on to say that at the current rate, population growth in India was steep, with the country adding an Australia every year. He said that it was in this context he used the clever but catchy phrase *"hum paanch"* (we five) -- husband, wife, and their three kids, which would in the next generation grow to twenty-five (*hamara pachhees*), and then to six hundred and twenty-five in the following generation. Was the explanation an afterthought? We don't know. But such was the atmosphere during the campaigning that every word of Modi's was dissected for its "communal content".

The pitch and fervor in the 2014 election campaigning was ratcheted up further. Everyone was accusing every other of the worst crimes and each day brought a new round of mindless and ugly rhetoric, and the Election Commission was flooded with hundreds of complaints. Smita Prakash wrote: "Political leaders began their election campaign of 2014 on the plans of development and stability, but it has not taken them long to slip into the tried and tested path of generating fear psychosis. And they are liberally using all tools available to them. Again tried and tested. Campaign speeches, advertisements, Facebook updates, tweets, carefully planted stories in newspapers and television reports, everything to drive away clear thought and reason at the time of voting. Rational debate has been poisoned for now".[208]

The Gujarat Intelligence Bureau (IB) recorded the Chief Minister's speech. This was not to the liking of Modi. Instead of gathering strategic and accurate data about anti- social and anti-national activities the Intelligence Bureau sought to keep tabs on what the Chief Minister was saying. Even if recording the speech was according to routine procedures, the perceived view in the public, and the administration was that the State's IB had acted as the hub of anti-Modi activity since the Godhra days and was bent upon harming his reputation at the behest of a few senior Congress Party leaders.

Was Modi's complaint far-fetched? Are India's bureaucrats neutral? Without sounding partisan, we can point out that whatever may be the rationale for Modi's "we five, our twenty-five" comment, it is indeed true that Indian bureaucracy has become politicized to such an extent that the nexus between politicians and administrators has become both worrisome and dangerous. It was said in the early days of the NDA government's first tenure that the political masters were prisoners of bureaucrats because most of the BJP ministers were novices in governing and relied on the bureaucrats to draft policy. The Congress Party was in power for nearly fifty years in Delhi and IAS, IPS, and IFS officers as well as bureaucrats in other areas had established a close connection with that political party. Similarly, in Gujarat, Modi had to deal with detractors within the bureaucracy.

The National Commission for Minorities asked the state government to submit a report on Modi's speech. The state IB sent Modi's speech, recorded as part of routine procedure, to the Commission. Modi was furious at the selective application of the Intelligence Bureau rules, and immediately transferred senior officers. Additional Director General Srikumar was transferred to the police reforms department, Deputy Inspector General of Police E. Radhakrishna, in charge of political and communal affairs, was shunted to Junagadh as principal of the Police Training College, and Deputy Commissioner of Police Sanjeev Bhatt, in charge of internal security, was made principal of the State Reserve Police Training College. All these off-field postings were seen as "punishment" postings. (Note: Sanjeev Bhatt continued to be a thorn in the side of the BJP and Narendra Modi. He filed an affidavit in the Supreme Court of India concerning Modi's alleged role in the post-Godhra riots. Known as a cunning and criminal mastermind, he was embraced by the Congress Party, but the Special Investigation Team looking into the post-Godhra riots accused him of forging evidence to malign Modi. See, "Sanjeev Bhatt forged evidence to malign Gujarat govt: Special Investigation Team," *DNA*, September 5, 2013.)

In his speech, Modi told the people that the Congress Party accused him of being communal for diverting the waters of the Narmada to the Sabarmati during the Hindu holy month of *Shraavan*. The river inter-linking project and the Narmada dam had

---

[208] Prakash, S. (April 21, 2014). "Fear and hysteria as campaign tools". *Mid-Day*.

already been completed, and Modi's decision to let the waters mix during *Shraavan* was based more on traditional expectations than on communal criteria. He ridiculed the Congress Party by saying that it was free to bring water during the Muslim holy month of *Ramadan*, if it so desired.

Modi also pointed out that there was a mushrooming of *madrasas* all over Asia, many funded by Saudi money. Modi spoke of the growth of these schools in Gujarat, especially on the border with Pakistan. He reiterated that every child -- Hindu, Muslim, Christian or of any religious faith -- had a right to primary education, but a child going to a *madrasa* was deprived of modern education. Modi wondered what such children did once they grew up. In Pakistan, of course such a child would become ideal fodder for fundamentalist parties and armies. Modi spoke of the need for Gujarat to have peace, and peace was possible only when a long-term plan for the development of the state was ready.

Modi's speech at Becharji was as usual full of pun, humor, and passionate appeal. Modi is a powerful and gifted speaker, and the people listen to him with rapt attention. Modi told the eager crowd that the Congress Party had chosen to abuse Gujarat and the Gujarati people. He took digs at Sonia Gandhi, calling her "Italy's daughter" and asking whether she had the right to insult Gujarat and its 50 million people. He asked how the Congress government had built a *samadhi* (resting place) for Sanjay Gandhi, the son of Indira Gandhi on government land in Delhi, and how they could not find one for Sardar Patel. Modi accused the Congress Party of seeking to erase Sardar Patel's memory, but he would never let such a thing happen.

No doubt, politicians play to the gallery. Modi too does, and he did so at Becharji. Did some of his statements hurt Muslim sentiments? Most probably they did. Were they too clever by half? May be they were. Were the comments blown out of proportion? Surely they were, for if anything characterized the nature of media coverage and analysis of the Gujarat situation in 2002, it was its effort to show that Modi was devil incarnate. When pushed to the wall, when demonized, when selected for such brutal disparagement, can one expect a person with self-respect not to fight back? Sure, Modi fought back, and he may have crossed the line sometimes. He would not have been Chief Minister of Gujarat if he were a docile man.

More important than the slanted remarks of Modi is the change in religious demography in the Indian sub-continent. In the book *Religious Demography of India* the authors reveal that the number of Indian religionists (those with allegiance to religious faiths founded in India – Hinduism, Buddhism, Jainism, Sikhism) declined 11 per cent from 1881 to 1991 (from 78 percent of the population to 67 percent) in the Indian sub-continent. According to the book, in two-thirds of India, the Hindu population is still about 90 to 95 percent. However, specific areas have seen some major changes: in the city of Hyderabad in Andhra Pradesh, northern districts of Karnataka and certain areas of Maharashtra, the growth of Muslims is higher than the national average. Similarly in the Mewat region and the Christian- dominated areas of Kanyakumari, the number of Indian religionists is going down. In other parts of the country, like Uttar Pradesh, Bihar, West Bengal, Assam and in the Ganga belt Indian religionists are about 85 percent. Moving towards the Northeast region of India, this number gradually declines from 85 per cent to 65 per cent.[209]

In the Northeast States of India, the number of Christians registered remarkable growth. Before India gained independence, only one state, Mizoram, was Christian dominated. Now, almost all of the "seven sisters" states in the Northeast have a Christian majority. Similarly in the Andaman and Nicobar Islands, which had only Indian religionists before independence, Christians now are over 70 percent. Similar to the trend in the U.S., where Whites will no longer be the majority by the year 2050, in India too, within the next 50 years Indian religionists would be less than 50 percent of the total population. Muslims would form the bulk of the remaining 50 percent of the population, the book pointed out.

The fear of being overwhelmed by the "other" is not particularly Indian, and we can see such fears being expressed not only in the U.S., but in Europe, Australia, and elsewhere. One can be politically correct and say that such trends are natural, and that those who fear the "other" are racists. However, when we see how deliberate choices are made about family size and family planning, and how religious edicts about populating the earth influence population trends, we can begin to understand the fear that people have about losing power, about being marginalized, and about losing identity. For example, the Christian belief that when the world's population becomes Christian then Jesus will appear again, and Pope John Paul II's call at the Asian Synod in 1999 urging his flock to make the third millennium an Asian millennium are indeed calls for "demographic wars". The Pope meant that Asia should be targeted for conversion to Christianity just as Europe was targeted in the first millennium and the Americas in the second millennium.

Thus, the Gujarat situation should be seen in this context, and while Modi's choice of sloganeering may be faulted, his concerns about population explosion, the lack of family planning among sections of the population, and the calls for demographic war are nothing to be scoffed at.

---

[209] Joshi, A. P., Srinivas, M.D., & Bajaj, J.K. (2003). *Religious Demography of India*. Chennai: Centre for Policy Studies.

CHAPTER XXVIII – ELECTIONEERING AND THE ELECTIONS

National institutions like the National Human Rights Commission (NHRC) and the Election Commission (EC) have been increasingly seen as having succumbed to pressure from certain sections of the media and the intelligentsia. The neutrality of such august institutions is at stake, and their selective activism in certain cases, and deafening silence at other times raise doubts in the minds of the people if indeed this is constitutional democracy at work or the railroading of process. Fairness and balance, just as in journalism, demand that the office bearers in such institutions not only believe in these edicts but are seen to act impartially and consistently.

However, it also happens that officers dealing with human rights and elections attract criticism not because they are not performing their duties, but because their actions can easily be interpreted as favoring one or the other political party. The presence of such institutions does augur well for democracy and freedom, no doubt. Independent institutions are the bastions of democracy in a civilized society where absolute power is held by none. The acrimony, arguments, and criticism of such institutions during elections should lead to a correct retrospective appraisal and even appreciation of work well done after the elections.

The BJP in Gujarat in 2002, and the Congress Party in Chhatisgarh in 2003 were asked to explain alleged misuse of government machinery to propagate their own political agenda. The EC notice to the Congress government of Ajit Jogi in Chattisgarh asked why the EC should not de-recognize the party. A shocked Congress Party struggled to respond believing that the EC would deal with it differently than it did with the BJP in Gujarat. Lyngdoh, the recipient of a Magsasay Award, had even more reason to act firmly and consistently.

Following the trend set by T.N. Seshan as CEC, Lyngdoh seemed to believe that he and the EC could right democracy's wrongs. However, as Swapan Dasgupta pointed out, to uphold the neutrality of the electioneering process is one thing but to pose himself as the arbiter of morality is another. Dasgupta cautioned, "The task of the CEC is simply to organise free and fair elections. He should remain single-mindedly devoted to that enormous task. By doing his job properly, Lyngdoh would be strengthening democracy and making Indian politics more wholesome. The task of moral cleansing should be left to others".[210]

During the Gujarat campaign certain groups with alleged affiliation to the BJP launched a provocative advertising campaign attacking the Election Commission, the NHRC, the NCM, and those they termed "anti-Hindu" political parties and politicians. The messages were in Gujarati. Some of them said:

---

[210] "Lyngdoh's Vigilantism", December 30, 2003, *Rediff on the Net*.

- *Election Commission stands for whom? Answer: For the minority.*
- *National Human Rights Commission stands for whom? Answer: For the minority.*
- *Minorities Commission stands for whom? Answer: For the minority.*
- *Congress stands for whom? Answer: For the minority.*
- *Samajwadi Party stands for whom? Answer: For the minority.*
- *Sonia Gandhi stands for whom? Answer: For the minority.*
- *Laloo Yadav stands for whom? Answer: For the minority.*
- *Mulayam Singh Yadav stands for whom? Answer: For the minority.*
- *Shankersinh Vaghela stands for whom? Answer: For the minority.*

The ad campaign suggested that secularism aimed at making India pro-Muslim and anti-Hindu. The ads went on to exhort in bold type: *Aapna mate kaun?* (Who stands up for us?) The answer appeared in the form of graffiti on the walls of Ahmedabad – "*Who belongs to you? Bharatiya Janata Party*"! Cleverly, supporters of the Congress Party erased the words "BJP" from the walls and wrote the "Congress Party" instead. Using the BJP's weapon against the BJP the Congress Party workers sought to undermine BJP's and Modi's popularity.

Another advertisement mentioned that elections were held in the Northeast Indian state of Mizoram and in Jammu & Kashmir despite the exodus of thousands of refugees there. It pointed out that elections were held with 30,000 refugees in Mizoram and 300,000 Hindu refugees in Jammu & Kashmir, and that by the same token the EC could not postpone elections in Gujarat where there were only five to ten thousand refugees. This ad campaign was appealing to many in Gujarat. These seemingly dual standards made people angry and they questioned the neutrality of the EC and its most public face, the CEC, James Lyngdoh.

The Congress Party protested the ads and the ad campaign on the eve of the elections. The ads made sense and resonated with the experiences of urban Gujaratis. Wherever one went in Gujarat, the oft repeated complaint was that the Congress Party had pandered to religious minorities, cultivated the habit of dividing Hindu voters by catering to caste equations, and deliberately ignored the dangers posed by fundamentalist Islam that had made inroads into Gujarat with the help of agents from across the border. Unfortunately, the Congress Party seemed caught in a time warp, wrapping itself in the "secular" fabric woven out of foreign thread, and giving credence only and to any complaint by minorities. This was democracy turned on its head, where the majority was cast as the devil, and sought to be sliced and diced into a shrinking bowl.

The Congress' myopic view worked well in the early years of an independent but partitioned India, but with the advent of the BJP, Hindus increasingly demanded that political parties consider their demands too. To stem this rise in Hindu awareness, some political parties chose to divide the Hindu community on the lines of caste. The BJP sought to unite Hindu society and have it transcend caste barriers. The politics of caste-based electioneering and the extension of reservation in jobs and education on caste lines seriously eroded Hindu unity and solidarity over the past seven decades. The deliberate efforts to divide and weaken Hindu society enjoy the support of an axis comprising mainly Left/Marxist, Christian, and Muslim fundamentalist forces, with some help from international agencies and governments. That the European Union sought to rap the Indian government on its wrists in 2002 was clear indication of the meddling nature of Western governments. That the same EU apologized for its stridency in 2003 was due to the Vajpayee government's effective and assertive diplomacy.

Officially, an outfit calling itself the "Gujarat Gaurav Samiti" or the "Committee for Gujarati Pride" had sponsored the ad campaigns that drew the ire of the Congress Party and the EC. The EC warned that it would prosecute anyone campaigning for votes on religious grounds. Hence the GGS instead of directly criticizing the Congress Party or the EC chose sarcasm as a rhetorical tool to sway the electorate. The BJP made it clear that freedom of speech was a fundamental right, and hence it was free to criticize the actions of the CEC or anyone else. BJP spokesperson V.K. Malhotra wondered why certain people were hyper-critical of the charges against the EC, and wondered whether the EC alone enjoyed the privilege of criticizing others. The BJP reminded the Congress Party of the several instances when in the past it had criticized the EC.

Lyngdoh labeled the situation in Gujarat as "nasty". The BJP took offense to this statement, and fired a salvo claiming it was Lyngdoh's statement that was nasty. The situation in Gujarat, nearly four months after Godhra, was better than in most other states that had seen such conflict or even in states where there was little communal violence but a lot else wrong: for example, in states like Bihar ruled by Laloo Yadav, or Chattisgarh ruled by a corrupt and autocratic Ajit Jogi. The BJP took righteous umbrage at the EC's sweeping statements.

Fatwas by the Imams

The Shahi Imam of Delhi's Jama Masjid, Maulana Syed Ahmed Bukhari said that the Gujarat poll would decide India's future. Addressing the weekly Friday congregation of Muslims after *"Juma Namaaz"* (Friday prayers), and on the occasion of the Islamic *"Jumatul Vade"*, Bukhari said that a BJP victory would be a victory for lawlessness. He appealed to the voters in Gujarat to "wipe out" those responsible for the violence there. It was not clear to which violence the Maulana referred -- the one against the Hindus in Godhra, or the one against Muslims in Naroda-Patiya, or the one against both the Hindus and the Muslims during the post-Godhra riots.

It was no surprise that the Maulana did not mention in this speech attacks by Muslim terrorists on September 11, 2001 or by a Muslim mob in Godhra on February 27, 2002, or the unremitting suicide bombings then in Israel by Palestinians. He blamed the Sangh Parivar for the Gujarat riots saying that the riots were not a sudden event, and that the Sangh Parivar had hatched the conspiracy earlier with the rioters and offered them training and rewards. Bukhari was also critical of those who attempted to teach secularism to Muslims. He said secularism should be taught to those who attack Islam and Muslims. Bukhari claimed that Muslims had always been loyal to India and stood for secularism. He chose to forget the partition of India and the role played by Muslims in one of the worst cases of ethnic cleansing, genocide and barbarity in human history. Recep Tayyip Erdogan, the Prime Minister of Turkey, once an Islamist, is credited to have said in 1997 that "secularism and Islam do not go hand in hand". Hence Bukhari was contradicting both local and international history and his own understanding of Islam. If Bukhari claimed that most Indian Muslims are peace loving, loyal to India and believe in secularism, he would have a point. But the sweeping generalization he made was both too pat and wrong. Attempting to propagate a pan-Islamic vision, Bukhari appealed to all Islamic countries to stand united against the "unholy" alliance of America and Western powers against Islam.

On this score, the concept of issuing *fatwas* (religious edicts) is contradictory to the practice of secularism and democracy in India. No religious leader -- Hindu, Muslim, Christian, Jew, Parsi, Buddhist, Jain, or Sikh -- has the right to tell others of his or her faith to vote for this party or that, and issue orders in the name of religion. *Fatwas* are issued by unscrupulous mullahs telling fellow Muslims to vote for a particular political party in the election. The very act of issuing a *fatwa* is a death knell to democracy. Such *fatwas* are routinely issued in favor of "secular" parties (every political party except the BJP), and hence the "secularists" in the media and the EC have remained quiet.

The most controversial event of the week prior to the elections was the so-called *fatwa* issued by the Uttar Pradesh-based All India Ulema Council. The "appeal", printed in the December 5, 2002 edition of *Gujarat Today*, a newspaper read mostly by Gujarati Muslims, asked people to vote for the Congress Party. The appeal was promptly reproduced in mainstream Gujarati newspapers by the VHP. Muslim organizations later said that the "appeal" was not a *fatwa* (religious edict) but just an appeal to the Muslim community to vote for the Congress Party, and that the BJP was technically wrong to dub it a *fatwa*. The BJP was not impressed. It reasoned that asking people of a particular community to vote for a select party was against the secular norms of India and hence undemocratic.

Modi brought copies of such *fatwas* to his public meetings and appealed to the voters to reject them, and told them that the time had come for the people of Gujarat to show to the rest of India that such edicts would not be tolerated. In openly challenging the *fatwa* game, Modi neutralized their effect, and created a sense of urgency among the BJP workers to ensure a large turnout on Election Day.

The Election That Shaped Gujarat

A Case Study: Juhapura

Ahmedabad is a city burdened by history and religious cleavages. The forced conversion of large masses by marauding Muslim kings upset the demographic structure of India, but the effects were devastating in Gujarat. Stories are still told about the sacking of Somnath, the carting away of thousands of beautiful Gujarati damsels, and the murder and plunder that devastated the region. The repercussions of such demographic damage are evident even today.[211] There are certain Hindu dominated localities in the city where Muslim residents are rare as rain in a desert, and similarly there are Muslim dominated areas where Hindus dread to go.

The area of Juhapura in Ahmedabad is one such area. It is dubbed as "mini-Pakistan" by many. Both the Congress Party and the BJP governments, and the municipal corporations had paid scant attention to the development of this area. It is a shanty-town with narrow lanes, much like the Palestinian areas in the Middle East. Power cuts were frequent, and the area had very little of modern roads. However, some well-to-do and rich Muslim families also live here, and there are impressive bungalows, along with small houses and apartments. It is estimated that nearly one million people (a large majority of them Muslims) stay in the Juhapura area. Crime was wide-spread and the place was akin to a ghetto. Hindus walking through this area for work were scared, as according to them Muslims stored bombs, swords, and other weapons at home, some even having secret alleys to escape a police raid, and that the Muslims started fights for no reason.

High walls divide Hindu and Muslim residential colonies. These walls are termed as the "border". On one side of the border live the Hindus, and on the other side the Muslims. Godhra released the pent up anger of the Hindu majority. According to newspaper reports, following the riots, both communities began to distrust each other.

An outsider passing through the Muslim or Hindu areas has to first reveal his identity, his antecedents, and the purpose of his visit before people open up to him. The most important criterion for agreeing to talk to a reporter was religious affiliation. Hindus talked to Hindu reporters, and Muslims talked to Muslim reporters. The distrust was complete.

There was one common topic between the two communities, and that was the talk about Modi. Many Hindus considered him nothing less a savior, whereas for many Muslims he had become a hateful figure.[212] Hindus accused the Juhapura Muslims of hoisting the Pakistani flag atop their homes. Muslims claimed that the white crescent and star on a green background are Islamic symbols and if the Pakistani flag uses such

---

[211] Lal, K.S. (1992). *The Legacy of Muslim Rule in India*. South Asia Books.

[212] Ashraf, S. F. (December 6, 2002). "Juhapura: Hemmed in by Prejudices", *Rediff on the Net*.

symbols they are not to be blamed. They argued that they hoist the Indian tricolor too, and yet they are branded as Pakistanis and terrorist sympathizers even though most of them are faithful to India.

Provocative statements by Muslim clerics instigated Muslim youths, and their actions earned a bad name for the entire Muslim community. However, a small group of moderate Muslims, led by prominent and successful socialites and businessmen, like Zafar Sareshwal, took the lead in trying to weaken the hold of the extremists. In this context, Madhu Kishwar's 2013-2014 reports and interviews from Ahmedabad, compiled into an e-book titled, *"Modinama,"* provide insights into the struggle between and among Muslims to come to terms with Narendra Modi, the post-Godhra riots, and the future of Gujarat.

The countdown began for December 12, 2002, the day when the 50 million people of Gujarat would decide the future course of democracy in India. Would the forces advocating justice for Hindu rights win or would the so-called secularists advocating the defunct form of Nehruvian secularism emerge victorious? Political pundits labeled the Gujarat elections as the make or break elections for the BJP. The BJP had earlier lost power in most major states in India, losing Maharashtra, Rajasthan, Madhya Pradesh, and also Delhi. The Congress Party under Sonia Gandhi had grown into a formidable force heading governments in 14 states. The Congress Party had not come to terms with coalition politics and hence advocated one-party rule. The mass base the Congress Party enjoyed was detrimental for the growth of strong regional parties. It was only with the rise of the RSS, and its political wing, first the Jana Sangh, later the Bharatiya Jana Sangh, and finally the BJP that the Congress faced a serious challenge.

Towards the end of the 1980's under V. P. Singh's Janata Dal government caste-based politics became more and more prominent. Caste equations gave rise to strong caste-based regional parties. Even casteless religions like Christianity, and Islam started demanding government reservations to the backward castes in their religions. It was also reported that lesser known Christian churches in some rural areas in India have special places for higher castes, and separate enclosures for the lower castes.

The Congress Party traditionally cornered the votes of Muslims and "backward castes", while the BJP won the votes of traders, businessmen, and the Hindu middle class. However, with the advent of the pro-Muslim Samajwadi Party (SP), Congress Party's Muslim vote bank saw a dramatic decline. The remaining support of the backward castes turned towards the pro-backward caste party the Bahujan Samaj Party (BSP). Without the support of these two sections of society, the Congress Party's electoral curve took a steep dive.

Under Sonia Gandhi's leadership, the party regained some lost ground. It developed strong regional leaders like Digvijay Singh (who was ousted in the December 2003 elections as Chief Minister of Madhya Pradesh), Ashok Gehlot, the Chief Minister of Rajasthan, who suffered a fate similar to that of Digvijay Singh, Vilasrao Deshmukh, and his successor Chief Minister of Maharashtra Sushilkumar Shinde, Chief Minister of

The Election That Shaped Gujarat

Punjab Amrinder Singh, Chief Minister of Delhi Sheila Dixit, Chief Minister of Assam Tarun Gogoi, Chief Minister of Uttaranchal Narayan Dutt Tiwari, Chief Minister of Chhatisgarh Ajit Jogi (who was also ousted in the December 2003 elections), Chief Minister of Kerala A. K. Antony, and Chief Minister of Karnataka S. M. Krishna. Hence the Congress Party ruled virtually every major state in India, but could not head the Central Government in Delhi.

Gujarat and the Congress Party

In Gujarat, the Congress Party's election preparations started the day Narendra Modi was announced as BJP's chief ministerial candidate. Both the BJP and the Congress Party left no issue untouched: Kashmir and Sonia Gandhi's Italian origin, Godhra and the definition of pseudo-secularism, post-Godhra riots, damage to Gujarati pride, demand for Modi's resignation, support for Modi by the masses of Gujarat, everything was hotly debated. It was probably one of the most keenly contested elections. Certain sections of the intelligentsia had convinced themselves that Modi would not win.

Modi appealed to both the Muslims and the Hindus. He told them that to make Gujarat more rich and prosperous people should rise above their religion and caste identities and work collectively to make Gujarat a developed state, and India a developed country. For Modi, nothing was more important than development, and for development, technology and technological advancement were essential. Modi believed that the youth of India would work to achieve India her rightful place among world nations.

The Congress Party tried to extend the dynastic rule of the Nehru-Gandhi family by displaying photos of Priyanka Gandhi-Vadra, the daughter of Sonia Gandhi, and grand-daughter of Indira Gandhi. The party's posters showed Priyanka, Sonia and Indira together. Boosted by the press blitzkrieg against Modi, the Congress Party made Narendra Modi its main target. But this is where they gravely erred, for the more they attacked Modi, the more Modi grew in stature among the Gujaratis. The Congress Party thus made a strategic error in targeting Modi, when they should have made their attack more impersonal and focused on the terrorist attacks and the increased violence under the aegis of the BJP government. The party even came out with posters showing Modi surrounded by "black cat commandos" against the backdrop of the Akshardham temple. It showed bodies lying scattered outside the temple. This particular poster, instead of increasing Congress Party's popularity, shocked people as the party had chosen to politicize the terrorist attack on Hindus at Akshardham.

Politicization of Events

As both Godhra and Akshardham incidents became politicized, the BJP too came out with a poster showing a horrified Modi looking at a picture of the burning Sabarmati Express and the Akshardham temple. The poster bore the slogan, "Be it Godhra or

Akshardham, we will wipe out terrorism." The EC objected to such posters claiming that they provoked people on communal lines.

In order to appease Muslim politicians parties organize *Iftaar* parties. This is done in the Muslim holy month of *Ramadan*. People break their daily fast in the evening. However, no political party felicitates Hindus on occasions like Diwali/Deepavali (the festival of lights), or Holi (festival of colors). By some strange twist of irony only Bihar's Lalu Prasad Yadav celebrated both Muslim and Hindu festivals, and publicly celebrated the Hindu festival of Holi. The Congress Party decided not to host *Iftaar* parties in 2002 as a mark of respect for the suffering people in several drought hit areas, and the victims of the Gujarat riots. The BJP at once labeled this move as yet another show of pseudo-secularism. By publicizing the issue of *Iftaar* parties, the Congress Party did not gain much Muslim votes. Instead, it merely reiterated its traditional support for Muslims. It would have augured well for the Congress Party if it had not mentioned anything about *Iftaars* at election time, for there was not much to gain, and a lot to lose.

Campaigning Fare

The Congress Party brought its MLAs and Chief Ministers from other states to campaign against Modi in Gujarat. Not to be outdone, BJP ran an aggressive election campaign involving twenty-two of its top leaders. Even Prime Minister Vajpayee took an active part in the electioneering, addressing multiple public meetings on December 5 and 7. Other senior leaders like Advani campaigned more extensively. Amitabh Sinha, BJP's media cell chief in Delhi, revealed that the party had planned to "carpet bomb" Gujarat with its leaders. Advani's first election meeting took place in the earthquake affected Bhuj region.

While Narendra Modi focused more on Godhra and Gandhinagar, his predecessor Keshubhai Patel campaigned in Bhotad and Vamipur areas. Party president Venkaiah Naidu campaigned in Vadodara, and then in Anand. Human Resource Development Minister Murli Manohar Joshi went to Ankleshwar, Bharuch, and Surat. Pramod Mahajan campaigned in the Saurashtra region, while Sushma Swaraj concentrated on Patan and Ahmedabad. Arun Jaitley coordinated the overall campaign and also went to Himmat Nagar to address public meetings. Uma Bharti visited Jetput and the pilgrim city of Junagadh. Former Chief Minister of Uttar Pradesh Rajnath Singh campaigned in Kheda and Godhra, while Sahib Singh Verma traveled to Bayad, Modasa, Bhiloda, and Idar constituencies. BJP Chief Minister of Jharkhand Marandi went to Faladara and Motishambadi. The BJP roped in film celebrities turned politicians -- Shatrughan Sinha and Vinod Khanna -- along with actresses like Hema Malini and Vijay Shanti to woo the masses.

About a week before the elections, the then Chief Minister of Uttar Pradesh Mayawati declared that though her party, the Bahujan Samaj Party (BSP), was contesting 31 assembly constituencies in Gujarat, she would campaign for the BJP in constituencies where her party had not fielded any candidates. Such a move by the "secular" backward caste leader was seen as a major step towards closer political ties between the backward castes and the BJP.

Winter Session of Parliament

Advani declared on the floor of Parliament that the government wanted free, fair and peaceful elections in Gujarat, and asserted that India could never be converted into a Hindu state, adding that the Indian people would neither condone communal violence nor tolerate pseudo-secularism.[213]

The Opposition parties attacked the BJP and the VHP, accusing them of trying to create trouble in Gujarat ahead of the elections. Some of them demanded the detention of leaders like Pravin Togadia till the completion of the election process. The motion, moved by CPI (M)'s Subodh Roy, to highlight the "failure of the government in curbing communal elements in the country, especially in Gujarat", was defeated by a voice vote.

The BJP, fed up with the Congress Party's slander in Parliament responded by accusing the Congress Party of attempting to polarize Gujarat for the sake of power. Defense Minister George Fernandes made a scathing comment on Sonia Gandhi and accused her of provoking her party members to create uproar in the House. "The leader of the Opposition is provoking her members. She is also chewing gum," he pointed out caustically.[214]

Declaration of Election Dates

The EC announced on October 7, 2002, that elections to the Gujarat Legislative Assembly would be held on December 12, 2002. It was an hour after the constitution bench of the Supreme Court passed its order upholding the EC's stance on Gujarat. Lyngdoh declared that the polls would be conducted in one phase. The last date for filing nominations would be November 25, with scrutiny taking place on November 26, and last date for withdrawals would be November 28. The counting of votes would take place on December 15, and results would probably be declared on the same day. The strict "model code of conduct" was enforced immediately. The EC asked for 400 companies of paramilitary forces. However, the Central government could provide only 353 companies, and hence the plan to provide one company with every returning officer was scaled down, and the companies were deployed only in sensitive or riot-prone areas.

Lyngdoh allowed foreign media and diplomatic missions to witness the elections, saying that they would be welcome to do so. They would get the same facilities they got during the successful Jammu & Kashmir elections. By asking foreign diplomats to witness the Gujarat elections, the CEC once again exceeded his authority, and seemed

---

[213] *The Hindu.* "India will never be a theocratic state", November 28, 2002.

[214] *The Hindu.* "Uproar over Fernandes remarks on Sonia". May 01, 2002.

willing to transgress the nation's foreign policy arena. No one objected but the absence of diplomats was a clear sign that Lyngdoh's scheme was flawed.

The entire electoral process for Gujarat, with a population of 50 million, and about 33 million registered voters, was to be completed by December 20. Lyngdoh said that the EC had found nearly 400,000 (about one percent of registered voters) people not residing at the place where their names were registered. Of these, about 176,000 wanted to re-register. For the mammoth task of conducting elections, more than 35,000 polling stations were set up. Electronic Voting Machines (EVMs) were to be used in all the constituencies. About 45,000 EVMs were shifted from Uttar Pradesh to be pressed into service on the day of election, while another 5,000 were kept as stand-by and ready replacement. Voting was scheduled between 8 a.m. and 5 p.m. on December 12, 2002. The cost of elections to the state exchequer was estimated at 400 million rupees ($ 9 million). Nearly 200,000 persons were trained to handle the EVMs, and to be in charge of polling stations. The polling stations were equipped with modern communication systems to report any untoward incident.

Voters could identify themselves through a variety of means. Relief camp cards, property documents, student identity cards and even railway and bus passes were considered valid proof of voter identity. Alternatives to the EC-issued voter photo identity cards included valid passports, driving licenses, permanent income tax account number cards, service identity cards issued by employees of the state and central governments, public sector undertakings, local bodies and private industrial houses. Bank and post office accounts opened prior to November 1, 2002 were also accepted as proof. Ration cards, scheduled caste, tribe and other backward class certificates issued by competent government authorities, property documents such as *"pattas"*/registered deeds, arms and weapons' licenses and photo certificates of physically challenged were also considered valid. Conductor licenses issued by the state transport authority, pension documents such as ex-servicemen's pension book/pension payment order, freedom fighter identity cards, domicile certificates issued by the state government, identity cards and house allotment letters issued by the Slum Clearance Board up to October 31, 2002, insurance policies and certificates of residence issued by village administration officers were all considered as valid proof. The EC's announcement allowing these myriad options was to ensure a large voter turnout, and enable all registered voters to cast their ballot with the least inconvenience.

Media & Elections

It was reported that on December 5, 2002 a younger brother of a Congress Party candidate walked into the office of a senior media editor in Saurashtra, took out two bundles of currency notes containing 10,000 rupees ($ 220) each and gave them to the editor along with four pages of handwritten notes.[215] It was the "fee" for printing the

---

[215] *Rediff on the Net.* "Media's Rs. 50 crore shame in Gujarat", December 7, 2002.

speech of Sonia Gandhi in the newspaper. In Rajkot, the same day, a BJP leader told a journalist to publish a speech delivered by Narendra Modi. He wanted his picture to go along with it. The "fees" was 160 rupees ($3.5) per column centimeter. This rate was perhaps on the lower side and could even go up to 800 rupees ($17) per column centimeter. Such "advertorials" and pictures have now become part of electioneering in India.

It was reported that each candidate had a budget of one million rupees ($22,000) to pay mainstream and regional newspapers for favorable publicity. Journalists received money for not publishing campaign reports of rivals. Vikram Vakil, Editor-Publisher of *Hotline Weekly*, said, "In Gujarat 400 candidates fight election seriously and they end up paying Rs. 50 crores ($11million) to editors and owners of newspapers".

Other Observers

The "Concerned Citizens Tribunal" headed by former Supreme Court Justice V. R. Krishna Iyer began an inquiry into Godhra and post-Godhra events even when an official judicial probe was underway. This extra-judicial activism took on a life of its own in India, drawing conclusions based on selective evidence, producing media-hyped controversies and exacerbating political and social conflict. Vigilance by citizens is a primary requirement for the sustenance of healthy democracies. However, unbridled activism and ideologically driven public posturing merely delay justice and development. When retired judges of the highest court in India come under a banner and form a parallel tribunal to examine and pass judgments it amounts to gross contempt of democratic institutions and the judicial system. Interestingly, Justice Iyer praised Narendra Modi in 2013, saying he was a good candidate to become Prime Minister of India.[216]

Nevertheless, the tribunal met people, examined evidence and delivered a verdict on Modi without inviting him or listening to the version of Modi. It demanded the arrest and prosecution of Modi stating that the large-scale violence that followed the Godhra carnage was directly related to his "inaction". This "judgment" by the tribunal just before the elections fouled the atmosphere further. The tribunal did not ask the BJP, RSS, VHP, and Bajrang Dal representatives to appear before it and refute the allegations. It was a one-sided affair, a kangaroo court no less. The state government said that the tribunal had no statutory authority to conduct an inquiry in such a matter and the findings of the tribunal were one-sided and not based on facts established in accordance with constitutionally sanctioned legal processes of law. The release issued by the state government cautioned people against being misled by such self-appointed guardians of law and order, and urged people to await the report of the Gujarat

---

[216] *IBN-Live*. "Ex-SC judge Krishna Iyer praises Modi, says he is a good candidate for Prime Ministership", September 19, 2013.

government-appointed Commission of Inquiry headed by Justice Nanavati to probe the Godhra carnage and the subsequent violence. The VHP too attacked the tribunal's actions and threatened legal action against those behind it. Pravin Togadia criticized retired judge Iyer for signing the report and said that he treated the report as an anti-Hindu pamphlet.

BJP Election Manifesto

The BJP manifesto focused on *"Saanskritik Raashtrawaad"* ("cultural nationalism") as the main electoral theme. The party believed that terrorism could only be successfully countered by cultural nationalism. The main issues for Gujarat elections were cultural nationalism, safety, security of the common man, and developmental work done by the BJP government during its tenure. The state BJP president Rajendrasinh Rana said that solving Gujarat's perennial water problem was the biggest achievement of the BJP government in its four and a half year rule.

No general election campaign in India can ever be complete without some reference to India's intransigent neighbor, Pakistan. After the attack on the Akshardham temple, Modi routinely expressed fears that Pakistan could intensify attempts to vitiate the communal atmosphere in the state through more attacks. He warned that Pakistan could pump in fake currency in order to destabilize the economy, and to disrupt the elections.

Trying to characterize a Congress Party victory as a win for Pakistan, Modi accused the Congress of speaking the language of the separatist *Hurriyat* parties in Kashmir, alleging the state Congress president Shankersinh Vaghela had on a recent trip to the U.S. promised to help a U.S.-based group to probe the communal violence in Gujarat, and blamed the BJP and its affiliates for provoking Muslims to commit the Godhra massacre.

In Karamsad, where the first public meeting after the declaration of elections took place, Modi made a mention of "check dams" and said that in the five years under BJP rule, the government had built 45,000 check dams to harvest rain water, compared to only 5,000 built in the previous 45 years under the Congress Party's "misrule". He said the BJP governments in Gujarat had outperformed themselves in virtually every sector, and cited the creation of a water grid – India's first -- inter-linking the river Narmada with the river Sabarmati. The BJP, he said, had plans to link all 24 rivers in Gujarat, and harness as much of the water as possible. He referred to the construction of an expressway between Ahmedabad and Vadodara as one of the achievements of the BJP government.

On October 30, when Advani inaugurated the BJP's election campaign, he too referred to the machinations of Pakistan. He charged Pakistan with wanting to avenge the creation of Bangladesh. In his speech at Bhuj, Advani warned Pakistan that there had been three wars already between the two nations, and hence a fourth war could once and for all decide issues between them.

Congress Party Campaign

On November 11, eleven days after Modi's Karamsad meeting, the Congress party chose the very same venue to launch its election campaign. At this meeting Congress party leader Kamal Nath said his party would dislodge the corrupt and inept BJP government led by Modi. It was a serious error on the part of Kamal Nath to accuse Modi of corruption. The people of Gujarat adore Modi because of his clean image.

Shankersinh Vaghela's speech focused on the failure of co-operative banks in the state that saw millions of rupees of middle class savings disappear. Vaghela tried to put the blame on the BJP, and said that Gujarat deserved better governance. He promised to set up special courts to try members of the current BJP government. Vaghela conveniently forgot that many in the Congress Party were involved in the scam as were BJP members.

While the BJP claimed to monopolize the advocacy of Hindu rights, the Congress found itself confused. Whichever issue it picked up, it embarrassingly found itself to be at its roots. Probably the most effective attack on the BJP would have been the security lapses that led to the Godhra massacre that in turn triggered the riots. But blaming the BJP for failing to protect Hindus was a double-edged sword for the Congress. It would mean fighting the BJP on BJP's own turf, with BJP's rules, and risking the loss of Muslim votes.

As Narendra Modi raised in his speeches the issue of Vaghela undertaking a "dollar yatra" to the U.S., and inviting a U.S.-based group to probe the communal violence in Gujarat, Vaghela clarified that though he had visited the U.S., and a panel on religion approached him to investigate the recent communal violence, he did not invite them. All he had done was to tell them that he would read their report. But the BJP countered by saying that without a probe, a report would not be possible.

As the election date approached, electioneering became increasingly shrill. Sonia Gandhi was sharply critical of the BJP, charging that that BJP was only talking about terrorism but had no idea about the kind of sacrifices required to fight the menace. Alluding to the assassinations of Indira Gandhi and Rajiv Gandhi, she said that the "cowardly people" who took terrorists like Maulana Masoor Azhar and others to Kandahar should not talk about terrorism.

Sonia Gandhi was referring to the jailed Muslim terrorists who were released by India in exchange for the safety of the passengers of the hijacked IC-814 Indian Airlines flight. The plane was hijacked by Pakistanis en route to Delhi from Katmandu. They diverted the plane first to Pakistan, then to the United Arab Emirates, and finally to Kandahar, Afghanistan, where the Taliban gave the hijackers safe refuge. The Pakistani terrorists released by India later organized themselves into "Jaish-e-Mohammad", a group banned in India, and labeled a terrorist organization by the U.S. Another terrorist released by India was the Pakistani national Omar Sheikh. Initially Pakistani authorities offered safe refuge to Omar Sheikh. *Who killed Daniel Pearl?* by the French author and philosopher Bernard Levy describes the deadly saga of Omar Sheikh.[217]

When the Indian government asked that these terrorists be repatriated to India to face criminal charges for the murder of the Indian passenger Rupin Katiyal on-board IC 814, Pakistani authorities refused to apprehend any of them. This failure of the Pakistani authorities gave the terrorists freedom to indulge in anti-Indian, anti-Jewish, and anti-American activities. Omar Sheikh was later arrested, tried and sentenced to death by the Pakistani government for the kidnapping and murder of Daniel Pearl. If the Pakistani authorities had acted earlier the life of Daniel Pearl could well have been saved.

The BJP- led NDA government was criticized for being weak in releasing known terrorists in exchange for Indian passengers. People cited examples of the Israeli action in Entebbe many years earlier in a similar situation. The BJP campaign to counter criticism included three well-made and effective ads that highlighted the Godhra incident, the attack on Akshardham, and on Islam-inspired terrorism. Another series of ads that were published in the print media proclaimed *"Gujarat's Gaurav"* and attempted to establish how the Congress Party had portrayed Gujaratis as violent and without remorse. The BJP believed that the reach of local cable networks was more extensive than the individual reach of popular news channels like *Zee*, *Aaj Tak*, and *Star*. Therefore, the party advertised Modi-centric campaign ads only on the local cable channels like *Alpha TV* and *ETV*, and the state-run *Doordarshan*. The BJP also launched its interactive website related to Gujarat.

After releasing the 15-page BJP manifesto titled "BJP: Savior of fifty million Gujaratis", Modi spoke about the social evil of coerced or forced religious conversions. He said that if the BJP was voted back to power, he would enact a law preventing forcible religious conversions in Gujarat. Such an anti-conversion law was necessary to prevent change of religion by people out of fear and greed. He said his government would study the law already in force in Tamil Nadu, Madhya Prasdesh and Andhra Pradesh and then enact a similar anti-conversion law.

Modi also proposed the creation of a new state commando force to counter terrorism. This proposed anti-terrorist training program would be named "Sudarshan Suraksha Kavach" (*Sudarshan* is the name of the weapon of Lord Vishnu, *suraksha* means security, and *kavach* is armor). Under this program identity cards would be issued to residents near areas bordering Pakistan, and training imparted in the use of modern weapons for self-defense to deter infiltration from Pakistan.

The Congress Party still had support in Gujarat. Muslims felt that Modi was the hero of Gujarati Hindus, and hence their vote really did not matter. Some Muslims, understanding the dynamic in the state, supported Modi. Those Muslims from Modi's village of Vadnagar campaigned for Modi. Moreover, Modi spoke of 50 million

---

[217] Levy, B. (2003). *Who killed Daniel Pearl?* Melville House.

The Election That Shaped Gujarat

Gujaratis, deliberately trying to play down caste and religious divides. For Modi this collective image was important, and he used the concept of Gujarati pride to try and bring Gujaratis together, albeit with the knowledge that he had been cast as anti-Muslim. Addressing a public rally in Maninagar (Modi's constituency) on the last day of electioneering, Prime Minister Vajpayee said that Gujarat had set a target of ten percent growth rate during the next five years, and a BJP government would be the right choice to fulfill this goal.

The BJP's main vote bank was the middle-class, the traders, and the upper castes. The question in everyone's mind was "Will BJP's vote bank vote?" In just two days from the closing of official campaigning, BJP would have to get some of their apathetic supporters to cast their ballot. Voting means standing in line, often under a blazing sun, and waiting for one's turn to cast the ballot. Many prefer to skip the exercise. Even though election days are usually declared government holidays, private offices are open. A low voter turn out would make things difficult for the BJP.

One BJP team was working behind the scenes, sending SMS messages to each and every mobile phone in Gujarat using the latest technology. The messages were couched in catchy slogans reminding people to cast their votes. These high-tech messages specially aimed at the younger generation did their trick. First time voters and college students were particularly impressed. Of those between the ages of 18 to 25, over sixty percent voted for BJP. The entire focus of the BJP was to ensure maximum polling. For this mammoth task the BJP had issued specific directions to its activists to concentrate on bringing voters to the polling booths and educating them on using the electronic voting machines (EVMs).

Election Day and After

In an interview on December 12, 2002 Advani expressed confidence in his party winning a comfortable majority. Advani said, "I have never witnessed such a campaign during the last 20-22 years since the BJP was formed or in the 50 years of the Jan Sangh's existence. Despite this, if people give another mandate to the BJP, it will be comparable to the one in 1977 when Jayaprakash Narayan and opposition parties were under attack... Another mandate for the BJP would mean that people in a democracy understood what was wrong and what was right...." The Deputy Prime Minister cast his vote at the Bhardiavas Municipal School in Shahpur constituency. Modi was an early voter in Sarkhej constituency in Ahmedabad, and described the poll as *"loktantra ka mahaparv"* ("The big festival of democracy").

Exit polls refuted Modi's claims that the BJP would get over 120 seats. They predicted a simple majority for the BJP. The *Aaj Tak* exit poll indicated around 93-109 seats for the BJP, and that the Congress Party might get between 72 and 88 seats in the Assembly. The *Zee News-Taleem* exit poll gave BJP and the Congress 101 and 69 seats respectively. Independents were likely to win 11 assembly constituencies. This poll covered more than 9,000 voters across 31 constituencies, and forecast that BJP would get 57 percent of the vote share against 34 percent for the Congress. Even region-wise, BJP would be well ahead of the Congress. In North Gujarat, BJP was expected to get 54 per cent of the vote share, and the Congress party 37 percent. In the crucial Saurashtra region, BJP was expected to get 48 percent of the votes while the Congress would get 40 percent. In central Gujarat, the BJP vote share was estimated to be 60 percent while the Congress share was expected to be a low of 34 percent. In South Gujarat, BJP would get 50 percent of the votes against 24 percent votes of the Congress Party.

Voting in Godhra was peaceful. There were stray incidents of stone throwing, when some miscreants hurled stones at correspondents of two television channels. At the hot spot of Signal Falia, the area where the Sabarmati Express was set on fire, long lines of voters could be seen. Women were allowed to vote first so that if trouble broke out they would be the first to return home. But the reason for women to vote first was simple and less dramatic. Women had to return home and cook for the family. Most voters in the locality are Muslims, and local Muslim leaders spared no effort to ensure that every Muslim registered voter cast his/her vote.

The elections ended peacefully. Statistics released by the EC showed that 61.52 percent of those eligible had cast their votes. According to a rough calculation made by Arun Jaitley, BJP should win 124 seats. But it performed even better. Areas worst hit by post-Godhra riots registered 65 percent polling. Panchmahal district in central Gujarat, which includes Godhra constituency, registered 60 percent voting. Districts of Kutch, Bhavnagar and Jamnagar in the Saurashtra and Kutch regions saw 55 percent voting. In urban Rajkot 60 percent of the electorate exercised their franchise while Valsad, Amreli and Gandhinagar areas polled 62 percent. Patan, Banaskantha, Sabarkantha and Bharuch polled 65 percent each. Dangs and Surendranagar districts saw 58 percent. Dahod witnessed 63 percent, Surat 65 percent and Junagadh 61 percent voting.

The BJP outdid the Congress Party in the battle of mobilization, though the Congress Party had begun with an advantage. The *fatwa* asking the Muslim community to vote for Congress was certainly an advantage. The Muslim community, which had suffered in the post-Godhra communal clashes in central Gujarat, was only too eager to vote *en masse* for the Congress Party. Some Muslim leaders openly declared that in the absence of Samajwadi Party (SP) – the pro-Muslim party advocating Muslim rights -- the Congress Party was a better choice than the BJP. Some circles boasted that there would be 100 per cent Muslim participation to defeat the BJP in Godhra. Such boasts were not hollow. The towns of Halol and Kalol, that experienced massive communal violence in March and April of 2002 against Muslims in retaliation to Godhra massacre, saw the entire Muslim population coming out to vote against the BJP.

Muslim voter turnout was particularly large in the riot-hit districts of Ahmedabad, Vadodara, Mehsana and Panchmahals, that includes Godhra. In Godhra, nearly 90 percent of the 40,000 Muslim voters cast their ballot, according to state election commission sources. BJP workers complained of large scale bogus voting. Shahpur, Kalupur, Mirzapur, Naroda and other parts of the walled city of Ahmedabad, which witnessed large scale communal violence, saw heavy polling with some areas witnessing more than 70 percent turnout. The female to male voter turnout of the Muslim community was almost equal, suggesting that the entire Muslim community was out at the polling stations casting their ballot.

The BJP had an advantage in Central Gujarat, where communal violence polarized the two communities. It had the clear backing of the majority Hindu community. The problem that faced the BJP was the well-known apathy of the middle classes towards elections. Coupled with this was the fact that December was the Gujarati marriage season. In fact December 12, 2002, was a particularly auspicious day, as per Hindu astrological calculations, for performing marriage and other ceremonies. However, Narendra Modi and his party effectively handled the situation. Gujarat saw a massive turnout of over 60 percent, higher than the usual average of around 55 percent.

The myth of Congress Party's field strength was shattered after the exit polls. As the smell of defeat came painfully close, Congress Party's so-called giant killer Yatin Oza blamed the media for creating the Modi phenomenon. He said that the satellite channels -- *Star TV, Zee TV, and Aaj Tak* -- which kept showing the attacks against the Muslims pushed the Hindus closer to Modi. Oza said that even before the elections he knew he would lose, but he still fought against Modi, respecting the party *diktat*. In an interesting turn of events, on the morning of the polls, Yatin Oza's father Narendra Oza, being a Modi supporter, wanted to join the Chief Minister at the polling booth to cast his vote, but Yatin Oza prevailed upon his father to spare him embarrassment.

Counting of votes took place on December 15. As voting was done using electronic voting machines, results were expected to be announced by afternoon. Foolproof security arrangements were made to ensure smooth counting in all district headquarters. Counting for the by-election to Mehsana Lok Sabha seat, held simultaneously with assembly polls, was also taken up on Sunday. In Surat City (West) assembly constituency, polling was countermanded following the death of BJP candidate who was Minister of State for Law Hemant Chapatwala. Re-polling was held on Saturday, December 14, in fifteen polling booths of seven assembly constituencies, where polling was marred by technical snags in the electronic voting machines, or by protests and stone throwing.

Awaiting results, Narendra Modi called H. V. Sheshadri, a senior and respected member of the RSS, to tell him that he had done his job, and was sure of a BJP victory. Modi then offered to quit as Chief Minister, and requested the BJP to elect someone else for the job. Whether Modi's offer to resign was an act of renunciation, or bluff to reinforce his position in the party, and quell any dissent after the victory, it is difficult to tell. But the position of Narendra Modi became stronger only after the Prime Minister expressed support for his leadership. It was a secret call, and not many knew about it.

Results

On the morning of December 15, when counting began, leading news channels still stuck to their forecasts and kept repeating that there was a tough fight between the Congress and the BJP. As the day progressed, and results started pouring in, the deception ended, and the massive BJP victory could no longer be denied. The English-language media that had launched a "remove Modi" campaign bit the dust. The people of Gujarat returned Narendra Modi with unprecedented majority, even greater than the coveted two-thirds majority. Gujarat gave Modi a 70 percent majority. BJP president Venkaiah Naidu termed it a victory for nationalist and patriotic forces. He said that the people of Gujarat gave a befitting reply to those who were running down Gujarat and its people not only in India, but also abroad. He congratulated Narendra Modi, the state leadership, and all the BJP workers for registering a brilliant victory over the Congress Party.

The BJP won 126 seats in the 182-member assembly, bettering its tally of 117 in the 1998 election. Congress, which had 57 members in the dissolved house, fared worse than predicted, getting only 51. Of the remaining four seats, independents and the Janata Dal-United (JD-U) won two constituencies each. It was the BJP's first major victory after a string of defeats in the previous two years.

The newly elected BJP legislators met on Monday, December 16, 2002 and elected the 52 year-old Narendra Damodardass Modi as their leader. Modi and a number of his cabinet colleagues romped home comfortably, but the BJP got a shock when former chief minister and industries minister Suresh Mehta lost the Mandvi seat in Kutch, as predicted in the election surveys. The loss of the veteran politician was both a shock and a boon for Modi, as Mehta could have possibly challenged Modi's position, having himself been a Chief Minister once. In the Maninagar assembly constituency, Modi beat Congress Party's Yatin Oza by a massive margin of over 75,000 votes.

The BJP made a clean sweep of the tribal-dominated eastern belt of Gujarat, winning all the 12 seats in the region, including Godhra. This was a major breakthrough for the BJP. In the Vadodara area, one of the worst hit by communal violence, BJP won all the 13 seats. Congress lost a prestigious seat when its candidate Mahendrasinh Vaghela, son of PCC president Shankersinh Vaghela, was defeated in Mashru assembly constituency. Prominent among Congress winners were Amarsinh Chaudhary from the tribal seat of Khedbrahma and Faroukh Sheikh in riot-hit Muslim dominated area of Kalupur in Ahmedabad city. BJP's performance in the Patel dominated Saurashtra region was poorer than before. Where it won 52 of the 58 seats last time, this time it yielded several seats to the Congress. Similarly, in the quake affected Kutch region, it lost some seats. The BJP did well in central Gujarat, including Ahmedabad, where it scored impressive victories in Naroda and Maninagar. Deputy Prime Minister Advani

The Election That Shaped Gujarat

and Modi described the verdict as the defeat of forces that had spread slander and venom against Gujarati people, administration and Gujarat's police.

A meeting of the BJP National Executive was called on December 22 and 23 to discuss election results, and prepare an action plan for elections in other state assemblies, one of them in the adjoining state of Rajasthan, then under Congress Party rule. The incumbent Congress lost the by-polls, and for the first time the BJP secured Sagwara, Bali, and Bansur seats. Hence Venkiah Naidu said that the BJP won not only in Gujarat but also Rajasthan. It was possibly a prelude to things to come, as in a year's time, the BJP came back to power in Rajasthan, Madhya Pradesh, and Chhattisgarh.

A jubilant Narendra Modi said that the Gujarat victory proved all the nay-sayers wrong. As results started trickling in, Modi headed for former Chief Minister Keshubhai Patel's house, where in an act of reconciliation he thanked Keshubhai for his help. Modi said that he needed the blessings of all the experienced leaders. He accused the media saying, "For the last ten months, you (media) people have been saying that Gujarat is burning. But the reality is that the riots occurred in only two percent of Gujarat... People have given their verdict and now it is the turn of the media to accept the truth and be accountable for its false propaganda in the past 10 months and try to build a rapport with the people." Addressing his first press conference at the BJP headquarters, Modi said the BJP victory symbolized Gujarat's *swabhiman* (self respect) and *gaurav* (pride).

Modi affirmed that BJP would implement its election manifesto and work towards development and peace. He asked the Congress to accept dutifully its constitutional obligations as the opposition, and play a constructive role so that Gujarat could progress. Modi pointed out that there were no full stops in politics, indicating that whether it was the BJP or the Congress in power, the progress of Gujarat ought not to stop. Modi said that he had begun his electoral campaign on October 31, the birth anniversary of Sardar Vallabhbhai Patel, and from the Sardar's hometown in Karamsad. The Karamsad leg began with a youth rally, in which Modi emphasized the importance of the role youths had to play in the development of India in the 21st century. Officially, the youth wing of the BJP – the Bharatiya Janata Yuva Morcha (BJYM) -- was in charge of the inauguration, and BJYM's national president G. Kishan Reddy, and BJYM Gujarat unit's president Amit Thakkar shared the stage with Modi. Modi thus gave the youth a platform at the historic birthplace of Sardar Patel, and appealed to the youth to take their rightful place in the progress of Gujarat and of India as a whole.

At the BJP headquarters meeting, when asked whether he had any message for the Muslims of the state, Modi declared that his message of peace and brotherhood was for the state's entire 50 million people and that he would not divide the people on the basis of religion. Modi's slogan of *Panch Karod Gujarati* (fifty million Guajratis) included Gujarati Hindus, Gujarati Jains, and Gujarati Muslims. Refuting the claim that his party won because there was a Hindutva wave in the state, Modi said "What wave existed is for the political and media analysts to say; I believe that our victory is because Gujarat's 50 million people wanted us back for all our good work."

On December 16, 2002, Modi was elected leader of the BJP legislature party in Gujarat, and six days later he was sworn in as Chief Minister. Senior minister Ashok Bhatt proposed his name and six legislators seconded it at a meeting attended by BJP's national president Venkaiah Naidu. Following Modi's election as BJP legislative party leader, Naidu felicitated him with a garland while former chief minister Keshubhai Patel presented him a turban.

Accepting defeat, Vaghela did concede that to the common man all that mattered was the Godhra incident. He pointed out, "Even the tribals voted for the BJP, saying they were Hindus first." The BJP and its affiliates have traditionally referred to the tribals of India as *Vanavasi* (*van* = forest, *vasi* = inhabitant), and hence the word *Vanavasi* meant an inhabitant of the forest, while the Congress Party referred to the tribals as *Adivasi* (*adi* = first, *vasi* = inhabitant), or the first inhabitants, similar to the aborigines of Australia. There is a fundamental difference between Hindus and tribals, according to the Congress Party's adumbration of Indian history. They claim that the tribals in India are the original inhabitants, that Hindus were invaders from Central Asia, and that therefore the later colonization of India by Muslims and the British was merely part of a long line of such invasions.

The tribal peoples have Hindu names, and they worship Hindu deities in addition to their own. The tribals have different rituals which resemble those of the Hindus. Hence they can be considered to belong to the Hindu fold. The tribals of India as the rest of Hindu India follow the Hindu way of life, which is pluralist, and allows various beliefs and rituals to mutually co-exist. For instance, Tamil Nadu was inhabited by Neolithic people about 3500- 4000 years ago. Some tribals preferred to live in their original habitats, while some migrated, settled down as agricultural communities in the river-fed plains and started moving into the bronze and iron ages -- developing language, arts, culture and trade and influencing and influenced by other peoples, technologies, cultures and philosophies (Vedism, Buddhism, Jainism, etc.).

By Sangam age (third century BCE – first century CE) Tamil-speaking people had become deeply influenced by Sanskrit, started revering the Vedas as sacred texts, and begun protecting Brahmins (who came from the north) as the keepers of the Vedas. But still a lot of the original tribal practices, customs, traditions, worship and deities remained with them, a phenomenon reflected in mainstream Tamil society to this day. For instance, Murugan, a tribal deity, although at some point in history became Sanskritised to "Karthikeya" and "Subrahmanya", is still worshipped as a stand-alone deity along with his tribal consort "Valli", by many non-tribal Tamils. Many Murugan temples in Tamilnadu are still officiated by non-Brahmins, as they do in many Shiva and Kali temples. In Tamilnadu, in the month of "*margazhi*" (December 15 to January 15) young unmarried girls wake up very early in the morning, walk around the neighborhood waking up more girls and waiting for them to join in singing the "tiruppavai" -- Vaishnavite hymns -- and go to the river to bathe. Some say that this is an ancient fertility rite, converted by Vaishnavites later into a bhakti procession. Similar tribal deities and traditions still exist among non-tribal Hindus all over India. There are countless examples all over Kerala. Jagannath of Puri is supposed to be a tribal deity too. There is similar speculation about the Tirupati deity – Sri Venkateshwara.

Long ago, the ancestors of today's tribals may have decided that their way of life was best and refused to migrate elsewhere. They decided to remain separate. Even today, tribals are a proud people. This is because the tribals lived their lives on their own terms for a very long time. They never considered themselves superior or inferior to anyone. It must be only in the last two centuries of rampant land-grabbing that they were exploited and their rights violated. The influx of Christian missionaries, both foreign and Indian, has generated conflict in Gujarat as elsewhere. Their attempts at converting the tribal population based on the definition of *Adivasi* have sparked a lot of social upheaval. The tribals were traditionally Congress Party supporters, and prominent Gujarat Congress leader Amarsinh Choudhary is a tribal. The statement of Shankersinh Vaghela that the tribals believed they were Hindus first and then tribals next should be seen in this context. Modi's statement of *Panch karod Gujarati* (fifty million Gujaratis) that transcended caste and religion brought into focus a unified Gujarati identity.

Modi declared that his government's motto would be "appeasement of none and justice to all", clearly indicating that his government would not victimize the Muslim community neither would it appease anybody. It would treat Hindus and Muslims equally. Modi hoped that the Congress would play a constructive role in the progress of Gujarat. He welcomed criticism, adding, "Criticism is needed in a democracy or else it will jeopardize the system, but it has to be within limits." Addressing a meeting of newly elected legislators of the BJP, Modi said that his landslide victory brought with it greater responsibilities, and his government would strive to fulfill all the promises made in the party's election manifesto.

Elections saw eleven out of the 36 women fielded winning seats in the assembly. Seven women candidates out of the eleven nominated by BJP emerged victorious, including the state's education minister Anandiben Pandya, while four Congress women candidates also won.

The Congress Party tried to gloss over this debacle, pledging a renewed commitment to protect and preserve the secular fabric of the Indian polity. It continued its affair with its special brand of secularism. Really, there was never a threat to secularism under BJP, as the party advocated appeasement of none and justice for all. Opponents of the party, however, routinely interpreted the "appeasement of none" part of the slogan as anti-Muslim. For example, the BJP opposed subsidy to Muslim pilgrims for the Hajj. It argued that no country in the world, including Islamic Republics, subsidized personal pilgrimage to the Hajj. It is only in India's strange interpretation of secularism that subsidies are given for Hajj, and not to Hindu pilgrims going to Ayodhya or Vaishnodevi (Hindu places of pilgrimages). The BJP tried to remove these inequalities, but ironically, and considering the dynamics of religion in India, the BJP-led NDA government increased Hajj subsidies during its rule in New Delhi.

Modi's Swearing-in Ceremony
On December 18, 2002, Gujarat's Governor Sunder Singh Bhandari formally invited Modi to form the next government. Earlier, Modi had met the governor and staked the claim of his party to form the government. December 22, 2002 was fixed as the date for the swearing in ceremony for Modi and his Cabinet at the Sardar Patel Stadium in Ahmedabad. After the formation of government, a brief session of the *Vidhan Sabha* (legislative house) was to be held by the end of the year.

On October 7, 2001, when Modi was sworn in as the youngest Chief Minister in place of Keshubhai Patel, it was on a helipad in Gandhinagar. Modi at that time had never contested any elections. A year later it was a different and more confident Narendra Modi. He had survived the Godhra massacre, the post-Godhra riots, the enormous press campaign to remove him, bitter in-fighting in his own party, as well as character assassination at the hands of the media and opposition elements. His government survived even the Akshardham temple attack, fought the elections and effectively countered Congress plans for a comeback. The Modi of 2002 December was very different from the Modi of October 2001.

For the swearing-in ceremony Modi chose a public venue, the Sardar Vallabhbhai Patel stadium. The event was open to public, and for the first time in Indian history, the Prime Minister of India was to attend the swearing in ceremony of a state chief minister. The Congress party objected to Vajpayee's attending the swearing-in ceremony, knowing well that Vajpayee and Modi belonged to the same party. A Congress Party spokesperson complained that the prime minister had "lowered the image of the office by attending the swearing-in ceremony of a chief minister". Such protocols and bureaucratic red-tape are the vestiges of colonialism, and continue to weigh heavily on the nation. While the Congress Party relished and indulged in the luxuries of imperialistic protocol, the BJP decided to adopt a more populist approach to governance.

On the eve of the swearing-in, one of Modi's confidants took a tour of the stadium to see how the stadium was being redied for the big day. Seeing the stadium draped in the Indian tri-color, he immediately called the Chief Minister and advised that the tri-color be replaced by saffron. When India became independent, the tri-color flag of the Congress Party became the nation's flag. The only change was the replacement of the central symbol of a *charkha* (spinning wheel) by the *chakra* (wheel) of the legendary emperor of India, the third century BCE ruler, Ashoka. The Congress Party even today has the same flag, and the central symbol of the spinning wheel is of the same color as the symbol of the centerpiece of India's national flag. From afar, the Congress Party flag looks very much like India's National Flag. The Congress Party's other celebratory symbols also have a tri-color combination without the centre-piece. Modi immediately ordered that the tri-color be replaced by saffron.

Prime Minister Vajpayee, Deputy Prime Minister Advani, Human Resources Development Minister Dr. Murli Manohar Joshi, Chief Minister of Tamil Nadu J. Jayalalithaa, Chief Minister of Haryana Om Prakash Chautala, Chief Minister of Goa Manohar Parrikar, former Chief Minister of Punjab Parkash Singh Badal, former Chief Minister of Jammu & Kashmir Farooq Abdullah, and other Central government ministers, and political leaders attended this gala event. Modi also invited the religious leaders of various Hindu organizations like the Swami Narayan Movement, ISKCON, and others. There was a special area cordoned off for the hermits, monks, and Hindu and Jain renunciates invited to the event. After being sworn-in Modi went to the enclosure of the holy men and took their blessings. Modi's then 85-year-old mother and his elder brother too came to participate in the event.

Huge television screens were installed in the stadium for viewers. The event was telecast live. Nearly 600 reporters from the state, national and international press were present to cover the event. This was the first time that the ceremony was held outside Gandhinagar, the state capital. The venue was shifted to allow the electorate of Maninagar to attend the ceremony. Modi was sworn-in amidst thunderous applause from the crowd that numbered well over a hundred thousand. Modi did not deliver a speech, and there was no talk of either Godhra or the riots or Akshardham. He waved to the crowd and sat in his chair, and witnessed the swearing-in of his cabinet colleagues. Nine Cabinet Ministers were sworn in along with Modi. After the ceremony, Modi sought the blessings of the senior BJP leaders in the traditional Indian way of touching the feet of the elders.

As Modi's vehicle left the stadium, it was surrounded by people. One man shouted, "Modi, the next twenty years are yours!" People were excited on the verge of hysteria. They were there not to see any film celebrity but their Chief Minister, the man whom the press had demonized. It took twenty minutes for his car to cover the one hundred meters from the stadium to the main road. As Modi's vehicle headed towards Gandhinagar, he asked those who were in the vehicle with him for their opinion. All that anyone could say was *"Na Bhuto"* (Never such a gathering in the past). The *Indian Express* newspaper reported of "the sea of humanity" at Modi's swearing-in ceremony. When Modi reached his residence, his young confidant greeted him by saying, *"Naye Mukhya Mantri ka swagat hai"* ("Greetings to the new Chief Minister). Modi replied *"Hum to purane hi hain, abhi aur mehanat karni hai, logon ki umeedoon ko pura karna hai"* (I am the same, but now I have to do more hard work to justify the love of the people").

Modi's Achievements

A close scrutiny of Narendra Modi's performance as Chief Minister, early on, shows him as an able administrator and a commanding leader: determined and tough (see Uday Mahurkar, 29 December 2003, "Beyond Saffron", *India Today*). He is acknowledged as a man who injected new life into a moribund administration. He has, according to Mahurkar, achieved this "through transparency in financial dealings, vision and commitment to development". While other Indian state governments have fallen prey to cobbling together "jumbo cabinets" in a bid to cater to every caste and regional demand, Modi has set a model for good governance, running the Government with the smallest cabinet in the country, comprising fourteen ministers.

In his two years at the helm, Modi brought down the state's revenue deficit to about 25 billion rupees ($500 million) from 67 billion rupees ($1.34 billion) through cost cutting and better financial management. He hiked user charges in education and irrigation, and brought ailing public-sector units out of the red, and implemented restructuring of the economy keeping at bay an Opposition constantly nipping at his heels. Modi worked wonders at the Gujarat Electricity Board (GEB), known as a den of corruption, by reducing its losses by over 10 billion rupees ($200 million) in just a year through steps ranging from checking power theft, slashing agriculture subsidy, and renegotiating old power purchase agreements.

Home Minister Amit Shah, who was also in charge of the Transportation Department, worked hard to increase the revenues by 2.3 billion rupees ($46 million) in just one year. Shah overhauled the Intelligence Bureau as well. Besides, he transformed the Anti-Corruption Bureau from a toothless body into an effective agency to curb corruption.

Mahurkar noted that Modi had won accolades from industrialists and economists for his plan to turn Gujarat into the "petroleum capital of India" by implementing a natural gas network for industrial and domestic use to reduce the state's dependence on coal and power. Within a year, vehicles in Ahmedabad, Surat, Vadodara and Gandhinagar were expected to run on compressed natural gas (CNG). By April 2004, gas would be made available for domestic as well industrial use in Vadodara and by the beginning of 2005 in Ahmedabad, Rajkot, Surat, Surendranagar and Vapi, thanks to a 35 billion rupees ($70 million) gas transmission pipeline being laid by the Gujarat State Petroleum Corporation in collaboration with private industrial houses. The Vibrant Gujarat Global Investor's Meet organized by the Modi Government in 2003 attracted investment proposals worth 560 billion rupees ($ 11.2 billion).

The Modi government sought to cut down revenue expenditure by four percent and increase income by 30 percent, saving three billion rupees ($60 million) in absolute terms through economic reforms and financial management coupled with a resolve to achieve a 10.2 percent growth rate during the Tenth Plan, to mark completion of the first year in office after the 2002 December elections.

Modi spelled out the initiatives taken by his government in the form of *"Panchamrit"*

The Election That Shaped Gujarat

-- a confluence of five powers/ingredients -- education, energy, water, power to the people, and security. Modi pointed out that Gujarat remained the only state in South Asia to create the largest Information Technology (IT) network through Gujarat Statewide

Area Network (GSWAN) for E-governance. Gujarat built a 40,000-km-long fiber optic cable network with the highest teledensity. The state created a world-class revolution of sorts in water management practices having laid a 1,400-km-long pipeline to carry Narmada waters. Surplus water from Narmada was diverted into Sabarmati, Saraswati, Banas Rupen and other seasonal rivers. He said that a permanent solution had been found to meet the perennial shortage of water in the drought-prone region with Narmada waters, bringing an end to the corruption-ridden practice of hiring water tankers to distribute water to villages. An ambitious river-grid project was also taken up to link the Damanganga River in rain-fed South Gujarat. While previous governments built 4,000 check-dams in 40 years, his government had built over 25,000 check-dams in just one year. Gujarat set an example in disaster management not only in the country but the entire world, following the 2001 earthquake, thus winning the prestigious United Nations' Sasakawa Award for disaster reduction.

It is said that many industrialists consider Modi more as a CEO of a successful company than a politician. Unfortunately, given the nature of Indian politics, a section of senior BJP leaders resented that as Modi was not known to dole out favors to his partymen. The Chief Minister also faced the charge that he doesn't believe in collective decision-making. Modi has also been accused of being autocratic in his functioning. Here we see the classic dilemma of states that have ushered in democratic form of governance before the emergence of institutions that make democracies strong and vibrant. Having put the cart before the horse, India can continue to face pressures internally as well as externally for "toeing the rules of democracy" even though that may mean corruption of politics and administration, the looting and wasting of the country's resources, and continued poverty of hundreds of millions of Indians.

But Modi was in some good company. For example, then Union Minister for Divestment Arun Shourie placed state-owned companies such as India's long-distance telephone company and its biggest auto maker in private hands. Despite considerable opposition, he sold off stakes in 34 state-owned companies -- more than the government had divested in the previous three decades. The Indian Government then began preparing to sell oil companies, shipping concerns, and hotels, but since the NDA Government lost the general election in 2004, all of these initiatives were curtailed or simply abandoned. With Modi now India's Prime Minister we may see an attempt to replicate these initiatives and programs to rebuild and develop India. For the first time since the end of British rule India began to redefine government's relationship to business. The Indian economy was expected to expand by at least seven percent the year ending March 2003. Here again, we find that the initiatives taken by the NDA government were abandoned by the UPA-I (2004-2009) and UPA-II (2009-2014) governments, and especially in the UPA-II tenure and corruption became rampant and growth stymied, so much so that Prime Minister Manmohan Singh's own media adviser ended up writing a scathing critique of the UPA-II administration (See, "The Accidental Prime Minister: The Making and Unmaking of Manmohan Singh", New Delhi: Viking, 2014.)

Some of Modi's staunchest supporters are the top bureaucrats who work with him. His Additional Principal Secretary Anil Mukim said that Modi had brought enormous changes in the short time he had been in office, and that government officers and offices were working differently. "You should have seen this place two years ago. It may seem to an outsider that things are not changing, but there is a major shift in the attitude and approach of administrators. The Chief Minister's style of functioning is impressive. Even his silences send a powerful message", he revealed in a long conversation with the authors. Mukim said that unless there were systemic changes in India, individual officers and politicians could only have small impact. It was heartening to see a copy of the *"The Federalist Papers"* on the desk of Anil Mukim, and we felt that officers who thumbed such a book would indeed provide good advice to the Chief Minister. John Jay, one of the revolutionary authors of *The Federalist Papers* said about the United States: "This country and this people seem to have been made for each other, and it appears as if it was the design of Providence, that an inheritance so proper and convenient for a band of brethren ... should never be split into a number of unsocial, jealous, and alien sovereignties". He argued that if the United States was truly to be a single nation, its leaders would have to agree on universally binding rules of governance. John Jay and his colleagues, Alexander Hamilton and James Madison, who shaped the American Constitution argued the implications of establishing a kind of rule that would engage as many citizens as possible, and that would include a system of checks and balances.

India's battle against feudalism and colonialism is fought not by the hyper-sensitive social activists who merely complain and work to feather their own nests, nor by the fickle media owners and prima donna editors, nor by academics who jet in and out of New Delhi peddling their latest treatises on India, but by tough political leaders and on-the-ground administrators who have the power to make a difference and who persist despite threats to their life and their reputation. In the choice of his close advisers and confidants Narendra Modi has shown that he indeed believes in hard work to strengthen the institutions of democracy.[218]

---

[218] Note: There has been much speculation about what Modi and his government would do to boost India's economy, spur development, and end large scale corruption, all leading to a major change in the feudalistic, paternal, big government approach to solving economic and social problems. A *Reuters* article, April 06, 2014, titled, "Advisers to Narendra Modi dream of a Thatcherite Revolution" speculated, using a Western trope they are comfortable with, that Modi's team would shrink the government's footprint, encourage free enterprise, and cut down on large, expensive welfare programs and dole-outs, privatize large and loss-incurring government enterprises.

Attacks on Modi

Modi has been so viciously attacked and his reputation so badly tarnished in the media and academe that if he were an ordinary person he would have quit office a long time ago. For example, when Modi visited England in August 2003 to urge Britain-based Gujaratis and the British industry to invest in Gujarat he was compared to the worst of the world's dictators and mass murderers. The Left-leaning *Guardian* newspaper compared Modi to war criminals of the 20th century. The *Guardian's* India correspondent Luke Harding profiled Modi as "the most controversial figure in modern Indian politics -- likened by his many enemies to Adolf Hitler, Slobodan Milosevic and Pol Pot". It said that Modi was "catapulted to infamy last year after presiding over India's worst communal rioting for a decade" which "left 100,000 people homeless, severely damaged India's credentials as a secular democracy and were described -- correctly -- as genocide".[219] Some activists in Britain sought to move the British courts to arrest Modi using the British precedent of arresting Chile's dictator Pinochet. Many of these Britain- based Indian-origin academics, artists, and gadflys have written open letters, harangued Members of Parliament, and threatened a variety of boycotts and protests, which the Left- liberal media in Britian have given much space late into the campaigning for the sixteenth Lok Sabha but it seems to little effect.[220]

The Guardian's flippant use of the term "genocide" is reflective of the attitude of many in the Left who have made it their agenda to demonize anyone who does not subscribe to a left/socialist ideology. "Genocide" does not accurately describe the violence that occurred in Gujarat. Genocide is "the systematic and planned extermination of an entire national, racial, political, or ethnic group," but there was no plan to exterminate Gujarat's Muslim population. There were roughly five million Muslims in Gujarat in 2002. The official death toll was about 1000, while newspapers like the *Guardian* claimed 2,000 had been killed, without any evidence for that claim. Most but not all of those killed were Muslims. The genocide charge was baseless because there was no noticeable exodus of Muslims -- a logical corollary of such persecution.

Critics pointed out that Muslims had been driven out of Gujarat and their businesses boycotted. Gujarat's Chief Coordinator of Relief S.M.F. Bukhari, a Muslim, noted that of the 133,000 refugees who had taken shelter in the 110 camps across the state, 12,229 were still living in the camps in July 2002, indicating that a significant number had already been rehabilitated. He stated that 680 million rupees had been given as compensation to the kin of the dead and injured. Bukhari also stated, "We

---

[219] *Rediff on the Net.* "British Media gives Modi the Cold Shoulder", August 18, 2003.

[220] *India Today*, April 22, 2014, "Indian-origin Academics in UK dread Modi in power, issue open letter."

could achieve 100 per cent success in rural areas where we involved local leaders and made them convince the refugees to return home. The state machinery behaved as a catalyst".[221] He added that the kin of 773 of the 925 dead had been fully compensated. He reported that money had been spent under seven categories of the rehabilitation program -- death compensation; injury compensation; cash doles; daily allowance; camp maintenance; housing compensation and distribution of earning assets.

Yes, there were complaints about the slow pursuit of criminal cases against those accused of murdering and raping Muslims in the riots following the Godhra massacre. The most public and controversial of such cases was the "Best Bakery Case". The Supreme Court of India chastised the Modi government of being both incompetent and obstructionist in this regard. It was inexplicable why a government that sought to put the past behind and to work towards raising the living standards of all Gujaratis did not appoint competent prosecutors to argue the cases in court and to punish those found guilty quickly. The Best Bakery case in Vadodara came under close scrutiny. As with so many of India's court cases in pursuit of those charged in riots, the twists and turns introduced by unwilling witnesses, witnesses who commit perjury, and by pressures on witnesses to recant or to mouth what human rights activits coached them to say, hamper police and even court processes. In this instance, one of the key witnesses, Zaheera Sheikh, who said one thing in the court absolving those accused of arson and murder, recanted her statement a day later in public. She became the poster girl for those actively pursuing the demonization of Modi, but the Supreme Court sentenced her to one year in prison for perjury, in 2006.

Zaheera's sister-in-law, Yasmin Sheikh, alleged that Zaheera and her mother had been bought over. Yasmin claimed that despite being a witness herself, she was not allowed to speak because Zaheera and her mother wanted to cash in on the controversial case. "I want to tell the truth. My mother-in-law did not get my name mentioned in the First Information Report. All these names are false. This was done as they were greedy and wanted quick money," Yasmin said.

Yasmin's version is a complete contradiction of what Zaheera had deposed at a press conference. Zaheera had accused Madhu Srivastava, a local BJP MLA and his brother, Chandrakant Bhattu from the Congress Party, of forcing her into changing her original statement in court. The sudden change in statement led to the collapse of the case and the acquittal of all 21 accused by a Vadodara sessions court. However, according to Yasmin, "Chandrakant Bhattu saved our lives. When we were attacked, it was he who called the police and told them what was happening" (*NDTV*, September 20, 2003). The clashing versions raised more questions over a possible political cover-up. That said, it would be naïve to believe that the nexus between criminals and politicians at various levels cannot keep even a strong administrator like Modi at bay. Since Modi is beholden to and works within a party system there could be a variety of

---

[221] *Times of India*, July 22, 2002.

pressures from people within his own party and elsewhere to suppress some and tom-tom other matters. It takes an adroit and sagacious politician to steer these matters to a rightful culmination but no one in India, either at the state level or at the national level has proved himself or herself more committed to and been able to bring change than Narendra Modi.

The denoument in the Best Bakery Case came when on July 9, 2012, the Bombay High Court, upheld the life sentences of four accused -- Sanjay Thakkar, Bahadursingh Chauhan, Sanabhai Baria and Dinesh Rajbhar -- on the basis of accounts by injured bakery employees who identified the accused. But the court acquitted five others accused -- Rajubhai Baria, Pankaj Gosavi, Jagdish Rajput, Suresh alias Lalo Devjibhai Vasava and Shailesh Tadvi, for lack of evidence. The Gujarat High Court had reprimanded NGOs and social activists for trying to railroad the justice system in pursuit of their agenda of demonizing Modi's government. Elaborating on an oral verdict dismissing the State Government's appeal for retrial on December 26, 2003, the court said there was a "conspiracy to malign people by misusing" Zaheera who could "play into the dirty hands of anti-social and anti-national elements". The High Court also passed strictures against the media and the NGOs who they said had attempted "to set up a parallel investigation". It said that the State's judiciary and "the system as a whole" were targeted because excessive publicity was given to a perjurer who had been made into an overnight celebrity by "rent-a-cause" human rights champions.[222]

Without waiting for the verdict, and with determined efforts to undermine institutions and subvert process, Modi's detractors spared no effort at running him down, and targeting his government. Numerous books on the post-Godhra riots have now been made required reading in top American universities. A multitude of activists who sought to implicate Modi were invited by American and European think tanks, official commissions of enquiry, and academic institutions to document the events in Gujarat. Plays were written, documentaries produced, and effigies of Modi burnt in protest marches around the world. Indian youth were coached and goaded to write articles and poems condemning Modi, and the most egregious like the ones below got published and widely circulated:

Oh, it's my finest hour
Look at that beatific smile on my face
Who says it's oily can't you see
My coiffured beard
My spotless white kurta pyjama
And freshly starched conscience
Don't tell me it's got the blood of innocent

---

[222] *The Pioneer*, "The Best Case". January 15, 2004.

Muslim kids and pregnant women
Have you forgotten Godhra?
Naroda Patiya was not just to avenge
The train massacre and restore Hindu pride
It was the beginning of the final solution
Oh, it's my finest hour

-- "Modi Rap" in Sanjay Trehan's "Appassionata"

How does one account for this split morality, angry judgmentalism, and willful caricatures? The simple reason is that one, democracies are messy; two, it is easy to be politically correct, to jump on the bandwagon of political fashion, and to attack those who have no chance of hitting back; three, Modi was/is an easy target for India's Westernized men and women who see Modi wielding power that they believe correctly belongs to them; and four, the attacks against Modi is part of a larger attempt to keep India in its place – either fractured, messy, and ungovernable, or an exotic "paradise" of multicultural maya. American legislators and policy makers fished in troubled waters, and continued to do so till the tide turned with the BJP-led NDA sweeping the 2014 general elections, and Modi chosen as the Prime Minister. The Europeans ramped down their shrill invective, which was evident early on, as they began to read and hear reports of the Chief Minister's initiatives, his hard work, and his focus on development. But President Obama changed his mind only late, seeking to reverse his former Secretary of State, Hillary Clinton's "get Modi" policy, and to bring some mature balance into the equation.[223]

---

[223] Nalapat, M. (April 19, 2014). "Obama quietly reverses Hillary's 'get Modi' policy," *The Sunday Guardian.*

CHAPTER XXIX – ENDS, MEANS, JUSTIFICATIONS

AND THE FUTURE OF INDIA

India is no ordinary nation. It indeed has a tryst with destiny. What that destiny is going to be – a beacon for other nations, or a battlefield for global conflict -- depends on how we analyze the threats it has faced and faces now, and the solutions we propose so that it stands for the comity and well-being of all peoples, for both material prosperity and spiritual quest, for freedom and for excellence in the pursuit of the global good, welding and harmonizing the best of India with the best of the rest.

We began with an analysis of how Indian problems have been misdiagnosed and misinterpreted, and how the varieties of dangers it faces from within and from outside its borders have been wrongly identified. Some of the biggest problems are the problems of misdiagnosis. There is still a lucrative business in academe, media and politics to sell India as a basket case of caste conflict, women's oppression, irredeemable poverty, religious conflict, and a nation being hijacked by Hindu fanatics. This case has sold well for a variety of reasons: India has always been a happy hunting ground for foreign marauders, and the effects of colonization has had far reaching effects, including making the majority of modern India's intellectual class and elites peddlers of self-defeat and alienation. They deliberately ignore the vast storehouse of knowledge and wisdom that is India, and instead use foreign tools – whether Marxist, feminist, postmodernist or whichever current, fashionable continental theory – to disembowel India of its traditional best.

Their analysis of modern Indian politics and society is based on both self-serving and foreign interests, and many who write in English are clueless of the realities on the ground. However, their positions in elite universities of the West make them "experts" and thus purveyors of advice and wisdom. Thus historian Sunil Khilnani, whose slim book on "imagining India" launched him on a career of India expertise, gets invited to speak to business leaders in India about India's future.[224] It is India's business leaders, technologists and scientists, doctors and engineers who have created the new wealth in India but somehow it is those who have written glosses on India's politics, society, and history who get to speculate about the future of India. It would be acceptable if such "experts" have something revealing or insightful to say but instead all that we get from them is the tired old rhetoric of "secularism", Hindu fundamentalism, women's oppression, Dalit liberation, and so on. They fail to acknowledge that prosperity will and usually does uplift all sections of society, maybe not at the same time, but surely.[225] They refuse to accept that India as a strong nation can be a bulwark against religious

---

[224] *India Post*, "Success of democracy can help 'branding' India: Khilnani", December 26, 2003.

[225] Das, G. (2001). *India Unbound*. Knopf.

fundamentalism -- especially of the monotheistic variety that has devastated large sections of the world culturally, economically, and environmentally. They loathe the home-made paper tigers but are sanguine about Islam-inspired terrorists who wish to make the world Muslim.

Many of these "experts" fail to acknowledge the hard economic analyses that show India becoming a leader of innovation and wealth creation, and as a major contributor to global culture. They ignore the fact that such analyses show India as "a market, a partner, a competitor, and a growing part of American culture itself" for it is India and the U.S., the two most important democracies in the world, that face the biggest threats to their multicultural and multiethnic societies by fundamentalist forces and by the "pie in the sky" supporters of such fundamentalists.

However, what our "India experts," both Indian and foreign wish to focus on is human rights, divisive issues, nuclear testing, poverty, and backwardness and superstition in India, while using caste and conflict as the predominant lenses for understanding and adumbrating about India. As one perceptive observer points out, there is also a contradiction between the U.S. government's positive new policies towards India and what many scholars, who are also political activists, seek to accomplish.[226]

Malhotra focuses on the three new threats that the U.S. faces -- Pan-Islam, China, and labor competition from overseas. For India, pan-Islamism is the greatest and most immediate threat. The Indian subcontinent is home to about 40 percent of the world's Muslims, and if moderate and apolitical Muslims are overwhelmed by determined fundamentalists then the world will be faced with a Muslim South Asia that has both a nuclear arsenal and the wish to use it. The Islamic threat was often seen as a disorganized and scattered force but after the attack on the World Trade Center on September 11, 2001 we know what determined *jihadists* can accomplish. We also know that Pakistan is the world's most dangerous country for both its nuclear proliferation,[227] and for its terrorist training camps. And Pakistan's obsession with India, with whom it has fought three major wars, should be acknowledged as the most serious threat to peace and stability in the region. Instead, many India experts, blinkered by ideology, continue to peddle a false version of the problems and the potential of India. On rare occasions, and in small does, however, we have a few who try to counter the deluge of disinformation and misinformation.

The vigorous engagement of the U.S. State Department, and especially the interest and support of Ambassador Blackwill at a very crucial juncture, at the turn of the century, made America realize the importance of India. In his address to the Institute

---

[226] Malhotra, R. (January 20, 2004). "America Must Re-Discover India", *Rediff on the Net*.

[227] Sanger, D., & Broad, W. (January 03, 2004). "From rogue nuclear programs, web of trails leads to Pakistan", *The New York Times*.

for Defense Analysis' Fifth Asian Security Conference, in New Delhi, on January 27, 2003, Ambassador Blackwill said that "cooperative relations between America and India will endure over the long run most importantly because of the convergence of their democratic values and vital national interests. Our democratic principles bind us -- a common respect for individual freedom, the rule of law, the importance of civil society, and peaceful state-to-state relations".

In 1998, when India tested nuclear devices, the U.S. imposed sanctions, and there was a huge ruckus both in the U.S. policy establishment as well as in the media and academe about the nature of the Vajpayee government, about India's goals and ambitions, and the political dynamic in the Indian sub-continent. The September 11, 2001 events made many in the policy establishment realize their mistake in branding India as maverick and unreliable. Those in academe and the media were not just slow but have failed to acknowledge their mistakes, and continue to repeat their old lies and newly minted fears. What they care not to know or acknowledge is what Ambassador Blackwill pointed out in his address: "The Prime Minister has spoken of India and the United States as 'natural allies'. He is right. Since September 11, 2001, five members of the Bush Cabinet have come to India, some more than once. Nearly 100 US official visitors to India at the rank of Assistant Secretary of State or higher have reinforced their efforts".

Ambassador Blackwill concluded his presentation by pointing out the risks that statesmen have to take: risks that analysts and academics don't have to, or if they do, do not have to be responsible for or to pay a price for what they say. He said that the transformation of U.S.-India relationship has been propelled by two statesmen -- President Bush and Prime Minster Vajpayee, and that the strategic vision opted for by both in January 2001 is now a growing reality. He said that ties between the United States and India were better today than at any time in a half-century. "Both governments are determined to keep it that way -- for their own sake and for an Asian security built on freedom, prosperity and peace" he reiterated. Alas, that dynamic got dissipated over the past ten years, and we don't how quickly they will regroup if Narendra Modi heading a new NDA coalition raises the tri-color in New Delhi.

This is counter to what the old Left in India, and its supporters in the U.S., do not want to see, given their "pie in the sky" attitude and their inveterate hatred of certain people and projects. Thus the academics and analysts who have built their careers and their reputation propagating particular pictures of the West and India want to continue to peddle them lest their tenures come to an end and their power wane.

If therefore the U.S. and the West are to articulate clearly their long range strategic vision, and India's place in it, they will look at the Gujarat riots of 2002 and the Gujarat elections in a whole new light. The battle for Gujarat was not just a local battle but which has worldwide implications. Gujarat was fighting both internal divisive forces and external enemies. The internal forces are the agents who seek to maintain if not exacerbate caste (or color) divisions through selective doles, who appease minorities for creating vote banks, who ignore economic development and education because they can continue to maintain an ignorant, poor, and gullible mass base for their invidious politics, and who turn a blind eye to agents of violent monotheistic creeds who wish to destabilize India either through violent means or through cultural desecration.

If the world has to learn about India and its potential to be a super power, not in a militaristic sense, but in terms of social, cultural, and political values, then it has to revise its understanding of India. Relying on benighted "India experts" and their skewed projections is assuring in the short run, for none of us wants to stop riding our pet hobby horses. For instance, the U.S. has repeatedly backed Pakistan and reduced it into being governable only by the military or by the mullahs. After the Soviet withdrawal from Afghanistan, U.S.-backed *mujahideen* reinvented themselves as anti-U.S. *jihadists* with the help of Pakistan-based clerics and the insidious secret military agency, the Directorate for Inter-Services Intelligence (ISI).

So, what are the dangers that India faces, and the Gujarat elections repulsed that we need to identify here? One, the increasingly Talibanized Pakistan military could launch another attack on India leading to a disastrous traditional war or nuclear holocaust; two, Islamic fundamentalism could spread into India using a combination of spillover from Pakistan and India's own Saudi-funded *madrasas* that use the same teaching curriculum as in Pakistan. Gujarat is the home of many of these extremist Islamic schools, and except for a rare investigative report in the Indian media, most have ignored their presence and the dangers that they pose; three, the focus on internal divisions and the proposal to make India a "commonwealth of nations" is a sure recipe for quicker and easier takeover by fundamentalists of all kinds and thus for the kind of boody civil wars we see in Iraq, Syria or the many African nations split between equally ferocious groups of Christian and Muslim fundamentalists; four, the demonization of Hindu nationalists and the soft-pedalling of the forces of monotheistic fundamentalism, including the dangerous Wahhabi religious movement in the Indian subcontinent, would assure the polarization and radicalization of Indian society; five, the destabilization of India would have a snowballing effect that could easily spillover to all of Asia, and in turn to the rest of the world; and six, Indian democracy needs to be strengthened through systemic changes and events like the Godhra massacre, if they cannot be thwarted, are quickly dealt with by an efficient and firm law and order machinery. The post-Godhra riots were an unhealthy response by a frustrated majority, and unless all political parties affirm their faith in equal rights and equal justice, India will continue to be buffeted by caste, class, and religion-inspired violence.

With the high-tech revolution of the past three decades, India is now one of the international centers of growth. India supplies to the world a well-educated army of engineers and technologists, scientists and innovators. India has become a leader in knowledge industries, and if India continues to be a stable nation, it can leverage that position to spread to the world the ideas of peaceful coexistence and prosperity, for after all India is home to many religions, Indians speak myriad languages, and they are the trustees of a vast storehouse of cultural riches. On the other hand, the forces of political and social destabilization are hard at work, and their willingness to destroy than to create points to catastrophes for which the whole world will have to pay dearly.

When the BJP-led NDA Government came to power in New Delhi leading a coalition of regional parties in 1998, the drumbeat of hate and opposition to the emergence of a Hindu voice was heard throughout the world, and especially in Western academe and media, fueled by the work and activism of "brown sahibs" whose blinkered approach to the Indian condition would be laughed away as ludicrous if not for the danger and threat they pose. Many of these India and foreign-based Indian academics, often in the garb of "human rights" activists, are conduits for channeling foreign intellectual and material support to agencies and individuals who exacerbate India's internal cleavages, including insurgencies in Kashmir, Nepal (now spilling over to India), Northeast India, and the variety of separatist movements in India based on caste, religion, language, ideology, and "race" (Aryan and Dravidian). Besides seriously dampening India's economic growth, these divisive forces, many of them working for and under the control of foreign agencies and institutions, will continue to act as India's "fifth column" keen on achieving their dream of a divided, fractured, and Balkanized India.

India's fate over the next quarter century will therefore depend on whom we listen to and how the West and the rest wish to cooperate with India. Are we willing to listen to those "India experts" keen on inflicting their version of a divided India, and creating the conditions for a global clash of civilizations, or are we going to strengthen the forces of a united India that will be a bulwark for democracy, and of mutual and peaceful coexistence? The more leverage and power the "Balkanizers" have, the more angry and violent will be the reaction from Hindu leaders and groups who fear the vivisection of India.

The consequence of a billion Indians achieving first class, world citizenship status would expand markets and allow the U.S., for example, to continue its role as the leader of innovation and prosperity. An economically strong India would lead to regional economic advancement and stability. Therefore, supporting a unified India should be a strategic imperative for U.S. interests to bring stability across Asia.

As Ambassador Blackwill noted a decade ago, the U.S. and India share many civilizational values and visions. India is one of the world's oldest crucibles for experimenting with pluralism. Its overall historical record is in sharp contrast to the way most other civilizations dealt with difference. India's tapestry of inter-woven communities is empirical evidence for India's culture of pluralism.

American businessmen and technologists, as well as astute politicians, understand the nature of Indian democracy and the vast potential the region holds for economic and spiritual prosperity. The problem is with the many India experts who have overinvested in old paradigms and become aggressive in their pursuit of power and influence at the cost of undermining the Indian ethos. Gujarat elections and the violence in 2002 can be seen either through the old, cracked and narrow lens of "India experts" or Gujarat can be seen as a case study, however messy, for recovering and reinstituting cultural, social, and economic growth and affirming democratic traditions.

We know that there are many, many more details to the story we have told. If one, however, is aware of this story, the complaint could be that our choice of details is partisan. These responses would reflect the classic problem of mistaking the trees for the woods. We acknowledge our biases. We do not claim that all that we have recounted is all that there is to be told. However, what we wish to urge for India and about India is neither partisan nor narrow-minded. We do not wish to make Narendra Damodardas Modi the "knight in shining armor" who saved Gujarat and India, but we wish to point out that he too is a visionary and that his vision for his state and for the nation is very much in consonance with the goals of democratic nations and free peoples all over the world. His demonization is at the behest of the perpetual malcontents who tinker with the world at others' expense, and part of their agenda is to lead the world to anarchism or to some unreal and historically false "idyll" of the past. Who we support therefore is of immense relevance and importance for the future of the world. Thus, this version of the story needed to be told.

On May 16, 2014 we learned the the results of the elections to the sixteenth Lok Sabha. Polls in early April 2014 had indicated the BJP winning, on its own 234 to 246 of the 543 seats in the Lok Sabha. When the results came in, the BJP had won 282 of the 543 seats, gaining an absolute majority on its own. The BJP knit a coalition before the elections, and announced who would be its Prime Minister if it were to form the government. The BJP's coalition partners won another 54 seats to give the BJP-led NDA a total of 336 seats in the 543-member Parliament. The election results ensured that there would be no horse-trading, unethical and unworkable alliances, and shoddy governance.

"Democracy is so over-rated", says the character playing the role of "President Frank Underwood" in the popular television series, "House of Cards". This may be the reaction to the kind of messy gamesmanship in American politics that has led to a variety of impasses over the past couple of decades, and especially since President Obama took office. There were many, biding their time and hoping, waiting to create a similar dysfunctionality in India if the BJP-led coalition did not gain a majority of the seats. While strong and clean governance with little hint of authoritarianism is a tough act, and which many fear may be impossible in an age of disenchantment and division, there is now some hope that India might have turned that corner, though it is just an year and a half since the new government took office, and Narendra Modi was sworn in as the fifteenth Prime Minister of India. Modi has been given the mandate to change India, and he may yet prove to be the leader who would get India on the path to self-sustenance, self-respect, and self- worth. He is not a magician nor is he a Superman,

The Election That Shaped Gujarat

though he seems to draw sustenance and energy from the daily practice of yoga, and from wisom gained on in his early years, as a young man, walking across the Himalayas in search of gurus and grace. Giving one the chance to accomplish good would need patience, sagacity, and goodwill. It may therefore be best to close with this *shanti mantra* from the Katha Upanishad:

Sarve bhavantu sukhinaḥ
Sarve santu nirāmayāḥ
Sarve bhadrāṇi paśyantu
Mā kaśchit dukha bhāg bhavet
Om Śāntiḥ Śāntiḥ Śāntiḥ

May all be happy;
May all be free from diseases; May all see things auspicious;
May none be subjected to misery; *Om*! Peace, Peace, Peace!

QUESTIONNAIRE – NARENDRA MODI

(Note: We sent this questionnaire ahead of time to the Chief Minister. At the time of our interview, in his office, between 10 p.m. and midnight on June 11, 2003 we were not able to touch upon all of these matters, and Mr. Modi's answers were general in nature, and mostly confirmed what he had said before about what he knew was happening as the riots broke out, or what he had said about his political opponents, about his dreams for the state and the nation. We have included this questionnaire for the sake of transparency and for archival purposes, lest someone at a future date seek to understand our own interest in and approach to this assignment.)

1. When you took over as Chief Minister in 2001, what were your main priorities for the State?
2. You had not then run for any political office. Why did you believe you could be an effective head of the Gujarat State government without administrative experience?
3. What was your assessment of the Hindu-Muslim relations in Gujarat at the time you took office in 2001?
4. What was your relationship with the Muslim leadership and community in Gujarat when you took office? Can you recall any seminal event or interaction that would symbolize your relationship with the Muslim community?
5. Who were your chief confidants/advisers when you became Chief Minister, and how did they you settle into your duties as CM?
6. What were the main challenges once you assumed office: intra-party conflicts? Relationship with bureaucracy? Communal conflict? State of the economy? Elaborate.
7. Though you were not the CM in 2001, the earthquake of 2001 must have shaken the BJP government– literally and figuratively: overall, do you think the BJP government successfully dealt with the aftermath of the earthquake? What symbolizes most effectively the achievement of the BJP government in dealing with the aftermath?
8. There were complaints that the RSS affiliated NGOs discriminated against the Muslim and Christian victims of the earthquake, and that caste conflict was evident too in how villages were reconstructed and compensation paid out. How did you deal with those complaints?
9. Why did you/your government not foresee any event like the Godhra massacre?
10. Was it not a failure of the Home Department, and failure of intelligence, just as 9/11 was a failure of the CIA in the United States? Do you not think that

intelligence agencies have not been able to penetrate deep into the Islamic anti-social groups and organizations?
11. What was your immediate reaction to the event: as an ordinary human being, as a Hindu, and as the Chief Minister of Gujarat?
12. What do you think were the reasons behind the massacre?
13. You have accused outside forces/terrorists for carrying out the crime. How close is the police investigation to finding the masterminds?
14. The national and international media, human rights observers, academics, and even foreign embassies have alleged that your government was either involved in carrying out the violence against Muslims, post-Godhra, or that your government was deliberately inefficient in containing the violence. What is your strongest defense to challenge that assessment?
15. One major accusation against you and Gujarati Hindus is that you/they have not shown remorse for the bloody violence. What is your response?
16. At the time of KPS Gill being appointed your Security Advisor, many in the State Bureaucracy, the State Police, and yourself seemed to be against his appointment. If that is the correct reading, why was the appointment opposed? Did you welcome KPS Gill's appointment? Do you think without KPS Gill the situation could have been brought to normal by the Gujarat Police?
17. How would you rate your relationship with the IAS bureaucracy in Gujarat? Some say you listen only to bureaucrats. Is it true? What is your philosophy/strategy for dealing with IAS & IPS bureaucrats?
18. How effectively have you been able to control corruption in the government?
19. Was your response to Godhra influenced by the fact that you are a former RSS pracharak? If so, how? If not, how so?
20. Looking back, what could or would you have done differently in response to the Godhra massacre, and the violence following it?
21. There are still some places in Ahmedabad called "Mini-Pakistans" like Juhapura, where there is severe theft of electricity, law & order problem, and anti-national, anti-BJP, anti-Modi feelings. What has your police department done to control such areas?
22. Godhra, Akshardham, and the killing of Haren Pandya: do you not feel that the BJP Government is weakening on the law & order front? Do you link the three incidents? How have your intelligence machinery been strengthened?
23. Post-Akshardham, there were no attacks against Muslims. Some say that this shows your government could have suppressed the violence post-Godhra. Comment.
24. In what ways was the VHP leadership influential in shaping the events, post-Godhra? Praveen Togadia and Ashok Singhal have made public statements

about the "Gujarat experiment" being repeated elsewhere in the country. What is your response?
25. When did you first realize that you have to seek a fresh mandate from the people, and what were your reasons for that assessment?
26. Did you think of resigning as CM: why, or why not? Was there pressure from within the BJP for you to resign?
27. What do you consider was the darkest hour in your first tenure as CM? Explain.
28. Why would President's rule not have been more appropriate before the next round of elections? What did you fear would happen if you resigned, and the State came under President's rule?
29. The Chief Election Commissioner and your administration were publicly at loggerheads. Do you think the CEC was politically motivated in the public stances that he took on the readiness of the state for holding elections?
30. Did you have personal communication with the CEC? What is your assessment, post elections, of the role of the CEC last year?
31. Some have criticized your "Gaurav yatras" even as the state continued to be troubled by communal conflict. What was your rationale for those ten Gaurav yatras?
32. What was your grand strategy for winning the election, and what were the most important tactics for carrying out that strategy?
33. Did you have any doubts about winning the election: if yes, at what points during the campaign?
34. Your win has been characterized by some as a win for the BJP over the dead bodies of Muslims. Your comments.
35. Now that you are Chief Minister again, with a more than 2/3rd majority, what are your three most important priorities for the State?
36. What drives you as a person: what are the most important goals in your life?
37. The national and international media, various human rights committees, Muslim groups, academics have all come together to condemn you and your government. They accuse you of being tardy in rehabilitation work, in apprehending the prime accused, and building bridges with the Muslim community. Tell us why they are wrong in their assessment.
38. How have the communal riots affected the government at the Center. Advani has apologized in London for the riots; Indian diplomats continue to be under pressure to answer questions about Gujarat; foreign embassies have reported negatively about the events. Has your relationship with the Center therefore been under strain?
39. Surely, Gujarat is going to be an issue in the next general elections. How do you see your role as a lightning rod for communal relations in the nation, and what do you portend for the next five years in the country in terms of Hindu-

Muslim relations, if the BJP or a BJP-led coalition forms the government, or if they are defeated?
40. Can Hindus and Muslims get along in Gujarat/India? What are the main threats to good community relations?
41. Observers have labeled the Gujarat elections of 2002 as "historic". Why do *you* think it is historic?
42. Prafull Goradia says that the Gujarat elections proved that Hindus too can consolidate politically. If that consolidation is to endure, he says, castes and classes that feel neglected have to be given more importance. How is this formula or response different from the kind of "quota system" that prevails elsewhere in the country when it comes to giving tickets for elections and to reserve berths in ministries, or the KHAM grouping previously in Gujarat? What are your plans to make this consolidation enduring?
43. Ashutosh Varshney ("Ethnic Conflict & Civic Life") says that communal conflict is less bloody and long lasting in cities where there is good interaction between Hindu and Muslim business and social/cultural organizations. Do you think that assessment is true, and if so, what will you do to help such interaction?
44. Who do you consider your political guru and mentor; your spiritual guru and mentor?
45. Which books have influenced you the most in your life? How?
46. Some say you have a larger ambition, and that is to lead the country. If one day you become Prime Minister, what would be your three most important priorities?
47. Prafull Goradia, writing in The Pioneer, says you have emerged as a national icon, and as a determined nationalist. Icons can be, however, objects of hate and fear to some, as Goradia points out. What is your response?
48. Ashis Nandy has characterized your personality as that of a potential mass murderer and genocidal dictator. How do you respond to such assessments? Do you lose sleep over such analyses? What do you think makes people allege that you are such a person? What will you do to disprove such assessments?
49. Should India be a Hindu rashtra/nation? What does the concept mean to you?
50. Many in the RSS are against globalization. But Gujarat and Gujaratis have prospered in a global economy, with the Gujarati Diaspora being a clear example of it. Are you for globalization, and what are your concerns about globalization?
51. What does secularism mean to you, and should India be a secular country?
52. Varshney says that Gujarati youngsters in the U.S. are being brainwashed by their parents to be anti-Muslim. Your comments.

Questionnaire

53. What is the role and influence of the Gujarati Diaspora in your government?
54. If you were an ordinary citizen of Gujarat, why would you vote for Narendra Modi?
55. How do you spend your time? What time you get up? What time do you go to bed?
56. What do you do on holidays? What are your hobbies?
57. Do you answer your emails by yourself?
58. What attracts you to Information Technology & Biotechnology?
59. Is it true that a whole team was working behind Narendra Modi for the elections, from media handling to message spreading through SMS, emails, and also interpreting scientific surveys data on a continuous basis? Would you say that the 2002 Gujarat State Assembly elections were the most technologically advanced elections in terms of strategy, and election handling?
60. As a border state, Gujarat is in the mix of any changes in Indo-Pak dynamics. Should India be talking to Pakistan now, and why?
61. Why have you remained single throughout your life?
62. If there is a next birth, what would you want to be?
63. What and how deep are your spiritual interests?
64. People say that Narendra Modi travels to the Himalayas? Is it true?
65. What do you like best about yourself?
66. What do you consider to be your biggest weakness?

BIBLIOGRAPHY

Ahmad, A. (1994) *In Theory: Classes, Nations, Literatures*. London: Verso.

Aiyar, V. S., Mahurkar, U. (March 18, 2002). "Gujarat wasn't a communal riot, it was a mass agitation," *India Today*.

Akbar, M.J. (1985). *India: The Siege Within: Challenges to a Nation's Unity*. Penguin Books.

Aljazeera, "European Court upholds France's face veil ban," July 1, 2014.

Anand, U. "From Shah Bano to Salma," *The Indian Express*, March 26, 2010.

Ansari, J. M. (July 8, 2003). "Congress begins fine-tuning poll strategy", *The Hindu*.

Ashraf, S. F. (December 6, 2002). "Juhapura: Hemmed in by Prejudices", *Rediff on the Net*.

Barber, B.R. (1996). *Jihad vs. McWorld*. Ballantine Books.

Berman, P. (2003). *Terror and Liberalism*. W. W. Norton & Company.

Bhatia, V. P. (April 21, 2002), "Godhra 1928: The story of Muslim war on Hindus as told by Gandhiji", *Organiser*.

Bhatt, S., & Prabhudesai, S. (April 12, 2002). "Modi gives in, submits his resignation." *Rediff on the Net*.

Bhattacharya, A. "Creating a Pakistan of Distortions", *The Daily Pioneer*, July 12, 2003.

Bidwai, P., & Vanaik, A. (2000). *New Nukes: India, Pakistan and Global Nuclear Disarmament*. Olive Branch Press.

Biema, D. V. "Missionaries Under Cover", *Time*, June 30, 2003.

Boorstin, D. (1974). *Democracy and Its Discontents: Reflections on Everyday America*. New York: Random House

Bose, A. C. (1954). *The Call of the Vedas*. Bombay: Bhavan's Book University

Broad, W.J., Sanger, D.E., & Bonner, R. (February 12, 2004). "A Tale of Nuclear Proliferation: How Pakistani built his Network". *The New York Times*.

Bunsha, D. "Hindutva's Triumph", *Frontline*, December 21, 2002.

Burke, K. (1984, 3rd Edition). *"Attitudes Towards History"*. University of California Press.

Choudhury, S. R. "Whose Democracy?" *The Hindu*, April 28, 1999.

CNN, "India: Damage Costs $5.5 billion or higher", January 30, 2001.

Coll, S. (2005). *Ghost Wars: The Secret History of the CIA, Afghanistan, and Bin Laden, from the Soviet Invasion to September 10, 2001*. Penguin Books.

Cook, D., & Allison, O. (2007). *Understanding and Addressing Suicide Attacks: The Faith and Politics of Martyrdom Operations*. Praeger SecurityInternational.

Das, G. (2001). *India Unbound*. Knopf.

Dasgupta, S. (December 30, 2003). "Lyngdoh's Vigilantism". *Rediff on the Net*.

Dasgupta, S. (January 05, 2004). "Lessons from Islamabad", *Rediff on the Net*

Dasgupta, S. (February 29, 2004). "Oh, these intellectuals!", *New Indian Express*.

Datta, V. N. (September 30, 2001). "Patel's Legacy", *The Tribune*.

Deccan Herald, "State ministry likely in two stages," DH News Service, October 14, 1999.

Deccan Herald, "40-odd member Cabinet to be sworn-in on Sunday: Muslims to get major representation in State", DH News Service, Oct 16, 1999.

Desai, B. (March 7, 2002), "Toll now 677 due to recovery of more bodies", *The Times of India*.

Desai, M. (1974). *The Story of My Life*. New Delhi: Macmillan India.

Dhulipala, V. (2015). *Creating a New Medina: State Power, Islam, and the Quest for Pakistan in Late Colonial North India*. Cambridge University Press.

Dinkar, C. (2002). *Veerappan's Prize Catch: Rajkumar*. Konark Publisher, Pvt. Ltd.

Elst, K. (1990). *Ram Janmabhoomi vs. Babri Masjid*. New Delhi: Voice of India.

Elst, K. (1991). *Ayodhya and After: Issues before Hindu Society*. New Delhi: Voice of India.

Elst, K. "Caste: Verdict from Belgium", *Hinduism Today*, September 1994.

Flood, G.D. (1996). *An Introduction to Hinduism*. Cambridge University Press.

Friedman, T. (March 06, 2002). "The Core of Muslim Rage". *The New York Times*.

Friedman, T. (January 29, 2004). "Elephants Can't Fly", *The New York Times*.

Frontline, "It must be retained, but its abuse prevented", July 04, 1998.

Fukuyama, F. (1993). *The End of History and the Last Man*. New York: Penguin Books.

Gall, C. (2014). *The Wrong Enemy: America in Afghanistan 2001-2014*. Mariner Books.

Gandhi, R. (September 16, 2001). "Not History". *The Hindu*.

Ganguly, S., "The start of a beautiful friendship? The United States and India", *World Press Journal* Volume 20, Spring 2003.

Gauchet, M. (1997). *The Disenchantment of the World: A Political History of Religion*. Princeton, NJ: Princeton University Press.

Government of India (November 6, 2001). "Protocol of Cooperation between the state of Gujarat and the Astrakhan region".

GSDMA (2002). "What has changed after Gujarat earthquake 2001?" PowerPoint presentation. http://www.jst.go.jp/astf/document/43pre.pdf

Gupta, G. V. (October 10, 1999). "IAS: God with feet of Clay", *The Tribune*.

Gupta, S., & Mahurkar, U. (May 20, 2002). "What can Gill do?" *India Today*.

Gurumurthy, S. (September 25, 2015). "Swami Dayananda: The Patriot Saint". The New Indian Express.

Hoagland, J. (January 8, 2004). "Nuclear Resolution", *The Washington Post*.

Hoffman, B. (June 2003). "The Logic of Suicide Terrorism". *The Atlantic*.

Huntington, S. (1996). *The Clash of Civilizations and the Remaking of World Order*. New York: Simon & Schuster.

IBN-Live. "Ex-SC judge Krishna Iyer praises Modi, says he is a good candidate for Prime Ministership", September 19, 2013.

India Post, "Success of democracy can help 'branding' India: Khilnani", December 26, 2003.

India Today, "Mixed Signals", October 20, 2001.

Bibliography

India Today "More than Modi". December 30, 2002.

India Today, "Godhra Carnage: On the Fast Track", July 21, 2003.

India Today, "Wanted Justice", July 21, 2003.

Jack, A. (December 1, 2013). "The Political Biography of an Earthquake, by Edward Simpson". *Financial Times*.

Jain, S. "Criminal Law, Secular Yardstick", *The Pioneer*, August 12, 2003.

Jain, S. (August 26, 2003), "Political lesson of Demography", *The Pioneer*.

Joshi, A. P., Srinivas, M.D., & Bajaj, J.K. (2003). *Religious Democgraphy of India*. Centre for Policy Studies.

Kak, K., "The Bloodstained Halo", *Vigil Online*, Vicharmala 49.

Kamath, M.V. (May 10, 2002). "Media Hypocrisy and Humbug", *Cybernoon*.

Kamath, M.V. & Randeri, K. (2009). *Narendra Modi: The Architect of a Modern State*. New Delhi: Rupa & Co.

Kaplan, R. (2000). *The Coming Anarchy:Shattering the Dreams of the Post Cold War*. Vintage Books.

Kapoor, C. (March 17, 2002). "Old Wine, New Bottle", *Indian Express*.

Kapur, D. "Europe's India Aversion," April 13, 2014, *The Business Standard*.

Kaur, N. (September 1, 2001). "Waiting for Justice", *Frontline*.

Kautilya (2000). *Arthashastra*. Penguin Classics.

Khilnani. S. (1997). *The Idea of India*. New York: Farrar, Straus & Giroux.

Krishnamoorty, D. "The Hindu, Hindus, and Hindutva", *The Hoot.Org*

Lal, K. S. (1992). *The Legacy of Muslim Rule in India*. South Asia Books.

Lavakare, A. (August 27, 2002), "The EC's Gujarat Order". *Rediff on the Net*.

Lavakare, A. (September 4, 2002), "The Gujarat Impasse". *Rediff on the Net*.

Lavakare, A. (February 13, 2003). "We need a CEC not a CEO". *Rediff on the Net*.

Lavakare, A. (November 18, 2003), "One Way Street", *Rediff on the Net*.

Levy, B. (2003). *Who killed Daniel Pearl?* Melville House.

Lewis, B. (2003). *The Crisis of Islam: Holy War and Unholy Terror*. Modern Library.

Madan, T. N. (1998). *Modern Myths, Locked Minds: Secularism and Fundamentalism in India*. Oxford University Press.

Madan,T. N. (2003). "Hinduism", in Mark Juergensmeyer (Ed.), *Global Religions: An Introduction*. Oxford University Press.

Mahurkar, U., "End of hope", *India Today*, April 15, 2002.

Malhotra, R. (January 20, 2004). "America Must Re-Discover India", *Rediff on the Net*.

Mander, H. (March 20, 2002). Hindustan Hamara. *The Times of India*.

Mander, H. (June 11, 2003) "In Search of Gandhi and Godse", *Frontline*.

Manji, I. (2004). *The Trouble with Islam: A Muslim's call for Reform in her Faith*. Random House.

Marino, A. (2014). Narendra Modi: *A Political Biography*. Harper Collins Publishers India.

Modi, S.K. (2004). *Godhra – The Missing Rage*. Ocean Books.

Nandy, A. (2003). *The Romance of the State and the Fate of Dissent in the Tropics*. Oxford India Press.

Pal, A. (July 2003). "Bush ignores India's Pogrom". *The Progressive*

Panagariya, A. "Narendra Modi's Real Report Card," *Business Standard*, October 28, 2013

Panagariya, A. "The Narendra Modi economic model offers a compelling alternative to the mess at the Centre," *The Economic Times*, June 29, 2013.

Pandey, S. (April 28, 2002). "More fall prey to police firings in Gujarat", *The Times of India*.

Pandita, R. (2013). *Our Moon has Blood Clots*. Random House India.

Philipose, P. (May 21, 2002). "Imagining a new beginning", *The Indian Express*.

Prabhupada, A. C. (1970). *Krsna – The Supreme Personality of Godhead.* Bhaktivedanta Book Trust.

Prakash, S. (April 21, 2014). "Fear and hysteria as campaign tools". *Mid-Day.*

Prasad, C. B. (July 20, 2003). "Are Brahmins Still our Shatrus?" *The Pioneer.*

Price, L. (2015). *The Modi Effect: Inside Narendra Modi's Campaign to Transform India.* Quercus.

Punj, B. (May 27, 2002). "The Roys in the Media are harming India and worse", *Outlook India.*

Purie, A. "Primal Fear", *India Today,* March 18, 2002.

Raja Mohan, C. (2003). *Crossing the Rubicon: The Shaping of India's new Foreign Policy.* Penguin Books.

Rao, R. (December 30, 2002). "Profile: Narendra Modi", *BBC.*

Rao, R. N. (2001) *Secular 'Gods' Blame Hindu 'Demons': The Sangh Parivar through the Mirror of Distortion.* New Delhi: Har-Anand Publications.

Rao, R. N. (August 19, 2002). "An Interview with Koenraad Elst". Sulekha.com

Rao, R.N, & Elst, K. (Eds.) (2002). *Gujarat after Godhra: Real Violence, Selective Outrage.* New Delhi: Har-Anand Publications.

Rebello, M. (December 02, 2013). "Sonia Gandhi is richer than Queen Elizabeth and the Sultan of Oman, claims 'Huffington Post' Report". *DNA India.*

Rediff on the Net, "NC expels Soz for life", April 19, 1999.

Rediff on the Net, "RSS forces Vajpayee to change tack on Modi issue", April 13, 2002.

Rediff on the Net, "Jana echoes RSS line on Minority Welfare", April 13, 2002.

Rediff on the Net, "Modi is scared of going to the polls: Congress", April 17, 2002.

Rediff on the Net, "SC should not answer Presidential reference on Gujarat Poll: EC," August 18, 2002.

Rediff on the Net, "EC versus Govt of India," August 20, 2002

The Election That Shaped Gujarat

Rediff on the Net, "Youth's testimony throws new light on Godhra attack", August 22, 2002.

Rediff on the Net, "Sonia asks Vajpayee to stop Gaurav Yatra," August 22, 2002.

Rediff on the Net, "Congress moves to counter BJP's Hindu card in Gujarat," August 22, 2002.

Rediff on the Net, "Only Musharraf's men will compare Gujarat with Kashmir". August 23, 2002.

Rediff on the Net, "Arrest Modi for planning Gaurav Yatra: Laloo," August 30, 2002.

Rediff on the Net, "Modi begins yatra with swipe at Congress," September 8, 2002.

Rediff on the Net, "Gujarat election on December 12: Election Commission," October 28, 2002.

Rediff on the Net, "Laloo accuses Modi of inciting communal tension," November 12, 2002.

Rediff on the Net. "Togadia barred from entering Godhra". November 16, 2002.

Rediff on the Net. "Yatra to take shape of public meetings: VHP", November 17, 2002.

Rediff on the Net. "Media's Rs. 50 crore shame in Gujarat", December 7, 2002.

Rediff on the Net, "No police lapse in Gujarat riots: Justice Nanavati", May 18, 2003.

Rediff on the Net, "Cabinet clears Bill on Cow Slaughter, CrPC", August 11, 2003.

Rediff on the Net. "British Media gives Modi the Cold Shoulder", August 18, 2003.

Rediff on the Net, "At least 48 Die in Mumbai Blasts", August 25, 2003.

Rediff on the Net, "Andhra CM hurt in Tirumala Bomb Blast", October 01, 2003.

Rediff on the Net. "US to make Pakistan non-NATO ally". March 18, 2004.

Roosevelt, T. (1910). Excerpt from the speech, "Citizenship in a Republic".

Sanger, D., & Broad, W. (January 03, 2004). "From rogue nuclear programs, web of trails leads to Pakistan", *The New York Times*.

Bibliography

Sanu, S. (April 25, 2014). "Modi, media and the theology of apology", *The Hoot*.

Saxena, S. N. (December 06, 2003). "Publicity Relations", *The Pioneer*.

Schwartz, R. (1998). *The Curse of Cain: The Violent Legacy of Monotheism*. Chicago: University of Chicago Press.

Sciolino, E. (February 11, 2004), "Ban passed on religious symbols in schools", *The New York Times*.

Sen, G. (September 02, 2015). "Integral Humanism of Deendayal Upadhyaya". *Indiafacts*.

Seshan, T.N. et al. (1995). *Degeneration of India*. Viking/Allen Lane.

Shah, J., & Jha, P.K. (July 4, 2010). "SWAGAT, says UN to Gujarat CMO's initiative". *Daily News and Analysis*.

Shahin, S. "The Criminalization of Indian Politics", *The Asian Age*, July 12, 2002.

Sharma, V. (August 7, 2003). "Strategic Interests v/s Superpower Seductions," Vishal Sharma, *Free Press Journal*.

Sharma, V. (August 14, 2003). "Human Rights Commissions – Trials, Retrials, or Satires," *Free Press Journal*.

Shashikumar, V.K. "Preparing for the Harvest…" *Tehelka*, February 07, 2004.

Shenoy, T.V.R., "Who will be Prime Minister, Sonia?" *Rediff on the Net*, December 31, 2003.

Shourie, A. (1992). *State as Charade*: V. P. Singh, Chandra Shekhar and the Rest. New Delhi: ASA Publications

Shourie, A. "The Comfort of Conspiracies", *Daily Excelsior*, February 26, 1999.

Shourie, A. (2000). *Harvesting our souls: Missionaries, their design, their claims*. New Delhi: ASA Publications.

Singh, A. (February 17, 1999), "Congress' soft Hindutva and Muslims", *Times of India*.

Srinivasan, R. "Blaming the Hindu Victim: Manufacturing Consent for Barbarism", *Rediff on the Net*, March 7, 2002.

Stiglitz, J. (2003). *Globalization and its Discontents*. New York: W. W. Norton & Company.

Sudarshan, V. (May 20, 2002). "To Bridge the Gulf". *Outlook India*.

Swami Dayananda Saraswati (July 9, 2003). "The specter of religious freedom". *The Indian Express*.

The Economic Times (June 14, 2003). "Jaya blasts Pope for views on anti-conversion laws".

The Economist, "Campaign Finance in India: Black Money Power", May 4, 2014.

The Financial Express (January 18, 2002). "Mr. Modi's Samras Gram Yojana pays rich dividends in Rural Gujarat".

The Hindu, "Gujarat Minister speaks out against CM", August 09, 2001.

The Hindu, "Paswan quits, to vote against Government", April 30, 2002.

The Hindu. "Uproar over Fernandes remarks on Sonia". May 01, 2002.

The Hindu, "Poll can wait, Mr. Modi must go", September 04, 2002.

The Hindu. "India will never be a theocratic state", November 28, 2002.

The Hindu, "Antony rejects deadline for rehabilitating the displaced in Marad", July 10, 2003.

The Hindu. "The Original Sin of 1984", November 1, 2012.

The Indian Express, "What the BJP leader said on TV reveals BJP's hidden agenda", September 26, 2001.

The Indian Express, "BJP fears more may follow Jaspal", December 30, 2001.

The Indian Express, "Dial M for Modi, Murder" March 24, 2002.

The Indian Express, "Gujarat Riots Probe: After Modi Justice Nanavati clears VHP, Bajrang Dal", May 20, 2003.

The Indian Express, "CBI begins probe in Satyendra Dubey murder case", December 13, 2003.

Bibliography

The Muslim News, "Gujarat riots inquiry commission, a whitewash", June 27, 2003.

The Pioneer, "The Best Case". January 15, 2004.

The Telegraph, "Advani pats Modi on Gaurav Yatra", September 16, 2002.

The Tribune, "Exit Polls are here to stay", October 11, 1999.

The Tribune, "Gujarat situation quite delicate: CEC". August 12, 2002.

The Times of India (November 23, 2001). "Modi's noise over Samras may backfire".

The Times of India, "Terrified in Godhra", March 1, 2002.

The Times of India, "Keshubhai to be weighed in blood," June 10, 2002.

The Times of India, "Godhra bogie was burnt from inside: Report", July 03, 2002.

The Times of India, "Gujarat tense after *rath yatra* related riots", July 13, 2002.

The Times of India. "Temple siege ends, commandos kill 2 militants". September 25, 2002.

The Times of India. "Narendra Modi hospitalised, advised rest". November 22, 2002.

The Times of India, "2002 attack was result of conspiracy: Medha Patkar", September 6, 2013.

The Times of India, "Thousands of voters' names go missing in Mumbai", April 25, 2014.

The World Bank (June, 2011). "Curbing Fraud, Corruption, and Collusion in the Roads Sector".

Trivedi, D. "Chhabildas sticks to his guns on minority votes", *Indian Express*, July 12, 1995.

USA Today, February 27, 2002, "Many in Islamic world doubt Arabs behind 9/11".

Varshney, A. (2002). *Ethnic Conflict and Civic Life*. Yale University Press.

Venkatesan, J. (March 07, 2002). "Arundhati Roy jailed for contempt of court". *The Hindu*.

Waldman, A. (September 8, 2003). "Shoes, and Religious Ire, Fall Away at a Saint's Feet", *The New York Times*.

Weiner, J. R. (2003). "Palestinian Children and the New Cult of Martyrdom". Harvard Israel Review.

Yadav, Y. "The Patterns and Lessons", *Frontline*, December 21, 2002.

Zakaria, F. (2003) *The Future of Freedom: Illiberal Democracy at Home and Abroad*. W. W. Norton & Company

Zakaria, F. "Is India's bold Prime Minister bold enough?" *The Washington Post*, September 18, 2014

Zakaria, R. (1998). *The Price of Partition: Recollection and Reflections*. Bharatiya Vidya Bhavan.

SUBJECT INDEX

9

9/11 attacks
  terrorism, 4, 203, 214

A

A. K. Antony, 43, 242
A.N. Jha, 146
Abdul Kalam, 156, 179
Abdul Qadeer Khan, 191
Acharya Dharmendra, 227, 229, 230
Advani, 50, 51, 53, 56, 87, 97, 115, 119, 124, 152, 155, 161, 173, 181, 198, 213, 243, 244, 247, 253, 258, 275, 287
  pat for Modi, GGY, 160
  rath yatra, 1980s, 137
Aga Khanis, 77
Ahmedabad
  Election Commission, visit, 148
AIADMK, 38, 39, 51, 52, 212
AIBMAC, 74
AIMPLB, 74
Ajit Jogi, 242
Akhil Bharatiya Vidyarthi Parishad
  ABVP, 71
Akshardham temple, 23, 88, 194, 196, 204, 230, 242, 247, 257
Akshardham Temple, 194
  attack on, 190
Alain Daniélou, 91
Allahabad High Court, 74
Alyque Padamsee, 97
Amarsinh Chaudhary, 55, 63, 132, 217, 253
Ambaji temple, 139, 140, 162
Ambedkar
  Bhimrao, 7, 22, 91
Amir Teheri, 98
Amrinder Singh, 242
Anand
  Amul, 168
Anand Sharma
  Congress spokesperson, reaction, 126
Andy Marino, xiii
Anil Mukim
  Additional Principal Secretary, 61, 223, 261
Annie Besant, 91

apartheid
  South Africa, 13
Archbishop of Ernakulam
  Joseph Cardinal Parecattil, 25
Arthashastra, 1
Article 174
  six-month limit, 152
Article 324
  interpretation by CEC, 152
Article 335, 30
Article 355, 115
Article 356, 114, 115, 146, 172, 203
  President's rule, 114
Article 370, 23, 51, 108
Article 44, 21
Article 46, 30
Articles 25-30, 17, 21
Arun Jaitley, 120, 124, 166, 215, 243, 251
  chief strategist, base camp, 170
  faction fights, Gujarat, 220
  Modi resignation, strategy, 126
Arun Shourie, 29, 45, 260
Arundhati Roy, 67, 95, 98, 121, 169
Ashis Nandy
  secularists, authoritarian, 186
Ashok Bhatt, 55, 255
Ashok Gehlot, 241
Asian Synod, 235
Atal Bihari Vajpayee
  foreign minister, 1977, 213
Aurangzeb, 75
Aurobindo Ghosh, 105
Ayodhya, 3, 12, 23, 49, 50, 51, 73, 74, 78, 81, 109, 110, 114, 137, 149, 150, 176, 185, 226, 227, 230, 257, 279

B

B.S. Tandon, 147
Backward Classes Commission, 30
Bajrang Dal, 57, 81, 82, 230, 286
Bal Thackeray, 115
Bangladesh, 42
Barack Obama, 265
Barber, 10, 278
Best Bakery case, 87, 97, 263
Best Bakery Case
  sentencing, 264
Bhagavad Gita

Mahatma Gandhi, 90
Bharat Ratna, 165
Bharatiya Janata Party, 2
    BJP, xii, 3, 7, 9, 12, 160, 237
Bhati Maharaj, 141
Bhati Sena
    disruption, GGY, 142
Bible, 18, 20, 27
Biju Janata Dal, 211
BJP
    Bharatiya Janata Party, 2, 3, 4, 7, 9, 12, 15, 16, 17, 32, 38, 39, 40, 50, 51, 53, 54, 55, 57, 59, 60, 63, 64, 65, 67, 70, 72, 73, 79, 81, 83, 87, 88, 95, 100, 102, 103, 106, 107, 110, 112, 113, 114, 115, 124, 142, 150, 237, 239, 243, 244, 271, 273, 274, 275, 276, 284, 286, 298
    Dalit MPs, 160
    fear of defeat, consequences, 181
    misgivings, CEC intent, 148
    opportunism, Indian politics, 131
    poll committee, indiscipline, 173
    poll forecasts, 185
    Resolution on Godhra, Modi, 133
    statewide survey, people's views, 131
BJP manifesto, 247
black cat commandos, 242
Blackwill, 267, 270
Bohras, 77
Brahmana
    Brahmin, 25
Brelvis, 77, 78
Brigadier Raj Seethapathy, 196
Buddhadeb Bhattacharjee, 106

C

C. P. Singh, 57
CEC
    powers, impeachment, 145
    Central Vigilance Commissioner, 63
Chaitanya Mahaprabhu, 105, 183
Chanakya
    Kautilya, 1
Chandrababu Naidu, 103
Chhabildas Mehta, 43
Chief Election Commissioner, 144, 275
Chief Minister, xi
    Gujarat, xi
Christian missionaries

proselytism, 33, 35, 36, 256
Christianity
    British patronage, propagation, 128
Christina Rocca
    American response, 121
Congress Party, v, vii, 8, 9, 13, 17, 29, 31, 38, 39, 40, 43, 50, 51, 52, 53, 54, 59, 64, 65, 66, 67, 71, 90, 105, 110, 111, 114, 124, 125, 126, 130, 132, 136, 137, 142, 149, 150, 164, 165, 176, 184, 187, 189, 217, 220, 233, 237, 238, 239, 243, 244, 245, 250, 252, 254, 255, 256, 257, 263
    "soft" Hindutva, 149
    double standards, 126
    family dynasty, 217
    ideological tweaks, 131
    opposition to GGY, 140
    spoilsport, Bihar, 115
CRPF
    Central Reserve Police Force, 116

D

Dahod, 74, 75, 77, 162
Dalits, 26, 27, 29, 32, 37, 176
Dandi
    Gandhi's salt march, 161
Daniel Boorstin, 14
Darikhan
    relief camp, 120
dar-ul Islam, 91
Daryakhan Ghummat, 119
Dave Commission, 81
Dawood Ibrahim, 110, 138
Davos, 6
Dayananda Saraswati, Swami, 35, 36, 286
Deendayal Upadhyaya
    integral humanism, 3
    integral humanism, official philosophy, 3
Democracy, 9, 10, 11, 13, 14, 39, 66, 278, 279, 288
    "over-rated", House of Cards, 271
Democratic Party, 20, 65
Demonization campaign, 133
Deobands, 77
Digvijay Singh, 67, 150
Direct Action Day
    infamous, 1946, 193
DMK, 38, 39, 212
Dr. Dholakia, 222

Subject Index

E

earthquake, 16, 60, 61, 173, 174, 218, 243, 260, 273
East Pakistan, 42
EC
   Gujarat visit, bias, 146
Ehsan Jafri, 81, 83
Election
   astrologers, palm-readers, numerologists, 167
Election Commission, 144
   fishing expedition, 172
Electoral rolls
   annual revision, challenges, 154
Enlightenment, 19, 21
European Union, 98, 238
   reaction, meddling, 121

F

Fareed Zakaria, 11, 15
Father Cedric Prakash
   USCIRF hearing, 2002, 122
Fifth Asian Security Conference, 268

G

G.S. Subba Rao
   Chief Secretary, 223
G.V.G. Krishnamurthy, 37
Gandhi
   critics, 91
   erratic policies, 91
   machinations, Nehru, 90
   Mahatma, 7, 20, 22, 41, 75, 76, 89, 94, 108, 164, 224, 237, 280, 282, 283
   non-violence, 137
   selective advice, 90
   Subhash Bose, undermined, 90
   yatras, political strategy, 137
Gandhian nationalism, 3
Gandhinagar, xi, 46, 49, 56, 68, 73, 79, 89, 112, 123, 139, 149, 159, 190, 195, 205, 223, 243, 258, 259
Gandhinagar Civil Hospital, 224
Gauchet, M., 34, 280
genocide, 262
George Fernandes
   Defense Minister, 244
Ghanchi
   caste, 84
Giriraj Kishore, 227, 230
globalization, 6, 9, 10, 18, 44, 45, 46, 47, 48, 276
Goa, v, 123, 126, 258
   BJP conclave, 123
Godhra
   1927 riots, 75
   massacre, riots, 2, v, ix, 1, 4, 5, 6, 8, 12, 23, 42, 59, 67, 73, 74, 75, 76, 77, 78, 79, 80, 81, 84, 85, 86, 88, 89, 93, 95, 96, 98, 100, 103, 112, 113, 117, 133, 140, 148, 173, 185, 186, 187, 204, 214, 215, 226, 228, 229, 243, 246, 247, 258, 263, 265, 269, 273, 274, 278, 281, 282, 283, 284, 287, 298
   riots, duration, 139
Gopinath Munde, 124, 125
   sangharsh yatra, 138
Gospel for Asia, 35
GSWAN, 61, 68, 260
Guardian
   provocative reporting, 262
Gujarat
   BJP stronghold, 130
Gujarat Gaurav Yatra, 141, 168, 184, 203, 216, 217, 220, 222, 298
   flagged off, 158
Gujarat police, 77, 85, 96, 116, 119, 196, 198, 204, 207, 229
Gummat
   relief camp, 120
Gurucharan Singh, 178

H

H. D. Deve Gowda, 51
H. K. L. Bhagat, 111, 112
H. V. Sheshadri
   RSS senior official, 252
Hajj subsidies
   BJP, NDA, 257
Hamas, 11
Haren Pandya, 55, 70, 103, 114, 123, 173, 181, 214, 219, 274
   withdrawal from race, 221
Hari Singh, 107, 108
Harish Salve
   Solicitor General, 155
Harsh Mander, 94
   false claims, rumors, 94
heart attack

Modi, ploy?, 222
Hedgewar
    Keshav Baliram, 71
Hillary Clinton, 265
Hindtuva, 7
Hindu nationalism, 3
Hinduism, vii, 9, 20, 24, 25, 26, 28, 35, 91, 128, 129, 141, 234, 279, 282
Hindus
    revenge, 83
Hindutva, v, 16, 21, 25, 50, 86, 93, 99, 102, 125, 128, 129, 130, 131, 132, 149, 150, 164, 165, 181, 229, 254, 278, 281, 285
Hum paanch, humare pachees, 232

I

I. K. Gujral, 51
Iftaar, 243
India-China war
    1962, 192
Indian Army
    high alert, Pakistan border, 134
Indian Communists
    factions, 212
Indian Institute of Management
    Ahmedabad, 46, 298
Indian nationalism, 3
Indian Police Service
    IPS, 57, 115
Indic traditions, 7
Indira Gandhi, 3, 18, 40, 49, 51, 111, 124, 131, 152, 163, 165, 168, 212, 218, 242, 248
    assassination, riots, election, 136
integral humanism, 3
intensive care unit, 222
Iraq, 10, 269
Islam, 9, 13, 18, 24, 28, 33, 35, 42, 77, 78, 79, 84, 109, 110, 116, 128, 166, 186, 190, 191, 192, 207, 208, 237, 239, 267, 279, 282
Ismailis, 77

J

J. S. Verma
    National Human Rights Commission, 145
Jagannath Rath Yatra, 182, 183, 228
Jaish-e-Mohammed
    JeM, 204

Jammu and Kashmir, 23, 51, 100, 146, 147, 154, 164, 201
Jana Krishnamurti, 123, 124, 134
Janata Dal (Secular), 211
Janata Dal (United), 115, 211, 215
Jaspal Singh, 57, 58, 59, 70
jatis
    caste, 14, 28
Javed Akhtar, 97
Jawaharlal Nehru, 2, 7, 17, 106, 107, 129
Jawaharlal Nehru University, 97
Jayalalithaa, 258
Jihad
    terrorism, 10, 278
Jinnah
    Pakistan, land of the pious, 193
    two-nation theory, 129
Jinnah, Mohammad Ali, 12, 13, 41, 42, 108, 193
Judicial enquiry commission
    riot-related grievances, 120
Juhapura, 240
Justice V. R. Krishna Iyer
    Concerned Citizens Tribunal, 246

K

K. Randeri, xiii
K. S. Lal
    slaughter of Hindus, 91
K.P.S. Gill, 115, 116
    NSG, Gujarat Police, 198
K.S. Sudarshan, 25
Kamal Mitra Chenoy
    USCIRF hearing, 2002, 122
Kanya Kelavyani Yojna, 69
Karamsad, 163, 165, 166, 169, 247, 248, 254
    birthplace of Sardar Patel, 216
Karnataka, 27, 29, 31, 51, 84, 100, 104, 234
Kashmiriyat
    Kashmiri identity, 23
Keshubhai Patel, 53, 54, 55, 56, 58, 60, 63, 72, 123, 130, 160, 166, 173, 181, 216, 218, 219, 243, 254, 255
KHAM, 15, 32, 276
Khilafat riots, 91
Kingsley Davis
    nature of India, Hindu influence, 128
Kirit Rawal
    Additional Solicitor General, 155
Koenraad Elst, 2, 28, 91, 98, 283, 298

Subject Index

Koran, 27, 117
Kripalani
   Acharya, 7, 90, 163
Kshatriya, 15, 25, 28, 32, 130, 141
Kushabhau Thakre, 125

L

Lalu Prasad Yadav, 104, 115, 145, 243
   corruption, fodder scam, 140
Lance Price, xiii
Lashkar-e-Toiba
   handiwork of, 199
   LeT, mastermind, 204
Lee Kuan Yew
   Singapore, democracy, 11
Liaquat Ali, 164
Lingayats, 31
Lord Chamberlain
   appeasement policy, 190
Lyngdoh, 236, 237
Lyngdoh, James
   CEC, 145
Lyngdoh, James Michael
   Modi, tactics, 175

M

M. V. Kamath, 96
M.V. Kamath, xiii
Madandas Devi
   RSS strongman, 220
Madhu Kishwar
   Modinama, 241
   reaction to Indian activists, 122
Magsaysay Award
   Lyngdoh, 148
Maha Gujarat Sant Sammelan, 149
Mahatma Gandhi, 2, 7, 26, 51, 89, 104, 161, 163
Mahatma Phule, 26
Mandal Commission Report, 29
Manohar Parrikar, 258
Maoist Communist Centre
   MCC, 105
McDonalds
   India, no beef, 141
McGreevey
   New Jersey Governor, Akshardham, 202
Medha Patkar, 67, 102, 287
Middle East, 10, 240
mini- Pakistan

Juhapura, 240
Minoritarianism, 23
Modi
   antagonism, CEC, bias, 145
   CEO, no political favors, 260
   false accusations, against, 95
   resignation, response, 133
   youngest Chief Minister, Gujarat, 257
Modi or Musharraf, 16, 41
Modispeak, 169
Mohammad Ali Jinnah
   Day of Direct Action, 158
Monotheism, 34, 285
monotheistic faiths
   Christianity, Islam, 18
Morarji Desai, 75
Mossad, 112
Mother Teresa, 106
Moving Pixels Company, 61
mujahiddeen, 109
mujahideens
   Taliban, jihad, strategies, 191
Mulayam Singh Yadav, 53, 176, 212, 237
Murari Bapu, 149, 150
Murli Manohar Joshi, 258
Musharraf, 16, 43, 53, 75, 144, 160, 191, 284
Musharraf, General
   Godhra, UN speech, 201
Muslim Brotherhood, 11
Muslim students
   final exams, exhortation, 134

N

N. Gopalswami, 178
na bhavishyati, 158
Nalin Bhatt
   State Assembly, dissolution, 134
Nanavati Commission, 81, 112
Narayan Dutt Tiwari, 242
Narayana Murthy
   Infosys, 27, 44, 45
Narendra Modi, vi, vii, viii, ix, xi, xii, xiii, 2, 5, 6,
   7, 12, 14, 15, 16, 33, 41, 43, 48, 49, 54, 55, 56,
   58, 59, 61, 62, 63, 64, 65, 70, 71, 73, 76, 78,
   81, 87, 89, 93, 95, 97, 98, 102, 113, 115, 120,
   122, 124, 130, 149, 165, 169, 181, 214, 216,
   219, 223, 224, 226, 餕231, 242, 243, 246, 252,
   254, 261, 264, 268, 277, 281, 282, 283, 298
   assurance to Muslim communities, 119
   GGY, 5,000 km., 168

Gujarat gaurav rath yatra, 138
performance as Chief Minister, 259
persona non grata, xii
popularity, 188
Prime Minister of India, 271
Narmada Bachao Andolan
   NBA, 67
Naroda Patiya, 83, 231, 265
National Commission for Minorities, 119, 202, 232
National Executive Committee
   BJP, 124, 133
National Human Rights Commission, 236
Navajivan
   Mahatma Gandhi, 76
Navsari, 161
NDA
   National Democratic Alliance, 8, 31, 38, 39, 49, 95, 106, 124, 211, 265, 268, 270, 271
Nehru
   Goa, Portuguese rule, 123
   Harrow, 90
   Jawaharlal, 2, 7, 13, 17, 21, 22, 32, 90, 91, 108, 163, 164, 216
   secularism, 128
Nehru, Jawaharlal
   appropriating Gandhian legacy, 165
   dislike for Sardar Patel, 164
   love of power, attention, 165
New Delhi, xi, xiii, 8, 16, 29, 33, 49, 61, 72, 73, 75, 98, 110, 111, 113, 146, 172, 185, 189, 219, 223, 261, 268, 270, 279, 281, 283, 285
NGOs, 1

O

Om Prakash Chautala, 258
Omar Sheikh, 249
Other Backward Castes
   OBCs, 29, 149

P

P.C. Pande, 85
P.V. Narasimha Rao, 51
paan
   voting for specific party, 150
Pakistan, 16, 18, 22, 37, 41, 42, 44, 52, 53, 73, 75, 82, 88, 100, 105, 107, 108, 109, 110
dialogue, 5, 7, 12, 13, 41, 47, 49, 52, 75, 82, 96, 103, 108, 185, 205, 234, 267, 277, 278, 279, 284
Panchajanya, 86
Parliament
   delays, ruckus, cost, 135
Patel, Sardar
   disenchantment, Nehru, 164
   Home Minister, unification, J &K, 163
Patels, 15, 216
Paul Johnson, 91
Pentagon, 78
People's War Group
   PWG, 103
Phagvel, 141
Pluralism, 4
polygamy
   Muslims, 11, 25
Pope John Paul II, 235
   anti-conversion laws, opposition, 128
Populism, 14
Porbandar
   Gandhi's birthplace, 162
pracharak
   role, activities, 223
   RSS, 54, 70, 93, 222, 274
Pramod Mahajan
   BJP's man Friday, 124
Pramukh Swami
   Swaminarayan sect, 142
Pravin Togadia, 226, 229, 244, 247
   arrest, 1997, 130
President of India
   Abdul Kalam, visit to Gujarat, 173
President's Rule, 114, 115, 135, 146, 156, 172, 176
Prevention of Terrorism Act
   POTA, 75, 135, 173
Prithviraj Chauhan, 128
Priyanka Gandhi, 242
Protestant Reformation, 19
Protestantism, 19
Purusha Sukta, 26
Purushottamdas Tandon
   Sardar Patel, Congress Party, 164

R

Rabindranath Tagore, 105
Rabri Devi, 104, 105, 115

Subject Index

Rafiq Zakaria, 12, 13, 41, 42, 113
Raj Dharma, 112
Raja Rammohan Roy, 26
Rajagopalachari, 7
Rajesh Khanna
    film actor, political contest, 213
Rajiv Gandhi, 17, 22, 50, 52, 111, 123, 124, 168, 218, 248
    election victory, 1984-85, 131
    parents, 175
    wooing Hindu voters, 1999, 150
Rajya Sabha, 115
Ram bhakts
    victory for, 226
Ram Temple
    BJP meeting, 1989, 124
Ram Vilas Paswan
    NDA partner, challenge, 135
Ramajanmabhoomi, 74
Rashtriya Janata Dal, 211
Regina Schwartz, 34
relief distribution
    riot-affected, 118
remorse
    Hindus, Modi, 89, 90, 92, 249, 274
Republican Party, 20, 65
Reservations
    caste-based, 28
Results
    election, 253
Rig Veda, 26, 27, 183
RSS
    opposed to Modi's removal, 125
    Rashtriya Swayamsevak Sangh, 7, 15, 25, 45, 51, 54, 71, 73, 86, 93, 125, 126, 130, 230, 273, 274, 276, 283
    Who is a Hindu?, 132
Russia, 64

S

S. M. Krishna, 242
S. Mendiratta, 146
S. R. Choudhury, 39
S.M.F. Bukhari
    Chief Coordinator of Relief, 147
Saanskritik Raashtrawaad
    cultural nationalism, 247
Sabarmati Assembly, 55
Sabarmati Express, 242
Saddam Hussein, 10

Samajwadi Janata Dal Party, 211
Samata Party, 59, 115, 127, 211, 212, 215, 220
Samras, 64, 65, 66
Sandhya Jain, 87, 88
Sanjay Dutt
    Bombay blast case, accused, 138
Sanjeev Bhatt, 233
Sankrant Sanu, 89
Sanskrit, 129, 139, 163, 255
Saraswati Vandana, 24
Sardar Vallabhbhai Patel Stadium
    swearing-in ceremony, 257
Sarvepalli Radhakrishnan, 21
satyagraha, 193
Saudi Arabia, 10, 25, 73
Savarkar
    Vinayak Damodar, 21, 130
Scheduled Castes, 15, 28, 30, 31, 99, 218
secular nationalism, 3
Secularism, 17, 18, 19, 20, 101, 172, 282
secularists, 3
Semitic traditions, 7
Shabana Azmi, 96
Shah Alam, 118
    relief camp, 120
Shah Bano, 17, 18, 22, 123, 150, 278
Shah Bano case, 17, 18, 22
Shahada
    martyrdom, 207
shaheed
    martyr, 207
Shahi Imam, 98, 132, 238
Shahibaug, 118
Shambhu Srivastava
    Samata Party, resignation, 127
Shamlaji, 163
Shankersinh Laxmansinh Vaghela
    switching allegiance, 130
Shankersinh Vaghela, 54, 55, 203, 214, 217, 237, 248, 256
    defeat, 253
Sharia
    Islamic law, 22
Shaurya Divas
    VHP rally, 230
Sheikh Abdullah, 107, 108
Sheila Dixit, 242
Shekhar Gupta, 95
Shiv Sena, 99
Shivaji, 51, 86, 184, 227
Shiv-Sena, 115, 181, 200
Shourie

Arun, 35
Shudra, 25, 27, 28
Siddhapur, 162
Sonia Gandhi, 40, 49, 50, 52, 53, 95
    Italian descent, target, 167
    support for Vaghela, 132
Soviet Union, viii, 1, 10, 46
Sri Aurobindo, 91
Srikrishna Commission, 110
Sthaapatya shastras
    temple architecture, 194
Subedar Suresh Chand Yadav
    hero of Akshardham, 198
Sufis, 77
Sundarji, 52
Sunil Dutt
    sadbhawna yatra, 138
Sunil Khilnani, 12, 13, 23, 266, 280, 281
Supreme Court
    Article 174, Assembly dissolution, 156
Supreme Court of India
    Encyclopedia Britannica, Hinduism, 129
Sushil Kumar Shinde, 87
Sushilkumar Shinde, 241
Sushma Swaraj, 155, 243
Swami Agnivesh, 96
Swami Narayan Movement, 258
Swami Prabhupada, 105, 183
Swami Vivekananda
    Vivekananda, 35, 105
Swapan Dasgupta, 236
swearing in ceremony, 257
Syria, 269

T

T. N. Madan, 18, 20
T. N. Seshan, 144
T.N. Seshan, 236
T.S. Krishnamurthy, 147
Tableeqi Jamaat, 77
talaq
    divorce, Muslim, 25
Taliban, 10, 191, 248
Tarun Gogoi, 242
Teesta Setalvad
    USCIRF hearing, 2002, 122
Tele-Fariad, 68
Telegu Desam Party, 115
The Guardian, 262

The Huffington Post
    Sonia Gandhi, wealth, 224
The New York Times, 6, 12, 98, 139, 267, 279, 280, 284, 285, 287
The Washington Post
    false reporting, 99
Theodore Roosevelt, xi
Third World Democracy, xii
Thomas Friedman, 6, 98
toll
    post-Godhra, 117
Transparency International, 63
Treaty of Westphalia, 19
Trinamool Congress Party, 106, 212

U

U.S. Constitution
    God, 20
U.S.-India relationship, 5, 268
Uma Bharati, 124
USCIRF, 33, 35, 37, 101

V

V.V. John, 22
Vadodara, 57, 58, 70, 72, 148, 188, 200, 205, 224, 243, 251, 259, 263
Vajpayee
    Atal Bihari, 31, 49, 50, 51, 52, 53, 61, 64, 82, 112, 115, 124, 125, 140, 155, 183, 228, 238, 243, 258, 268, 283, 284
Vajubhai Vala, 63, 70
Vallabhbhai Patel, 7, 13, 51, 90, 163, 254
Valli Gujarati, 86
Valson Thampu, 96
Vande Mataram, 24
Vatican, 33, 35
Veerappan, 104, 279
Venkaiah Naidu, 124, 173, 178, 243, 255
VHP
    aid to victims, 118
Vijay Diwas, 227, 230
Vikram Sarabhai
    Abdul Kalam, 174
Vikram Vakil, 246
Vilasrao Deshmukh, 241
Vinod Mehta, 95
Vishwa Hindu Parishad

Subject Index

VHP, 71, 74, 130, 177
Vishwanath Pratap Singh, 50
Vokkaligas
   Gowdas, 31
Vyshya, 25

W

Wahabism
   Saudi Arabia, radical Islam, 192
Wahhabi
   Sunni, Islam, 10, 77, 269
Western countries
   church affiliation, 20
World Bank, 45, 46, 61, 63
World Trade Center, 61, 78, 79, 194, 267

Y

Yatin Oza, 55
   blames media, 252
   opposing candidate, Modi, 220
yatras, 137, 138, 169, 181, 183, 275
Yoganand Paramhamsa, 105
Young India
   Mahatma Gandhi, 76

Z

Zaheera Sheikh, 87, 263

ABOUT THE AUTHORS

Ramesh N. Rao is a Professor of Communication at Columbus State University, Columbus, Georgia, in the United States. Ramesh Rao has a Ph.D. in Communication from Michigan State University.

He has taught a variety of communication courses since 1987 including public speaking, intercultural communication, mediation, conflict resolution, mass communication, and persuasion. He has co-authored the book, *Intercultural Communication: The Indian Context* with Avinash Thombre, published in 2015 by Sage (India).

Ramesh Rao is also the author of *Secular 'Gods' Blame Hindu 'Demons': The Sangh Parivar through the Mirror of Distortion* and *Coalition Conundrum: The BJP's Trials, Tribulations and Triumphs*, both published in 2001. He has edited a book with Koenraad Elst titled *Gujarat after Godhra: Real Violence, Selective Outrage* (2002).

Ramesh Rao has written op-eds for *India Abroad*, and his essays and commentaries have appeared in the *St. Louis Post-Dispatch*, *Rediff on the Net*, *India Post*, *India Currents*, *Columbia Daily Tribune*, *The Washington Post*, *The Guardian (London)*, and on a variety of Internet portals, including *Sulekha.Com*, *Hamarashehar.Com*, *NewsInsight.com*, *Patheos.com*, etc.

Ramesh Rao lives with his wife Sujaya and son Sudhanva in Columbus, Georgia.

Vishal Sharma studied at St. Xavier's College, Mumbia, and at the Indian Institute of Management, Kolkata. He was an op-ed columnist for *The Free Press Journal*. Vishal served for 15 months as Officer on Special Duty to Narendra Modi, and was intimately connected with the election analysis process in 2002. Additionally, he was also assigned the work of extrapolating the Gujarat Gaurav Yatra data to general support for the BJP.

Vishal likes to paint, read, and understand the esoteric meanings common in world cultures. His paintings usually are metaphysical representations of common human aspirations. Vishal has also taught students from over 60 countries as a summer faculty member at the SIS program of the Leysin American School in Switzerland. He is a Salzburg Alumni and an invitee of the U.S. State Department for the IVLP program. Vishal has served as a Member of the Board of Governors of SPIPA (Sardar Patel Institute of Public Administration) – Gujarat Government's nodal body imparting good governance training to Gujarat state cadre officers. He manages an asset investment company in Mumbai.

Vishal is married to Pooja, and they are expecting their first child in December 2015.

www.ingramcontent.com/pod-product-compliance
Lightning Source LLC
Chambersburg PA
CBHW051646040426
42446CB00009B/994